Conditions of Marginalised Communities in the Globalised Era

Conditions of Marginalised Communities in the Globalised Era:

Challenges and Responses

Edited by

Dr. Gnanapragasam Lazar

Prof. N. Sudhakar Rao

GYAN

Published, 2021

Published by

Gyan Publishing House
5, Ansari Road
Daryaganj, New Delhi-110002
Phone: 011-47034999, 9811692060
www.gyanbooks.com
E-mail: books@gyanbooks.com

Printed at: Gyan Press, Delhi.

Cataloging in Publication Data—DK
Courtesy: D.K. Agencies (P) Ltd. <docinfo@dkagencies.com>

National Seminar on "Conditions of Marginalized Communities in the Globalized Era" (2020 : Hyderabad, India)
Conditions of marginalised communities in the globalised era : challenges and responses / edited by Dr. Gnanapragasam Lazar, Prof. N. Sudhakar Rao.
pages cm
"... Two-day National Seminar on "Conditions of Marginalized Communities in the Globalized Era" organized by the Institute of Dravidian Culture and Research, (SANSKRUTI), Hyderabad, India, on January 31 and February 1, 2020"—Foreword.
ISBN 9788121220231

1. Marginality, Social—India—Congresses. 2. Dalits—India—Social conditions—Congresses. 3. Dalits—India— Economic conditions—Congresses. 4. Women—India—Social conditions—Congresses. 5. Women—India—Economic conditions—Congresses. 6. Immigrants—India—Social conditions—Congresses. 7. Immigrants—India—Economic conditions—Congresses. 8. Globalization—Social aspects— India—Congresses. I. Lazar, G., editor. II. Sudhakar Rao, N. (Nemalladinne), 1953- editor. III. Society of the Divine Word. Sanskruti, organizer. IV. Title.

LCC HN690.Z9M26 2020 | DDC 305.560954 23

Contents

Foreword

This book is the product of a Two-day National Seminar on "Conditions of Marginalized Communities in the Globalized era" organized by the Institute of Dravidian Culture and Research, (SANSKRUTI), Hyderabad, India, on January 31 and February 1, 2020.In all 32 research papers were presented by eminent scholars from various disciplines.

In this volume attention is directed upon what are considered as marginalized groups (social products) and its connotation is indiscriminately employed also for the deprived and the exploited groups. More important may be to consider the point that being marginalized is the product of the event of marginalization which is discussed in some of the papers.

Globalization is the buzzword today and it is used in different contexts for so many different purposes that it is difficult to determine what is at stake in the globalization: what is problematic and precisely what effects it has for contemporary scenario, especially on the marginalized groups in India such as the tribals, Dalits, women, migrants, etc, with reference to their social, cultural and ecological aspects? A few of the papers in this volume venture to throw some light on such of these questions.

There is a new 'postmodern' intellectual movement which eschews all embracing theory and sees meaning as integral to context and the way people live. Broad theories may or may not have relevance in a particular context. In other words understandings are seen to relate to particular situations rather than all situations. The papers in this volume may be understood in this light.

Visakhapatnam

Prof. K.E. Rajpramukh
University of Andhra Pradesh

Preface

This book arose from our puzzlement at the paradoxical state of marginalized communities in the globalised era. The beginning of the new millennium has witnessed a groundswell of proposals for the transformation of marginalized communities underpinning neoliberal globalization. These proposals challenge our sociological imagination and belie the fatalistic ideology that 'there is no alternative' to globalization. The initiatives are as diverse as the network advocating them as the case studies in this book lay bare.

Eminent University Professors, inspiring college lecturers, progressive activist-researchers, people of faith, social activists and members of marginalized communities came together to collectively conceive global identities and empowerment of marginalized communities. The wide array of contributions in this book will spur an unprecedented effervescence of debate and experimentation in international level. This book is also a fervent experimentation with scholarly creativity at the grassroots level of the intellectually challenging and politically compelling aspects of globalization and marginalization. The effort to bridge the diverse between globalization and Marginalisation, academic work and political engagement made the process of producing this book an exceptionally challenging and stimulating transnational endeavour.

The specific contribution of this volume and the common thread running through all its chapters lies in the particular, bottom-up perspective on globalization and marginalization that it advances and empirically illustrates. This perspective has analytic and a political dimension. Thus, this volume looks more closely into the dominant sociological approaches and inquires into the reasons why they have rendered invisible grassroots resistance to globalization. Throughout the chapters, the book describes, the case studies contained in the remainder of the book and point to the ways in which, in my view illustrate the exigent conditions of marginalized communities.

Dr. G. Lazar SVD
Director
SANSKRUTI
Institute of Dravidian Culture and Research (IDCR).
Hyderabad

List of Contributors

1. **Prof. Virginius Xaxa:**

   He has obtained his Doctorate in Sociology from IIT Kanpur in 1978. He had the honour of teaching Sociology at Delhi School of Economics, Delhi University till 2011, and served as Pro Vice-Chancellor in TISS at Guwahati. His books *Economic Dualism and Structure of Class: A Study of Plantation and Peasant Settings in North Bengal* (1997) analysed the micro-level situation in the plantation of North Bengal. His *State, Society, and Tribes* (2008) unlike the conventional scholarship on tribal people in India, explores and evaluates the question of citizenship rights, moving on to long-standing debates on tribal movements. His edited volume with Dev Nathan titled Social Exclusion and ;Adverse Inclusion: Development and Deprivation of Adivasis in India (2022) explores various issues pertaining to Adivasi exclusion in India. Email ID: virg1978@gmail.com

2. **Prof. Vijoy S Sahay**

   He is an Emeritus Fellow (U.G.C.), Department of Anthropology, Ranchi University, Ranchi. Former Head, Dept. of Anthropology, University of Allahabad. Editor-in-Chief, The Oriental Anthropologist (A Biannual International Research Journal of the Science of Man) E-mail: vijoysahay@gmail.com

3. **Prof. Raja Mohan Rao**

   He is serving as Professor & Head, Centre for the Study of Social Exclusion and Inclusive Policy, University of Hyderabad, Telangana, India. He is currently heading the Center for the Study of Social Exclusion and Inclusive Policy at the University of Hyderabad in India. He is an Experienced Professor with a demonstrated history of working in the Education Sector as professor of Economics in the University system. Lecturing, International Relations, Policy Analysis, and Data Analysis. Strong research professional with an M.A. M.Phil., and Ph.D. focused in Development Economics and International Development. Email ID: rmrao.bdu@gmail.com

4. **Prof. Tinku Paul**

She is the current Superintendent for the Directorate of Legal Affairs, Sam Higginbottom University of Agriculture, Technology and Sciences (SHUATS), formerly Allahabad Agricultural Institute is an autonomous state government university located in Allahabad, India, Prayagraj- 211007. Email ID: tinksmiles@gmail.com

5. **Prof. Yazahi Josphine**

She has been rendering her service in JNU (Eco of Education), Dipl. Edu. Plng IIEP-Paris) & DAP (Rome). Former Prof at NUEPA, Social Development Entrepreneur in Global Consultancy, New Delhi. 9811344378(M) Currently serving as a founder member and Director of Peoples Development Academy, New Delhi.

E-mail:dryazali@gmail.com/y_josephine@yahoo.com———

https://nuepa.academia.edu/YazaliJosephine/Papers,https://www.facebook.com/dryazali

https://www.linkedin.com/pub/prof-yazali-josephine

6. **Prof. P.P.D. Satyapal**

He is currently serving as Professor and Head, Department of Anthropology, Andhra University, Visakhapatnam-530003. He has been specialised in areas such as Social Inequality Caste & Tribe Cultural Capital Nomadic Satellite, Dalit Communities Democracy and Human Rights. Mob: 9866326301.

Email ID: satyapalpd@gmail.com

7. **Prof. Victoria A. Masih**

She is working as Associate Professor, Department of Agricultural Economics, Director of Directorate of Legal Affairs. Mumbai.

8. **Prof. Jesurathnam**

He is an Associate Professor, Department of Anthropology, Pondicherry University, Puducherry – 605014, India, Cell: 07598485109.

Email ID: drjesudev@gmail.com

9. **Dr. Sharon Sucharitha Gold**

She is the Academic Consultant, Department of Psychology in Yogi Vemana University, Kadapa. Andhra Pradesh. Email ID: sharon-nemalladinne@yahoo.com

10. **Dr. James Ponniah**

At present he is an Assistant Professor, Department of Christian

Studies, School of Philosophy and Religious Thought, at University of Madras. Email: jamesponniah@gmail.com

11. **Prof. Amitha Sandiago**

    She is working as Professor and Head, Post Graduate Department of English, Bishop Cotton Women's Christian College, Bangalore. She has been teaching and doing scientific research for about 21- years. She is specialised in Cultural Studies; South Asian Studies; English Studies; Postcolonial Studies; Gender Studies; Religious Studies; Theology; Critical Theory, Email-ID: amithasantiago@gmail.com

12. **Sr. Velangini**

    She is the Principal and Head, Department of Cultural Studies, St. Pius X, PG College for Women, Nacharam, Hyderabad, Telangana.

13. **Dr. R. Komala**

    She is the Head, Department of Physics. St. Pious X, PG College for Women, Nacharam, Hyderabad, Telangana.

14. **Aarthi Deepak**

    She has been serving as Faculty Lecturer, Department of Political Science, St. Pious X, P.G. and Degree College for Women, Nacharam, Hyderabad.

15. **Dr. Jose D. Maliekal SDB**

    He is the Principal and professor of St. John's Regional Seminary (Institute of Philosophy and Religious Studies and Social Sciences), Kondadaba, Vizianagaram District, Andhra Pradesh, India. He is also the co-editor of the book published (2020), by Association of Christian Philosophers of India (ACPI). His areas of research are subaltern perspectives on the production of knowledge, Dalit identities and the impact of religion on socio-economic transformation.

    Email ID: jose.maleikal@gmail.com

16. **Dr. G. Jagadeesh**

    He is a Social Activist and Research Officer, IV State Finance Commission, Tadepalli, Guntur District, Government of Andhra Pradesh, Email- jagadeesh.hcu@gmail.com

17. **Prof. Srikanta Swamy**

    He is the Academic Consultant, Research and Analysis Wing of NAAC, Former Additional Director, Centre for Research, Christ University, Bengaluru, India.

    Email ID: swamysrikanta1950@gmail.com

18. Dr. M.G. Selvin SJ

He is a Social Activist and Director, CITRA - Centre for Information, Training, Research and Action, Jesuit Community, 12-1-334/17/1, Lallapet, Secunderabad - 500 017, Telengana State, INDIA. Mobile: 9951136558, 7550139095. Email ID: mgselvinraj@gmail.com

19. Dr. A. Mary Dayana

She is the Head, Department of Social Work, CTTE College for Women, Perambur, Chennai.

20. Dr. A. Vasantha Jeyaseelan

He is the Head, Department of Social Work, Thiruthangal Nadar College, Chennai.

21. Ms. Bhargavi Das

She is a Ph.D, research scholar, University of Hyderabad. Cell: 9515750855

22. Prof. Maria Arul Raja SJ

He is the Director of the IDCR (Institute of Dialogue with Cultures and Religions) affiliated to Madras University - situated within the campus of Loyola College- Chennai. With his interdisciplinary approaches in humanities from subaltern perspectives, he has authored 10 books and contributed over 160 research articles to various reputed journals. He lectured and presented papers in USA, Australia, South Korea, Philippines, Hong Kong, Indonesia, Thailand, and Sri Lanka. He continues his dialogical engagement with various People's Movements and subaltern groups like Dalits, Women, and Migrants.

23. Prof. Paul Roche

He is an Eminent Anthropologist of Vienna Circle, Austria. He was the former Contract Curator, Royal Ontario Museum, Toronto, Canada. Former Editor-in-Chief of *Metroscope,* a weekly newspaper published in Toronto. Edited and published *Catalyst,* the monthly social pastoral magazine for Melanesia, and *Point Series* the Forum for Melanesian Affairs. Email ID: palayamroche@gmail.com

24. Prof. Savarirayan SVD

He is the Director of Divya Vani, Bhopal (SVD Biblical Centre). Former Rector and Dean in Khrist Premalaya Regional Theologate, Ashta, Bhopal. Email ID:savarirayansvd@yahoo.co.in

25. Dr. Jose K. SVD

He is the Founder-Director of SANSKRITI – NEICR, Guwahati. Member of Anthropos International, Founder and Managing Editor of Anthropos India, and President of Association for Mission Education Research (MER). He has authored 3 books and edited 15 books on Anthropology and Sociology. Email ID: kjosesvd@gmail.com

26. Thomas Kavumkattayil SVD

He is an educationist and Research Scholar, Centre for Study of Social Exclusion and Inclusive Policy, School of Social Sciences, University of Hyderabad. Email ID: tkavumkatta@gmail.com

27. Prof. John Peter

He served as a Consultant in Philosophy Department at Indira Gandhi National Open University (IGNOU) for a couple of terms developing M.A. Philosophy Programme. He has been also Treasurer and Secretary of Association of Christian Philosophers of India. He is now pursuing his post-doctoral studies in Paris, France.

Email ID: petercapu@gmail.com

28. Dr. S. Janet Mary

She is a well-known specialist in Media Communications, Assistant Professor, Dept. Journalism and Communications in Madras Christian College, Tambaram, Chennai. A social activist worked among the marginalised communities of Bihar, Maharashtra and Tamil Nadu. Email ID: jmwater15@gmail.com

29. Dr. Surojit Sen Gupta

He is an Assistant Professor and Head, Department of Sociology, Maharaja Bir Bikram College, Agartala, West Tripura.

Email ID: meghaboy@gmail.com

30. Dr. Wesly Kumar

He is the Assistant Registrar and professor at School of Social Sciences, University of Hyderabad. Email ID: weslyhcu@yahoo.com

31. K. Sai Jaahnavi

Little Flower Degree College, Uppal, Hyderabad. Email ID: JKALLAKURI@gmail.com

32. C. Vanisree, N. Swathisree, Syeda Meher Afreen

Department of Bio-Chemistry, St. Pious X, PG Women's College, Nacharam, Hyderabad.

33. Dr. G. Lazar SVD

He is a specialist in Indology and Sociology of Religions, founder Director of Institute of Dravidian Culture and Research – SANSKRUTI, Hyderabad, visiting faculty in 12 academic institutes in India and abroad, published 4 books and edited 8 volumes of Anthropological and Sociological concerns.

34. Dr. Joachim

He is a retired professor and HOD of Social Work, Loyola College, Chennai. He had served as Chairman of Board of Study for Social work, Madras University. He has been actively involving in organizing seminars and conferences in social work in his academic career. A repatriate from Myanmar was amazed to observe the discriminative inhuman practices that prevails in Indian society and that prompted him to take up M.Phil and Ph.D studies on Christian SC.

General Introduction

SANSKRUTI - Institute of Dravidian Culture and Research (IDCR) conducted its 7th National Seminar on January 31 and February 1, 2020 in Hyderabad. **"Conditions of Marginalised Communities in the Globalised Era: Challenges and Responses"** was the main theme of this annual research seminar. Over 32 research papers were presented by eminent academics and scholars from various disciplines.

The Society of the Divine Word (SVD) inherited from their Founder Arnold Janssen, a strong tradition of study in the natural sciences and the humanities. Dr. Wilhelm Schmidt SVD, linguist, ethnologist, historian of religions, established *Anthropos Journal* in 1906.[1] Although research and publishing in the field of Anthropology have continued to the present day, the ways of the sciences have seen the emergence of other sciences as a distinct filed in the meantime. The growth of the study of social nature of humankind has focused different studies and different academic research besides the anthropological concerns. Accordingly the Divine Word scholars from south India have an organization of Sociology and Anthropology called SANSKRUTI (Institute of Dravidian Culture and Research).

Globalisation is a phenomenon that expands interconnectedness in the world. It is not just an economic phenomenon - it also affects cultural,

---

1. Dr. Wilhelm Schmidt SVD was an *Austrian linguist, anthropologist, and ethnologist.* Schmidt's contributions to the method of culture historical ethnology, which also became known as the culture circle method, on which he built his theory of the very early monotheism of the representatives of the earliest people, is quite remarkable. As one of the originators of this theory and as a prominent figure in the area of ethnology and the science of religion in the first half of the 20th century, he became the founder of the Vienna School of Ethnology. He was not only its best known representative, but also its most controversial. Schmidt's main passion was linguistics. His early work was on the Mon–Khmer languages of Southeast Asia, and languages of Oceania and Australia. The conclusions from this study led him to hypothesize the existence of a broader Austric group of languages, which included the Austronesian language group. Schmidt managed to prove that Mon–Khmer language has inner connections with other languages of the South Seas, one of the most significant findings in the field of linguistics.

political, social, legal and religious life. These aspects of globalization interact with each other and there are feedback loops between them. These effects may be unexpected and contradictory.

The term 'marginalization' refers to individual or groups who live at the margin of society. Their situations may be historical or cultural as they suspend between social classes or cultural groups, without being fully integrated to it. The term has different connotations and nuances in the modern era of post-colonial, postmodern period and in the world that is predominantly driven by market forces. In cultural anthropology marginalization is a major subject of study in which ethnic groups and their social situation are explained. It may have various forms like, class, caste, gender, community and so on at one level and at other level groups who are subjected to economic and social hardships. These groups may still be marginalized at multiple levels in a country like India, which has witnessed tremendous socio-political changes in both pre-independence and post-independence period. The concept of marginality rose to its high prominence while globalization started to hold its sway in the world.

This volume looks at the most important changes and challenges that are associated with globalisation and marginalization and then examines which groups have been most affected. It analyzes the changing process of marginalisation and how this benefits certain communities, in part to the detriment of others. Globalisation is a disruptive and destabilizing force, simultaneously opening up and narrowing down opportunity structures for different groups. To understand the impact of globalisation it is necessary to focus on drivers within the nation state, as well as forces that operate outside the domestic context. The essays will examine evidence about the impact of globalisation on domestic sources of inequality and disadvantage, and whether it is mistaken to suggest that national governments are increasingly impotent in the face of globalisation challenges.

The overall picture of marginalisation is arguably more complex – certainly more so than two decades ago – partly as the result of larger global trends. Increased mobility and fluidity combined with global economic, social and political integration is creating additional variance and transience in the patterns and processes of marginalisation. Many issues and concerns have become less clear-cut.

Marginalisation can be defined spatially, in terms of place and the geography and dispersal of power. This is important because where people live is an increasingly important determinant of subsequent life chances, and should be central to any credible account of the dynamics of social inclusion. But understanding the impact of place alone is insufficient.

There is an opportunity to develop new paradigms that are able to shape public debate and public policy in relation to social inclusion and marginalisation. Globalisation is still a widely misinterpreted and often ill-defined concept. It may, however, provide the stimulus that is needed to revise the basic analytical frameworks that must underpin future approaches to social exclusion, providing a much stronger international and global orientation.

In general, globalisation has been accompanied by market-oriented development strategies, which, for the most part, have adversely affected the livelihoods of marginalized people. Social scientists have strongly opposed the exploitative and exclusivist models of development associated with globalization and advocated a more people centric development paradigm.

In India the women, children, scheduled castes and scheduled tribes, persons with disabilities, migrants, women and aged are regarded as marginalized or vulnerable groups. These people are socially, economically, politically and legally ignored and excluded in Indian society. The health status and utilization patterns of ST's and SC's and backward classes give an indication of their social exclusion as well as an idea of their linkages between poverty and health. The economical dependence, politically powerless and culturally subjugated of ST's and SC's and backward classes to upper castes affects their overall lifestyle and access to food and health, etc.

From a human rights perspective, all citizens should receive adequate health, education, food and nutrition, housing, participation, equal treatment, and freedom from the discrimination and violence. However, these marginalized groups (STs, SCs, children, physically challenged, migrants, and elderly) are often marginalized and overlooked in the public delivery system and also subject to multidimensional problems whose underlying factors are intertwined.

In the globalized era, emphasis on the social mobilization of marginalized groups is witnessed. Some political and social activists focus on the movements of Dalits or Tribal rights. These activists highlight the historical and structural marginalization of Dalits, Tribal, and landless laborers. The Social and political activists working in the field of rights of marginalized use the term people rights to emphasize the collective characteristics of their rights and to focus on political aspects of their rights.

Therefore, from the mid-80s there have been continuous efforts to describe and re-articulate the rights of Dalits and Tribals over natural resources, etc. This became more articulated and vocal, when the issue of displacement because of large dams, developmental projects, forestry projects, mining companies, etc., came into existence. Most of the sufferers of these displacements were Dalits and Tribal people. The movement like Narmada Bachao Andolan, the Fish worker's struggle, and Dalit movements brought the issue of the marginalized communities into the mainstream political discourse in India. The spirit which permeated this consultation was that of understanding the plight of the marginalized communities. This does not mean that there was a total consensus in all the presentations and discussions. There were variety of ideas, some consonant, others more contrasting and even opposing. But throughout the two days, it was clear that there was a sense of common searching, a collective effort to find what was of worth and value in the life of the marginalized communities in the face of the threat to its sovereignty brought by the modern trends of globalization.

On the growing globalised consumerist culture Mahatma Gandhi commented, "The mind is a restless bird. The more it gets the more it wants and still remains unsatisfied. Our forefathers knew that if we set our hearts on such things we would become slaves and lose our moral fibre". ..."The incessant search for material comforts and their multiplications is such an evil; and I make bold to say that the Europeans themselves will have to remodel their outlook if they are not to perish under the weight of the comforts they are becoming slaves".

This volume on **"Conditions of Marginalised Communities in the Globalised Era: Challenges and Responses"**, is an attempt to examine the theoretical and epistemological engagement of globalisation, on the one hand, and to provide ethnographic and empirical information on the other. Furthermore, it seeks to analyse various facets of marginalisation from political, economic, social, gendered, and caste perspectives. Therefore, this volume is an earnest attempt to provide an interdisciplinary examination of globalisation and marginality in India today.

Dr. G. Lazar. Director,

Prof. Sudhakar Rao,

Hyderabad Central University (retd),

SANSKRUTI

Institute of Dravidian Culture and Research

Hyderabad

1

Globalisation and Marginalised

— Prof. Virginius Xaxa

Introduction

This paper attempts to address and examine the issues of the marginalised in the context of the globalised world. As to who is marginalised is located on the basis of certain economic, social, and cultural characteristics. In India, for long, this had come to be associated with people known as the untouchable caste who were at bottom in the hierarchical structure of caste. The other groups which to be associated as the marginalised were those delineated as tribes. They were treated as primitive and live in economic, social and cultural backwardness. Accordingly, the constitution of India has laid down special provisions for their upliftment and development. The idea of marginalised has undergone changes and with this other groups and categories have come to be seen as the marginalised because of the systemic discrimination they have been subjected to. The OBCs and women fill this category. In course of time, number of groups treated as the marginalised has grown both in official and non-official documents and reports. There is hardly any doubt that the globalisation has bearing on all segments of the marginalised. However, it is not possible to discuss its bearing on the different segments and hence I have restricted my discussion keeping one of the segments in mind viz. the tribal people in India. The paper is divided into four sections. In the first, it engages with the idea of marginality. The broad features of globalisation are laid out in the second section. The third situates the broad consequences of the globalisation on the marginalised group as a whole. The fourth section examines the consequences of globalisation on tribal people of central India.

Conceptualising Marginality

A number of terms are used in engagement with the question of marginality. These are margin, marginalisation, marginalised and marginality. These points to different dimensions of the issue of marginality. Margin points to location in relation to the whole. Marginality is a state or condition of being at margin. Marginalisation is the process through which condition of marginality is created and people who are product of the process may be referred to as the marginalised. Marginalisation invariably points to process at work in society and history causing it. However, after lapse of years and decades, the historical process is forgotten and the marginalised or margin is at times taken as the natural and original state of being.

Marginality is thus a relational term. It can only be understood reference to larger segment of the population in society or community. It is a pointer to its location in the whole. In spatial terms it means at the edge of physical/ geographical space. In social relation term or in respect of social space it refers to people who are on the margin viz. those denied from things accessed by other members of the society/ community. In other words, margin cannot be understood outside of the centre of the whole. A physical and geographical structure can be treated as periphery or margin only in relation to physical/ geographical space treated as the core or centre. The delineation of core is contingent on things or space that a society values. Now in almost every society there are things that are things that are greatly valued. Broadly, these are status (prestige/ honour), income or source of income and power. On these three axes people in society are differentially situated leading to hierarchisation and inequality in the society.

Thus, inequality in distribution of thing valued in society is at the root of locating the people at the margin. Even geographical understanding of core and periphery is driven by premium put to region marked by economic activity such as industry, trade and commerce which is then conceptualised as the core. The areas devoid of such activities are taken as the periphery. Indeed the centre-periphery or core-periphery perspective has become an important framework of understanding the world economy or world social system world political system in social science disciplines. Such perspective has also been used to understand the similar phenomena at national and regional level. The contour of centre-periphery is visible in the study of marginality. After all, marginality can only be studied in relation to others, other here people or groups who enjoy status, power and wealth. It is the extreme negation of these that constitute marginality. The bases on which this is constructed are primarily economic and political and social privileges which are denied to others. Often margin is couched in terms of degree of relative access to things valued in society. Those having the things valued in society in plenty are the most privileged and form the core or centre of society and those with the least of these at the lowest end of the margin. Marginality is thus marked by deprivation and exclusion of things values in society viz. income or source of income, status and power. The deprivation of these is the axial principle of marginality. Each of these can be worked out in details to understand the features in terms of which marginality can be understood. Whereas the most excluded/marginalised may be easily discernable, the same may not necessarily be the case in respect of intermediate groups viz. those between the most marginalised and the most privilege. Margin may be measured in terms of continuity by locating the groups in terms of relative access to things so valued.

Inequality at the root of marginality has taken different form in society. The predominant forms in society have been class, caste, race, ethnicity, gender and religion. At times, even language and religion assume such forms. These different forms of inequality, far from being dispersive, are in empirical social reality overlap and combine one or more of such forms of social inequality. Thus, the people at the margin not only point to different forms of marginality combine different form social inequality that mark any society. Thus, those at the extreme end of marginality may not only form at the bottom of the class structure, but they may also form a segment of population distinct in race, caste, language/ ethnicity and, religious identity.

As observed earlier, the margin cannot be understood outside of the whole. Hence, what is that whole or the unit in terms of which one intends to explore the question of marginality? The point of departure for such exploration can be micro social reality or macro social reality. Given the complexity of Indian society, the study of margin at the micro social reality may be very delimiting though it may give deep insight into the way and processes through which marginality has evolved. The location and understanding of marginality within wider framework and macro setting provides a space for understanding marginality from multidimensional perspective and also wider social process at work that impinge and shape the marginality at the periphery. Here India is being taken as reference for understanding the issues of marginalised.

The issue of marginality/marginalised is not recent phenomena. It has been there all though the history since the emergence and growth of social inequality in society. Indeed for a long stretch of human history, inequality has been treated as something desirable and legitimate in the society. This had been evident in dominant values of society. Given this inequality was taken as normal. All the same from time to time there has been challenge to such inequality. Indian history is replete with such cases. The Buddhism and Jainism may be taken as instances. However, such protests could not uproot the dominant values and ethos of hierarchy and inequality that pervaded society. The major challenge to this dominant idea in history came in French Revolution. For the first time in history, society was being envisaged based on an idea of liberty, equality and fraternity in place of hierarchy and inequality. This ethos and values captured the imagination of the people. The old system built on values of hierarchy, inequality and lack of freedom was dismantled and new society build on idea of freedom, equality and fraternity was inaugurated. Since then this new ideas and ethos have spread far and wide and taken deep roots in the consciousness of the people. It gave birth to new political system where sovereignty lay with people. The idea of liberty, equality and fraternity began to be translated into rights of the people thereby introducing or reinforcing the idea of citizenship which was confined to the few privileged. Rights of the people gradually evolved and took three major forms in Europe viz. civil rights, political and social rights. In fact, these assumed the major components of citizenship rights in Europe.

The citizenship is the status of full membership in the society. This was a distant dream in Indian society which was founded on the principle of hierarchical structure of caste. This underwent radical change after India's independence following the adoption of the Indian constitution. The constitution laid the foundation for building a new society which was diametrically opposed to the old one. It transformed people from being a subject of the state to citizen of the state irrespective of their caste, class, creed, race, language and religion. The entitlement of citizenship was thus a major step towards addressing the problem of marginality that a large chunk of people suffered in Indian history. Yet this entitlement was not sufficient and hence the constitution provided for special provision for addressing the issues of marginalised especially those at the bottom of the society. This has been evident in provision of reservation for the marginalised in the sphere of politics, state employment and higher educational institutions. It is also evident in the various economic and social development policies and programmes directed towards the uplifting the economic and social situation of the marginalised in accordance with the directive principle of the state in the Indian constitution.

Following such constitutional provisions and the policies of economic and social development, there is no doubt some gains have been made. Till the adoption of the constitution, there was negligible presence of the marginalised in the decision-making bodies at different levels of the governing institutions of the state. Now, the marginalised groups have their presence in these institutions. Similarly, they now have their share in state employment as institutions and enterprises controlled and run by the state. And so has been the case in higher educational institutions. All these have been possible because of development at the economic and social levels. Had there been no such development, the marginalised would not have able to have their share in state employment and other state controlled organisation? In fact the share of the marginalised in these institutions was not automatic but was rather contingent on required educational attainment and competence. Yet they fall far short of the share in proportion to the size of the respective population especially in higher level posts. Similarly their share or enrolment in institutions of higher education falls far short of their population size. Even while there is still a long way to address the exclusionary features of the marginalised, the policy of liberalisation, privatisation and globalisation adopted by the Indian state in 1991, has adversely impacted the marginalised communities in their march of development and empowerment.

Broad Features of Globalisation

The basic idea underlying globalisation is increasing interconnectedness and interdependence of people and countries coupled with changes in laws, policies, institutions at national and international with a view to promote such interconnectedness and interdependence. The role technology has been critical in shaping of the globalisation. Globalisation can be seen at different levels, be they economic, political and cultural. At the economic level, the globalisation means increasing movement of goods, commodities, services, technology, information, capital etc across countries thereby breaking the earlier boundaries. With this, every aspects of economy acquires global character. At the political level, globalisation points to a kind of world political system, which may lead a degree of erosion of power and autonomy of the state or nation state. The third dimension of globalisation is talked about at the level of culture. In the context of culture, the globalisations is primarily referred to in reference to transmission of ideas, values and other visible cultural elements such as music, cuisine, dress etc which influence and affect the existing ideas, values and cultural elements at national, regional and local levels.

India had begun its journey of integration to global economy in 1980s. However, the formal announcement came with the adoption of the New Economic Policy in 1991. The policy aimed at major structural economic reforms encompassing almost all sectors of the economy viz. industry, trade as well as the finance. The thrust of the reform was the integration of the economy with the global economy, dismantling controls, welcoming foreign investment and technology, promoting productivity and restructuring public sector. An important aspect of the reform was the programme of deregulation, which increased the scope of the private sector in the economy. In short, the thrust of the reform has been in the direction of liberalisation, privatisation and globalisation. This was contrary to the policy that aimed at building a socialistic pattern of the society. Hence laws, policies and programmes were mainly oriented towards safeguarding and protecting the interests of the common people including the tribal people. Such protectionist arrangements, however, came under threat with the inauguration of new economic policy. This paper focuses on the influence and impact of the economic and political globalisation on the marginalised communities with special reference to tribes in India.

Consequences on the Marginalised

Whereas there are great many advantages of globalisation, there are also disadvantages. In fact, the latter may not only outnumber former advantages but also of much greater adverse consequences on the marginalised such as the dalits and adivasis/tribes. One of such consequences has due to the declining role of the state and ascending pre-eminence of the market as a part of the structural adjustment programme of the World Bank and International Monetary Fund, promoter of neo-liberal market economy. In view of such shift, the safeguards the marginalised enjoyed are increasingly being eroded. A good example is the state employment. As noted earlier, the constitution has provision for reservation for communities hailing from the marginalised communities. Hence increase in state employment provides for greater share of absorption in stare employment. However, with liberalisation, privatisation and globalisation, it is exactly the opposite that is happening. The state employment is steadily shrinking. Earlier, there were four categories of state employment. These were grouped as class I, II, III and IV or A, B, C, D. The group D which provided large employment to people from the marginalised groups has disappeared from the lexicon of state employment. The size of group III or C has been greatly truncated. Thus, the key state employment is generally available only at the highest level of employment. All these jobs were contingent on certain level of educational attainment. However, educational attainment required for such jobs, were poor then. Now that the educational attainment has grown and pool of eligible and qualified candidates has seen increase, such jobs have been either done away with or have been greatly reduced. This being the case, they have forced to fall back on the private sector which does not make provision for reservation. Thus, the marginalised communities have to compete with others in job market in the private sector where their chances of making to the jobs are thin because of caste discrimination and prejudices that is pervasive in the society. The result is thrown in to the unorganised sector which is neither governed by any act nor by any government rules and regulations. Correspondingly, they suffer from irregular employment and wage/salary. Thus, they suffer from insecurity of job and may remain without jobs and months. Further, even when in jobs, their wages are low, working conditions poor. They live in congested colonies and slums without adequate, electricity and sanitation facilities. In short, they live a precarious life.

Multinational Corporations –Avatars of Globalisation

The state of Odisha in Eastern India can be taken as illustration. In pre-1990s, the state of Odisha used to be in news for large scale starvation deaths especially in Kalahandi and other neighbouring districts. Today, Odisha has been in news for different reasons viz. as ideal destination for investment of private capital- Indian as well as foreign. The tag of backward state that it is associated with is being attempted to be dispelled by sheer volume of new investments and investment proposals that have been pouring since 1993. During 1995-96, Odisha received the largest amount of private investment in India both foreign and domestic (Singh 1997). Underlying this unprecedented investment boom and proposals lie a number of factors.

One is the announcement of new industrial and mining policies. The industrialisation in Odisha has been mainly linked to mining. That mining occupies preeminent place in the industrialisation of Odisha is evident in successive Industrial and Mining policies of 1992, 1996 and 2001. The policies envisage the growth of private investment in the areas of infrastructure development, mineral-based industries and mega industrial projects. All these policies have been framed in the context of the liberalisation polices framed at the centre. The policies of 1992-2001 tried to simplify the procedures for higher investment through institutional support from within the government departments in large Industries and mining sector. The process of land acquisition was supposed to be done through bodies like Industrial Promotion and Investment Corporation of

Odisha (IPICOL), Industrial Development Corporation of Odisha (IDCO) and Directorate of Industries. The emphasis was on fast track single clearance windows known as the "Shilpa Jyoti". These bodies have been playing an important role regarding the dissemination of information to attract credit and investment opportunities for industrial development.

The new power infrastructure that has emerged in the context of disinvestment process has been the other stimulant of investment in Odisha. Odisha is the first state, which has taken the lead in the privatisation of the power sector with the dismantling of the Odisha State Electricity Board and inviting private investments in power plants. Another factor of attraction for investment in Odisha is the fact that the state of Odisha is rich in mineral resources. The state of Odisha has been showcasing the mining sector for the entry of private capital

In addition, the state government has been offering huge subsidies to investors in the form of guarantees, tax concessions, investment subsidy etc. Some of the subsidies extended to private investment are: 30 percent investment subsidy to new industrial units, capital investment subsidy on energy conservation equipment, sales tax exemption for new industrial units for 5 years, octroi exemption on machinery and equipment, minimum charge and electricity duty exemption for power generating unit for 5years, allotment of government land for industrial projects at pre-determinate rates, free of cost water drawn by new industrial unit from natural sources. Besides these, 8 districts of Odisha enjoy the special status of backward area given by the Central Government under which these districts enjoy special tax concession (*ibid.*).

The MNCs have been entering in a big way in the last one decade in the state of Odisha. They are engaged in projects of mineral exploitation and mines based industrial development. Infrastructure development such as power has also been one of the main concerns. Their entry has been made easy and smooth by the IFIs not so much by extending financial supports to their projects as by creating favourable climate and conditions, which in case of India was bought about by the economic reform of 1991. The entry of the IFIs in India is not new. Quite a number of projects have either been sponsored by the World Bank and other IFIs or the financial support has been made available for them from time to time. The governments through its Public Sector Undertakings have executed most of such projects. Even today, the World Bank and other such international financial institutions have been supporting a number of projects in different parts of India including Odisha. Indeed, coal mines and coal fired power have become one the IFIs the main preoccupation in Odisha today. Other financiers of Odisha's industrialisation are G-7 countries.

The New Economic Policy provided for greater autonomy and power to states to mobilise and restructure their economy. Most of the states with high concentration of tribal population and rich mineral and other resources such as Odisha, Jharkhand, Chhattisgarh, Andhra Pradesh, have taken advantage of the new policy and have opened up their states for private investment including the MNCs. Memorandum after memorandum has been signed with private investors. In Jharkhand, for example, between 2003 and 2007, 67 MOUs have been signed with different companies. In Chhattisgarh, in the period between 2001 and 2005, 51 MOUs have been signed and in Odisha the number has till the end of 2009, 80 MOUs have been signed. Most of these MOUs in all these states are to do with either the steel or aluminium or power projects. In Odisha, for example, of 80 projects as many as 57 were steel projects, 6 aluminium and 15 power projects. In Jharkhand, an overwhelming number of projects are to with sponge iron, steel and power and so has been the case with Chhattisgarh. The projects under MOUs are at different stages of their work. Some have already begun the first phase of their production, some have already purchased and some others are still in the process of submission of application and acquisition of land (Govt. of Odisha 2009; Govt. of Jharkhand 2008; Govt. of Chhattisgarh 2006).

The projects require land and the projects that are tied to mining lease require much more land than others. In fact, the six aluminium projects in Odisha have shown requirements of lands as high as over 12,350 acres. Similarly power projects, which again happens to be another mode of important development projects in tribal areas require vast amount of land. In Odisha, for example, 15 power projects have made demands of as much as over 19200 acres of land. Land to be made available for such projects happens to be either private or common or government land. The result is private land belonging to tribals and other cultivators are increasingly being acquired by the state for such development projects.

Alienation of Land from Tribes to Non-Tribes

The development and infrastructure projects both owned and controlled by the state or the private companies and the MNCs has not benefitted tribes in any way. At least this is the story of the last 70 years. Rather, such projects have attracted the non-tribal people from the state or outside to migrate for work in these projects. Gradually others too come as it provides opportunity for trade, commerce and other kind of services. In course of time, townships have emerged and people who have moved in look for land to make house and expand their enterprises. Though land cannot be transferred from tribes to non-tribes, they use various fraudulent ways to grab land. In fact, the movements of non-tribes in tribal areas have led to rampant alienation of land from tribes to non-tribes despite protective mechanisms. Dr. EAS Sarma who was commissioner for tribal welfare in the early 1980 in Andhra Pradesh narrates the story well. He tells as to how most teachers in schedule five areas came to be non-tribals. Even the Girijan Cooperative Corporation which traded in tribal produce was mostly controlled by non-tribals. The latter started in money lending and indulged in land grabbing (CPR 2013:14-15). The statistics available with the Ministry of Rural Development bear witness to the scale and magnitude of this problem. As per the information available with the Ministry of Rural Development in January 1999, 465 thousand cases of alienation of tribal land covering an area 917 thousand acres had been registered in the states of Andhra Pradesh, Assam, Bihar (Jharkhand), Gujarat, Himachal Pradesh, Karnataka, Madhya Pradesh (Chhattisgarh), Maharashtra, Odisha, Rajasthan and Tripura (Govt. of India 2001).

Dispossession and Resistance

Since a large number of projects have been welcome, land acquisition has assumed a scale unprecedented in the past resulting in large scale displacement of the population. Tribal people have suffered displacement all through the post-independence era of the national reconstruction process without any proper resettlement and rehabilitation and even without any adequate compensation. Further, they did not benefit much from any of such development projects. That has been the case even today. Rather, it is the outsiders who have benefited from such projects. In view of such experiences there has been now wide spread resistance against such development projects. Even in areas or regions which did not have to go through such experience, resistance against projects have been on rise because of what it has done to the tribal people elsewhere in state or region. The resistance to the projects has either taken the form of people's movement or the legal intervention. The former tends to be the most dominant form of the struggle against the project. In such movements tribals have found support from certain kinds of civil society organisations, activists, intelligentsia, academic and so on. Some of the key resistance/ struggle against the projects have been resistance against Polavaram dam in Andhra Pradesh, Jindal steel plant in Ghatsila sub-division in Jharkhand, Tata Steel plant at Kalinga Nagar and Vedanta Alumina at Lanjigarh in Odisha etc. In Kalinga Nagar on 2nd January 2006 when Tata's bulldozers started to move the earth under the community's paddy fields, the local inhabitants went to stop them with axes and bows resulting in a sort of battle leading to the killing of 12 tribal people and one policeman. One more tribal person died subsequently. Similarly against the Vedanta, the Dongria Khond took to resistance through meetings, rallies and protests including demonstrations in Bhubaneshwar, the capital of Odisha. Many such rallies and meetings were disrupted and disturbed by the state police and company goons. The Initial resistance was confined to households and villages, which were stated to be displaced. However, as the other Kondhs came to know of the proposed mining on their sacred mountain Niyamgiri, they also joined the protests and had even staged demonstration in Bhubaneshwar against the projects in 2005. In order to plan, coordinate and sustain the struggle, the Kondhs and other affected people formed themselves into an organisation called Niyamgiri Surakhya Samiti (Niyamgiri Protection Committee). As a consequences of their long and sustained struggle, they have been so far successful in halting the project (Xaxa, 2012). Similarly, tribes have waged a long struggle against the Polavaram dam beginning from 2004 through rallies, dharnas, relay hunger strike, foot-march etc (Bondla and Rao, 2010). In a way resistance against projects that displace them from their land and habitats have been wide spread in tribal areas in the globalised phase.

Deteriorating Social Development

The regions referred above are rich in mineral and other natural resources. Hence there has been strong intrusion of the MNCs in states such as Jharkhand, Odisha, and Chhattisgarh. In view of dispossession from land and other resources due the projects of the MNCs, people have been increasingly losing control of their land and other life support system. Dispossession from the land has either turned them into landlessness or into marginal and small farmers. Due to these, they have been forced to move out of their place either within or outside the state in search of livelihood. In fact, the volume of migration of tribal people from these states is largely the result of such developments that have got accelerated post-1991 development. This has begun to have bearing on tribal demography of the region. In Jharkhand, such trend has been visible even before the reform period. However, the pace and degree in decline of tribal population has sharpened in post-reform period. In 1991, the tribal population stood at 27.67 percent, which has gone down to 26.3 percent in 2001. Somewhat similar trend is discernable in other states especially at the local level. The similar trend seems to have begun to emerge in other state as well. The above has been due to increasing proletarianisation of the tribal people. The number of landlessness has been on the rise. Even with those with land, the size is steadily on decline. This is most evident in case of Odisha. The percentage distribution of marginal, small, semi-medium, medium and large farmers shows steady decline between 2005-06 and 2010-11. The percentage of marginal farmers was 54.79 in 2005-06, which has increased to 66.61 percent in 2010-11. The number of small farmers has declined from 29.6 to 23.55 percent between 2005-06 and 2010-11. And so has been the trend with semi-medium, medium and large. The semi-medium and medium declined from 12.46 to 8.3 and 2.14 to 1.46 percent respectively between the two periods. Even in case of the large farmers there was decline from 0.21 to 0.08 percent. The trend is similar in case of Chhattisgarh. Since the data in case of Jharkhand for 2005-06 is not available, the trend cannot be shown. However, as per 2010-11 agricultural census, the proletarianisation is glaring in Jharkhand too. In 2010-11, as large as 60.86 percent were marginal farmers, 17.75 percent small, 13,15 percent semi-medium, 6.97 medium and 1.27 large famers (Govt. of India 2013: 276).

The linkage between large-scale land alienation and displacement of the tribes and high incidence of poverty among them cannot be ruled out. The size of poverty in Jharkhand and Odisha, which have witnessed wide spread displacement of tribal population seems to be pointer in the direction. This has clearly been the case with Odisha. In 1993-94, the people living below poverty line were as high as 71.26 percent. This has increased to 75.6 percent by 2004-05 (Govt. of India, 2000; Govt. of India, 2007). In 2004-05 the states of Jharkhand and Chhattisgarh had 54.2 and 54.7 percent of people below poverty line respectively, which was much higher than the national average of 47.3 percent. (Govt. of India, 2007). In fact, these states fall under the extreme incidence of poverty among scheduled tribes in different states (Govt. of India, 2013:93: 291).

In 2001 the literacy rate of the tribes stood 47.1 percent at the national level. However, in states like Odisha, and Jharkhand, the literacy rate was lower than the national average. Jharkhand had literacy of 40.7 percent and Odisha 37.4 percent. Chhattisgarh was 52.1 and Andhra Pradesh 37.0 percent (Govt. of India, 2007)

The picture is no different in respect of health of the tribal population. The infant mortality rate and under-five mortality of the tribal population was 84 and 123 per 1000 population respectively in India in 2001-2011.

During the same period, the figure was 92 and 137 per 1000 population in case of Odisha and 95 and 143 per 1000 for Chhattisgarh. Jharkhand was somewhat better at 77 and 112 per 1000 population in respect of infant mortality and under-five mortality (Govt. of India. 2013: 201-202).

Conclusion

To conclude one can see the impact of globalisation in the most vivid manner in the context of tribal people in the eastern-central India As it is, they have been one of the most marginalised sections of the Indian society. This was evident in varied indicators of development. It is to address these that the constitution laid down various provisions for them. Due to such provisions, some benefits have reached them. However, a lot remains to be done. There is a paradox with tribal development. Whereas, on the one hand there are special allocation of resources and different programmes and schemes for their development, there is also a process of dispossession of tribes from their land by the state as well as the larger general population. This phenomenon has further led to their economic and social deterioration. The marginalised has further been being marginalised, more so with the advent of the globalisation.

References

Bondla, D J Narendra, Rao Sudhakar. 2010. "Resistance against Polavaram", Economic and Political Weekly, XLV (32), 93-95.

Centre for Policy Research. 2013. Consultation on the Fifth Schedule and Tribal Rights. Occasional Paper No. 21.

Govt. of India (Ministry of Tribal Affairs). 2013. Statistical Profile of Scheduled Tribes 2013.pdf.

Govt. of India (Planning Commission). 2001. Report of the Steering Committee on Empowerment of the Scheduled Tribes for the Tenth Five Year Plan.

Govt. of India (Planning Commission). 2007. Report of the Working Group on Empowerment of Scheduled Tribes for the Eleventh Five-Year Plan (2007-12).

Govt. of Jharkhand (2008): MOU List.

Govt. of Chhattisgarh (2006): MOU List.

Govt. of Odisha (2009): MOU List.

Singh, Kavaljit.1997.Odisha: From "Backward" to "Investor's Paradise" http:www.saanet.org/kashipur/articles/kaval.htm, accessed on 1July 2020.

Xaxa, Virginius. 2012. Identity, Power, and Development: The Khonds in Odisha, India in Susana Sawyer and Edmund Terence Gomez (ed.), The Politics of Resource Extraction: Indigenous Peoples, Multinational Corporations, and the State. Palgrave Macmillan &UNRISD: Hampshire.

2

Marginalised Groups in a Globalised World: With Special Reference to Caste System in India

— Prof. Vijoy S Sahay

Marginalisation, social marginalisation, social exclusion, and globalisation as well; have today, become 'buzzwords'. According to available sources, the term 'globalisation' first entered into the Oxford Dictionary in 1952, and the term 'social exclusion', (*a synonym of 'marginalisation'*) was first used in 1974 in France by Rene Lenoir- the French Social Action Secretary of State in President Chirac's government. However, anthropologically speaking, neither marginalisation nor globalisation, are any new phenomena. Both have been present ever since man's appearance on earth. They have been perennial throughout the known history of mankind.The task of an anthropologist is not merely to document a social or cultural phenomenon at the synchronic level at a given time and space, but his ultimate task is to attempt to discover the 'causal explanation' of the phenomena under study.

Any discussion on globalisation at this juncture would be, I think, out of the context and scope of this brief paper. However, when I assert that marginalisation has been a perennial phenomenon world over; it is by no means to justify any case of marginalisation of any social group at any time and space. Nevertheless, it is also unquestionably true that marginal groups could be ubiquitously found at all phases of human history. Even a very casual search into the Internet would approve that in every continent and in every nation of the world, the 'marginal groups' have been present. The degree of 'marginality' may vary from one place to another or one nation to another; but its omnipresence cannot be denied. Not only horizontally, but even if we examine the phenomenon vertically, i.e., at the dichromic level, we would discover that marginalisation of certain groups in the name of birth, gender, colour, faith, beliefs, rituals, religion, economy, or political status have always existed in all times and space.

After all, why has it been so? An anthropologist should at least attempt to examine that what are the forces that compel a social group to be marginalised? A psychological-anthropological attempt to examine the causal explanation of marginalisation or social exclusion of a group suggests that it is because of the very basic biological and social instincts that are inherent in man. Paul J Magnarella, (1993), in his book *Human Materialism* suggests that besides many other factors; inherent bio-psychological characteristics in man, such as love, sex, anger, hatred, jealousy, competition, rivalry, etc. play great roles in determining the social structure of a group at any given time and space. In addition to the above, the instinct of 'pugnacity',which leads men and societies so often to enter blindly upon deadly contests, has been a principal and one of the most powerful features of social evolution since man's appearance on earth. In the same vein, Malinowski (1944), in his book *A Scientific Theory of Culture*, talks about the 'derived needs' of man as a social animal. He calls it 'imperatives.' Without going into the details of his theory of needs, it is sufficient to say that one of the imperatives, according to him, is the 'exercise of authority', which is equipped with powers at the hands of an individual or a group for the forceful execution of its orders. In response, at the cultural level, it gives rise to different forms of political organisations.

In brief, because of the above bio-psychological factors in man, in every human society and in all types of political organisation and government; be it an egalitarian society like that of a band, or a tribal society, or a chiefdom, or a kingdom, or an empire, or an autocracy, or an oligarchy, or a theocracy, or a democratic republic, or even a communist society and government; at all times in history, we find some groups that have always remained privileged, while some others have remained unprivileged and marginalised. I also regretfully assume that in future also, howsoever technological advancement may take place in the world, and man can boast of reaching the Mars or any other planet of the galaxy; and at the same time, howsoever stringent measures are adopted to ameliorate the menace of marginalisation or social exclusion of all forms in the society, by the planners and policy-makers of any government; nevertheless, there would always remain some groups marginalised, and socially excluded from the mainstream, and some not. And, this would be so, not because of any deliberate attempt to do so by any individual or group, but this would happen spontaneously, because of the above referred biological, social, and psychological characteristics and instincts inherent in man.

From the above discourse, it may appear that my views on marginalisation or social exclusion are pessimistic. But it is not like that. Rather, despite envisaging a gloomy future in the above paragraphs, I am and would always remain very optimistic. My optimisms are based upon certain historical facts and sociological and economic concepts.

Sometime in the 1970s, I read a book named *Hundred Great Thinkers of the World* published by the Reader's Digest publication. It was about the life and contributions of 100 great thinkers, beginning from Hammurabi (c 1810- c 1750 BC) to Jean-Paul-Sartre (1905-1980). The book suggested in its Introduction that during the last three thousand years, there had been more than 6000 recorded wars in which millions and millions of people have been killed. Man is perhaps the only species that has killed its co-species more than any other species on this planet. Yet, man and man alone, is such a species, which is worried for the survival of mankind. No other species in the world is worried at all for the survival of its co-species. Here, one may ask a question, why is it so with man and man alone?

It is, I think, because of inherent capability of 'normative behaviour' found in man, which is not to be found in any other animal. This quality of normative behaviour of *Homo Sapiens* enables every group or community to decide and frame its own yardstick of, what is right or wrong; what is good or bad; what is desirable or undesirable; what ought to be done by the members of the group, and what ought not be done, and likewise.These become the values of the group, and thus, the values are gradually established and followed by the subsequent generations.

Today, at the first quarter of the 21st Century, the bulk of nuclear arsenal that different nations have piled up can no doubt, destroy the entire planet in minutes only. But I am sure that howsoever an autocratic leader or nation may attempt to wipe out any nation or group, the world community will unanimously come together to save the mankind. Here, I am reminded of French sociologist Emile Durkheim's (1858-1917) maxim '*society sui generis.*' According to him, society is though composed of individuals, but it is also independent of individuals. Society has a life of its own; it ensures its own survival and continuity.

In the same vein, I would also like to mention about the great economist, Thomas Malthus (1766-1834). In his 1798 book, *An Essay on the Principle of Population*, he proposed that while the food production in the world increased arithmetically, population increased geometrically, i.e., manifold as compared to food production. This gave rise to the hypothesis that the 'doomsday' had arrived, and the battle to feed all humanity was over. Sooner or later, there would be catastrophe. However, the proponents of this 'catastrophic theory' have perhaps failed to notice the closing lines of the second edition of the same book (1803), that raises a very positive hope, in which Malthus points out that "our future prospects are far from being entirely disheartening because of gradual and progressive improvement in human society". Today, world population has reached over 7.7 billion, but the dooms day has not arrived. Man is inventive by nature. He will find out the solution of any such problem that would be threatening to the very survival of the society. This also attests Durkheim's maxim that society ensures its own survival.

To sum up, I would reiterate that on one pretext or another, marginalisation of different social groups in all the nations of the world, including India, is a 'social fact.' One has to admit it without any justification. However, owing to normative behaviour of mankind, every nation, in its own way, attempts to improve the lot of the socially excluded groups through various socio-economic and political measures, though with varying degrees of implementation.

Caste System in India: with a focus on the marginalisation of *Dalits*

A few years back, I had been approached to write the Foreword of a book, entitled *Dalit Issues: Strategies for Comprehensive Escalation and Progress*, edited by Sangita Sinha (2017). In this brief paper, my views on the issue have been largely and liberally adopted from that Foreword.

One of the most deplorable forms of social exclusion could be found in the institution of 'caste system in India'. Umpteen number of books and articles have been written on the subject explaining the magnitude of atrocities perpetrated by the so called 'higher castes' upon the so called 'lower castes', especially, the '*Dalits*.' The biggest menace of this institution has been that it provides all the privileges to some select groups, and deprives any privilege to some other; and that too by birth. It has been even to the extent that a number of Holy Scriptures of the Hindus, imposed sanctions and punitive measures against the unprivileged groups in India. In ancient times, all the social, political, and economic norms in India were laid down by the priestly class of the *Brahmins*; who were considered at the helm of the caste hierarchy since millennia.

In ancient India, the concepts of 'purity' and 'pollution' remained the criteria for determining the social hierarchy of a group. As a result, the priestly *Brahmins,* and the pugnacious *Kshatriyas* remained the dominant groups. Mutually, both helped one another to ensure their supremacy and dominance in the society. The *Kshatriyas* had leverage over land, and the *Brahmins* had monopoly over the knowledge of the Holy Scriptures. The *Kshatriyas* patronised the priestly *Brahmins*; and in turn, the *Brahmins* ensured the well-being of their patrons in this life and also afterlife, by performing elaborate rituals and sacrifices for them, prescribed in the Holy Scriptures. Thus, they connived and maintained their dominance and supremacy for the longest period in Indian history.

The result of their supremacy and dominance was rampant exploitation of the weaker sections of society, chiefly the *Shudras*- many of whom were considered 'untouchables.' In today's vocabulary, they are called *Dalits*. All such groups considered as untouchables, were forbidden to enter any temple, to draw water from any well, they could not walk along the thoroughfares used by the upper castes; and even to the extent that the quantum of punishment for the same crime also varied from caste to caste, as per their position in caste hierarchy. Maximum punishment was prescribed for the lowest caste, whereas for the same crime, minimum punishment was prescribed for the priestly *Brahmins,* and the members of the other castes as per their hierarchical order. The extent of segregation and atrocities on such groups were even worse than perhaps the middle-age-slavery in Euro-American society. One can find unaccountable number of books and articles in the shelves of any library across the country that discusses the atrocities of various nature perpetrated by the twice-born castes on the *Dalits* in ancient and medieval India. Even today, every now and then, we come across the news of atrocities perpetrated on the *Dalit* in newspapers and television channels.

Even during the six hundred years of Muslim rule in India, and also in spite of large-scale conversion to Islam, chiefly to due to atrocities on them by the upper caste Hindus, the condition of the untouchables and their rung in the social hierarchy did not improve.Their socio-economic and political position remained *status quo* despite their conversion to alien faith. This is one good reason that of the entire Islamic world, caste system as such, could be observed only among the Muslims of the Indian subcontinent.

With the advent of the European missionaries in India, and particularly after the establishment of the British rule in the country, the conditions began to change. The European missionaries opened schools and hospitals in far flung areas of the country. The Britishers established a number of schools, colleges, and universities in the subcontinent. A large number of members of the upper castes, as also that of lower castes, received education in India as well as in England. This new class of educated Indians were thus exposed to the liberal western philosophies and style of life. In addition, various means of communications, such as roads and railways developed. Groups of people, irrespective of their caste belongingness, began to travel together in a bus or a railway compartment. Cumulative effect of all this was that the caste rigidity that prevailed for centuries, began to loosen.

Though, it is not that efforts were not made earlier to improve the lot of such marginalised communities in India. In fact, the backlashes against the rigidity and menace of caste system in India, has given rise to a number of religious and political movements during the chequered history of two and a half thousand years of the country. Many such movements laid down the foundations of new 'religious sects' in India. All such movements, be it religious or political, were aimed at ameliorating the evils that plagued the Indian society due to discrimination and marginalisation of various downtrodden communities, and that too, ascribed by birth in a particular caste.

Historically, over two thousand five hundred years ago, the *Buddha* was the first to categorically denounce discrimination against any caste or community by birth. Thereafter, a number of social and religious reformers all through the ages, attempted and condemned the orthodoxy and rigidity of caste system in India. Many of such movements gave rise to several sects in the country, such as, *Guru* Basweswara founded the *Lingayat* sect in South India in 12th century; *Guru* Ravidas, estimated to have lived during1450-1520 in North India, founded the Ravidassia faith: Guru Nanak Dev, during 1469-1539, founded *Sikhism* in Punjab, Chaitanya Mahaprabhu, during 1486-1533 founded the Gaudia Vaishnavism, Guru Ghasi Das, during 1756-1850 founded the Satnami sect in Central India; Raja Ram Mohan Roy during 1772-1833 founded the Brahmo Samaj; Dayanand Saraswati, during 1824-1883 founded the Arya Samaj etc. However, maximum momentum for the cause of the most marginalised communities in India, of which, enormous social and political impact could still be found in the country, received from Jyotirao Govindrao Phule (1827-1890), popularly known as Jyatiba Phule, founder of the Satyashodhak Samaj; Periyar E V Ramasamy (1879-1973), founder of Self Respect Movement and Dravid Kazhagam; and of course, the most significant momentum to the cause, was given by Baba Sahab Dr. Bhim Rao Ambedkar (1891-1956) by introducing *Neo-Buddhism*.

During the first half of the 20th Century, Baba Sahab tirelessly organised a number of societies to forge unity and solidarity among the marginalised groups; such as Bahishkrit Hitkarini Sabha in 1924, Samata Sainik Dal in 1927, Depressed Class Education Society in 1928, People's Education Society in 1946, All India Schedule Caste Federation in 1942. Himself being one of the most educated, able, and qualified leaders of his time, Baba Sahab emphasised upon imparting education among the marginalised groups. He believed that ultimately, education alone could emancipate the Dalits and every marginal group from their age-old socio-economic, political, and psychological depression and deprivation.

The Present Scenario

The present scenario relating to caste system in India and its implications is a mix of paradoxes. On the one hand, due to education, technological advancement, development of various means of communications, industrialisation, urbanisation, economic liberalisation and globalisation, and above all, enormous constitutional privileges and safeguards enshrined in the Indian constitution through various Articles to the marginalised groups after the enactment and implementation of the Constitution; a number of caste-based prejudices, orthodoxies, and rigidities have obliterated with the passage of time. Now, no one can prevent anyone to fetch drinking water from any well, nor could anyone be prevented from entering into a place of worship, just because of his birth in a so called 'low caste' category. If anyone or any organisation does so, there are adequate laws to deal with and protect the interest of the victims.Today, no one is bound to practice his traditional occupation only. One is free to choose profession of his like or dislike, as per his or her abilities, skill, and education. There are umpteen numbers of instances where we find top most services of the country occupied by the persons belonging to the marginalised communities. It is even to the extent that out of 14 full-time Presidents of the Republic of India (including the current one), this top most office of the nation, has been twice occupied by the persons of the most marginalised communities. Thus, the criterion that a caste is necessarily 'an occupational group' does not hold true today, as it did earlier.

However, this is only one side of the coin. The other side of the same coin is that because of the political reasons, the menace of casteism in the country has risen to such a height that had never been witnessed before. Casteism has virtually damaged the very spirit of all-round progress of the country. Untouchability and restrictions to entry in a temple or a place of worship may have, by and large, become a phenomena of the past; people of different castes might be seen dining together on specific places and occasions; inter-caste marriages might have become commonplace today; however, paradoxically, it is also true that chiefly because of political reasons, in different regions of the country today, one caste appears to be pitted against another, or a group of castes pitted against another group. I think that the nation is at the crossroads of the menace of casteism.

After all, why has it been so even after seven decades of independence of the country? The social scientists in general and anthropologists in particular have to come forward to furnish the 'causal explanation' of such deplorable phenomena that plagues the nation today. And one must speak the truth without fear; of course, at the same time, without having been influenced by any political ideologue or ethnic bias. It has been observed that the most of the books and articles written on the issue are guided by one political or ethnic bias or another. We hardly find any objective analysis on the subject seeking causal explanation of the problem.

Keeping the above objectives in my mind, and by reason of being a professional anthropologist, I have never been immune to any socio-economic, cultural, and political developments taking place in the country. It is true that generally anthropologists prefer to study any little community, be it a band, or a tribe or a village, and lately they have started studying cities also. But even a macro-study like that of a nation is not out of the scope of the discipline.

Though I have not done any empirical research on the subject, however, by dint of my anthropological orientation, I put before you some of my hypotheses that are as follows:

1. That, though, democracy is the most ideal kind of political organisation that mankind has achieved so far, but the democratic structure of our nation, despite being ideal; it has given rise to various problems in its practice, including the problem of casteism in the country.
2. That the first prerequisite of a democratic nation is the proper education of its citizens. With regard to it, barring a few exceptions, the standard of education in our schools, colleges, and most of the universities have deteriorated to such an extent that we have been distributing degrees only, and producing 'merely literates', not 'really educated' persons. In my opinion, *an educated person is he, who does more creative thinking than it is required for his survival*. I would also add that for creative thinking, any degree of a school, college, or university is not necessarily required.

3. That, Indian democracy, or for that matter any democracy in the world, is a game of numbers. It is axiomatic that in democracy, the majority will prevail over the others in struggle for power. Therefore, the will of the majority will also prevail over the will of the minority. Accordingly, in case of our nation, the will of the 'illiterates' and 'merely literates', will prevail over the 'educated persons'.
4. Any discussion on marginalised communities in India, and too with reference to caste system, would remain incomplete without any reference of the most controversial and politically most igniting and sensitive issue of 'reservation policy.'
5. While the laws dealing with reservation policy have been enshrined in the constitution with the best of the motives as per the need of the hour; however, as an anthropologist, I also assume that laws of any land is the product of, besides many other factors, its existing social, demographic, ecological, economic, political, technological, and cultural conditions. And also, that the said factors never remain the same. They are always susceptible to change.
6. Therefore, any law is never perennial. Had it been so, then the Law of Hammurabi (1810-1750 BCE) that "tooth for tooth, and eye for eye", codified sometime almost 4000 years before, would have remained in practice even today! Similarly, the ancient Roman law of *patriapotestas*, under which the father in the family had absolute right over his wife, children and slaves, even to the extent that he could give capital punishment, would have also survived. Henry Maine (1861) in his book *Ancient Law* has discussed about it in detail, and called it a '*legalfiction.*'
7. Undoubtedly, ever since the known history of India before independence, neither during the 600 years of Muslim rule, nor even during the British rule, any significant legislations were made to ameliorate the conditions of the most downtrodden and marginalised communities of the country. Therefore, in the very right perspective, the founding fathers of our constitution introduced a lot of legal provisions for the uplift of such marginalised communities. It was the need of the hour. However, even Baba Sahab also envisaged it as a temporary provision.
8. But today, ever after seven decades of independence, it appears to have become everlasting, despite the fact that the social, political, economic, demographic, technological, and many other factors

have changed since independence. Do we not require rethinking over the issue, and make suitable amendments, if the need be, as per the need of the hour?

9. The needle of the clock now appears to have been running reverse. With a view to bridge the gap between the privileged and the under-privileged groups, founding fathers of our constitution very adequately framed constitutional privileges and safeguards, and I very firmly believe that it must have been in their mind that if all these provisions are made everlasting, the clock would turn revers; that means that if it remains perennial, one day, today's under-privileged would become privileged, and the *vice versa*. Thus, the very purpose of the provisions of the constitution might be defeated perhaps.

Well, to conclude, I would only leave it the enlightened readers of this paper, and the future research scholars to judge, whether my hypotheses are credible or not???

References

Magnarella, Paul J. 1993. *Human Materialism:* University Press of Florida.

Maine, Henry 1861. *Ancient Law: Its Connection with Early History of Society, and its Relation to Modern Ideas*: London, John Murray.

Malthus Thomas Anonymously published. 1798. *An Essay on the Theory of Population.*

Malinowski, B. K. 1944. *A Scientific Theory of Culture and Other Essays.* Chapel Hill, N. Carolina: The University of North Carolina Press.

Sinha, Sangita 2017. *Dalit Issues: Strategies for Comprehensive Escalation and Progress*; B R Publishing Corporation, New Delhi.

3

Marginalised People's Resilience towards COVID – 19

— Dr. M.G Selvin Raj. S.J

COVID-19 pandemic has brought the humanity on their knees all over the world. We have become weak and vulnerable. Even the powerful countries are driven to face a great challenge and made to realise their helplessness and powerlessness. Though we boast of our achievements in inventing sophisticated modern technologies, harnessing the earth, space and sea, this barely visible minute virus has taught the world how brittle, weak and fragile are we and what we posses. Almost half a million population lost their lives because of the deadly virus. All over the world 2,35,86,641 people are affected and 8,12,537 have died and in India alone 31,06,348 are affected and 57,692 persons have died (till 24th August 2020). The smallest of the creatures has become a giant threat to the entire humanity.

The Virus Covid - 19 has disturbed the planet and destroyed the whole system of living. Human proximity and even touch has become suspicious and deadly. Everyone stands before the other as an untouchable. People's movements in and around their localities have almost been considered a criminal offence as violation of law and order in a civil society. Applying and obtaining e-pass to travel to inter-state is a herculean task. Everything has become hotchpotch. Lots of people have fallen into deep depression leading to suicide. There is an increase of alcoholism and domestic violence as the lockdown has ceaselessly continued. The poor, migrants, underprivileged, disadvantaged, marginalised who live at the peripheries of cities and towns and largely the Dalits and the Tribal people in small communities are the ones most affected by this pandemic. They are deprived of work, regular wages and money that guaranty their safety and security for their life. They are totally bereft of their livelihood opportunities and destined to face starvation and death in many parts of our country and in the world at large.

We don't know how long this pandemic would last. Everyone is extremely afraid of the virus and people are more cautious about it. This life threatening critical situation has brought us face to face with new revelations about our world, our attitudes, our behaviours, our choices and our priorities. We are rushing to safer places leaving behind our well cherished places of living, works, worship, business and study. We could not trust the places we lived in and people we lived with so long to be safe anymore. There is also an increasing urge in us to hoard food and other supplies with the fear of shortage in course of time. It is also saddening to see the plight of the marginalised people during the pandemic and how little and insufficiently the central and state government authorities cared for them. Amidst fear, anxiety and uncertainty people have learnt new ways of living their life. Covid -19 is not only a real threat to everyone's life but also a challenge to the resilience of the people and the marginalised ones in particular.

What do we mean by marginalisation and who are the marginalised people?

The Oxford English dictionary definition of marginalisation is: "To render or treat as marginal; to remove from the centre or mainstream; to force (an individual, minority group, etc.) to the periphery of a dominant social group; (gen.) to belittle, depreciate, discount, or dismiss." The term is being associated with other similar terms, such as 'vulnerable groups', 'seldom heard groups' or 'hard-to-reach groups'. The process of marginalisation leads to unequal outcomes.

The marginalised people are the ones affected by unequal outcomes of the social process, namely they are the socially excluded people. In the given Indian context they are the Dalits, tribals, unorganised labourers, trafficked women and children, LGBTQI, and many others.

They belong to such groups or even being perceived to belong to them heightens the risk of inequalities in terms of access to basic human rights, access to public services and goods in a variety of domains. They are denied proper access to education, employment, health, social and housing assistance. They constantly seek protection against domestic or institutional violence, and justice. They are considered socially downtrodden, economically poor, politically vulnerable, religiously impure, culturally low graded and physically malnourished. The resilience of such people against Covid -19 pandemic is a topic of worth study and the research interest of this paper.

What is resilience?

Resilience is the ability of people or things to feel better quickly after something unpleasant, such as shock, injury etch. Or the ability of a substance to return to its original shape after it has been bent, stretched or pressed (Oxford Advanced Learner's Dictionary, 9th Edition 2015). No doubt, Covid-19 pandemic poses a great challenge to the humanity in general and in particular how to understand and assess the resilience of the marginalised people in India and around the world.

Resilience of the marginalised people

Resilience of the marginalised people in any community is based on their in-depth understanding of water, land, forest and other natural resources available to them. There are three properties sustain the world and its population. One, the public property (ex. Railways, post office, pubic parks and public roads etch.) that belongs to the state all people who resides in the state enjoys the public property. Second, the private property (ex. Private house, land, bank account, vehicles etc.) which belongs to certain individuals who own them. The third, the common property (ex. Air, water, natural resources etc.) neither the State nor the private individuals own them. Common property belongs to all humans, living on this earth. The marginalised people posses only this common property wherever they live. So they have a very strong symbiotic relationship with all these common and natural sources of their livelihood wherever they live. They neither posses adequate private property, nor have access to public property. They solely depend on common property which is freely available at their disposal. If anything that ruptures their symbiotic relationship with those common properties, their life is in great peril. Any repeated attacks on these sources of their livelihood make them more vulnerable. However, they are able to withstand in due course of time, they find very hard to recuperate fully. Their innate ability to return to normalcy is nothing but their resilience. Covid – 19 also has affected badly their life by eroding their natural resources (common property) found in their environment.

In fact, for the marginalised people, resilience is rooted in their traditional knowledge and their capacity to adapt to changes in their environment. Covid – 19 has pushed them to the edge of their vulnerability.

When the media projected the hasty spread of this pandemic in China, US and other European countries they are in shock because of the seriousness of this virus which endangered their life and environment since there is no hope of bringing it under control completely. The world has not yet found an effective vaccine to curb this pandemic till today. Those who have high immunity in their body are likely to survive and rests are doomed. Naturally the poor and the marginalised are malnourished and are in great danger. The resilience of those people is put to test and they continue to live amidst sudden shock, dreaded fear, deep anxiety, hopelessness and uncertainty of their continual existence.

Resilience depends on their local knowledge of available natural resources

The intimate relationship with the natural surrounding is an important source of resilience for the marginalised communities. Their resilience depends on their ability to nurture and manage this symbiotic relationship uninterruptedly. Unfortunately Covid-19 pandemic alienated the marginalised people from the available natural resources and use of their indigenous knowledge.

Victoria Tauli-Corpuz (2010), Executive Director of Indigenous Peoples' International Centre for Policy Research and Education, points out that indigenous knowledge is locally fine-tuned, which is essential for climate change adaptation and long-term community resilience. The remedies for the symptoms of Covid-19 are not sought after from the indigenous medicinal practices available among the people rather the people are instructed with various precautions which are completely alien to their culture and indigenous knowledge.

Resilience depends on their social capital

The social capital necessary for community resilience (captured in rules and regulations, "ceremonies" of sharing and reciprocal support) is threatened when elements of social cohesion and identity fade away. This happens mainly because in the context of Covid – 19 pandemic, numerous migrant labourers from the cities returned back to their villages and they were not fully accepted into their communities. They were suspected of infection and probable carriers of this deadly virus. This affected their group solidarity. They remained the villages disassociated with the rest of the community members.

Due to continuous imposition of social distance and extension of lockdown, people are not able to meet each other in common places (fields, places of work and worship etc). People are prohibited to gather at the local markets in their villages and all the social and religious gatherings are prohibited. This badly affected their economy and livelihood. Examples of this degradation include formerly cattle-rich pastoralists became poor, women became more dependent on their husbands, men succumbed to alcoholism, children are left free without attending to schools.

In the process of adaptation to such changing scenario, indigenous communities will not be what they were before. Their resilience is further weakened. They will have to accept the challenge of societal transformation. This will require new institutional settings and shifts in societal hierarchies and power.

Resilience depends on their traditional work culture

The survival of the indigenous marginalised small communities very much depends on their traditional works, which are closely linked to their culture. Some of the nomadic tribes in India traditionally use domesticated animals to perform magical feats on the roads and street corners. They dance to the tune of drums and pipes attracting crowd to earn their living. There are many people from small traditional communities earn their daily living by carrying lamps during the procession conducted at the time of social gatherings and celebrations such as marriages and religious festivals. Stage performances are done by many local artists and artisans to earn their living. But during the lockdown social gatherings are totally banned. During this period they were driven to find alternative works for their survival. They were completely neglected and were not provided alternative opportunities to earn their survival needs. Thus, their resilience is very much eroded by the Covid-19 pandemic.

Revival of "*Gutti Pani*" a tool to strengthen resilience

The unpublished doctoral thesis of Selvin (2020) with the title "Cultural Resistance and the Process of Development through Participatory Action Research (PAR): A Case study of *Savara* Tribe, Andhra Pradesh" makes reference to the practice of *"Gutti pani"* (Group work) among the *Savara* tribe in Seethampeta on the hills of Palakonda in Srikakulam District of Andhra Pradesh. The study recognizes that the work culture of the *Savara* tribe is very much depended on community involvement in *Gutti Pani*, where everyone's land on the rocky hills is attended to by the members of the same *Savara* community. The repeated cyclonic storms (between 2014-20) uprooted countless fruit bearing trees and plants on the hills such as cashew, jack, custard apple, pine apple, ginger and turmeric plants. They are faced with the challenge of reviving their agriculture work, which involved considerable amount of investment on cleaning the fallen trees and wild thorny bushes. In such circumstances their traditional practice of "*Gutti Pani*" became very handy. Revival of *Gutti pani* practice enabled them to attend to their fallow land on hill terrains. In course of time they are eventually changed into cultivable land by the village community by utilising the credit facilities obtained from Micro-Credit Unions initiated through the Participatory Action research. The Micro-Credit available to them and the learned practice of circulating the money among them greatly enabled them to withstand the hard time of Covid-19 pandemic.

These stories illustrate hope and resilience of indigenous communities around the world, dealing with impacts from climate change to economic development to health hazard. Already, seasonal rains arrive late or fail completely or down pour excessively impinging their regular life style. The mobile pastoralists are led to sedentary lives. People are deprived of the forest produce. Fishing communities are not permitted to enter into sea and open their fish markets. The settled agriculture communities are discouraged to work in their own land. Economic activities remained standstill due to lack of credit affordability and failure to find alternative works. Covid – 19 isolated people belonging to the indigenous small and traditional communities in their own land. Their communal solidarity which sustained their resilience became more vulnerable.

It is high time to introduce new and innovative strategies to protect the nature and people from all these natural and man-made calamities. We need to promote economic development and enhance the lives of the marginalised communities around the world. Long term goals which are sustainable to the generation after us could be planned.

Sustainable Development Goals (SDGs)

In 2015, the world agreed to an ambitious set of Sustainable Development Goals (SDGs). From ending extreme poverty and hunger, to ensuring resilient communities, to ensuring water security, to sustaining life on land and life below water. This agenda defines the world we want in 2030. Achieving these goals will require a significant departure from business idea perpetuated by private corporate sectors as usual and moving towards imbibing corporate social responsibilities (CSR).

Considering the environmental degradation taking place at present it was presumed that – we will lose 68 percent of biodiversity by 2020. We are losing a rhino every eight hours, and an elephant every 15 minutes. Losing biodiversity also hurts the economy.

UNDP believe that no one actor – not governments, not companies, not cities and not NGOs – can achieve the SDGs alone. Local action will be an essential component to achieve the set goals. Local communities and indigenous peoples face the very real consequences of biodiversity loss which can mean life or death for their families, communities, and ways of life.

In Kenya, for example, Mikoko Pamoja is the first community-based initiative of its kind to sell carbon credits generated through the protection of mangrove forests. The community reinvests income from these credits into clean water and education, providing a virtuous cycle of development dividends that deliver on SDG1 (no poverty), SDG4 (quality education) and SDG6 (clean water and sanitation), in addition to SDG13 (climate action), SDG14 (life under water), and SDG15 (life on land).

Investment on nature strengthens resilience of small indigenous marginalised communities

Equator Prize winning communities show that investing in nature is an effective and efficient pathway to sustainable development which strengthens resilience. For example, the village of Bang La in Thailand was largely spared by the devastating force of the 2004 Indian Ocean Tsunami, because its mangroves were intact. The Bang La Community formed an association called the Mangrove Forest Conservation Group to legally protect their mangroves for future generations, at a fraction of what the cost of rebuilding a devastated community would be.

"As our natural world faces a range of unprecedented challenges, the Equator Prize lifts the curtain on a range of exceptional nature-based solutions pioneered by local communities and indigenous peoples," says UNDP Administrator, Achim Steiner.

Human right violations and anti-poor policies of the government

Many of the indigenous communities around the world are increasingly facing an erosion of their rights through land grabs, illegal mining, government sponsored road extension projects; industrial development and construction of mega dams undermine resilience-building efforts. The rights of the indigenous peoples and local marginalised communities have to be protected. This awareness is very much lacking not only among the indigenous and marginalised communities in India but also among the policy makers.

Community initiatives by the people and for the people

In Algeria, there is an interesting fusion is emerging of modern and traditional solutions deployed to prepare, respond and recover from COVID-19. At the sight of life-threatening nature of the global pandemic, there are instantaneous transformational changes taking place towards e-commerce in economies. At the same time, in villages across the country many communities are using their traditional bonds and community structures to help defend against the spread of the disease.

A crisis unit COVID-19 Tifilkout was formed to prepare and manage the confinement, led by civil society and "Tajmaat" the ancestral village assembly that usually organizes, traditional celebrations, volunteering for the cleaning and beautification of village. They also take up the responsibility of fund-raising for the poor and sick.

Amel Mohandi, a journalist from Tifilkout in Algeria explained how the ancestral tradition of wise men played a key role in responding promptly to the pandemic. The COVID-19 Tifilkout (2020) crisis unit prepared for the confinement with food supplies, gas and goods, organised outreach campaigns to each house. They delivered soap dispensers in each water fountain of the village. The group of volunteers stand at each access point of the village and sanitise the cars coming from outside. The crisis unit solicited local tailors to make fabric masks. To intensify social distancing among people a group of volunteers was assigned to make the rounds to take regular delivery orders from households. Tifilkout also has a health unit and an ambulance is donated by the Diasporas of the village.

Not all initiatives were welcomed. Funeral ceremonies are banned as protection measures. Even if someone dies of natural causes, the burial in Tifilkout had to take place without a ceremony. It was a big challenge for the crisis unit to convince the residents to abide by the rule, given to their strong cultural rituals and spirit of community solidarity.

Local experiences spark new ideas

Indigenous and local communities make careful observations about their natural resources. They exchange information and experiences, to plan for the future. New ideas spring up based on centuries-old knowledge found in their culture and tradition. It is a healthy sign of partnerships between indigenous and marginalised peoples and modern scientists. Together they produce new knowledge to address the challenges and threat to life and wellbeing of people countering Covid – 19.

A way forward

The measures taken to prevent the pandemic outbreak like quarantine, lockdown, social distancing has made people isolated and introverts. At the same time meditation, yoga, other spiritual and physical exercises had a positive impact on both the mental health and physical well being of people during the lockdown period.

The increasing rate of recovery gives hope that this pandemic is not as monstrous as we all had thought. It enables us with courage to face difficulties amidst this out-break. Historically, we see that pandemics have forced humans to break with the past and imagine their world anew. Therefore it is time now to bring greater awareness among people towards newness.

In this process of building resilient communities we cannot simply belittle the commitment and perseverance of small groups or individuals who strive to change the world for better. The works of medical and para-medical professionals and the service of the sanitary workers are marvelous during this period of pandemic. There is hope amidst chaos, showing us that local action can create powerful impacts on people.

At this situation recognition of indigenous rights and respectful two-way collaboration is the path to build better early warning systems. We need to support local efforts towards building resilient communities. Building resilience among the indigenous and marginalised communities is the moral responsibility of every responsible citizen of this country. Thus, the role of the government in every level is very crucial not only from the point of allocating needed funds but also sort out measures efficiently to see that the allocated funds reach the deserving people and departments in time to bring under control the pandemic more effectively.

References

Victoria Tauli-Corpuz (2010). Reflections on the Role of the United Nations Permanent Forum on Indigenous Issues in Relation to the Millennium Development Goals, *International Journal on Human Rights,* Vol. 7, No. 12, p. 78, June 2010.

Kristy Galloway McLean (2012). Land Use, Climate Change Adaptation and Indigenous Peoples. https://unu.edu/publications/articles/land-use-climate-change-adaptation-and-indigenous-peoples.html#info

Gnana Selvin Raj M (2020). Cultural Resistance and the Process of Development through Participatory Action Research (PAR): A Case study of *Savara* Tribe, Andhra Pradesh (Un published).

UN Sustainable Development Goals:

https://www.un.org/sustainabledevelopment/sustainable-development-goals/

Equator Prize winners inspire indigenous and innovative ways of coexisting with nature: https://www.undp.org/content/undp/en/home/news-centre/news/2020/11th-equator-prize-.html

Hamdi Sellami (2020), Traditional and modern ways to approach COVID-19 in Algeria. https://www.undp.org/content/undp/en/home/blog/2020/traditional-and-modern-ways-to-approach-covid-19-in-algeria.html

4

Post-Globalisation and the Predicament of the Marginalised in India

— Prof. P.D. Satya Pal

Introduction

'Marginalisation' refers to the relegation of some groups to the fringes of society resulting in their lack of access to rights, resources and opportunities. Marginalised people might be socially, economically, politically and legally ignored, excluded or neglected. The concept of marginality is generally used in the analysis of social-economic, political and cultural spheres, where disadvantaged people struggle to gain access to resources and full participation in social life. Marginality is based on the binary opposition of center and periphery. Marginalisation is a multidimensional, multicausal, and historical phenomenon. The analytical tools that can be used in most cases include class, race, caste, gender, religion and region in relation to specific social, cultural, economical and political conditions as well as ideological enforcement. The terms such as exclusion and deprivation are used as synonyms to marginalisation although conceptually exhibiting minor variations.

The nature of marginalisation varies in different settings. Social Marginalisation refers to the study of underlying factors responsible for the social inequality, social injustice and exclusion. Spatial Marginalisation indicates the geographical regulation of habitations and spacial segregation of sections of people owing to ideologically defined pollution, stigma and lowliness. The marginalised groups are kept away from access to resources and relegated to unfavourable spaces.

Various sections such as Afro-Americans, Native Americans and Hispanics in the United States of America, Gypsies and ethnic minorities in Europe, Australian Aborigines and other religious minorities including women suffer from being banished to periphery in their respective societies. It is pertinent to note that in other countries world over, it is the minority who get marginalised. But in India, it is the majority of the population that are marginalised. The present endeavour is to delineate the manifestations of marginalisation of majority despite a democratic constitution envisioning a just society.

Caste and Exclusion

Caste based exclusion in India resulted in the most severe and intensely discriminate form of deprivation. The Varna - Caste system, also known as the Brahminical system has regulated the life of the people over centuries in which the organisational scheme is based on the division of people into endogamous caste groups and the civil, economic, political and religious rights of each individual caste are ascribed unequally by birth and made hereditary. Exclusion of some castes from the rights and privileges enjoyed by others is enforced by several instruments of social ostracism (Thorat, 2008).

This systemic exclusion, the manifestations of which could also be found in geographical, gender and other areas is basically conceived by the Brahminical ideology and its rationalisation is being drawn from the concept of natural inequality and this ideology of exclusion permeates all facets of social-economic and political life. It forms a **majority exclusion** where in few privileged castes enjoy absolute rights and majority castes are denied equal privileges and basic human rights. The majority producer castes have been arranged in the system of graded degradation and subjected to physical and mental subjugation. Complete ban on education, accumulation of property, arms and authority dubbed them into enforced poverty and marginalised existence.

Constitution of India and the Marginalised

The Constitution of India founded on the ideals of Liberty, Equality, Fraternity and Justice is the culmination of several social movements against the Brahminical system for securing civil and political rights. Contemporary Constitutional authority, Granville Austin has described the Constitution of India as 'first and foremost a social document with three broad objectives-ensuing unity, democracy and creating a social revolution.' The majority of India's Constitutional provisions are either directly arrived at furthering the aim of social revolution or attempt to foster this revolution by establishing conditions necessary for its achievement."

The Constitution of India bears the impression of Ambedkar's thought as a key instrument for National Reconstruction. In order to establish an inclusive society, Ambedkar looks at democracy, not as a political arrangement, but as a mode of associated living. "The roots of democracy are to be searched in social relationship, in terms of the associated life between the people who form the society" (Keer, 1962:480). He highlights fraternity as the root of democracy and without fraternity other ideals of democracy like equality and liberty cannot endure. He defined democracy as a "form and method of government where by revolutionary changes in the economic and social life of the people are brought about without bloodshed" (Keer, 1962:61).

Affirmative and Transformative Agendas of the Constitution

The Constitution of India, in order to reconstitute the society on the democratic foundations incorporated legislations for equality and equal opportunity in all spheres of life. Ambedkar engineered the category **'Socially and Educationally Backward Classes'** with three principal components, the Scheduled Castes, the Scheduled Tribes and the Other Backward Classes as the marginalised majority. Road map is laid for a democratic and inclusive society through reservations as representations in education and public employment. These affirmative measures have been incorporated in the Fundamental Rights.

The transformative component is found in the Directive Principles of State Policy which is made duty bound to strive for creating a Welfare State and a just social order. Making the State responsible for social change, Article 38 contains the essence of these principles: "The State shall strive to promote the welfare of the people by securing and protecting as effectively as it may a ***social order*** in which justice–social, economic and political – shall inform all the institutions of national life".

However, the entrenched castes that have been controlling all portals of power are managing to keep the Constitutional goal of establishing a just society at bay. As observed by Ambedkar that "Today, India is governed by two ideologies. The ideology enshrined in the Constitution promises a life of Liberty, Equality, Fraternity and Justice. But the ideology that governs the life of the people denies them". By several deliberate and discrete means to maintain the marginalisation of the Scheduled Castes, Scheduled Tribes, Other Backward Classes and those who converted in to other religions from among these groups, the conscious and determined minority always create changing conditions in their favour over an ignorant and amorphous majority. The operationalisation of the ideology of marginalisation is apparent in manipulating the policies and programmes of the state in order to deny the rights and entitlements to the socially and educationally backward class citizens.

Globalisation, Libertarianism and Post Globalisation

Economic globalisation which is referred to as neo-liberalisation came in handy to the entrenched castes of India to disregard the constitutional democratic foundations and unleash Liberalisation, Privatisation and Globalisation. Brought into India in 1991 the successive governments have started converting the public resources as private goods. In 2002, the union government established a Ministry of Disinvestment for furthering the process of globalisation. The economic philosophy of globalisation which is known as Libertarianism proposes the movement of capital across sovereign countries for investment by Multi-National Corporations (MNCs). The governments are required to free the capitalist of taxes, permits and regulations and assist in the enhancement of private profits. The capitalist after realising profits will make charities known as Corporate Social Responsibilities. The democratically elected governments facilitate the MNCs in providing unbridled access to all resources. Libertarianism has its roots in Social Darwinism of Herbert Spencer and William Sumner who proclaim that one need not worry if 'certain sections of people get crushed under the wheels of progress'.

In India, those who have been getting trampled by the ideological adversary and its adopted policies are the historically marginalised populations. Whatever respite and promise that the democratic constitution provided them to become equal citizens has been put to severe erosion. The traditional business castes in India became global corporates and associates. With unleashing the process of globalisation, chunks of lands have been doled out to the corporates, protective and sensitive forests in the Scheduled Areas are being cleared for mining resulting in large scale displacement, loss of livelihoods and deprivation of the historically marginalised. It has been the experience that governments are increasingly becoming the facilitators and collusive of such 'development'.

Globalisation is a process and usually every process gets altered after two decades. By the advent of the first decade of 21st century we observe almost a reversal of the phenomenon which can be termed as Post Globalisation. The torch bearers of seamless investments across 'global village' have become 'inward looking'. Prioritisation and protection of national interests overtook the scenario. Manifestations like 'America is for Americans', building walls, Brexit from European Union, curbs on immigration by Australia and New Zealand are few examples. Such a situation became a boost to the traditional business houses in India in filling up the spaces and capitalising on the liberalised economy. With the government deliberately siding with the markets, the contemporary situation turned out to be perilous for the historically marginalised.

Contemporary situation

After seven decades of constitutional governance, a look at the situation of crucial indicators progress is crucial to assess the course that India is taking and to understand the quandary of the marginalised population. Although there has been some progress in the lives of the historically marginalised, the efforts are found not being enough to the task.

Social Dimension of Marginalisation

The constitutional agenda enjoins all spheres of inequality and anticipates to make heterogeneous groups divided on the lines of caste, class, region, religion and gender into a civil society. Making the State responsible for desired social change, Article 38 contains the essence of striving to promote

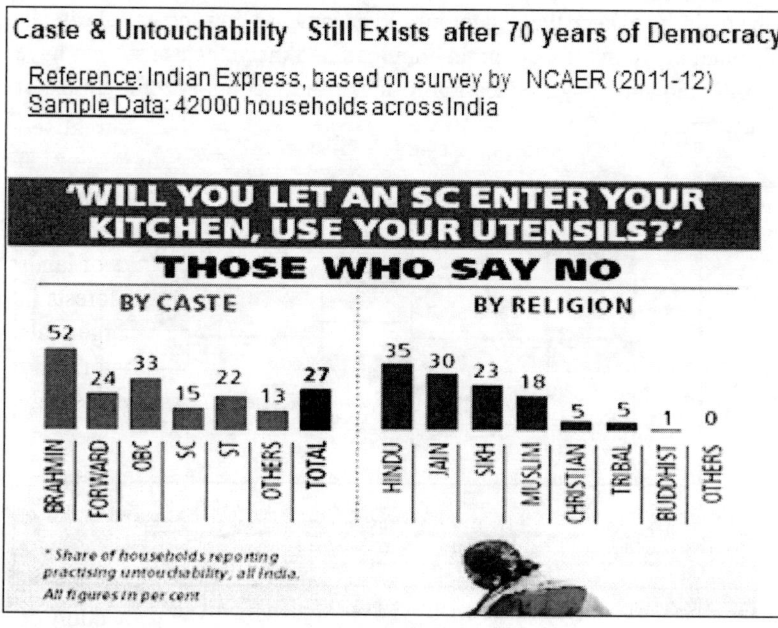

Source: The India Human Development Survey (IHDS-2)

Fig. 1

the welfare of the people by securing and protecting a new *social order.* These aspirations refer to the duty of elected governments in annihilation of caste and establish a just society. On the contrary we still see that caste remains the organising principle of the society and people arrogating themselves in the name of caste. Spatial segregation of households on the lines of caste in village India do not show any signs of weakening and caste-based gated communities started appearing in cities. The existence of caste is the standing denial of democracy. On the other hand we find some 'caste blind' assertions especially in urban, educated, private enterprises that caste and its entailing marginalisation became the things of the past. However, we find several researches proving the stranglehold of caste in all walks of life. Figure 1 illustrates that the ideology of Brahminism effectively informs the daily lives of people in India and regulates the thought and actions resulting in the continuation of discriminatory practices.

Education and Marginalised

India has an inglorious history of denial of education to the majority for centuries. The makers and upholders of the unnatural caste system that benefits the minority have understood the necessity of banning education to the majority to keep them ignorant and become wanton and wilful vassals. All social movements against the inhuman and inequal caste system have been the movements of education to make the victims become aware of their trammels.

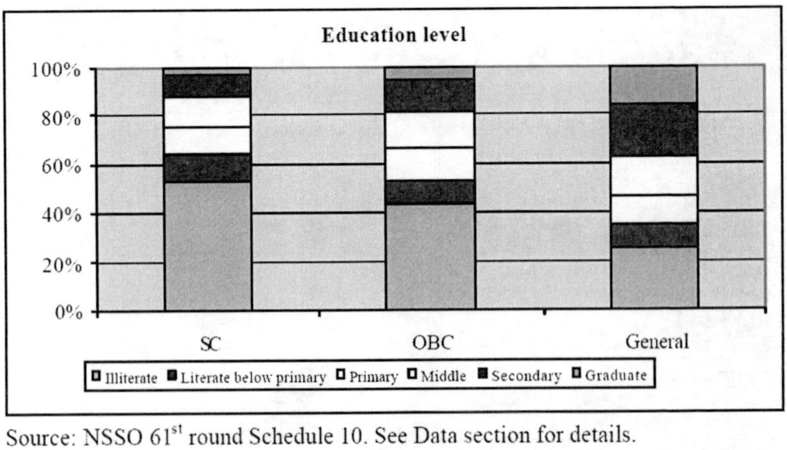

Source: NSSO 61st round Schedule 10. See Data section for details.
Note: All figures in this paper relate to prime-age adults (aged 20 to 65 years).

Fig. 2: Educational Attainment in 2004-05

The constitution of India has made the governments duty bound to impart education to all. Article 45 is the sole statute which has a temporal frame, i.e within ten years all children under the age of fourteen should get free and compulsory education. For the past seventy years governments have been shifting the goals of imparting educating the citizens. It is evident from figure. 2 that the historic inequalities are still maintained. The efforts have been concentrated in getting enrollment leaving aside the concerns of equity and quality of education. There has been promotion of inequality in education by recognizing different parallel boards in school education. The spending on education has been grossly inadequate and recruitment of teachers is not corresponding with the need. Culmination of such impediments reflects in the gap of literacy to the historically marginalised. It is found that there has been a significant dropout from these sections at secondary education. Even those who attained education, the quality of education is alarming. ASER (Annual Status of Education Report) by NGO Pradham reveals that 73.4% of students in class 8 cannot subtract, and 68% cannot recognize numbers between 10 and 99. Similarly 49.7% students of class V cannot read books of class II and the differentials category wise are presented in Table no.3. Students from marginalised sections receive education in government run schools and have to compete with the privileged students who received better education in private schools in the common entrance examinations.

Table 1: Subject-wise Mean Achievement Score of Students at National Level

National Average Mean Score		English	Mathematics	Science	Social Science
		250	250	250	250
Gender-wise	Male	248	250	250	250
	Female	252	250	250	250
Area-wise	Rural	244	247	247	247
	Urban	263	256	257	257
Category-wise	SC	238	240	239	240
	ST	241	237	235	239
	OBC	245	250	249	249
	Others	267	260	263	260
Institution Mgmt-wise	Govt.	236	239	239	238
	Govt. Aided	246	248	248	248
	Private	277	269	270	271
Overall Finding (In Percent Correct)		41	40	43	47

Source: National Achievement Survey (NAS) Class X- 2015, NCERT.

The governments have allowed private institutions in higher education thus paving way for the commercialisation that eluded the marginalised communities to attain adequate higher education. Those students from historically marginalised communities who can afford expensive private education suffer from institutional discrimination that affect their levels of confidence. There has been proliferation of private education institutions (Fig 3) run by political leaders fleecing students by collecting huge sum of fees.

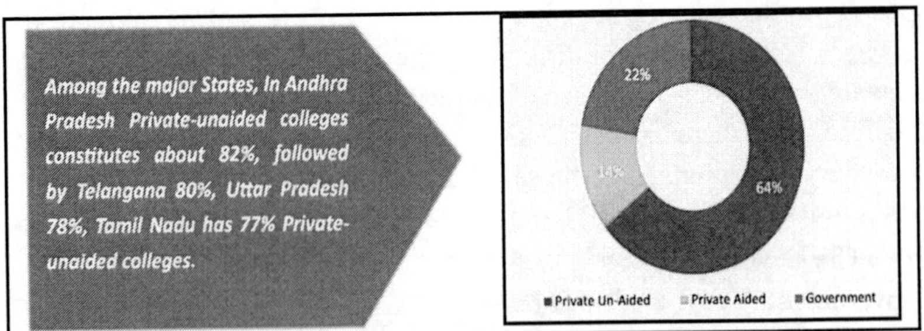

Source: All India Survey on Higher Education (AISHE) Report 2019, Ministry of Human Resources, Govt. of India.

Fig. 3: Privatisation of Higher Education.

These higher education institutions although referred to as private cannot be technically called as private because all are registered as not-for-profit institutions and enjoy concessions from the government in getting lands, water, communications and several amenities at subsidised rates and yet do not bother to implement constitutional requirements. As such we find skewed representation of the marginalised communities in appointments to teaching and support staff.

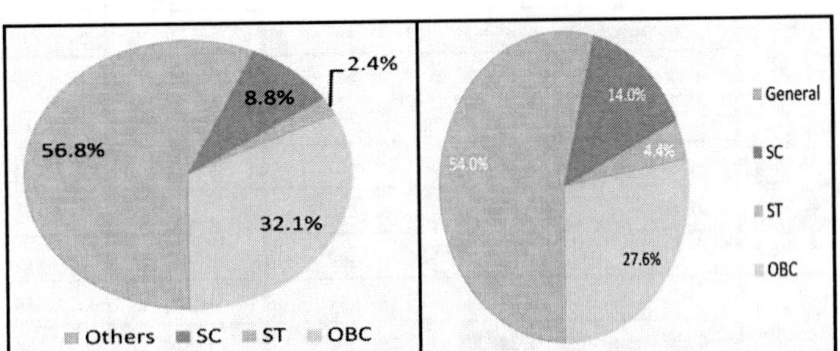

Source: All India Survey on Higher Education (AISHE) Report 2019, Ministry of Human Resources, Govt. of India.

Fig. 4 & 5: Higher Education: Social Category-wise Teaching and Non-Teaching Staff.

Similarly gender representation is a matter of grave concern in these institutions as shown below:

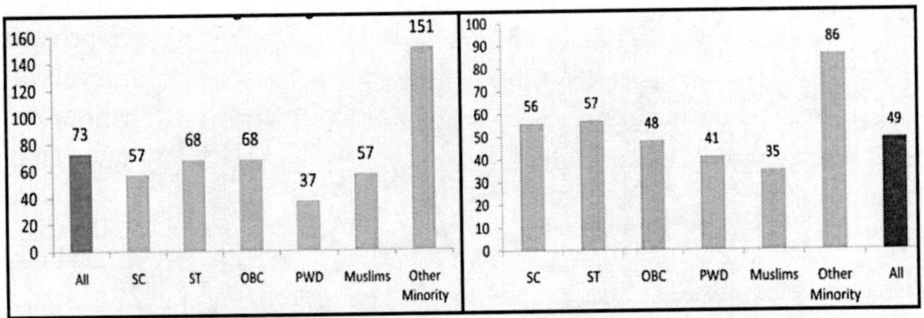

Source: All India Survey on Higher Education (AISHE) Report 2019, Ministry of Human Resources, Govt. of India.

Fig. 6 & 7: Representation of social categories, gender, religion in Teaching and Non- Teaching Staff.

The situation is much worse for the marginalised communities in the government-run premier institutes such as Indian Institutes of Technology and Managements. There is gross disregard for constitutional representations and have become the monopoly of the entranched minority. In IITs, of the 8,856 sanctioned faculty strength, 4,876 are from the general category, 329 are OBCs, 149 are SCs and a mere 21 are from the ST community. In effect, across 23 IITs, including new and old, only 9 percent of the current faculty are either SCs, STs or OBCs.

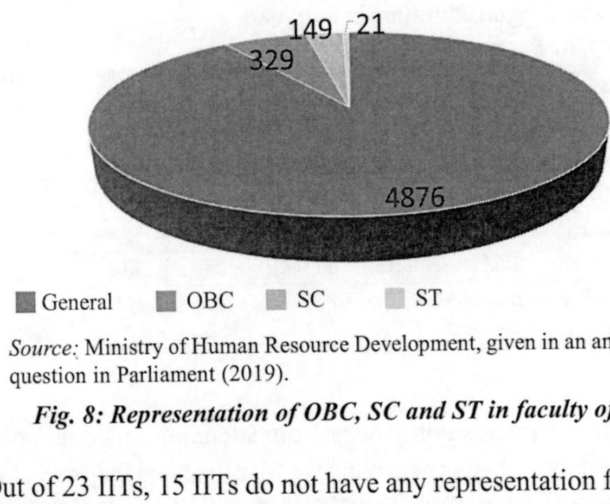

Source: Ministry of Human Resource Development, given in an answer to a question in Parliament (2019).

Fig. 8: Representation of OBC, SC and ST in faculty of IITs.

Out of 23 IITs, 15 IITs do not have any representation from STs in the faculty. These include the the IITs in Bombay, Kanpur and Kharagpur. Out of 18 IIMs as many as 16 had no ST, 12 had no SC and 7 had no OBC in their faculties. And in January 2020, all IIMs have written to Govt to exempt them from Reservation because they are 'Institutes of Excellence'!

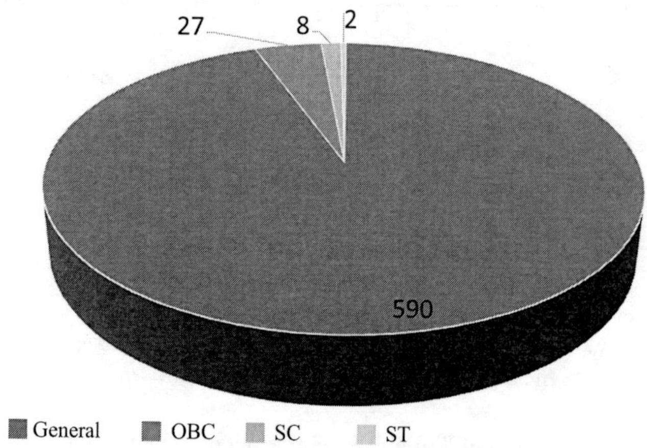

Source: Data submitted by the MHRD in Parliament (2019) for 18 IIMs.

Fig. 9: Representation of OBC, SC and ST in faculty of IIMs.

The world average spending on education is 6% of GDP. The spending on education in India did not cross 3% in the last seven decades. It is quite alarming that the spending has come down from 1.06 to 0.62 % in the last four years.

Spending on education in four years of the Narendra Modi government

	HRD Ministry budget (₹bn)	Total central budget (₹bn)	Gross national income (₹bn)	(% of GNI)	(% of central budget)
2014-15	1,103.51	17,948.91	104,122.8	1.06	6.15
2015-16	966.49	17,774.77	112,463.05	0.86	5.44
2016-17	926.66	19,780.6	120,347.13	0.77	4.68
2017-18	796.85	21,467.34	128,350.04	0.62	3.71

Fig. 10: Government Expenditure on Education.

While the government shying away from spending on education, it is leading to the privatisation thus depriving the marginalised majority students who are the future of the nation. The New Education Policy-2020 is also promoting private players in education sector. It is prioritising Vocational education to at least 50% of learners. Promoting distance mode and online mode of learning, this policy is pushing a scheme of training the majority marginalised as Hands and the privileged minority as Minds.

Youth Development Index shows that India has more number of youth in comparison to other countries of the world. About 65% of Indians are below the age of 35 years and the average age of 50% Indians is 26. The substantial youth belong to the marginalised communities as they form the majority of the country. Thus, there is enormous potential if these youth are educated and skilled. However, in Global Development of Youth, India ranks at 133 in 183 countries. Nepal (77), Bhutan (69) and Sri Lanka (31) stand much better. The indicators of youth development and India's hapless position is an indication of education, health, employment and participation of the youth in the country.

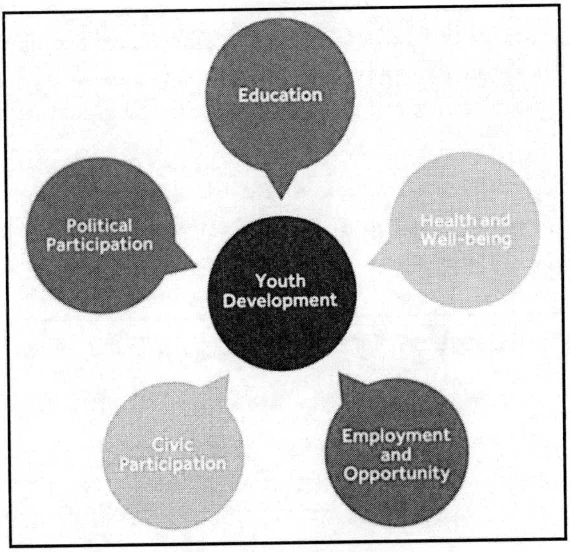

Source: Commonwealth Secretariat website.

Fig. 11: Youth Development?

Economic Dimension of Marginalisation

Economic well being of the citizens is an important indicator of governance. Article 39 of the Constitution makes the state responsible to see that 'there shall not be concentration of the wealth in the hands of the few' thus wants the state to oversee equitable distribution of wealth and resources among the people. However, we find that things have not moved in that direction. The reasons are to be found in the unique caste-based mode of production and division of labourers in India.

Enforced Poverty and Cultural Capital

Ambedkar is the first social scientist to find out several facets of dehumanisation in the caste system, powered through the engine of religion. "The Hindus are the only people in the world whose economic order – the relation of workman to workman is consecrated by religion and made sacred, eternal and inviolate". His diligent exposition of the economics of Brahmanism as the *law of enforced poverty* based on the *dogma of predestination*, conditioning the victims as willful vassals reveals the *third dimension of capital, i.e. the Cultural Capital* (Satyapal, 2010). While economic capital refers to the command over economic resources, social capital relates to the resources based on group membership, relationships, networks of influence and support. Cultural capital on the other hand, concerns forms of knowledge, skills and advantages that confer power and higher status in the society. Culture shares many of the properties that are characteristic of economic capital that any 'competence' becomes a capital in so far as it facilitates appropriation and unequal distribution thereby creating opportunities for exclusive advantage to individuals or groups in the society.

Ambedkar presented an elaborate illustration of such cultural advantages which are monopolised by the twice-born and are used to condition the behaviour and attitudes of the servile castes for the social,

Brahminical Capitalism: Drain of Wealth from Bahujans to Dwijas

Year	Population	Wealth	Remarks
2019	10%	77.40%	
2012	10%	62.52 %	Source: Oxfam India Inequality Report 2020 (Table 4, Page 28) shows richest 1% hold over 51.53% share in wealth (mostly Dwijas).
2002	10%	53.87 %	
1991	10%	51.61 %	The same report tells us that bottom 50% (mostly Bahujans) held only 9% of total assets in 1991 which came down to 5.3 % by 2012.

- **Attempts to underestimate poverty of Bahujans through definition of Poverty Line (BPL)**
  - ✓ Rs 27 per day spending per person in Rural India
  - ✓ Rs 33 per day spending per person in Urban India

Source: Suresh Tendulkar Committee Report 2011-12

Fig. 12: Brahmanical Capitalism.

economic and political dominance of the leisure castes. He was the first to trace out the relation between Brahaminical ideology, caste system and economic exploitation. These notions were comprehensively developed later into the concept of Cultural Capital.

Even after 70 years the majority of the population are under Below Poverty Line. Economists indicate certain states as BIMARU states as they lie at the bottom of the Human Development Indices. However, their analysis stops at showing certain states, i.e. Bihar (Jharkhand), Madhya Pradesh, Rajasthan and Uttar Pradesh are low but do not explain who are *bimaru* and why? A cursory look reveals the fact that where the ST, SC and OBC population is high, those areas report low HDI figures. Today there is growth without equity and 75% people in Agriculture have just 16% share in GDP. The economic inequalities are so skewed that the Oxfam India Inequality Report, 2020 shows just 1% rich control 53% of the total wealth of the country, and they belong to the entrenched castes.

There have been some revisions in the estimation of poverty doing away from nutritional calculations. The Multiple Poverty Indices include different pointers of living standards, education and health. Going by this calculation it becomes evident that the poverty rates have gone down but the gaps remain unchanged among SCs, STs, OBCs and others.

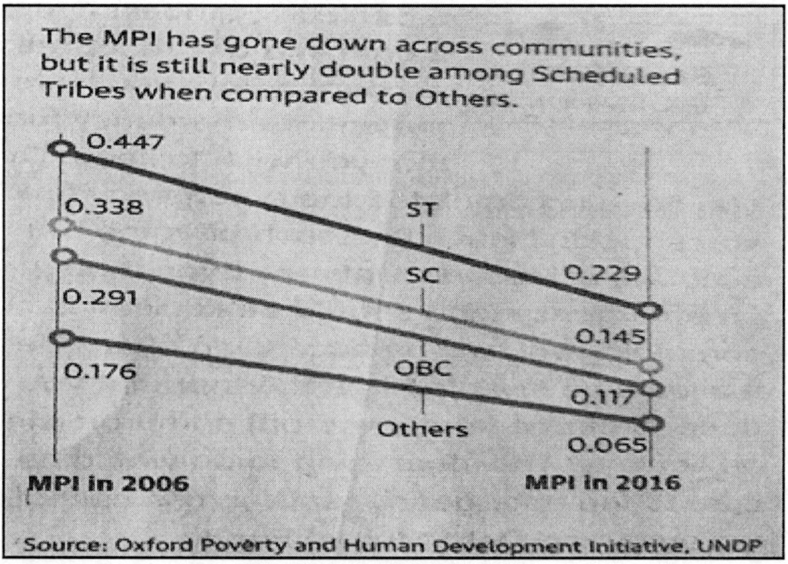

Fig. 13: State of Poverty.

Similarly poverty calculations across the states, social categories and rural and urban locales also indicate that the historically marginalised communities showed higher levels of poverty as against entrenched castes.

Table 1: Prevalence of poverty-BPL (2004-05)

S.No	States	Rural				Urban			
		ST	SC	OBC	Others	ST	SC	OBC	Others
1	Andhra Pradesh	**30.5**	15.4	9.5	4.1	**50**	39.9	28.9	20.6
2	Assam	**14.1**	27.7	18.8	25.4	**4.8**	8.6	8.6	4.2
3	Bihar	**53.3**	64	37.8	26.6	**57.2**	67.2	41.4	18.3
4	Chhattisgarh	**54.7**	32.7	33.9	29.2	**41**	52	52.7	21.4
5	Delhi	**0**	0	0	10.6	**9.4**	35.8	18.3	6.4
6	Gujarat	**34.7**	21.8	19.1	4.8	**21.4**	16	22.9	7
7	Haryana	**0**	26.8	13.9	4.2	**4.6**	33.4	22.5	5.9
8	Himachal Pradesh	**14.9**	19.6	9.1	6.4	**2.4**	5.6	10.1	2
9	Jammu & Kashmir	**8.8**	5.2	10	3.3	**0**	13.7	4.8	7.8
10	Jharkhand	**54.2**	57.9	40.2	37.1	**45.1**	47.2	19.1	9.2
11	Karnataka	**23.5**	31.8	20.9	13.8	**58.3**	50.6	39.1	20.3
12	Kerala	**44.3**	21.6	13.7	6.6	**19.2**	32.5	24.3	7.8
13	Madhya Pradesh	**58.6**	42.8	29.6	13.4	**44.7**	67.3	55.5	20.8
14	Maharashtra	**56.6**	44.8	23.9	18.9	**40.4**	43.2	35.6	26.8
15	Orissa	**75.6**	50.2	36.9	23.4	**61.8**	72.6	50.2	28.9
16	Punjab	**30.7**	14.6	10.6	2.2	**2.1**	16.1	8.4	2.9
17	Rajasthan	**32.6**	28.7	13.1	8.2	**24.1**	52.1	35.6	20.7
18	Tamil Nadu	**32.1**	31.2	19.8	19.1	**32.5**	40.2	20.9	6.5
19	Uttar Pradesh	**32.4**	44.8	32.9	19.7	**37.4**	44.9	36.6	19.2
20	Uttarakhand	**43.2**	54.2	44.8	33.5	**64.4**	65.7	46.5	25.5
21	West Bengal	**42.4**	29.5	18.3	27.5	**25.7**	28.5	10.4	13
	All India	**47.3**	**36.8**	**26.7**	**16.1**	**33.3**	**39.9**	**31.4**	**16**

Correspondingly, the labour participation among the marginalised communities is higher as revealed in Table 2.

Table 2: Labour Force Participation Rate (per 1000 persons) according to usual status (ps+ss) for different social groups all-India

Social Group	Rural			Urban			Rural+Urban		
	Male	Female	Person	Male	Female	Person	Male	Female	Person
ST	569	362	468	534	212	378	565	349	460
SC	558	273	419	567	186	385	560	256	412
OBC	548	271	412	559	155	366	551	241	400
others	563	204	391	558	121	350	561	171	375
all (incl. n.r.)	556	265	414	559	146	362	557	233	400

NSS Report No. 543: Employment and unemployment situation among social groups in India

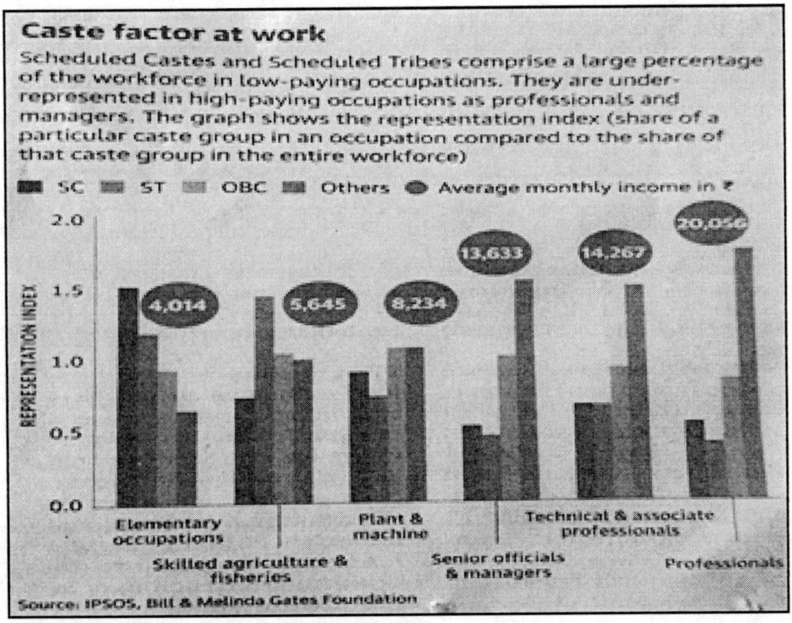

Source: Data Point, The Hindu Daily, 18-10-2018.

Fig. 14: Caste Factor at Work.

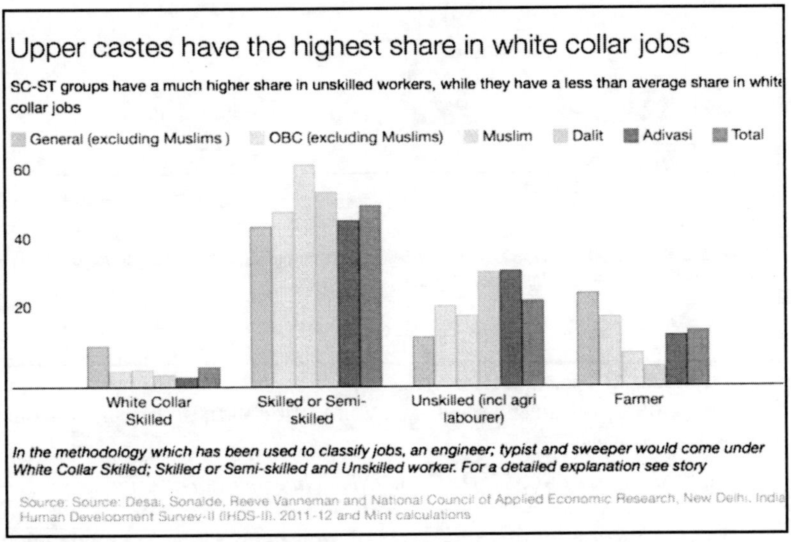

Source: Livemint, 21 October, 2016.
https://www.livemint.com/Politics/ino3tfMYVsd6VVGUdWXB8H/Themany-shadesof-casteinequality-in-India.html

Fig. 15: Status of SC, ST, OBC and Others in employment & industry.

The nature of work and incomes as assessed by the caste groups reveal that Scheduled Castes and Scheduled Tribes are mostly engaged in elementary occupations which provide low incomes while their participation in the high-paying occupations such as managerial and professional occupations is significantly low (Fig. 14). The entrenched castes almost monopolise the high pay jobs as is presented in Fig. 15:

The continuance of the discriminatory ideas of pollution associated with Scheduled Castes can be attested from the data presented in Fig. 16 wherein both rural and urban locales show very few food related industries owned by the Scheduled Castes. The overt forms of untouchability might have been on the decline but various subtler forms of discrimination are experienced by the members of Scheduled Castes often. However, sporadic violent episodes of caste conflicts, rapes and humiliations are organised to remind them of their lowly status in the caste hierarchy.

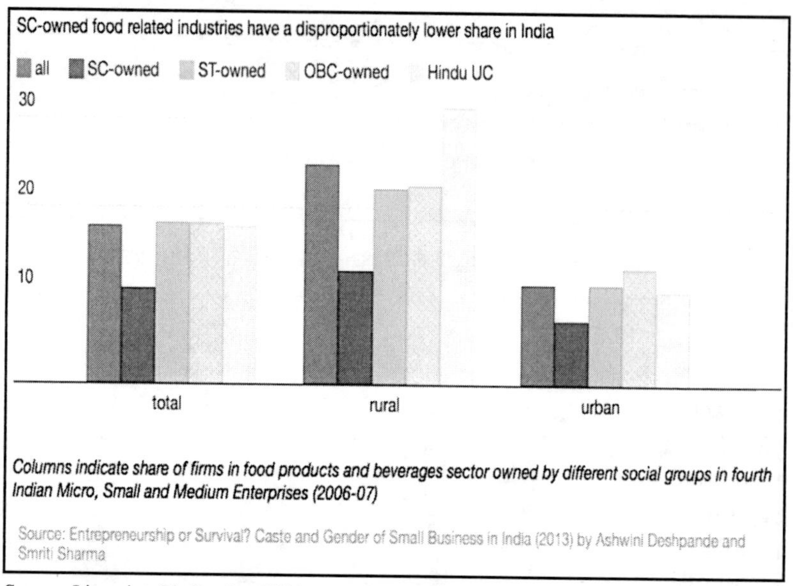

Source: Livemint, 21 October 2016.
https://www.livemint.com/Politics/ino3tfMYVsd6VVGUdWXB8H/Themany-shadesof-casteinequality-in-India.html

Fig. 16: Status of SC, ST, OBC and Others in employment & industry.

It is not surprising that the levels of well being (Fig. 17) aggregated from different indices of the plane of survival of the communities in India are correlative of the caste hierarchy. The historically marginalised communities continue to languish in the relatively deprived conditions.

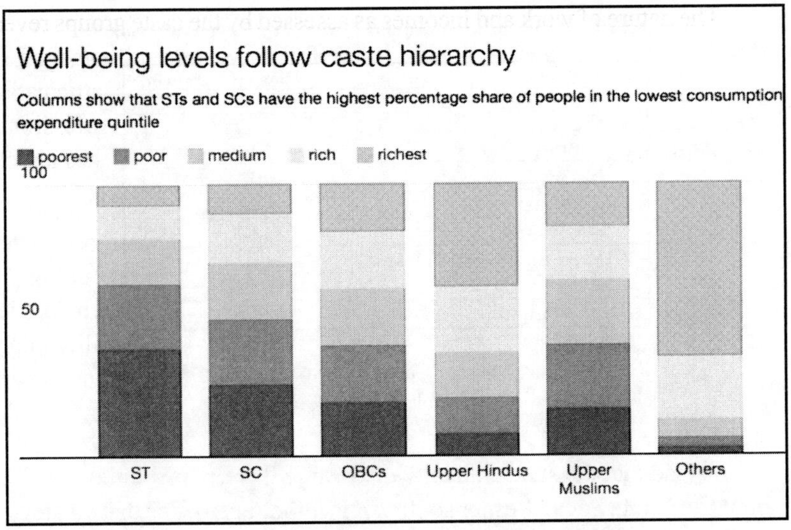

Source: 2011-12 NSSO Data from Indian Labour and Employment Report, 2014

Fig. 17: Well-being Level of SC, ST, OBC, Muslims.

Information Technology and Corporate Sector and Caste

Conditions turned too favourable for the entrenched castes after globalisation. The booming economic growth in India is attributed to the success of the service sector, which today contributes more than half of the country's GDP (Sen, S, 2010:101). This most promising fall-out of globalisation for the Indian economy has been limited to those sections that control the financial capital and cultural capital. Several studies reveal that never in Indian history have there been so many entrepreneurial and managerial Brahmins as can be seen in the software industry now (Adams, 2001; Das 2001; Fromhold-Eisebith, 2000), and in particular most of them are from South India (Kapur & Ramamurti, 2001; Merchant, 2002). The recruitment process is tailor-made for people from better-off families. The studies also point out that networking is prevalent and the background is most often to be found in a South Indian Brahmin family and upbringing (Thorat, et al. 2005, pp. 25-29). A study on technical and scientific manpower indicates that the lower castes are represented much below their share in the population (Deshpande, 2000; Xiang, 2002; Fromhold-Eisebith, 2000).

Economic globalisation has become not merely 'crony capitalism' but indeed 'caste capitalism' with the factors of production – land, labour, capital, entrepreneurship, technology and human capital and the control of markets being owned by few privileged castes.

Table 3: Representation of Social Groups in Corporate Boards

	Caste	Numbers	% to Total
1	Forward caste	8,387	92.6
	Of which		
	(a) Brahmin	4,037	44.6
	(b) Vaishyas	4,167	46.0
	(c) Kshatriya	43	0.5
	(c) Others#	137	1.5
2	Other Backward Classes	346	3.8
3	SC/ST	319	3.5
4	Total (1 to 3)	9,052	100.0

Refers forward castes (like Syrian Christians).

Ref: Corporate Boards in India Blocked by Caste? D Ajit, Han Donker, Ravi Saxena in Economic and Political Weekly, August 11, 2012, Vol. xlvii, No. 31.

We find that the state gradually disowning its responsibilities but talk about Corporate Social Responsibility. It is important to note that whatever the claims made for its efficiency and effectiveness, the so called private sector in India, which is in the hands of a few privileged castes, has never been renowned for its adherence to such collective goals as equity, social justice or social inclusion. The resultant phenomena is the strengthening of Brahaminism and Capitalism which were declared by Ambedkar as the twin enemies to the society as a whole.

Political Dimension of Marginalisation

The Constitution of India conferred the right of adult franchise to all citizens which heralded a democratic revolution in the lives of historically marginalised communities. It is envisaged that one man-one vote and one vote - one value would lead to a democratic society. However the entrenched castes have been conscious and highly manipulative in keeping the power *status quo ante.* The marginalised communities could not assert their political representations owing to lack of economic power and the divisive machanisations.

It can be attested from Fig. 18 that the historically marginalised communities continue to be on the peripheries of the portals of power. On the path to attain the goal of One Man- One Value, Ambedkar highlighted 7 challenges before the parliamentary democracy in India-Absence of glaring Inequalities; Need of strong Opposition; Equality in Law and Administration; Observance of Constitutional Morality; No Tyranny of Majority over Minority; Moral order in the Society and Strong presence of Public Conscience. We find all these challenges have not been tackled by the Indian polity but contributed to promote them.

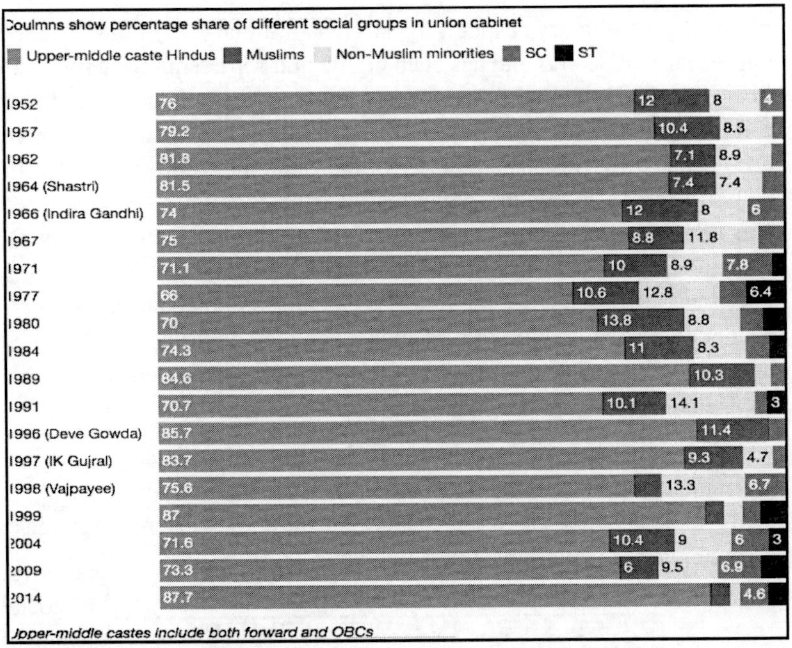

Source: Livemint, 21 October 2016,
https://www.livemint.com/Politics/ino3tfMYVsd6VVGUdWXB8H/The-many-shadesof-casteinequality-in-India.html

Fig. 18: Representation of Social Groups in Union Cabinet (1952-2014)

'Democratic Deficit'

India today is in a situation which the Political Scientists refer to as 'Democratic Deficit' wherein "the failure of an elected government to fulfill the promises to the electorate". This type of democracy can also be understood as plutocracy, which is in fact a *compromise between the 'power of the vote' and the 'power of business'*, with the governments negotiating the interface between the two. It is too well known that the 'corporate welfare' always wins out over 'social welfare' when economy gets tight. Hence Ambedkar warns "What they are doing is not to make India safe for Democracy but to free the tyrant to practice his tyrannies…Let not tyranny has the freedom to enslave".(p.238).

Judiciary and the Marginalised

Judiciary has been the most important organ of the constitution and is assigned the task of proper interpretation of the constitution and to oversee the conduct of other organs such as legislature and bureaucracy. Common citizens, especially the marginalised approach judiciary for justice and protection. Judiciary, especially Higher Judiciary in India assumed unprecedented powers and has been highly non-representative with regard to marginalised communities. Commenting on the conduct of judiciary former Judge of the Supreme Court, Dr. Justice K. Ramaswamy observes (2003) that "till Thomas case (1976), the Supreme Court interpreted the constitution to elongate social justice and economic empowerment and other human rights by the deprived social segments. But in the later judgments, starting from Indra Sawhney's case (1992), deprivatory interpretation has become the order… The glorious contents of social and economic justice and process of judicial review be used as a shield but unfortunately used as sword against the deprived social segments namely, the Dalits, Adivasis and the OBCs."

The composition of the judiciary is an important factor in making the judiciary participatory. Representations are of late observed in the lower judiciary and Fig. 19 presents that the judges from marginalised communities are grunting being filled up.

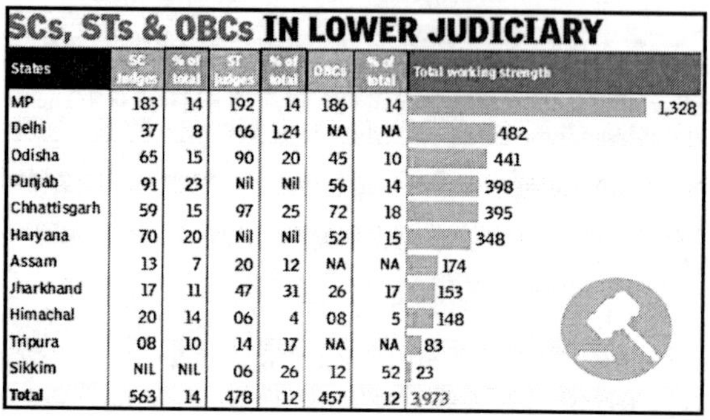
SCs, STs & OBCs IN LOWER JUDICIARY

States	SC Judges	% of total	ST judges	% of total	OBCs	% of total	Total working strength
MP	183	14	192	14	186	14	1,328
Delhi	37	8	06	1.24	NA	NA	482
Odisha	65	15	90	20	45	10	441
Punjab	91	23	Nil	Nil	56	14	398
Chhattisgarh	59	15	97	25	72	18	395
Haryana	70	20	Nil	Nil	52	15	348
Assam	13	7	20	12	NA	NA	174
Jharkhand	17	11	47	31	26	17	153
Himachal	20	14	06	4	08	5	148
Tripura	08	10	14	17	NA	NA	83
Sikkim	NIL	NIL	06	26	12	52	23
Total	563	14	478	12	457	12	3,973

Source: Newsclick, Feb 2018; Law Ministry; https://www.newsclick.in/castediversityindianjudicialservices-stilldream-saysnew-report

Fig. 19: Representation in Judiciary

In the last two decades, some major judgments were decided against the marginalised communities by the higher judiciary where the court betrayed a lack of sensitivity towards their rights. The judgments delivered in SC, ST Prevention of Atrocities Act; interpreting Reservation as enabling rights and not as Fundamental rights; OBC reservations in premier institutions; reversing the Samata judgment; transferring land in Scheduled Area in BALCO judgment; Govardhan case of right to habitat; and the May 2019 judgment of eviction of tribes from forest; keeping the

Economically Weaker Section Reservation case pending etc. are some instances of intense anxiety of the marginalised communities.

Authoritarian Populism and the Marginalised

In their book, *How Democracies Die,* Steven Levitsky and Daniel Ziblatt (2018) referring to the global trend of democracies being infected and leading to breakdowns explain the emergence of elected despots. In the Indian context, we are reminded of the analysis that Ambedkar made in 1945 about the role of majority in democracy. He explained that there are two majorities in Indian society- Political Majority and Communal Majority and among the two he finds the former better as it could be changed at the hustings. He warns that if a political majority joins hands with a communal majority, it leads to a Fascist state. In such a state, on the pretext of national interest, the fundamental rights of the individual-which are paramount in the Constitution, shall be curbed (BAWS, Vol. 17:2). This is the peril that India and its democracy faces today. Hence Ambedkar warns "What they are doing is not to make India safe for Democracy but to free the tyrant to practice his tyrannies…Let not tyranny has the freedom to enslave". (p. 238).

It becomes evident that the prospects of the marginalised communities in India are tied up with the democracy. The success of democracy requires responsible citizens who not only realise the necessity to save but to make democracy work. Therefore, it is imperative that the marginalised communities, especially the youth of India who constitute the majority should realise the dangers to democracy in India and must prevent it dying from within.

References

Ambedkar, B.R. 1956. "Prospects of Democracy in India" in (ed) Hari Narake., et.al 'Dr. Babasaheb Ambedkar Writings and Speeches' 2003, Vol. 17, No. 3, Education Department, Government of Maharashtra, pp. 519-520.

Arjan de Hann 2008. Social Exclusion : Towards a Holistic Understanding of Deprivation, Critical Quest, New Delhi.

Beall, J and Piron, L.H. 2005. "DFID Social Exclusion Review", Department for International Development, May, United Nations.

Clert, C. 2000. 'Social Exclusion and Globalisation: Implications for Social Policy and Urban Governance', Paper prepared for the African Technical families – Macro Economics 2, Washington DC: The World Bank.

Estivill, J. 2003. "Concepts and Strategies for Combating Social Exclusion: An overview", International Labour Office.

Foucault, Michel 1970. The Order of Things: An Archeology of Human Sciences.

Frazer, N. 1989. Unruly Practices: Power, Discourse and Gender in Contemporary Social Theory, Cambridge: Polity Press.

Kabeer, Naila 2008. Social Exclusion, Poverty and Discrimination: Towards an Analytical Framework, Critical Quest, New Delhi.

Kosambi, D.D. 1957. Exasperating Essays, People's PublishingHouse, New Delhi.

Lal, Deepak 1988. Hindu Equilibrium, Cultural Stability and Economic Stagnation, Vol.1, Oxford: Clarendon.

Lukes, S. 1974. Power: A Radical View, London, Macmillan.

Nayak. P. 1994. 'Economic Development and Social Exclusion in India' in Social Exclusion and South Asia, Labour Institutions and Development Programme, DP/77/1994, Geneva.

Satyapal, P.D. 2010. From Culture of Reservations to Culture of Representations: Phule-Ambedkarite Agenda for Social Inclusion in India in V. Subrahmanyam (ed) Social Exclusion, Integration and Inclusive Policies, Jaipur, Rawat Publications.

Satyapal, P.D. 2010a. Dr. B.R. Ambedkar's Exhumation of Cultural Capital and its Dynamics in Indian Society in The Eastern Anthropologist, Vol.

Satyapal, P.D. 2011. The Ideology of Exclusion and Cultural Politics in Indian Society, Vol. V. No. 3 July, The IUP Journal of History and Culture,The Icfai University Press.

Sen, Amartya 2004. Social Exclusion: A Critical Assessment of the Concept and Its Relevance, Critical Quest, New Delhi.

Silver, H. 1995. 'Reconceptualizing Social Disadvantage: Three Paradigms of Social Exclusion' in Social Exclusion: Rhetoric, Reality and Responses, (eds). G. Rodgers, C. Gore and J. Frizegald. (ILO/UNDP).

Thorat, Sukhadeo and Kumar, Nagendra 2008. B.R. Ambedkar: Perspectives on Social Exclusion and Inclusive Polices, Oxford University Press, New Delhi.

5

Marginalised Communities in the Globalised Era

— Prof. S. Srikanta Swamy

General Introduction

Community is the word which is used in different context. But from the sociological perspective community refers to group of people living together in a region or country having certain norms, beliefs which are in common. The structure and functions of community keep on changing due to social change. The dynamic nature of society is also responsible for this change. Ever since the formation of society, some categories of people are socially excluded due to various reasons such as age, health, cultural factors, educational status, economic status and political reasons. They are referred as socially excluded groups and are named as marginalised groups. They suffer from discriminations at different levels and are denied the opportunity of joining the mainstream. Through education, and other welfare measures by the government and other agencies attempts are being made to bring the marginalised communities to the main stream. But, the scenario has not changed much and continues to exist across the globe even during the process of globalisation. There are studies highlighting the reasons for the continuous existence of the marginalised groups without being benefitted significantly.

In this paper, an attempt is made to analyze the problems and also suggestions through which marginalised communities can be made to get the advantages of the globalisation process and come closer to the mainstream of the society.

Introduction

Every individual is born with certain biological potentials which make him to be unique. As and when an individual grows, the influence of environment makes him/her to acquire certain behavioural characteristics. In the name of socialisation the individual develops a personality which is very unique and possess social behaviour to become the member of a social group. The group may be primary wherein there will be more cohesiveness, frequent face-face interaction with greater degree of solidarity. Primary groups are considered as small, and are long term groups. Member of these groups acquire values, beliefs and attitudes in the name of socialisation. The other type is also referred as secondary group which is usually exists for a short period. They are formed because of common interests, values and also goals. According to Dunbar's number, an individual in this type of group cannot have social relationships with more than 150 individuals!

Talcott Parsons, a well known American Sociologist of 20th century, who contributed to 'Social Action theory' and 'Structural functionalism', opines that "if one has to have stability, order, and uniformity in society there must be a mutual understanding among people by having certain values that should be acceptable by everyone in society and viewed as good for all." Further, he says that Stratification takes place from these common values, and through these values a person is judged and positioned in society at certain ranks. So, one who performs well and follows all the common values of society will be ranked at the top and one which performs badly will be placed at the bottom. This is how stratification is seen in the human society, which in turn responsible in pushing certain categories of people and is marginalised. Parsons is of the opinion that stratification is unavoidable and found in all societies irrespective of any human society. Stratification is not an undesirable thing, since it is based on the common values shared by the members of society. But what about marginalisation? Is it desirable for a progressive society? The answer may be no to a greater extent.

Community

It is also a social group in which Individuals share common interests, common heritage and lives in a closed region or area. Thus, a community is considered as sociological Construct and in a broader sense, it includes set of interactions and human behaviours which have common meaning and shared expectations among its members. It is not so easy to understand how the communities are formed, functions and changes as per the social change. Similarly, with respect to the marginalisation of the community. Communities may be recognised as, urban community, rural community, local community, village community and so on.

Communities are also seen across the globe.

Marginalisation

The concept of Marginalisation was first introduced by Robert Park. It refers to "a processes by which individuals or groups are kept at or pushed beyond the edges of society" (Park, 1928). Encyclopedia of Public Health defines marginalisation as, "to be marginalised is to be placed in the margins and thus excluded from the privilege and power found at the centre" (2002). According to Gurung and Kollmair (2005), the concept of marginality is generally used to analyze socioeconomic, political, and cultural spheres, where disadvantaged people struggle to gain access to resources and full participation in social life. Thus, people belongs to marginalised community are deprived of social, economical and political status and are aspiring to join the mainstream of the society.

It is a process denying opportunities and outcomes to those 'living on the margins' and enhancing the opportunities and outcomes of those who are 'at the centre'. Marginalisation combines discrimination and social exclusion. It offends human dignity and it denies human rights, especially the right to live effectively as equal citizens. Exclusion keeps segments of the population out of social interaction, or casts them out from it. Those who are at the centre have benefited from globalisation, but those who are already marginalised are often left further behind. What is New about Globalisation Today? It varies from culture to culture and happens simultaneously at the micro and macro levels. It occurs at different levels, such as individual, group, community, and global discriminates across different social institutions, such as family, schools and neighbourhood, at work places, or places of worship. There are various marginalised groups, which includes, women, people with disabilities schedule castes, scheduled tribes, elderly or aged people, children and sexual minorities.

Types of Marginalised Groups

(i) Socially Marginalised Groups

(ii) Economically Marginalised Groups

(iii) Politically Marginalised Groups

Following are some of the characteristics of Minority groups:

(1) They share a sense of collective identity and common burdens.

(2) They suffer from discrimination and subordination.

(3) They have physical and/or cultural traits that set them apart, and which are disapproved of, by a dominant group.

(4) They have shared social rules about who belongs, and who does not.

(5) They have a tendency to marry within the group (Devesh Saxena).

Issues

It is commonly observed that women from the marginalised community are not considered for certain jobs and occupations. They are always marginalised relative to men. Women belonging to lower classes, lower castes, illiterate, and the poorest region have different levels of marginalisation than their better-off counterparts (Ramakrushudu, B. 2015); In India women are expected to adhere to strict gender roles. It is observed that they are affected by more health problems when compared to men. There are many factors because of which the health conditions of women are affected such as, economic dependence, experience of violence and gender bias.

Apart from this, discrimination also exists in some groups, because of other factors like educational status, urban or rural background or health conditions. In the working place, discrimination is also shown by

- Denying of academic or professional opportunities based on identity (i.e. racism, sexism, ableism).
- Use of preferred pronoun without bothering its effect on their status.
- Criticizing or interfering with culture or language usage issues.
- Denying equal access to certain facilities.
- Abusing cultural practices related to marriage and ceremonies.

Challenges

The following are some of the challenges related to marginalisation, especially with respect o women:

- Interference of social stigma
- Competing with gender related issues
- Problem of getting good education
- Overcoming the exploitation
- Difficulty in getting facilities for maintaining good health
- Overcoming the stereotype threat
- Discomfort participating in class discussions, study groups, student organisations, intramural sports and other institutional sponsored events
- Poor academic performance on exams and/or assignments due to negative impacts on concentration and emotional well-being
- Internalisation of negative messages

Ineffective coping such as disengaging, avoidance, and substance used

Marginalised Community

It is a community which experience discrimination and exclusion from the mainstreams because of unequal power relationships across economic, political, social and cultural dimensions. Socially excluded groups of people for different reasons, like age, physical or mental disabilities, economic status, access to education, or live in isolated places or depressed areas. Whereas, Marginality is an experience that affects large number of people throughout the world. People who are marginalised have relatively little control over their lives, and the resources available to them. This results in making them handicapped in contribution to society. A vicious circle is set up in which their lack of positive and supportive relationships prevents them from participating in local situations. This in turn leads to further isolation. This has a tremendous impact on the development of human beings, as well as on society at large.

Since the focus of development is to create an enabling environment for people to enjoy a productive, healthy, and creative life, it is important to address the issue of marginalisation. Development is always broadly conceived in terms of mass participation. Marginalisation deprives a large majority of people across the globe from participating in the development. It is a complex problem, and there are many factors that cause marginalisation. This complex and serious problem needs to be addressed at the policy level. Hence there is a need to address the problems associated with the groups suffering from marginalisation and suggest measures to reduce the gap.

The Encyclopedia of Public Health defines marginalised groups as, "To be marginalised is to be placed in the margins, and thus excluded from the privilege and power found at the center". Latin observes that *"'Marginality' is so thoroughly demeaning, for economic well-being, for human dignity, as well as for physical security. Marginal groups can always be identified by members of dominant society, and will face irrevocable discrimination."*

Categories

Categories consist of individuals that are similar to one another in a certain way, and members of this group can be permanent members or temporary in group members. Examples of categories are individuals with the same ethnicity, gender, religion, or nationality. This group is generally the largest type of social group.

Problems faced by working women in India

It is the human tendency that every family wants to increase their standard of living so that they can lead comfortable life. This has lead women to go for higher job oriented courses leading to more job opportunities. Especially in cities, men prefer to select their life partners who are working or prefer them to work. This trend is spreading everywhere and helps the family to have better accommodation, food, clothing, and good education to their child/children. As a consequence, the home-makers are forced to go for jobs and some of them are taking risks and working.

Thus, women workers are faced with lot of problems. In India, even today, many of the families are dominated by men, and educated women with higher educational status are not treated properly and are not involved in making decisions. However, in the employment market the demand for women employers are increasing day by day. According to Wentling (2003), the twin roles of women cause tension and conflict due to social structure which is still more dominant in the lives of people. In her study on working women in Delhi, she has shown that traditional authoritarian set up of Hindu social structure continues to be the same basically and hence women face problem of role conflicts.

Ali, J.S. (2011) investigated the challenges facing women in career development. She found that most of the women employees were dissatisfied with career development programmers and women were discriminated against in career development opportunities;

- In the traditional Indian society, women had low status when compared to men. As and when the educational opportunities increased, greater percentage of women acquired higher qualifications and moved to job market, thus bringing a paradigm shift in their status. Though, economically.
- Their status has increased, their double responsibility at home as well as in the working place has created lot of problems. According to Chandrima Chatterjee and Gunjan Sheoran (2007) in Indian society women face double discrimination being members of specific caste, class or ethnic group apart from experiencing gendered vulnerabilities. The working women in the modern society face lot of problems such as:

  Occupational stress

  It is also called work related stress. According to World Health Organisation, "it is the response people may have when presented with work demands and pressures that are not matched to their knowledge and abilities and which challenge their ability to cope." (2003). There are other factors associated with the Occupational Stress namely,

- Discrimination at Workplace
- Sexual harassment
- No Safety for Working Women
- Lack of Family Support
- No freedom to use her own earnings
- Insufficient Maternity Leaves
- Job insecurity
- Under-employment
- Gender discrimination
- Marginalisation
- Workplace Adjustment

Nagda (2001) Community survey includes 230 women in tribal areas of Rajasthan and found that among tribal women, 62 percent women were physically beaten by their husbands at least once a month. Majority (83 %) of females reported was verbally abused by their husbands, in-laws and other family members at least once a week. About 39 percent women suffered mental and physical tortures in the family. Sometimes in extreme forms of violence the victim may be killed.

Further, it was reported that more than two-thirds of the tribal women were abused by their husband, having fights regularly in evening and being insulted, taunted and criticized. Despite of this the majority of wives who suffered in domestic violence are also suffering in many health hazards like reproductive tract infection/STD, depression anemia, blood pressure, somatic disorders and broken family etc.

Globalisation

It is a phenomenon that brings interconnectivity among the members of the world. It has brought lot of significant changes in the field of education, economy, technology, culture and religion. Globalisation era is the spread of products, technology, information, and jobs across national borders and cultures. In economic terms, it describes an interdependence of nations around the globe fostered through free trade.

On one hand, globalisation has created new jobs and economic growth through the cross-border flow of goods, capital, and labour. On the other hand, this growth and job creation is not distributed evenly across industries or countries. Specific industries in certain countries, such as textile manufacturing in the U.S. or corn farming in Mexico, have suffered severe disruption or outright collapse as a result of increased international competitor.

The vision of globalisation is very idealistic, as well as opportunistic; it has both positive as well as negative impact. The open global market has brought more trade, easy availability of commodities, greater opportunity for the work force and corporation sectors. At the same time, it has affected the cultural, political, legal and religious life domain and social life.

Task force report on Globalisation and Marginalisation (2006) has identified some of the tensions produced due to the process of globalisation:

- Openness and universality versus neocolonialism and imperialism;
- The expanded freedom of the individual versus the resurgence of new communitarian projects;
- The tendency to 'homogenize' cultures versus the strong emergence of individual and group-identities;
- Consumerism versus sustainable development;
- Local versus global citizenship;
- A guarded attempt to downplay institutional religion versus the rise of neo-conservative religious expressions.

In the context of Globalisation, we are witnessing a world in which increasingly a smaller proportion of global resources and trade activities are shared among a larger number of economies and vice versa. The result is the widening gap in income between poor and rich nations.

According to Castells (1998), "The polarisation between the rich and the poor, is a consequence of ICTs, which have also had the effect of heightening the speed of the globalisation process. He also makes a link between the rise of information technologies and the growth of a global currency market with financial services industries centered in the global cities of London, New York, and Tokyo. Areas of the world and people that are unable to access the new technologies will not only fail to tap into the benefits of globalisation but also risk being further sidelined or pushed to the margins of global trade, and other types of socio-economic and political activities".

Action Suggested

In the context of Globalisation, following are the actions suggested;

1. Provide access to gender sensitive primary healthcare to improve the diverse health needs of women.
2. Establishment of more and more Anganwadi and ICDS centers in tribal and rural areas so that the marginalised women can be prevented from malnutrition. This can be done with the help of International Voluntary Organisations.
3. Proper implementation of laws to prevent and to protect the marginalised groups from domestic violence, physical and sexual abuse in urban as well as rural areas and also to create awareness about free legal aid.
4. More freedom to marginalised women with respect to their sexuality, including their sexual and reproductive health, and free from coercion, lack of information, discrimination and violence.
5. Provide social security for unorganised workers through redressal mechanisms against sexual harassment at the workplace.
6. To build a support network with campus groups or organisations so that diversity could be honoured, and also encourage women to become the members of self help groups to improve their financial sustainability.
7. Establishment of Counseling Centers with professional staff to assist the women for health, education and employment.
8. Provide Adult and functional education with more emphasis on training in technological tools (ICT) so that women from marginalised community can be socialised so that they can move freely with the main stream and encourage them to participate in campus such as C.A.R.E Dialogues that address issues of marginalisation and oppression.
9. Encourage women from marginalised community to improve their educational status through Open University (Dr. BRAOU, IGNOU, etc.)
10. Implement the constitutional provisions and the initiatives of the government effectively to be studied.

Conclusion

Globalisation has brought many significant changes in all walks of life. The impact of globalisation may vary from country to country and from society to society. Its impact is seen more by the urban society when compared to rural society. It has marginalised people in the field of education, economy social status. More so with marginalised communities. The general perception is that globalisation has reduced disparities among different social groups. In fact, it may be true to some aspect. But, still in reality marginalisation do exist as evident from the incidents that are happening in the developed countries. Upcoming and progress of marginalised communities are blocked in spite of constitutional support. The marginalised groups such as, women, children and other deprived groups are denied of good health, economic, political and social status. Hence, higher education institutions, governmental and non-governmental organisations and legal aids have to play a vital role. This will provide liberation and helps the marginalised groups to fulfill their aspirations and contribute for the welfare of a society.

References

Parsons, Talcott (2010). *The Structure of Social Action: A Study in Social Theory with Special Reference to a Group of Recent European Writers*. New York Free Press; London Collier Macmillan.

Lester Breslow, Lawrence W. Green, and Bernard Goldstein (2002). *Encyclopedia of Public health.*

Zulufkar Ahmad Khanday, Mohammad Akram (2012). *Health Status of Marginalised Groups in India.* International Journal of Applied Sociology 2012, 2(6): 60-70 DOI: 10.5923/j.ijas.20120206.02_

http://article.sapub.org/10.5923.j.ijas.20120206.02.html#Sec9

https://www.lawctopus.com/academike/problems-marginalised-groups-india/

https://www.investopedia.com/terms/g/globalisation.asp

https://en.wikipedia.org/wiki/Social_group

https://www.lawctopus.com/academike/problems-marginalised-groups-india/

https://en.wikipedia.org/wiki/Robert_E._Park

https://www.bing.com/search?q=talcott+parsons&FORM=AWRE&cc=IN&setlang=en-US&cvid=b74d32f2f39a4edcbc84213b217692be&qs=SW&nclid=8B77E4A2486644DEE4625830F7AA7F22&ts=1598922427988

http://cec.vcn.bc.ca/cmp/whatcom.htm

http://www.sjweb.info/documents/sjs/docs/GlobalisationandMarginalisationDiscussionGuide.pdf

http: //www.sjweb.info/documents/sjs/docs/GlobMarg_ENG. pdf

https://www.oneindia.com/politicians/yanamala-ramakrishnudu-46365.html

https://www.pramanaresearch.org/gallery/prj-p407.pdf · PDF

https://www.citypopulation.de/php/india-madhyapradesh.php?cityid=23421

http://cris.unu.edu/sites/cris.unu.edu/files/Globalisation%20and%20the

https://www.emerald.com/insight/content/doi/10.1108/13673270310463

http://www.cehat.org/go/uploads/Hhr/vulnerable.pdf

6

Feminisation of Agriculture: The Economy of the Resultant Workforce as an Impact of Globalisation

— Dr. (Mrs.) Tinku Paul

Introduction

International Rural Women's Day declared by the United Nations observes October to highlight the contribution of rural women to the world's economic growth. The Government of India in consonance with this declared October 15, 2017 as Rashtriya Mahila Kisan Diwas. But the state of women as farmers remains unchanged. With broadening and deepening of agricultural contributions resultant upon male migration to urban fringes, globalisation has put up multiple challenges for women and their survival in agriculturally dependent economies. The paper specifically focuses on the condition of women with marginal landholdings or who are landless belonging to low social and economic categories with respect to their occupational status, quality of living, indebtedness etc.

Women and the World of Work

Women's employment is directly linked to the role of women in the family and the disproportionately high burden of domestic responsibility, acts as a barrier to entry into the labour market. The problems relating to work participation of women can be both pre and post labour market entry. Also after the entry into the labour market women face and suffer a number of hardships and problems. These problems can be related to availability and opportunity to avail better income earning opportunities, irregular and low payment of wages due to submissive attitude and lack of bargaining power among women. Also women are found to occupy the lower positions in the hierarchical order of the work structure i.e., in the low paid and low skill jobs. Within the unorganised sector, women have an overwhelming presence in agriculture, forestry, fishing, plantation and allied activities with the highest proportion working as agricultural labour.

The seasonality of work in this sector and the lack of other avenues of work make them vulnerable to a range of exploitative practices. They predominate in certain industries such as garments, textiles, food and electronics. They remain the most vulnerable and the poorest. And yet they are economically active and contributing to the national economy. Thus, we may summarise the post-labour market problems of women as the ***gender division of labour, which tends to confine women to relatively subordinate and inferior positions in the organisation of monetized production, is not overridden by "flexibilisation".*** It is indeed due to the fact that ***'flexibility' operates in a gendered fashion***.

The **level of employment,** its **composition** and the **growth in employment opportunities** are not only critical indicators of the process of development in any economy but also indicators that, in most cases, directly capture the economic attainments and hence the level of well-being of individuals. **The employment of women and young girls are always a strategy to reduce cost when there exists a comparable difference in the wages between male and female workers.** However, with the swelling rates of unemployment among males, combined with the high insecurity in employment, the reservation prices of male workers seems to have gone down, making them as cheap as that of women counterparts. This is found to deny women access to employment in jobs where the relative wages are high with better skill requirement.

The important trend that needs to be highlighted is the considerable increase in the number of women engaged in trade, hotels and restaurants of which retail trade accounts for majority of the workers. Considerable change is visible in the community, social and personal services of which, excepting personal services all other categories have registered growth.

The findings of the study are based on the empirical survey based on the study of 448 female respondents aged above 15 years, selected from the 6 villages of Handia (206) and Chaka blocks (242) of Allahabad District. In the following section a detailed description of the demographic and socio-economic status is presented.

Empirical Findings

1. Demographic Profile

The proportion of respondents in categorised age groups increases from 5.4 percent in the age group 15-24 years to 36 percent in age group 25-34 years, and then falls steadily to 23 percent in 35-44 years, 14 percent in 45-54 years, 11 percent in 55-59 years and in 60 and above age groups. The decline after age 25-34 reflects the normal pyramid shape of population's age distribution.

Table 1: Village-wise Age-group Categorizes of Respondents

<table>
<tr><th rowspan="3">Age</th><th colspan="6">Age Groups</th></tr>
<tr><th>15-24 Yrs</th><th>25-34 Yrs</th><th>35-44 Yrs</th><th>45-54 Yrs</th><th>55-59 Yrs</th><th>60 & above</th></tr>
<tr><td>24
(5.4)</td><td>162
(36.2)</td><td>104
(23.2)</td><td>61
(13.6)</td><td>48
(10.7)</td><td>49
(10.9)</td></tr>
<tr><th rowspan="3">Head of the Hhd.</th><th colspan="6">Head of Household's Relation with the Respondent</th></tr>
<tr><th colspan="2">Self</th><th colspan="2">Husband</th><th colspan="2">Others</th></tr>
<tr><td colspan="2">88
(19.6)</td><td colspan="2">331
(73.9)</td><td colspan="2">29
(6.5)</td></tr>
<tr><th rowspan="2">Type of Family</th><th colspan="2">Nuclear</th><th colspan="2">Joint (without in-laws)</th><th colspan="2">Joint (with in-laws)</th></tr>
<tr><td colspan="2">220
(49.1)</td><td colspan="2">99
(22.1)</td><td colspan="2">129
(28.8)</td></tr>
<tr><th rowspan="2">Marital Status</th><th colspan="2">Currently Married</th><th>Widow</th><th>Separated</th><th colspan="2">Deserted</th></tr>
<tr><td colspan="2">403
(90.0)</td><td>32
(7.1)</td><td>3
(0.7)</td><td colspan="2">10
(2.2)</td></tr>
<tr><th rowspan="2">Caste</th><th colspan="2">SC</th><th colspan="2">OBC</th><th colspan="2">General</th></tr>
<tr><td colspan="2">230
(45.3)</td><td colspan="2">104
(23.2)</td><td colspan="2">141
(31.5)</td></tr>
<tr><th rowspan="2">Education</th><th>No Education</th><th colspan="2">Up to Primary</th><th>Middle</th><th colspan="2">Up to High School</th></tr>
<tr><td>315
(70.3)</td><td colspan="2">69
(15.4)</td><td>36
(8.0)</td><td colspan="2">28
(6.3)</td></tr>
<tr><th rowspan="2">Avg. Hhd. Size</th><td>Kazipur</td><td>Kanakpur</td><td>Rikhipur</td><td>Chak Garibdas</td><td>Chak Abhayram</td><td>Chak Kriparam</td></tr>
<tr><td>8.0</td><td>13.1</td><td>11.3</td><td>6.3</td><td>8.1</td><td>6.4</td></tr>
</table>

Source: Field Survey, July-September, 2005.

One out of five households was found to be female headed. With the male partners migrating in search of better income generation activities to places like Surat, Rajkot, Delhi and Mumbai, the female members with little capital assets in their control are left behind bound to hearth. Reviews on feminisation of poverty reflect that female-maintained households are very often among the poorest because of wage discrimination, occupational segregation patterns in the labour market and other gender-based barriers. Family disintegration, population movements between urban and rural areas within countries and internal displacements are factors contributing to the rise of female-headed households. In nearly three-fourths of the households husbands were heads of the households. 50 percent of the sample families were nuclear families.

No unmarried respondent were in the sample. 9 out of 10 ever married respondents were currently married. Almost 3 percent of the female respondents were separated or deserted.

7 out of 10 respondents were illiterate. Among those who were literate, the proportion of respondents with education up to primary education was high.

The average household size was highest in Kanakpur village followed by Rikhipur both in the Trans Ganga region of Allahabad District.

2. Social Profile

Caste: Nearly 45 percent of the respondents belonged to the SC category followed by 23 percent of OBC category and the rest 32 percent of general category. The proportion of scheduled castes was higher in the Trans Yamuna region as compared to the Trans Ganga region.

Education: The education levels of respondents have an important bearing on the status of empowerment of women. Several studies have proved that educational attainments have direct relationship with the enhancement of decision-making capacity, capabilities, health-seeking behaviour etc. and makes women more receptive to social changes.

Table 2: Village-wise Caste Category

Sample Village	*Caste of the respondent*			*Total*
	SC	*OBC*	*General*	
Kazipur	28 (57.1)	10 (20.4)	11 22.4%	49 (100.0)
Kanakpur	15 (26.3)	19 (33.3)	23 40.4%	57 (100.0)
Rikhipur	35 (35.0)	19 (19.0)	46 46.0%	100 (100.0)
Trans Ganga	**78 (38)**	**48 (23.3)**	**80 (38.8)**	**206 (100.0)**
Chak Garibdas	72 (62.1)	14 (12.1	30 25.9%	116 (100.0)
Chak Abhayram	35 (40.2)	28 (32.2)	24 27.6%	87 (100.0)
Chak Kriparam	18 (46.2)	14 (35.9)	7 17.9%	39 (100.0)
Trans Yamuna	**125 (51.7)**	**56 (23.1)**	**61 (25.2)**	**242 (100.0)**
Grand Total	***203 (45.3)***	***104 (23.2)***	***141 (31.5)***	***448 (100.0)***

Source: Field Survey, July-September, 2005.

In our study nearly seven out of ten rural women are illiterate, followed by 12 percent respondents with at least primary school education. (Table 3) Illiteracy was found more pronounced in the Trans Ganga region as compared to the Trans Yamuna region i.e., 14 percentage points higher in the Trans Ganga region. Interestingly education beyond middle school was nil in the Trans Ganga region. This has its implications on the nature and quality of the working status of rural women. This has been discussed in the next section of this Chapter.

Table 3: Village-wise Educational Status of Respondents

Sample Village	*Educational Status of the respondent*				*Total*
	No Education	*Up to primary School*	*Middle School*	*Up to High School*	
Kazipur	40 (12.7)	7 (10.2)	2 (5.6)	0 (0.0)	49 (10.9)
Kanakpur	50 (15.9)	6 (8.7)	1 (2.8)	0 (0.0)	57 (12.7)
Rikhipur	82 (26.0)	13 (18.8)	5 (13.9)	0 (0.0)	100 (22.3)
Trans Ganga	***172 (83.5)***	***26 (12.6)***	***8 (3.9)***	***0 (0.0)***	***206 (100.0)***
Chak Garibdas	54 (17.1)	24 (34.8)	20 (55.6)	18 (64.3)	116 (25.9)
Chak Abhayram	56 (17.8)	17 (24.6)	6 (16.7)	8 (28.6)	87 (19.4)
Chak Kriparam	33 (10.5)	2 (2.9)	2 (5.6)	2 (7.1)	39 (8.7)
Trans Yamuna	***143 (59.1)***	***43 (17.8)***	***28 (11.6)***	***28 (11.6)***	***242 (100.0)***
Grand Total	**315 (100.0)**	**69 (100.0)**	**36 (100.0)**	**28 (100.0)**	**448 (100.0)**

Source: Field Survey, July-September, 2005.

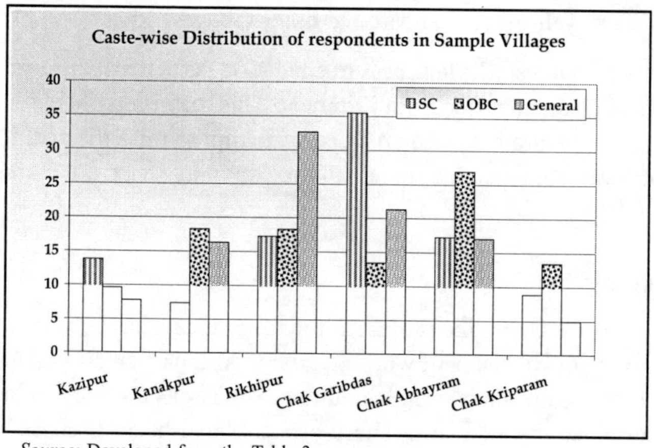

Source: Developed from the Table 3.

Chart: 1

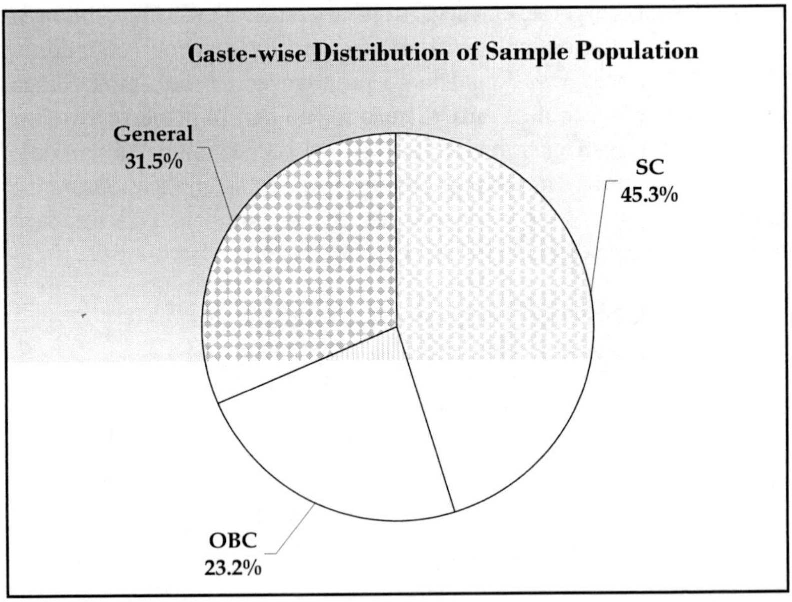

Source: Developed from the Table 2.

Chart: 2

Chak Garibdas recorded the highest literacy rate. More than 50 percent of the respondents have attained education upto primary or more than primary. Except for Chak Kriparam village of Chaka block, illiteracy is highest in the villages of Handia Tehsil. Chak Garibdas has number of private schools apart from government primary school. Due to access to education facilities apart from its vicinity to the Chaka town, the education standards are well-off as compared to other villages.

Women have very little access to education particularly in rural areas, hence most of them suffer from illiteracy. This may be probably because of the fact that there has been no sincere attempt to raise the position and status of rural women and a social stigma continues to exist towards their education.

3. Economic Profile

The study of the economic profile of the respondents has been made with respect to their own status of work i.e., their work participation rates, type of land ownership, status of indebtedness with respect to the productivity or non-productivity of loans. These aspects have been discussed under following sub-sections.

- **Work Status:** The Work Participation Rates (WPR) of the rural women in the sample villages as shown in the Table 4 presents a profile of their working status. In our field work in the Trans Ganga and Trans Yamuna regions of Allahabad district the nature and quality of work differed to a large extent which has its reflection on the status of empowerment of women. For instance the nature of economic activity in the Trans Ganga region was predominantly agriculture and was of subsistence in nature.

Table 4: Village-wise Status of Employment

Village	*Status of Employment*		*Total*
	Worker	*Non Worker*	
Kazipur	26 (53.1)	23 (46.9)	49 (100.0)
Kanakpur	28 (49.1)	29 (50.9)	57 (100.0)
Rikhipur	41 (41.0)	59 (59.0)	100 (100.0)
Trans Ganga	***95 (46.1)***	***111 (53.9)***	***206 (100.0)***
Chak Garibdas	51 (44.0)	65 (56.0)	116 (100.0)
Chak Abhayram	46 (52.9)	41 (47.1)	87 (100.0)
Chak Kriparam	26 (66.7)	13 (33.3)	39 (100.0)
Trans Yamuna	***123 (50.8)***	***119 (49.2)***	***242 (100.0)***
Total	**218 (48.7)**	**230 (51.3)**	**448 (100.0)**

Source: Field Survey, July-September, 2005.

This was observed to be especially true for the female-headed agricultural households. Though, according to secondary statistics the average FWPR is higher in the Trans Ganga Region as compared to the Trans Yamuna Region, the selected villages present a contradictory profile.

- **Ownership of Agricultural Land:** Ownership of landholdings pattern reflects on the economic status of the respondent especially in a rural framework. The concept of ownership here is not concerned with the ownership of the land by the female respondent but concerns with the family ownership. Of the total households surveyed, 46 percent households were landless. These landless families mostly belonged to the lower order of the social strata. Half of the sample households had access to land holdings, whereas nearly four percent held land on *adhia batai* or were share croppers.

- **Status of Indebtedness:** The Table 5 presents the purpose and the amount of loan taken by the sample households from various sources. The proportion of non-institutional debts (including debts taken from money lenders, thakurs or even friends and relatives) was 53 percent and 47 percent depended on institutional borrowing including banks or SHG funds. Nearly six percent women respondents were unaware of the source of debts as they just had the idea that their spouse must have had taken some debt from somewhere. Nearly 7 out of 10 sample households were indebted. It is especially alarming to find that 68 percent of loans were taken for unproductive purposes like marriage, illness, gambling, to fight legal cases or even to meet household needs.

Table 5: Purpose-wise Amount of Debt

Purpose	*Debt Amount*				*Total*
	Less Than 1000- 5000	*5000- 20000*	*20000 or more*	*Can't say*	
Unproductive Debt	80 (38.1)	65 (31.0)	27 (12.9)	38 (18.1)	210 (68.0)
Productive Debt	10 (13.7)	54 (74.0)	1 (1.4)	8 (11.0)	73 (23.6)
Both	2 (7.7)	21 (80.8)	3 (11.5)	0 (0.0)	26 (8.4)
Total	92 (29.8)	140 (45.3)	31 (10.0)	46 (14.9)	309 (100.0)

Note: The figures in parentheses show row percentages and the last column shows column percentages.

Source: Field Survey, July-September, 2005.

Also a very important fact to worry about was that 15 percent or three out of 20 female respondents did not have the knowledge about the debt amount. More strikingly this unawareness was higher in the case of unproductive debts. This reflects on the patriarchal pattern of decision-making on financial matters within the households and exclusion of women in such decisions. This fact comes out very strikingly in the discussion on women's participation or autonomy in decision-making in critical issues discussed in the third section of this chapter.

4. Status and Quality of Employment

In the sample villages of Trans Ganga and Trans Yamuna agriculture was the backbone of the rural economy. This was more prominently visible in the Trans Ganga region. The division of rural women workers according to their work category shows that 62.3 percent of women earned their livelihood from agriculture working as cultivators, agricultural labourers, share croppers etc. These rural women working in the farms, participate in a wide range of farm activities by slogging alongside with men in the field as well as taking care of the home and children, thereby performing dual role that of a homemaker and of a partner in the farming activities outside the home. As is clear in the Chapter III, nearly 78 percent of the rural female working population is engaged in agriculture either as cultivators or as agricultural labourers. ***Allahabad has the largest number of rural women workers in Uttar Pradesh which accounts to nearly five lakhs.*** (4, 86,248).

Rural farm labourers work under severe limitations, their contribution towards agricultural production and development is noteworthy. Apart from the job they do outside the household, the unpaid activities in the domestic sphere go unnoticed and unrewarded. Women workforce outside the four walls is larger in rural areas than in urban India. For the present study, the women performing agricultural operations have been classified into four categories:

(1) Women working in other's fields for cash or kind technically termed as agricultural labourers;

(2) Women working in their family owned land as labourers. The research indicates that it is this section of working women who are most susceptible to underreporting. They neither own any agricultural land nor are paid any form of reward in form of cash or kind in compensation for their hard toil;

(3) Women supervising the agricultural operations performed by the labourers in family owned land. This category of workers is again similar to the above mentioned third category.

(4) Women working and supervising work in their own land, or cultivators. Share croppers have also been included in the cultivator's class.

Forty-two percent of the rural females depend on agriculture by working as labourers, who possess no land of their own. Women possessing small landholdings work in their own farm and also work as labourers for wages on other's farms, thereby, supplementing the family's income. Women who supervise the farm activities performed by the labourers generally belong to higher social strata. The study reveals that almost 70 percent of landholdings more than a hectare, were owned by high caste Brahmins and Thakurs whereas 54 percent of the landless agricultural or non-agricultural families belonged to the scheduled castes. During the survey it was found that most of the women worked in own (family) farms from dawn to dusk but did not consider themselves as workers. When asked are you employed?

The spontaneous answer was ***"I don't get free time from my family responsibilities like working on farm, feeding cattle and weeding the fields etc. I have to work and supervise in the fields from dawn to dusk."***

Quality of Work of Rural Women as Reflected by Census 2001 in the Sample Villages

The Table 6 presents the distribution of rural working women according to main and marginal categories in the Census 2001. As is clearly visible 92 percent of the workers in the Trans Ganga region were marginal workers i.e., working for less than 183 days of work.

Table 6: Work Participation Rate of the Sample Villages

Name of the Village	*Status of Employment*				*Total Female Sample Population*
	Worker	*Work Participation Rate*	*Non Worker*	*Percentage of Non-workers*	
Kazipur	26	53.1	23	46.9	49
Kanakpur	28	49.1	29	50.9	57
Rikhipur	41	41.0	59	59.0	100
Trans Ganga	***95***	***46.1***	***111***	***53.9***	***206***
Chak Garibdas	51	44.0	65	56.0	116
Chak Abhayram	46	52.9	41	47.1	87
Chak Kriparam	26	66.7	13	33.3	39
Trans Yamuna	***123***	***50.8***	***119***	***49.2***	***242***
Total	**218**	**48.7**	**230**	**51.3**	**448**

Source: Field Survey, July-September, 2005.

Table 7: Distribution of Female Workforce by Main and Marginal Category

Name of Village	*Total Workers*	*Main Workers*	*Marginal Workers*
Kazipur	147 (36.3)	6 (4.1)	*141* *(95.9)*
Kanakpur	91 (29.1)	8 (8.8)	*83* *(91.2)*
Rikhipur	10 (1.7)	6 (60.0)	*4* *(40.0)*
Trans Ganga	***248*** ***(19.1)***	***20*** ***(8.1)***	***228*** ***(91.9)***
Chak Garibdas	92 (13.4)	41 (44.6)	*51* *(55.4)*
Chak Abhaydas	196 (36.8)	135 (68.9)	*61* *(31.1)*
Chak Kriparam	89 (37.7)	44 (49.4)	*45* *(50.6)*
Trans Yamuna	***377*** ***(25.9)***	***220*** ***(58.4)***	***157*** ***(41.6)***
Total	***625*** ***(22.7)***	***240*** ***(38.4)***	***385*** ***(61.6)***

Source: UP Census Abstract, 2001.

Similarly, four out of 10 workers in the Trans Yamuna region were marginal workers. This status of employment has an important bearing on the earning and sustaining capacity of women.

Table 8: Category-wise Distribution of Female Workers in the Sample Villages

Name of Village	*Cultivators*	*Agricultural Labour*	*Hhd. Worker*	*Other Workers*	*Total Workers*	*FWPR*
Kazipur	5 (19.2)	20 (76.9)	0 (0.0)	1 (3.8)	26	**53.1**
Kanakpur	7 (25.9)	13 (48.1)	5 (18.5)	2 (7.4)	27	**47.4**
Rikhipur	17 (40.5)	20 (48.8)	1 (2.4)	4 (9.5)	42	**42**
Trans Ganga	***28 (29.5)***	***53 (55.8)***	***6 (6.3)***	***8 (8.4)***	***95***	***46.1***
Chak Garibdas	3 (5.9)	10 (19.6)	1 (2.0)	37 (72.5)	51	**44.0**
Chak Abhaydas	9 (19.6)	17 (37.0)	0 (0.0)	20 (43.5)	46	**52.9**
Chak Kriparam	1 (3.8)	8 (30.8)	2 (11.5)	15 (57.7)	26	**66.7**
Trans Yamuna	***13 (10.6)***	***35 (28.5)***	***3 (3.3)***	***72 (58.5)***	***123***	***50.8***
Total	**42 (19.3)**	**88 (40.6)**	**9 (4.1)**	**79 (36.2)**	**218**	**48.7**

Source: Field Survey, July-September, 2005.

At this juncture it is also interesting to point out that in 80 percent of the women cultivators were either deserted or separated or their spouse had migrated (made yearly visits) in search of work. The impact of male labour migration or absence on women taking up family responsibilities either as cultivators (including share croppers), agricultural labourers, etc. leads to high responsibility for keeping the family farm imposed on women left behind. However, in the paucity of the resources for enhancing productivity, the yields are not satisfactory. The remittances by migrants go to meet social and religious obligation etc. These findings drive home the point that responsibility on women does not make for more equitable gender relations. While family farm management does provide for a measure of food security it is laid unilaterally on the shoulders of women.

Caste-wise Female Work Participation Rate

As is clearly visible the Female Work Participation was high among the scheduled caste category. The participation rate in the general category was merely 23.4 percent. This substantiates the findings of the Table 9.

Table 9: Status of Employment by Caste Categories

Caste of the Respondent	*Status of Employment*		*Total*
	Worker	*Non Worker*	
SC	140 (69.0)	63 (31.0)	203 (100.0)
OBC	45 (43.3)	59 (56.7)	104 (100.0)
General	33 (23.4)	108 (76.6)	141 (100.0)
Total	218 (48.7)	230 (51.3)	448 (100.0)

Source: Field Survey, July-September, 2005.

Occupational Categorisation of Rural Women Workers

Not confining to the definition of cultivators in the Census 2001 (as in Table 10 developed from the available primary data and categorised restricting to the Census concepts), the Table 10 shows supervisory work in family land and working on family land as separate categories. Share croppers have been merged with cultivators. This is done to demarcate the nature or pattern of female work. Confining to the definition of cultivators in the Census 2001 (see Chapter IV) only 2.8 percent of the agricultural

Table 10: Occupational Category according to Age Groups

Main Occupation	*Age of Respondent (in completed years)*						*Total*
	15-24	*25-34*	*35-44*	*45-54*	*55-59*	*60 & above*	
Agri. Labour	0 (0.0)	20 (22.7)	35 (39.8)	19 (21.6)	10 (11.4)	4 (4.5)	88 (100.0)
Self Employed	1 (2.3)	25 (58.1)	12 (27.9)	1 (2.30	0 (0.0)	4 (9.3)	43 (100.0)
Regular Employed	0 (0.0)	5 (38.5)	0 (0.0)	5 (38.5)	3 (23.1)	0 (0.0)	13 (100.0)
Casual/ Contractual	0 (0.0)	2 (7.7)	7 (26.9)	3 (11.5)	4 (15.40	10 (38.5)	26 (100.0)
Cultivator	1 (0.0)	0 (0.0)	7 (83.3)	4 (16.7)	0 (0.0)	0 (0.0)	12 (100.00
Working on family land	0 (0.0)	12 (38.7)	10 (32.3)	5 (16.1)	3 (9.7)	1 (3.2)	31 (100.00
supervisory work in family land	0 (0.0)	0 (0.0)	1 (20.0)	2 (40.0)	2 (40.0)	0 (0.0)	5 (100.0)
Non Workers	22 (9.5)	98 (42.4)	32 (13.9)	22 (9.5)	27 (11.7)	29 (13.0)	230 (100.0)
Total	24 (5.4)	162 (36.2)	104 (23.2)	61 (13.6)	48 (10.7)	49 (10.9)	448 (100.0)

Source: Field Survey, July-September, 2005.

workers in the sample were categorised as cultivators. Despite efforts made over the years to improve coverage of women's work in rural areas by proper inclusion of unpaid productive work, there have been only marginal improvements in this direction. The definition of cultivators relies on the ownership of land cultivated. This ironically eliminates women who work from dawn to dusk as workers in family land or even as supervision work in family land as they do not own land.

Leaving aside these technicalities, no one can deny the fact that women continue to be immersed in agriculture and bear heavy burden of farming tasks with less access to on-farm work than men.

Thus, in an effort to net the contribution of these workers who are mostly under-reported, let us widen our horizons and include women working in family land and women performing supervisory work in family land. Thus, after incorporating these two categories of women, (workers who are often unacknowledged as workers) the proportion of 'cultivators' to the total agricultural workers rises to 19 percent.

Chart No. 3

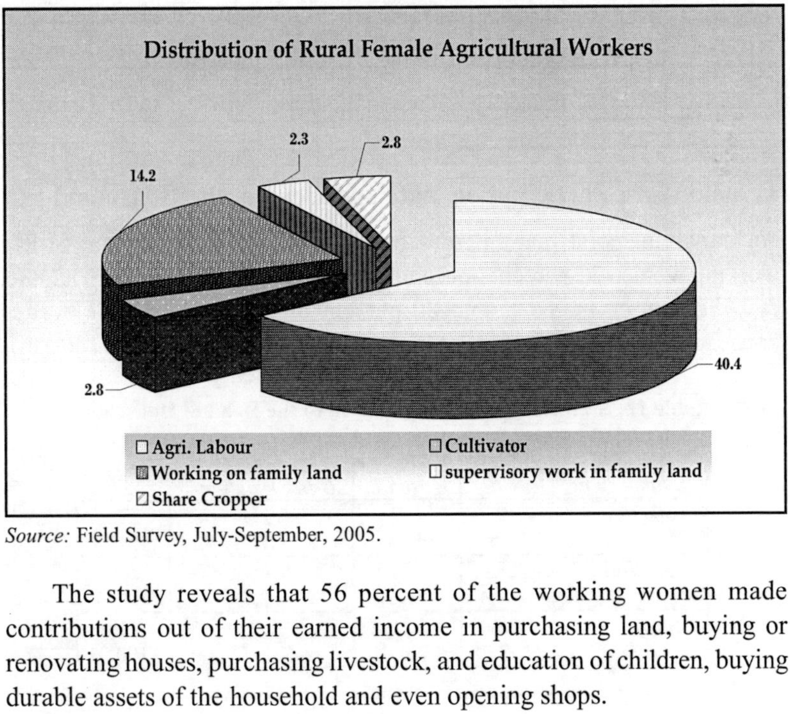

Source: Field Survey, July-September, 2005.

The study reveals that 56 percent of the working women made contributions out of their earned income in purchasing land, buying or renovating houses, purchasing livestock, and education of children, buying durable assets of the household and even opening shops.

The Table 11 points out that the illiterate females were mostly engaged as agricultural labourers (88 percent) or as casual or contractual workers (100 percent). This implies that the educational standards have an implication on the quality of employment. Regular and salaried workers were mostly educated up to middle or even up to higher secondary. These included teachers in primary schools, ANMs, daais, cooks in aganwadis, and other aganwadi workers.

Table 11: Education Specific Category-wise Status of Work

Main Occupation	*Educational Status of the Respondent*				*Total*
	No Education	*Up to Primary*	*Middle School*	*Up to High School*	
Agri. Labour	77 (87.5)	9 (10.2)	0 (0.0)	2 (2.3)	88 (100.0)
Self Employed	26 (60.5)	6 (14.0)	6 (14.0)	5 (11.6)	43 (100.0)
Regular/ Salaried Employed	1 (7.7)	0 (0.0)	8 (61.5)	4 (30.8)	13 (100.0)
Casual/ Contractual	26 (100.0)	0 (0.0)	0 (0.0)	0 (0.0)	26 (100.0)
Cultivator	36 (75.0)	11 (22.9)	0 (0.0)	0 (0.0)	48 (100.0)
Non Workers	149 (64.5)	43 (18.7)	22 9.5%	17 (7.4)	230 (100.0)
Total	315 (70.3)	69 (15.4)	36 8.0%	28 (6.3)	448 (100.0)

Source: Field Survey, July-September, 2005.

Female Work Participation Rate and Head of the Household

An important point that emerges from this Table 12 is that out of 218 working women 32 percent households were female-headed. Also another fact that can be traced is that 80 percent of women in female headed households were working.

Table 12: Status of Work and Relation to the Head of Household

Status of Employment	*Relation to the Head of the Household*			*Total*
	Self	*Husband*	*Other Relations*	
Worker	70 (79.5)	137 (41.4)	11 (37.9)	218 (48.7)
Non Worker	18 (20.5)	194 (58.6)	18 (62.1)	230 (51.3)
Total	88 (100.0)	331 (100.0)	29 (100.0)	448 (100.0)

Note: Figures in brackets show column percentages to the total.

Source: Field Survey, July-September, 2005.

Consumption Status and Burden of Responsibility

Almost 4 out of 10 working women responded that they had to skip meals so that the rest of the family could have sufficient meals. This proportion was ten percentage points lower for the non-working females. Though women's employment is necessarily related to the alleviation of poverty, yet a look at the occupation-wise consumption pattern portrays a different picture.

Table 13: Consumption of Meals a Day by Occupational Categories

Main Occupation	*Meals Skipped*		*Number of Times Meals a day*			*Total*
	Yes	*No*	*once*	*2 times*	*3 times or more*	
Agri. Labour	56 (63.6)	32 (36.4)	1 (1.1)	61 (69.3)	26 (29.5)	88 (100.0)
Self Employed	11 (25.6)	32 (74.4)	0 (0.0)	14 (32.6)	29 (67.4)	43 (100.0)
Regular/ Salaried Employed	0 (0.0)	13 (100.0)	0 (0.0)	9 (30.8)	4 (69.2)	13 (100.0)
Casual Labour	13 (50.0)	13 (50.0)	4 (15.4)	18 (69.2)	4 (15.4)	26 (100.)
Cultivator	3 (25.0)	9 (66.7)	0 (0.0)	7 (58.3)	5 (41.7)	12 (100.0)
supervisory work in family land	0 (0.0)	5 (100.0)	0 (0.0)	0 (0.0)	5 (100.0)	5 (100.0)
Working on family land	2 (6.5)	29 (93.5)	0 (0.0)	8 (25.8)	23 (74.2)	31 (100.0)
Non Workers	73 (31.7)	157 (68.3)	1 (0.4)	120 (52.2)	109 (47.4)	230 (100.0)
Total	158 (35.3)	290 (64.7)	6 (1.3)	239 (53.3)	212 (47.4)	448 (100.0)

Source: Field Survey, July-September, 2005.

Chart No. 4

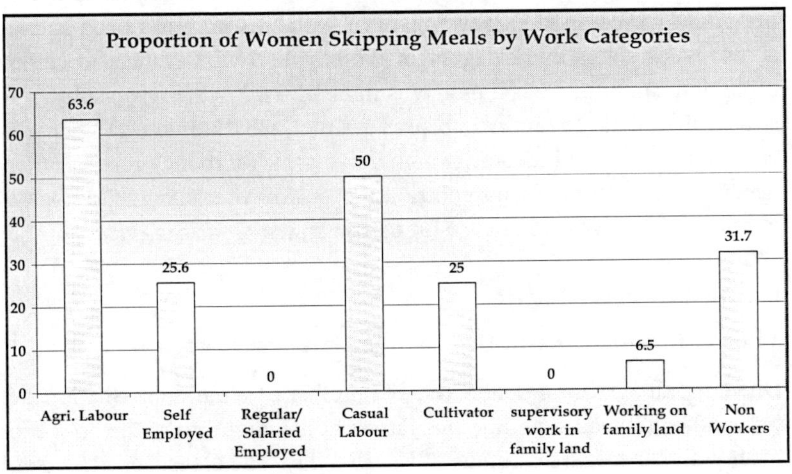

Source: Developed from Table 13.

This fact somewhere points to the casual and marginal nature of work and their meagre earnings i.e., even below subsistence levels. Fifty four percent of the working women could afford only two meals a day. (refer Chapter II, hypothesized relation number one)

Case of Shushila Devi

Village: Kanakpur, **Tehsil:** Handia, **Age:** 35 years

Sushila is a mother of seven children (still expecting another). She works in others fields for petty wages (Rs. 30 a day or five kg paddy or wheat) apart from bidi making for which she earns a paltry sum of Rs. 28 for 1000 bidis. Her husband off and on job as a painter mostly within the village premises. His income hardly meets the domestic requirements as most of his earnings is spent on drinking, gambling and other vices. Thus, the whole burden of family's sustenance is on Shushila. When asked,

She bluntly says, my children have not had proper diet for days. When I can't meet feed my children a proper meal a day how do you expect me to eat!

Interestingly Shushila fought for the post of pradhan in the panchayat elections on being provoked by her husband. Paradoxical to what is viewed of an empowered female pradhan, Shushila does not even know about her family indebtedness. She blindly okays her husband and puts signature (which she can crudely make) on any document.

Access to and Control over Resources

Access to and control over resources has been considered to be a very important indicator of empowerment of women which has been studied across work status and category of employment with respect to certain proxy indicators like when money is tight who takes the responsibility to stretch it so that the family expenses are met, what do you do with your earned income/saved income, whom do you ask for money for your petty needs, have you made any contribution out of your income/savings to purchase land, livestock, house for marriage, etc.

Case Study of Dhanraji

Village: Rikhipur, **Tehsil:** Handia, **Age:** 35 years

Dhanraji, an agricultural labourer, is a mother of 6 children. She lost her husband eight years ago. She finds it very difficult to make the both ends meet with her meagre earnings of Rs. 30 a day. The eldest son (15 yrs. of age) is working in Mumbai and supports the family with his income. Her only asset is a thatched hut which badly needs maintenance. Her parents have disowned her as a witch who has responsible for the predicament of her family. She is regular subject to tortures by her brothers-in-laws who have disowned her of any share in the property. With her hard earned money (sleepless nights to make bidis) she saved money to buy a buffalo. Now her agricultural income is supported by her dairy income. Now all what she aspires is to get her daughter out of this hell and give her a decent life. Lastly she laments, "

– " i.e. For a woman to live without her husband is just like dying each day to live the next day.

Thus, we may conclude that migration consummates in feminisation of agriculture wherein more and more women are absorbed (both with broadening and deepening of agricultural performances) in agriculture and allied activities. As per the Census 2011, there has been a 24 percent rise in the number of women agricultural labourers from 2001 to 2011, i.e. from 49.5 million to 61.6 million. With 98 million Indian women agricultural workers 63 percent are agricultural labourers. Let us rethink on this issue of concern!

7

ECO-ORPHANS: Marginalised Farmers as Victims of Globalisation

Dr. John Peter Vallabadoss

Introduction

Orphans are real existing beings with ignorance or denied knowledge of their parentage. Cut off from their roots and their parents of origin, the orphans are left to survive either by themselves or by compassion of adaptation. Surveillance over the experimented globalisation policies in contemporary times, highlights the perils of those denied of their rightful belonging to their origins and rooted existence in their own land, due to the utopian imagination of global village. Highly-fantasied castle of globalised one-world community for about three decades from 1990s has proved to be no 'haven' for all, and a no 'dwelling place' for those marginalised farmers. Affecting the sectors of food and industrial products on a large scale, the globalisation has triggered enormous rise in international trade, economics, political policies, development, technological exchanges and logistics.

The developmental strategy of globalisation has negatively impacted the environment and those directly connected with it, especially the large community of food growers, the farmers. Moreover, the ecological awareness in the developed countries has compelled the largely polluting industries to have the disposal of waste, including e-waste and nuclear waste, in the underdeveloped and developing countries. The land which is the parental home for the farmers, has become dumping ground, stressed out over-grower of large scale food production, sterile soil with non-manageable chemical fertilisers and readily available uncultivatable plots for real estate businesses and for special economic zones for multinational companies. As a result, the children of the soil, the farmers have become 'eco-orphans,' those who have lost their home (*oikosas* in Greek) and cut off from their parental roots.

This paper attempts to explore the reality of marginalisation of farmers from victim point of view as globalisation has advanced, and tries to propose 'eco-parentage' of 'return to the land' through indigenous techniques of farming, whereby one could mitigate the negative effects of globalisation, and reclaim their 'belonging.'

1. Impacts of Globalisation

Globalisation as a paradigm of economic activities, growing inter-connectedness and liberalisation of trade, reduction of restrictions and tariffs, has encouraged international and multinational big business companies to expand their activities. Their influence with the governmental acting in their favour, has resulted in their less fair and ethical policies contributing to more negative than positive impacts.[1] After 1990s, market economy introduced, international trade and special economic zones have contributed to the growths, with foreign and capital investments. Globalisation as a more integrated world community brings both benefits and problems for all.[2] The complex phenomenon of globalisation affects both positively and negatively human life worldwide. With globalisation comes increased trade where many communities have access to previously unavailable foods, medical facilities and living necessities.[3] The effects of globalisation are not separate but multifaceted phenomena, affecting the growing of crops, contributing to food scarcity crises and to some extent introduction of new diseases to particular regions.[4]

At the wake of cutting edge competition in business, companies using globalisation paradigm, sought to lower prices, more choices and better services for consumers by having a cheap, forced labour, sometimes encouraging human trafficking of labourers, especially in industrial production units. Due to globalisation many farming communities were forced to lose their jobs in their sector and become easy prey to be people of cheap labour in these industries of multinational companies. With less than ideal conditions for the environment and health security of labourers, ethics and integrity of trade policies were compromised with corruptions prevalent in socio-economic-political scenario of exploited (developing and under-developed) countries.[5]

2. Effects on Environment

The surge in international trade has brought along with its economic progress various effects on the environment: emissions and environmental damage associated with the physical movement of goods, excessive use of fossil fuel, oil spills, extinction of species and introduction of exotic species, etc.[6]The increase in the consumption of products available through globalised markets and movement of goods anywhere in the world has impacted the ecological cycle. Eventually the increased consumption led to an increase in the production of materials, especially putting stress on agrarian goods from the land and marine foods from the sea, impacting the environment. Transportation of raw materials and food products from one corner of the world to the other, the consumption of fossil fuel for such transportation, increased not only the pollution levels but also on the depletion of rare, non-renewable sources of energy. Industrial wastes dumped in the oceans and on the landfills, along with gases emitted from various transporting facilities have increased the greenhouse effect in the skies and killed many organisms on the earth.

Globalisation, liberalisation and privatisation in the nineties have made big effect on economy, production, distribution. The climate change talks in Paris at the end of 2015 showed just how fragile the global environment is and the impact of climate change on the world, and the role that globalisation plays. Public sector industries in most countries, especially in India, suffered a decline due to lack of support from social welfare schemes of the government and lack of cooperative participation of people. Globalisation favoured the private sectors who were concerned only in increasing their business and exploiting the labour and the resources. The defence of environmental concerns and land protection was termed as business-hostile. The defending forces of people and activists were labelled as anti-developmental, rebellious, traditionalists, anti-national, primitive and under developed. The poor are always found fault with. They become the victims of exploitation of the natural resources by the free-trade, liberalisation and globalised economy. With increased displacement and economic migrations, the poor farmers are given the burden of bearing the weight of ecological crisis accelerated by globalised industrial activities.[7]

3. Recycling Hypocrisy

Globalisation has succinctly licenced the global North to marginalise further the exploited countries. The people of these countries are made to live upon the waste dumped by multinational companies and governments of global North. A leak of an internal World Bank memo signed by chief economist Lawrence Summers, in which he appeared to urge World Bank economists to encourage pollution intensive industry migrate to developing countries,[8] proves the fact of blatant privilege taken by these globalisation forces. Tighter rules adopted by different countries have prompted western nations to send rubbish elsewhere. Using the provisions of special economic zones (SEZs) and of export oriented units (EOUs) which allowed businesses to procure resources from abroad, United Kingdom and other countries were sending plastic waste to India. China which was the world's biggest importer of scrap plastic implemented a ban on western imports of waste.

After China banned the import of scrap plastic in 2018, Malaysia, Vietnam and Thailand have been the main destination for British plastics. Following China, India banned imports of waste plastic to tackle environmental crisis. To uphold the principles of sustainable development and ensuring minimal impact on the environment, the Indian Government has now completely prohibited the import of solid plastic waste.[9] Most of the waste currently circulating in the world's oceans is thought to originate in developing countries which failed to have effective waste management infrastructure. After the ban announcements of China over 'foreign garbage' UK's environment secretary Michael Gove has said that the country would 'stop offshoring our dirt.' In the name of liberalisation of economy and starting of special economic zones, globalised markets have been used as 'dumping grounds' with no responsibility for their waste production and disposal.[10]

For many economically rich nations, the last step of waste management depends heavily on a cluster of countries in Asia and Africa. The economic superpowers are working to find a new strategy to find a new home. The reverse course of countries in Asia with notice of waste import ban have asserted that they could no longer be the waste destination. The import ban is indicative of growing trend for a major domestic clean-up effort, along with its own domestic gradual crackdown on all single-use plastics. Crying over the ban, the developed countries have opined that these would create a host of other problems. The manufactures after losing valuable scrap materials, will turn to virgin materials thus creating greater energy requirements and increasing greenhouse gas emissions. The quick problem solving method used by waste exporters is by looking for the possibility of either towards less resistant and ecologically conscious countries, which they wilfully call as 'right kind of partner' or towards a more permanent, home-grown solution.[11] Therefore, despite the efforts of countries to stop this globalised mess of waste from exploiting (developed) countries, the recycling hypocrisy continues.

4. Contemporary Neo-colonialism

Globalisation as monopolising culture, continued with colonial tints. Modern colonial tactics with one particular ideology of production, distribution and consumption are in principle defying the natural law of multiplicity and diversity. Patent rights, free-trade zones, liberal economy of moving capitals and manufacturing in other countries, especially where there is a cheap labour markets and utilisation of carbon resources of water and land, are all critiqued as new vistas of neo-colonisation in the name of globalisation. The countries which have polluting industries are free to move to other countries not only to pollute their host environment but also continue to accuse them of carbon emissions and to teach them of reduction of greenhouse gases.

Monopolising culture of globalisation influences the introduction and promotion of genetically modified seeds to colonise and control the food production world-over. Indian environmental activist, Vandana Shiva working on anti-globalisation and organic farming by women, opinions that mechanical science and reductionist biology were hailed by globalisation. The scientism has killed the complex unity of a system of corporal and material existence into single units of physical, chemical and biological properties.[12] Analysis and discoveries are applauded but the consequences of them have led to the monolith-singular explications of life made of complexities and compositions based on interdependence and co-existence. The river is not merely a source of energy as in hydroelectric ideology, as reservoir serving purpose of supply of drinking water and irrigation through canals. The reductionist approach to organism sees cells and genes as mere master molecules.

The reality of life is contrary to such totally unfounded central dogma of monolithic practices. The life organises itself, with its complexity. Vandhana Shiva criticised the 'green revolution of India'[13] through promotion of monocrop farming through chemical fertilisers, and the introduction of GMOs as forms of scientism and bio-terrorism, crushing the real knowledge and wisdom of the earth and the traditional human practices and heritage. Calling it as 'monoculture of mind' she says that it has destroyed the food system and its cycle. If green revolution has been growing enough food, half of India would not be starving today. Industrial farming is the cause of climate change, soil and water pollution, depletion of water tables. Having promised to end famine and eradicate poverty, the intensive industrial farming has only resulted in more the problem than the solution. Monocrop culture boosted by globalisation has transformed the land of abundance of food in terms of pulses and cereals and millets into soil-factory manufacturing food of just few kinds in abundance only for humans and has maliciously labelled diaries, poultries and animal husbandries, only in terms food producing units. It is indeed a contemporary new way of colonisation![14]

5. Farmers as Victims

From its introduction as economic policy, globalisation has had far-reaching effects on modern lifestyle with its faster access to technology, improved communication, shared innovation, multi-cultural interactions. The economic prosperity opening up vast channels of development through globalising activities, has created various concerns and debates extensively on environmentalism and plight of the poor and marginalised.[15] Anthony J. McMichael asserts that the effects of globalisation are not separate but multifaceted phenomena, affecting the growing of crops, contributing to food scarcity crises and to some extent introduction of new diseases to particular regions. With climate change affecting the agriculture in various ways, with more or less rainfall, extreme temperature, introduction of new pests and changes in nutritional factors of carbon and nitrogen levels.[16] The impact of globalisation directly on the farmers, is very well seen in the growth of noxious weeds and plants. The toxic wastes from chemical fertilisers have interfered in the genetic make-up of many plant species. The non-biodegradable products such as plastic and electronic wastes are major threat to farming lands and eco-system.

The globalised marketing strategy marginalised Indian agriculture, not creating employments for farming sector. Farmers have been identified as suffering the damaging consequences of globalisation. It has a direct impact on people's potential to develop and achieve their potential to be physically labouring on the land. Pain and disruption in social health and other services associated with structural adjustment policies resulting in negative consequences. Fertile lands have become vast barren lands which have been encroached by 'developers and promoters' for housing units and industrial sites or roads. Farmers are excluded in any policy making, with regard to developmental projects and industrial growths. Economic recovery programmes which are meant for social developments of 'excluded' individuals and communities, have been only on documented papers. The farmers have become the most affected victims of globalised economy and development.

6. Anti-globalisation- Lobbying and Resistance

The anti-globalisation movement on fighting against patent rights over indigenous products, introduction of genetically modified seeds, monocrop agriculture and industrial/corporate farming, is making some headway. The corporate lobbying and money power are instrumental in buying the policy-makers to act in their favour. Even international organisations both legislative and regulatory authorities are roped in to support the big businesses. The ideological mafias with corporate interest work hand in hand with governments and organisations to spread the ills of globalisation. Anti-globalisation movements through local and international channels like World Social Forum, are succeeding in stopping momentarily the negative impacts of globalisation. Few victories as far as Indian groups are concerned, give certainly a confidence in counter-lobbying and resistance. For instance, one could cite the examples of the victory of Chipko in saving the forest, fight against Himalayan hydro-electric projects, defeating the WR Grace's claim of Neem patent, contesting introduction of GMOs and BT cotton and bringal, etc. Yet, the task is enormous as India is facing multidirectional attack by polluting industries, exploiting business, stealing knowledge of traditional medicines by pharmaceuticals, indirectly gaining access to patents over indigenous seeds.[17] Fighting against these strong forces of globalisation, for Indian socio-economic, ecological groups, has become a Herculean task.

Meanwhile, rise of anti-globalisation has seen a light of the day all over the world. The sense of loss of individual, communal and national identities has compelled each group of people in every country to voice out against globalising trends. Mounting anti-globalisation sentiments have engulfed the Global North, North American countries who were strong architects, proponents and promoters of globalisation three decades ago. With the neglect of local products and introduction of all imported goods produced and manufactured elsewhere, every country tries to reverse the impacts of globalisation. In such context, the question arises about prospects of 'de-globalisation.' The current 'de-globalisation' trend among number of environmentalists, nationalists, anti-capitalist economists, is equally argued against creating harmful consequences for the environment. In the absence of globally available products, each country would have increased economic activity which might lead to greater emissions of industrial pollutants and more environmental degradation.[18] With help of WTO (World

Trade Organisation) the enthusiasm for sustainable development and environmentally friendly trade policies, directions are in place for green provisions to protect human, animal or plant life and conserve the natural resources. With de-globalisation, isolating countries become likely be responsible for the environment and lose effective bargaining strategies to demand environmental accountability from trading firms.[19] From globalisation one could take the transfer of intermediate, capital goods and clean state-of-the-art technologies, environmentally friendly technological innovations.

7. 'Eco-Parentage'

To minimise the negative impact of globalisation on environment in general and on farmers in particular, we propose 'eco-parentage.' Normally parentage is understood as the transmission of kinship when a person descends from another. While consanguinity within the family relationship binds the individuals by degree of genetic similarity, kinship links individuals down the line of offspring with social and cultural ties. In modern anthropological discourse we have three types of parentage of legitimate, natural and adoptive. Biological kinship from the social kinship is distinguished by D. Schneider[20] and patrilineality-matrilineality in question, there is no single parentage principle for Rodney Needham.[21] Today conformity with a uniform model is unlikely. The question of filiation directs towards inheritance and of familial authority. Sociologically speaking, parentage determines the identity of a person in a group, an individual in a society, with rights of titles, status, privileges and obligations. We apply these principles of social anthropology on 'parentage' to current issue of marginalisation of farmers as victims of globalisation and as ecological orphans.

Farmers have ecological kinship with their land. Land is their identity, right and heritage. Globalisation is killing their space, cutting their link with the land is driving them out of their home. 'Eco-parentage' is an ideological hypothesis tracing the kinship relation of farmers specially to the land, as 'eco-kinship.' Satish Kumar says that we are all related to and dependent on the soil. Humans have such link with soil, *humus*. Modern life style, economy, education has estranged humans from the soil. Wishing to change the perspective of contempt for soil, dirt, 'peasant' he promotes 'touch of the soil,' saying, "We are all part of this healthy web of life maintained by soil."[22] Farmers are dignified humans and the noblest of all, as they are the ones who are in touch with the soil. The soil levels all our identities and our status. It is a soil-status that makes us all equal; solely the social status identified with money and power, has hierarchical structure, with someone as superior or inferior, as higher or lower, as better or worse. The earth as the home and the soil as the mother provide 'ecological kinship' to humans and 'eco-parentage' embraces all.

8. Returning to the 'Eco-cycle'

Law of Nature is to give. Humans have learnt only to take it. We need to return to nature and learn to give. Recycling is a good practice of reusing the resources we took from Nature. It would also reduce dependence of further resources from Nature. Nature needs only the returning to Nature what is taken from it. Returning back to Nature as humans interconnected to it, is better than just Re-cycling. Food cycle in eco-system is very much affected by globalised economy and production. Nature produces plenty, not only for humans but for all. The humans need to give it back to Nature what they do not need and it would give in return abundantly. To counter the hypocrisy of recycling, a cry of 'no recycling,' but 'return to the eco-cycle' should be heard loud and clear and implemented effectively.

The estrangement from nature enables human to think contrary to ecology and nature. As Vandana Shiva says that service for the earth calls for a paradigm of thinking that we are not separate from the earth and what tries to separate it from us in name of science and technology, economy and development, has certain form of violence built in to it. What could be learnt from the earth is that of 'non-separability' in the world where there is exclusion, domination, fundamentalism, the principle of segregation.[23] The human society by its very nature of forming and functioning, and the natural character of the earth and the soil, are that of diversity which is the condition of existence. Interdependence is the part of existence where one is not the single organism but punch of composition of various parts and organisms.

Promoting indigenous seeds Vandana Shiva says that these natural seeds have inbuilt capacity of multiplying, whereas laboratory seeds have to be produced every time with the manipulation. These seeds only produce onetime crops and become sterile for next cycle of life. No GMO seed is to produce another seed and every time it is laboratory produced. Whole cycle of life is cut and artificially produced and manufactured. The estrangement of Nature becomes the brilliant ways of preventing multiplication of seeds through genetic engineering. These terminated seed with exclusive patent rights of certain companies makes it illegal to produce seed from the seeds bought. And they prevent farmers to save their seeds and make them buy every time they need.[24] Such practice leading not only to biocide (killing of pests and germs) and genocide (farmers' suicide) but also 'ecocide' (killing of eco-system), can be reversed only if we return back to biodiversity.

9. Abandoning Mono-crop Cultivation

The dominant model of monocrop agriculture after industrialisation and globalisation separated the land for agriculture from other activities of humans. To counter such paradigm, areas are managed with biodiversity conservation and food production. Expansion of land areas and continuous activities of utility of artificial growth promoters and machinery tools, not only destroy the ecological systems in various parts of the planets but leave behind the land inutile for decades. Increasing the mass production of crops by using biotechnological methods and industrial farming, has given negative result from the beginning of this millennium. They not only have increased the demand for food supply as projected to satisfy the world hungry mouths, but also raised concerns over the left-behinds of globalised form of mono-agricultural practices and experiments.

While the market economy and liberalisation in the globalised era has ensured the movement of farm goods of food, vegetables and fruits to be stored and distributed worldwide, the evil effects are by such mass production and monocrop cultures destroyed the local life and made them dependent always on the market. The lands have been de-fertilised and became barren, just after few years of depositing poisonous chemical fertilisers, pesticides and herbicides. The biocides from these hybrid crops and chemicals have killed the very life of the microbes which helped the soil fertility conservation and sustainable farming activities. The industrial farming has reduced the natural supply of organic biomass and sustainable fertilisers and microbes.[25] Moreover, the cost of production has increased the farmers and producers to look forward to financial supports to continue their activities of farming. The lenders have always calculated returns and the infertile lands have not given them hopes for such returns. The best option for farmers is then to abandon mono-crop cultivation.

10. Promoting Eco-agriculture

Only agro-ecology (eco-agriculture) can save the world, feeding the entire humanity world-over. Eco-agriculture has been developed to guarantee the conservation of ecosystem providers such as water, air and soil, the sequestration of trees and shrubs, the protection of natural habitats of bees and insects for natural pollination, and preservation of traditional seeds of indigenous varieties. Locally grown indigenous farm products are proven to be healthy and climatically adapted to the local geographical region, and seasonally life promoting and sustainable. Such practices have longstanding heritage of protecting natural resources. Eco-agriculture develops strategies for managing landscapes for increasing agricultural products and raising farm income for the producing communities. The eco-agricultural practices have a principle of providing ecosystem services and be served by them. They allow production of crops and at the same time protect the environment, by conserving natural resources and biodiversity, including microbial protection for soil enrichment.[26]

What makes this method different from other sustainable agricultural activities is the management of landscape. The landscape approach integrates farmlands, protected areas and natural resources. Same as the driving need for survival in the humans the eco-consciousness allows us be sensitive to the survival of other creatures and earth resources. While conservation of these resources are aimed at the far end survival of humans, it has a wider scope for sustainability of non-human species and material beings also. All of them, humans, plants, animals, insects, microbes and even non-living beings, work in synergy for farm production activities. The key ingredients of this agriculture are firstly the self-recognition of the farmers themselves and being recognised by others as equal partners in profession. The non-human creatures quickly do that miracle and participate willingly in the sustainable farming methods.[27]

11. Indian Innovators in Natural Farming

New wave of returning to natural way of farming has been witnessed in contemporary India. Many discarded farming due to unbearable debts, failure of water conservation, and influence of mono-crop cultivation and chemical fertilisers. Returning back to natural farming through various methods like Zero-budget natural farming of Subhas Palekar, adopting to permaculture, natural way organic farming by Namazhvar have made awareness of shunning away from chemical fertilisers, developing indigenous methods of water conservation, creating biodiversity in and around the land, multi-crops cultivation, seasonal crops, raising indigenous species of live-stocks, etc.[28] The confidence in a sustainable natural environment which supports life would boost the farming communities to turn challenges from globalisation into opportunities for growth with human dignity and labour. Self-reliance of farmers with efficient agro-economy is promoted by local processing units for millets and oilseeds, and marketing facilities for fruits and vegetables. Then, the bank loans and non-banking sectors' credit schemes along with governmental and corporate lobbies are not needed for farmers adapted to natural way of farming.

As claimed by globalisation, production locally for the globe has failed to have equitable distribution. For, the production of monocrop continually in a particular region has not only reduced the capacity of the land, but also failed to provide for all other needs of people in the locality. It made them utterly dependent on the global supply which was manipulated by the markets. Paradigm is changed of not only acting locally but thinking locally. Globalisation has helped only the middle men and markets. True globalisation is by localisation of production and distribution. Local markets are to be promoted with community supported agriculture where there is common production and consumption. Value addition to natural farming products makes the price of domestic goods affordable, the production less expensive and competitively capable. Changes from production to consumption practices, along with realisation of individual and collective potential enable self-reliance of farmers and resist further marginalisation of food producers with debts and global market dependency. Preventing the victimisation of farmers is by returning back to natural way of cultivating which not only heals them but also cures the ecological crisis.

Conclusion

The process of globalisation which it was claimed would bring the world together has proved to be widening the gap between the global South and the global North. It has provoked tension and division, protest and violence, contest and confrontation among many national and international governments and organisations. A common need for and a right to a fair share of natural resources is not met by globalisation. Further the challenges of environmental degradation by globalisation have direct social and economic consequences in life of people especially the farmers. The threat of non-accessibility of resources for them renders them 'ecological orphans,' with loss of identity, dignity and life. While reversing globalisation seems impossible today, developing effective mechanisms to reduce its impact on environment and the marginalised communities is encouraged to take forward the economically feasible and environment-friendly developmental policies, projects and practices.

From estrangement of humans from the Nature caused by globalisation we propose that all human activities should be in harmony with the environment for the survival of human race, all living and non-living beings, dependent on the resources of the planet earth, their home. Returning to the Nature, not mere 're-cycling' resources, is the prophetic call of the day. What we need is not an 'eco-orphanage' to the care of the farmers as ecological orphans, but consciousness of 'eco-parentage' of feeling of kinship with land and of returning to natural way of farming with multi-crops cultivation and catering to biodiversity. Denying the marginalising efforts of globalisation, we rely on the Nature that embraces and sustains all. Nature is not out there, but we are part of it.

Notes

1. Anna Roberts, "The Negative Impacts of Globalisation on the Environment" https://bizfluent.com/info-8528910-role-multinational-companies-human-rights.html, accessed on 24 Oct, 2019.
2. "Globalisation and the Environment," in https://www.ifsw.org/globalisation-and-the-environment/ accessed on 24 Oct, 2019.
3. Ravi Fernando, "Sustainable globalisation and implications for strategic corporate and national sustainability," *Corporate Governance,* Vol. 12, Issue: 4, (2012), 579-589.
4. Megan Nichols, "Globalisation and its Environmental Impact,"https://magazine.scienceconnected.org/2019/04/globalisation-and-its-environmental-impact/accessed on 24 Oct, 2019.
5. Halil Ibrahim Aydin, et al., *Economic Development: Global and Regional Studies* (Istanbul: IJOPEC Publication, 2017), 190. And also, *Op.Cit.* Anna Roberts, "The Negative Impacts of Globalisation on the Environment."
6. Carol McAusland, "Globalisation's Direct and Indirect Effects on the Environment," in *Global Forum on Transport and Environment in a Globalising World* (Mexico: Guadalajara, 2008), 5.
7. Peter Newell, *Globalisation and the Environment: Capitalism, Ecology and Power*(Cambridge: Polity Press, 2012), 1932-1935.
8. Highly published event, John S.Rosenberg, "Summers in Summary," *Harvard Magazine,* May-June 2001, 59. See also, "Toxic Memo," interview with Pritchett, https://www.harvardmagazine.com/2001/05/toxic-memo.html
9. Vishwa Mohan, "Govt puts Complete ban on Import of Solid Plastic Waste," in *Economic Times,* 7 March, 2019. https://economictimes.indiatimes.com/
10. Josh Gabbatiss, "UK now exporting more waste to countries with highest levels of ocean plastic pollution," in *Independent,* 14 June 2018.https://www.independent.co.uk/
11. https://www.tes-amm.com/waste-import-bans-in-china-india/ accessed on 27 April, 2020.
12. Refer, Vandana Shiva, *India Divided: Diversity and Democracy Under Attack.* New York: Seven Stories Press, 2005.
13. Refer Vandana Shiva, *The Violence of the Green Revolution: Third World Agriculture, Ecology, and Politics.* Kentucky: University Press, 2016.

14. Rebecca Todd Peters, *In Search of the Good Life: The Ethics of Globalisation* (New York: Continuum, 2004),139-165.
15. https://www.environment.co.za/environmental-issues/globalisation-and-its-impact-on-the-environment.html accessed on 24 Oct, 2019.
16. McMichael, A. J. "Globalisation, Climate Change, and Human Health," *The New England Journal of Medicine*, Vol.368,(2013),1335-1343.
17. This is 'bio-piracy' as Vandana Shiva calls it. Fighting of pharmaceuticals that were trying to steal India's bio genome of various herbs and plants and for medicinal purposes they are trying to patent it and capture that knowledge and prevent Indians from making any medicines on those formulas. Refer, Vandana Shiva, *Biopiracy: The Plunder of Nature and Knowledge.* North Atlantic Books, 2016.
18. Arguing against globalisation has the risk for the countries wishing to go green – the risk of depending on local firms with no energy-efficient production processes; less specialisation in many sectors depending on competition; inefficient allocation of resources leading to the dissipation of scarce natural resources; duplication in production processes and increase in local emissions.
19. Sylvanus KwakuAfesorgbor & BinyamAfewerkDemena, "Globalisation may actually be better for the environment," published 24 April 2018, http://theconversation.com/globalisation-may-actually-be-better-for-the-environment-95406 accessed on 24 Oct, 2019.
20. David M. Schneider, *A Critique of the Study of Kinship* (Michigan: University Press, 1984), 189.
21. Rodney Needham, *Remarks and Inventions: Skeptical Essays about Kinship* (London: Routledge, 1974), 38.
22. Satish Kumar, *Soil, Soul, Society: A new Trinity for our Time* (Brighton: Ivy Pres, 2017), 12-13. The Latin word '*humus*' means soil. The words 'human, humility and humanity' all come from the same root. When humans lose contact with soil, they are no longer humans.
23. Vandana Shiva, Introduction, *The Vandana Shiva Reader* (Kentucky, University Press, 2014), 1-5.
24. Refer, Lionel Astruc, *Vandana Shiva pour une déobéissance créatrice – Vandana Shiva for CreativeDisobedience*(in French), Actes Sud, 2014.
25. G. Nammalvar, *IyarkaiVelanmai – Natural Farming* (Karur: Vanagam, 2004), 30. Referalso, Sandrine Bélier et Gilles Luneau, *La Biodiversité, une chance – Biodiversity: A Chance* (in French) 2013.
26. Pierre Rabhi, *L'agroécologie: une éthique de vie – Agro-ecology : Ethics of Life* (in French), (Arles, France: Actes Sud, 2015), 32-41.
27. G.Nammalvar, *Thai Man – Mother Soil* (in Tamil) (Karur: Vanagam, 2013), 20. Refer also, Jacques Caplat, *L'agriculturebiologique pour nourrirl'humanité – Biological Agriculture for Feeding Humanity* (in French). 2012.
28. Sridhar, V., Amarnath Surendranath, *An Economic Analysis of Organic Farming in Tamil Nadu.* Lambert Academic Publishing, 2013.

8

Rohingya on the Move: Story of Global Irresponsibility and Indifference

— *Dr. Jose D. Maliekal S.D.B.*

Introduction

This paper intends capturing in broad outlines, the saga of displacement and statelessness of the Rohingya, especially from the perspective of the response of the international community to their plight.

1.0 Rohingya Presence in Burma (Myanmar) from a Historical Perspective

The 1982 Citizenship Law of Myanmar denied the Rohingya identity in the name of indigenous ethnic group. The Rohingya Muslims from Arakan, who are ethnically closer to Bangladeshi Muslims, have now become *de jure* stateless in Burma. Despite the argument of the current government of the Union of Myanmar that the Rohingyas are Bengalis, they themselves claim to have their roots in Arakan, the northern part of today's Rakhine State in Myanmar.[1]

Rakhine Buddhists and other Burmese leaders often raise the question as to why the Muslims of Arakan did not call themselves Rohingya at the time of Burmese independence. In addition, Rakhine leaders have claimed that Arakanese and Buddhism are synonymous and that the Rohingya are outsiders who have nothing related to the word Arakan/Arakanese. Rohingya Solidarity Organisation-President Mohammad Yunus responded, saying that, "...after independence when Burmese politics was developed based on ethnicity and questions arose about our identity. During that time some influential groups accused that we are Bengalese. Then our leaders stressed that we are Rohingya, the original inhabitants of Rohang, the old name of Arakan, and not immigrants from Chittagong."[2]

It is clear that some Muslim groups were living in Arakan State before the Burmese and British colonisation. One point of agreement is that Rohingya inhabitants of Arakan as one of the major Muslims groups in Burma are entirely different ethnically from other Muslims. They have a long history and have been involved in different political processes in Arakan since ancient times. Their indivisible identity was not questioned before the enactment of the 1982 Citizenship Law. Interviews and various statements made by Rakhine leaders provide support that the Rohingya have a strong attachment to Arakan. Discussion with Arakanese communities leads to the conclusion that the identity of Rohingya rests on the fact that they were inhabitants of "Rohang"—the ancient name of Arakan.[3]

Due to ongoing denial of citizenship, and being vilified as aliens, by the military-dominated government of Myanmar, the Rohingya has been in a state of statelessness and those denied citizenship, in their own homeland. They find themselves as refugees, in the neighbouring Bangladesh, India, Thailand, Malaysia and other countries.[4]

According to the Article 1. A. (2) of the 1951 Refugee Convention, a refugee is a person who,

> [O]wing to well-founded fear of being persecuted for reasons of race, religion, nationality, membership of a particular social group or political opinion, is outside the country of his nationality and is unable, or owing to such fear, is unwilling to avail himself of the protection of that country; or who, not having a nationality and being outside the country of his former habitual residence as a result of such events, is unable or, owing to such fear, is unwilling to return to it.[5]

Though all these concepts focus on individual persecution excluding people fleeing from war and civil strife, every Rohingya falls under the universal concept of 'refugee'. Each Rohingya is being persecuted due to state's repression and is also unwilling to avail himself of the protection of that country. Myanmar's two most brutal campaigns against Rohingyas namely 'Operation Dragon King (1978)' and 'Operation *Pyi Thaya* (1991-1992) created risk of persecution in their state of origin through mass killing and expulsion of Rohingyas from their land which led thousands of Rohingyas to flee as well as seek refuge in another place. Later, in the mid-2012, another case of violence against Rohingyas once again led them to seek refuge in neighbouring countries. The United Nations, therefore, defines Rohingyas as the most persecuted community in the world.[6]

1.1 Rohingya on the Move: A Saga of Displacement(s) and Statelessness

The latest instance of the protracted Rohingya refugee crisis which began 25 August 2017 with the influx of several hundred thousand refugees from Myanmar to Bangladesh, the day after the release of the Advisory Commission report chaired by late United Nations (UN) Secretary-General Kofi Annan is an enormous challenge for the international community.[7]

The recent mass influx of several hundred thousand Rohingya refugees from Myanmar to Bangladesh was shocking and dramatic, but not unprecedented. Smaller yet significant forced movements of ethnic Rohingya to Bangladesh occurred in 1942, 1978, 1991, 2012 and 2016. Over the years, thousands of individual Rohingya have travelled to Bangladesh for medical treatment and studies prior to the most recent influx. Some never returned home. In the 1990s as a result of closed camp settings and the absence of long-term integration prospects, a repatriation exercise based on a memorandum of understanding (MOU) between the Bangladesh government and the Office of the UN High Commissioner for Refugees (UNHCR) took place between 1993–1997, with some 230,000 Rohingya returning to Myanmar. Sub-standard living conditions, the absence of legal and human rights protection, political exclusion, questionable voluntariness and returnees being poorly informed of what they would encounter once back in Myanmar resulted in this operation being soundly criticized. The presence of a large number of armed officers engaged in the repatriation exercise in the 1970s has been also been acknowledged. Indeed earlier attempts at repatriation of Rohingya refugees in the 1970s and 1990s are regarded as regrettable low-points in UNHCR's operational history in the Asia region.[8]

What is different this time in the quest for repatriation is a vigorous response on human rights and accountability issues initiated largely through the UN. There is also enormous media attention to the crisis, and credible claims of crimes against humanity and possibly genocide having taken place. Within the UN, the Human Rights Council (HRC) established an Independent International Fact-Finding Mission (FFM) on Myanmar comprised of eminent jurists and human rights experts Marzuki Darusman from Indonesia, Radhika Coomaraswamy from Sri Lanka, and

Christopher Sidoti from Australia.[9] The FFM investigated and prepared comprehensive reports on the events which gave rise to the 2017 exodus. The FFM's findings are based on detailed interviews with hundreds of survivors and government officials, UN and NGO staff, in addition to field visits and forensic and other evidence collected and vetted by a team of experts on sexual violence in conflict, international criminal law, and military operations.

The FFM's 444-page report released in September 2018[10] and its subsequent reports[11] provide an unprecedented amount of information including names of individuals alleged to have committed the most serious crimes and human rights violations against Rohingya men, women, and children. The FFM's work continued through the presentation of its final report to the UN Human Rights Council (HRC), while in March 2019 FFM Chair Darusman noted that there has been very little progress, since they presented their report to the [UN] Human Rights Council, General Assembly and Security Council at the end of [2018] ... To the contrary, the fighting has continued in Rakhine and in the Northern States of Kachin and Shan and tensions are escalating in other regions. Human rights violations have not stopped, nor are victims seeing justice. There is an acute need to continue to thoroughly document the patterns of violations being committed, as we speak.[12]

Some 600,000 Rohingya are estimated to remain in Rakhine State. They continue to be subjected to discriminatory policies and practices, including segregation and severe restrictions on their movements; deprivation of citizenship; denial of economic, social and cultural rights; physical assaults constituting torture or other cruel, inhuman or degrading treatment or punishment; arbitrary arrest; and, in some areas, hostility from members of ethnic Rakhine communities that the mission found also to constitute persecution and other prohibited crimes against humanity. The Government of Myanmar claims that it would welcome back Rohingya returnees from Bangladesh. In the light of the continuing persecution of remaining Rohingya, the legal conditionalities placed on return and the unacceptable living conditions that await returnees, the mission regards these statements and associated measures as lacking sincerity. In May 2019, the tripartite memorandum of understanding between [UNHCR], the United Nations Development Programme and the Government of Myanmar aimed at creating conducive conditions for the voluntary, safe, dignified and sustainable repatriation of refugees from Bangladesh was extended for one year. The mission concludes, however, that the Government [of Myanmar] has not taken the steps necessary to put the requisite conditions for the return of the refugees in place.[13]

In presenting the final report to the 42nd session of the Human Rights Council on 17 September 2019, FFM Chairman Darusman employed even stronger language in noting that there was a strong inference of continued genocidal intent on the part of the State in relation to the Rohingya, that there was a serious risk of genocide recurring and that Myanmar was failing in its obligations under the Genocide Convention to prevent genocide, to investigate genocide and to enact effective legislation criminalising and punishing genocide. He emphasised that whatever policies, laws, individuals and institutions that laid the groundwork for the brutal "clearance operations" in 2016 and 2017 remain in place and strong.[14]

The FFM's findings fed into another mechanism established by the HRC, the Independent Investigative Mechanism for Myanmar (IIM) which is tasked with "collecting, consolidating, preserving and analysing evidence of the most serious crimes and violations of international law committed in Myanmar since 2011."[15]

At another level, the UN General Assembly in its 22 December 2018 resolution on the 'Situation of human rights in Myanmar' *inter alia* calls for a wide range of operational and related accountability measures including

> "… a full and independent investigation of the human rights violations and abuses committed … against the Rohingya Muslims and persons belonging to other minorities … to ensure that those responsible for such crimes are held accountable; … and requests the Secretary General to call the continued attention of the Security Council to the situation in Myanmar with concrete recommendations for actions towards resolving the humanitarian crisis, promoting the safe, dignified, voluntary and sustainable return … and ensuring accountability for those responsible for human rights violations …. [16]

The UN Presence in Myanmar: Towards Stocktaking

In Myanmar, UN entities have for decades been between a rock and hard place operating in a country which imposes firm controls. UN officials have limited freedom of movement and access. This limits the ability to conduct needs assessments and plan, deliver and monitor humanitarian assistance and other interventions. Concerns that perceived overstepping may lead to admonishment or being asked to leave by the authorities can result in limited engagement, extreme secrecy and self-censorship. Lack of sharing information even between offices of the same organisation is the way some UN actors and agencies have operated for years. Even at the senior level, it is a rare official who risks speaking out on human rights issues while posted and residing in a country like Myanmar. Personal risks are high and the track record of the UN supporting its own, when an official takes a courageous stand resulting in being made *persona non grata* does not instill confidence in staff.

Leadership also sets the tone, and as suggested by the 'Rosenthal report',[17] UN operations in Myanmar predominantly engaged in 'quiet diplomacy'. While often pragmatic and effective, this approach can also have serious limitations. Against the background of the latest crisis and subsequent developments including calls for justice and accountability, the UN continuing in the same tracks may be untenable. As one important element, a more consistent and system-wide human rights focus is strongly encouraged.[18]

Limited humanitarian access and being unable to move and operate with autonomy in addition to leadership concerns and reports of lack of inter-agency cooperation and unnecessary secrecy and mistrust,[19] exposed the UN in Myanmar to criticism. Claims of some UN entities being unable or unwilling to raise human rights issues despite the aspirations of the Human Rights Up Front initiative,[20] in addition to robustly engaging in early warning activities, appear to have motivated the FFM's recommendation to conduct an inquiry into the UN's work in Myanmar.

In his report, Mahony further notes:

> Regrettably, engaging in 'negative coping strategies' appears to be the way the UN has chosen to operate over many years. The international organisations on the ground and the diplomats in the [Myanmar] capital keep silent as a general rule because they believe this silence to be a necessary condition of operating smoothly in the country. Humanitarians often apply the phrase "negative coping strategies" to certain self-destructive approaches chosen by populations and individuals under duress. A "negative coping strategy" is an equally apt description of how these organisations and bilateral donors chose to quietly sustain Myanmar's internment camps for the Rohingya for over 5 years. The government also allowed humanitarians to provide a fraction of the food needs of a starved Rohingya population of northern Rakhine state for two decades, on condition that they stay mostly silent about one of the worst ongoing child malnutrition situations in the world, and they obeyed. Adding insult to injury, Myanmar in recent years has demanded that the internationals inside Myanmar refrain

from using the word "Rohingya" at all when speaking of this persecuted minority, and nearly all have consistently complied, thus assisting the state in erasing this minority's identity. Such compliance and silence made ethnic cleansing easier.[21]

A decade ago the UN and other humanitarian organisations exhibited similar obedience to the Sri Lankan government. First they kept quiet about mass killings and war crimes, and after the war they funded and managed state-run internment camps for ethnic Tamils. The subsequent scathing internal UN investigation prompted a new UN-wide doctrine called "Human Rights Up Front", imploring UN leaders and other international organisations to behave more courageously. In the ensuing years, many meetings were held, papers and manuals were published and countless Powerpoint-based trainings were delivered to thousands of UN and NGO staff all over the world – including in Myanmar. But for Myanmar's Rohingya, this doctrine can only be characterised as a complete failure. At their expense, the mistakes of Sri Lanka are still being repeated, and their suffering continues.[22]

Rosenthal rightly concludes that the brunt of the responsibility rests squarely on Myanmar regarding the nature and scope of violations of international humanitarian and human rights law that have occurred and continues to occur. Notably there is an absence of any evaluation of institutional or professional accountability. His conclusion that there was an absence of a unifying strategy at the highest levels of the UN Secretariat is also nothing new. What appears to have taken place is an attempt by UN country team leadership to emphasize development work at the expense of human rights. Rosenthal suggests a United Nations "observatory" in Rakhine State would have offered a measure of confidence to "oppressed minorities that their basic human rights would be respected, and that the root causes that led to their forced emigration would be addressed by the national authorities".[23]

How the UN can engage in a repatriation scheme with a credible monitoring role and the ability to engage in robust advocacy for the Rohingya remains unclear at best, and is unlikely given the current political scenario.

Vitiated Political Atmosphere, Ongoing Conflict and the Vilification of the Rohingya

As an ethnic group the Rohingya, 'the world's most persecuted minority' have been historically demonised.[24] Not dissimilar to propaganda campaigns against Jews and other religious, ethnic and sexual minorities in Nazi and

Fascist occupied Europe, the 'fear of outgroups'[25] appears to be actively tolerated in Myanmar making it unlikely the Rohingyas will ever be accepted as equals.[26]

Christine Fair, an American political scientist and terrorism expert has written that in spite of the grotesque brutalities the Rohingyas have endured, they have not articulated an Islamist or separatist demand. Their demand is simply to return to Myanmar with citizenship and, problematically, with government recognition as a distinct ethnic group. The Rohingya have not given rise to many violent non-state actors claiming to represent them. One of the few violent groups that have emerged in recent years is the Arakan Rohingya Salvation Army (ARSA). While many in the "Islamist terrorism" industry have been quick to paint ARSA with the jihadi brush, she stated that she was sceptical of ARSA's Islamist *bona fides*. ARSA has assiduously rejected Islamist appeals. However, other Islamist groups in the region have identified the Rohingya as a *cause celebre*, including the Pakistan-based Lashkar-e-Taiba (LeT), the Islamic State, and al-Qaeda Indian Subcontinent. The longer the Rohingya remain cramped in inadequately-appointed camps in Bangladesh or countenance ongoing ethnic cleansing in Myanmar, the more probable it becomes that either the ARSA will bend towards Islamism and/or Islamist militant groups will conduct violence on their behalf.[27]

While there is considerable support and growing calls for justice and accountability of both institutions and individuals before the International Criminal Court and the International Court of Justice, with notably the Gambia taking the lead to file a case under the 1948 *Genocide Convention* against Myanmar,[28] these developments and legal actions[29] may paradoxically make finding a return solution more challenging by creating contradictory pressures on the Myanmar authorities.[30]

The Myanmar military (Tatmadaw) holds the reins of power with respect to creating conditions to permit the Rohingya to safely return home. As noted by the FFM, the Tatmadaw's domination in politics remains absolute and secure. League for Democracy (NLD) being in power, the Government remains a quasi-civilian one at best. The 2008 Constitution was designed by the military to retain its dominant role in politics.[31] International accountability measures against the state of Myanmar including towards senior Tatmadaw officers are not recognised by the Myanmar. It is quite possible that a return solution for the Rohingya may be used as a bargaining chip in an attempt to diminish or by-pass accountability efforts.[32]

A Geo-Political Archaeology of the Inaction by the Security Council

Why the events of August 2017 did not prompt decisive Council action in what may be considered a textbook case envisioned by the Responsibility to Protect regime can be summed up in a few words: *lack of collective political will.* Permanent members China and Russia in particular have not to date agreed to any Security Council action against Myanmar.

On 21 August 2019 the Security Council engaged in consultations on Myanmar and was briefed by the UN High Commissioner for Refugees and UNDP. While the general position remains to support voluntary repatriation in principle, there remains a lack of consensus and specific action by the Council to move forward the required elements in Myanmar to instill confidence for returns including granting the Rohingyas' demands for human rights enfranchisement, including the grant of citizenship. An Arria-Formula meeting was held on 23 August on *'Mass Atrocity Crimes in Myanmar: Where do we stand on accountability'*. The Council was briefed by FFM member Radhika Coomaraswamy, journalist Esther Husan, and Wakar Uddin of the North American Burmese Rohingya Association. The meeting reportedly did not result in any Council decisions.

Ms Coomaraswamy gave a briefing to the UN press corps on 22 August 2019 upon the release of the FFM report on 'Sexual and gender based violence.[33] Of particular interest she described that apart from ongoing (albeit limited) engagement of the ICC and potentially ICJ, the FFM recommends establishing an international mechanism as the best way forward to deal with accountability issues.

Despite the current political impasse, as an executive organ with authority to take action under Chapter VII of the *UN Charter,* the Council should have a clear obligation to act when credible allegations of genocide or crimes against humanity are brought before it.[34] While some commentators and political leaders have suggested UN peacekeepers or international observers or monitors be deployed to ensure the safety and security of the Rohingya upon return, that too is a far reach without the full agreement of all Security Council permanent members.

Questions of state sovereignty and non-interference aside, hallowed principles in the ASEAN context, perceived international interference in the treatment of religious and ethnic minorities in the territory of Council member states is also acutely at play. Moreover the importance of maintaining positive bilateral and economic relations and trade may trump the importance of ensuring the human rights of the Rohingya.[35]

As noted by Simon Adams of the Global Centre for the Responsibility to Protect (R2P), eight months after so-called "clearance operations" began in Rakhine State, the UN Security Council did, however, undertake an official visit to the region. During April 2018 Council members visited Rohingya refugee camps in Bangladesh. While in Myanmar they met with political and military leaders, including *de-facto* head of state Aung San Suu Kyi and Senior General Min Aung Hlaing [...] On the flight to Rakhine State the ambassadors flew over scorched villages and several of them photographed the charred landscape below, noting that they could still see the outline where the huts and homes of the Rohingya had once been. Entire communities had clearly been purged. The visit had a profound impact on several of the ambassadors and although a group of states on the [Council] have worked to keep the issue of the Rohingya in the Council's focus, as of October 2019, there had still not been a single formal resolution adopted to name the nature of the crime committed against them, nor to hold the perpetrators accountable.[36]

Aside from R2P and SC inactivity, another element which has thus far failed to take root is the principle of responsibility sharing in refugee law. While celebrated by major states in the *UN Global Compact on Refugees* and the earlier *NY Declaration*, 'responsibility sharing' has failed to materialise in practice in the Rohingya context with no major offers to date to resettle or provide temporary protection to ease the pressure on Bangladesh.

Even a neighbouring country like Japan, while showing strong support for Bangladesh and the humanitarian plight of the Rohingya and remaining a generous donor country, was among a handful of states, including India, who abstained during voting on General Assembly and HRC resolutions on human rights in Myanmar.[37] While in principle abstaining is neither voting for or against a resolution, the perception appears to be that not voting for a resolution critical of Myanmar may permit privileged diplomatic access. At the time however, this may not have been appreciated by the country hosting close to a million refugees, and Japan's perceived indifference and interest "to promote foreign business opportunities in war-torn Rakhine state" has been criticized.[38]

Similarly, India has a keen economic interest in Myanmar as a part of its Act East policy and a potential land bridge into Southeast Asia. Notwithstanding head of state level diplomacy which resulted in agreement for the "safe, speedy, and sustainable" repatriation of the Rohingya,[39] the Hindutva-movement and perceived view by the Indian authorities concerning the national security implications of Rohingyas residing in their territory has resulted in deportations to Myanmar.[40] Although UNHCR has registered some 40,000 Rohingya refugees under its mandate in India, a pending Indian Supreme Court challenge may determine the fate of those remaining in the country.[41]

For both Japan and India, Myanmar is a key bridge country for their economic ambitions. The geo-political interests and economy of these countries and how it may play out to counter China's presence and domination may explain why regional responses and powers have been unwilling or ineffective to pressure Myanmar. Furthermore, China, as a permanent member of the SC, has not taken a lead to move things forward in the Council. Beyond geo-political considerations there can be a reluctance to set a precedent through the Council acting to resolve a major refugee crisis which fails to serve the economic interests of key powerful states.

The economic ambitions of China in Myanmar are clearly apparent. China wants access to the Bay of Bengal as part of its Belt and Road Initiative (BRI), and a direct line from China to this strategic maritime route is through NRS state. An empty and unhindered geography could facilitate infrastructure development and security while serving any interest to repopulate NRS with Bamar Buddhists. With China's economic and military might and regional leadership, it can be expected any future development of NRS will see their continued involvement and influence.[42]

Another factor which can impact finding a repatriation solution for the Rohingya is a chauvinistic attitude towards Bangladesh. Economic exchange between Myanmar and Bangladesh is not particularly high compared to other regional trading partners and the Rohingya crisis has made the trade picture increasingly less favourable. Bangladesh may also be viewed as a predominantly Islamic country which threatens Buddhist dominant Myanmar. The Rohingya crisis repeating itself since before the formation of the Bangladesh state naturally aggravates bilateral relations. Security concerns are also being raised by both the Bangladesh and Myanmar authorities concerning the Rohingya.

Finally, the long history of conflict in Myanmar which relies on contraband trade to finance both state and non-state actors strategies and political aspirations is yet another factor working against refugee return. Widespread corruption and militant and criminal enterprises operating on various borders throughout South and Southeast Asia and China contributes to trade in illegal arms and human trafficking. There are regular reports from national human rights bodies and NGOs and the media concerning allegations and in some cases criminal convictions of government officials having committed heinous crimes including human trafficking. It remains a relevant consideration at a time when many voices are calling for repatriation of the Rohingya to Myanmar.

Conclusion: Options for a Way Forward

Short of decisive action by UN and regional institutions or bodies including the SC, ASEAN or the Organisation of Islamic Cooperation (OIC), or significant political developments in Myanmar which would permit safe and sustainable repatriation as a preferred solution,[43] there are other interim solutions and mitigating actions which deserve attention. While many Rohingya refugees have themselves expressed the desire to return "home", many have not. What they all largely agree upon is ensuring several reasonable demands are in place before returning to Myanmar. These include justice for the wrongs committed and reparations for losses suffered; recognition of and ensuring their protection and human rights including physical protection in Myanmar; the grant of civil status including full Myanmar citizenship[44]; in addition to being able to return in safety and dignity and to their home villages and regions in Myanmar.[45]

While the emphasis on repatriation should not be diminished or abandoned, other solutions should be given serious consideration by concerned state actors, international organisations and other interested parties in the interest of making them operational. They are granting the Rohingya: (1) Access to Education, Work Rights and Other Services with Government Support, (2) Promoting Third Country Resettlement and Regional Responsibility Sharing, (3) The importance of Diplomacy and Rohingya Participation, (4) Pursuing accountability of those who have perpetrated crimes against humanity to the Rohingya and violation of their human rights and (5) Reparation for the Rohingya.

Of particular importance is accessing education, as this could prevent another lost generation given the current figures of 70-plus percent of Rohingya being illiterate and innumerate. Increased access to public services with government support would permit more individuals to benefit, and the quality of services in education and healthcare in particular could significantly improve. Assuring them legal protection for their work and Engagement of the International Labour Office (ILO) in supporting job skills training and creating job opportunities for the Rohingya, similar to initiatives for Syrian refugees in Jordan, could also be explored and promoted in Bangladesh.

Another solution is third country resettlement. While some limited movement of Rohingya refugees directly from Myanmar and Bangladesh to third countries is taking place, this is often done through irregular channels and at great cost and personal risk.[46] Over the last decade, several thousand Rohingya refugees have benefitted from being resettled from Malaysia to several countries including Canada, the United States, Japan and New Zealand.

A basic element in preparing for repatriation is to ensure each individual refugee can make an informed choice concerning his or her decision to return, including any benefits or restrictions they may experience in their country of origin. Administering a transparent, well-informed, safe and sustainable voluntary repatriation exercise is not something the UN can achieve on its own. The responsibility lies first and foremost with the country of origin, Myanmar.

The international community and UN institutions cannot overlook or minimize the serious violations of human rights and purportedly criminal conduct experienced by the Rohingya. Beyond individual and state accountability as part of an eventual criminal process and proceedings before the ICC and ICJ, the FFM has suggested the international community embargo Myanmar business interests and impose targeted sanctions against companies tied to the Tatmadaw. This would serve to cut off financial and other support for Myanmar's armed forces which has used "its own businesses, foreign companies and arms deals to support brutal operations against ethnic groups that constitute serious crimes under international law, bypassing civilian oversight and evading accountability."[47]

The importance of ensuring international and national accountability, justice and reparations to victims of serious human rights violations including refugees[48] cannot be understated. Failing to take decisive action sends a signal such occurrences can happen again with impunity. In addition to directly impacting victims, accountability through a criminal justice process provides psychological closure for families and communities. While lost property or loved ones may never be returned, those who are responsible for the loss and harm can be punished for their crimes. Different approaches, including establishing truth and reconciliation commissions and even amnesties, may also provide an effective route to healing and accountability.

Article 75 of the *International Criminal Court* (ICC) *Statute* recognises the need to establish principles relating to reparations to victims including "restitution, compensation and rehabilitation". This provision permits the Court on its own initiative or upon request, to "determine the scope and extent of any damage, loss and injury to, or in respect of, victims and will state the principles on which it is acting."[49] Apart from the *ICC Statute*, there is a significant body of jurisprudence based on international civil liability and other international law which provides reparations and damages for injury to aliens and others as a result of wrongful acts by states or state agents.[50] There is also scope to seek reparations from the International Court of Justice if any contracting state were to bring a claim against Myanmar under the *Genocide Convention*.[51]

A former UNHCR Head, the late Sadako Ogata, once stated that there were no humanitarian solutions to humanitarian crises, but only political solutions. It should be recalled however that the UN and UNHCR in particular have protection mandates. In this vein a political solution for the Rohingya refugee crisis is insufficient, but hand in hand there is a need to promote and implement protection and rights-based solutions in the interim and long term.[52]

Powerful states which have influence can and should leverage Myanmar to ensure conditions, protection and monitoring measures are in place to make any potential return process feasible and sustainable. No one knows what may happen if the Rohingya refugees are left without a future. Resentment and anger can only lead to greater hardship, difficulties and risks. Refugees themselves are not a security concern, but failing to find solutions for refugees can lead to security risks at various levels.[53]

Looking ahead, inclusive and systematic refugee representation in important decisions which affect them, especially around repatriation, is a must. Failure to engage with and include the Rohingya will limit or prevent buy-in to whatever is negotiated on their behalf. As with other refugee groups, the Rohingya, in all their diversity, need to be a part of and own any proposals or solutions which impact them. It will take mobilizing and consolidating *collective political good will* with sustained international pressure and crucial support from civil society and the Rohingya themselves, in addition to institutional courage and commitment from the UN, to find lasting solutions.[54]

Notes

1. Md. Mahbubul Haque, "Rohingya Ethnic Muslim Minority and the 1982 Citizenship Law in Burma", *Journal of Muslim Minority Affairs*, 37:4 (2017), 461, https://doi.org/10.1080/13602004.2017.1399600, accessed on 1/6/2020.
2. Haque, "Rohingya Ethnic Muslim Minority and the 1982 Citizenship Law in Burma," 463.

3. Haque, "Rohingya Ethnic Muslim Minority and the 1982 Citizenship Law in Burma," 462-463.
4. See Sultana Yesmin, "Policy towards Rohingya Refugees: A Comparative Analysis of Bangladesh, Malaysia and Thailand," *Journal of the Asiatic Society of Bangladesh* 61/1 (2016) 71-100, for analytical treatment of the shifting approaches of the governments of Bangladesh, Malaysia and Thailand, towards Rohingya refugees.
5. The 'well-founded fear' limits the scope of being 'refugee' under law. It means "the people who face a genuine risk of persecution in their state of origin are entitled to the protections". See James C. Hathaway, "Well-Founded Fear," *The Law of Refugee Status*, eds. James C. Hathaway and Michelle Foster (Cambridge: Cambridge University Press, 2014) 91.
6. Syeda Naushin Parnini, Mohammad Redzuan Othman and Amer Saifude Ghazali, "The Rohingya Refugee Crisis and Bangladesh-Myanmar Relations", *Asian and Pacific Migration Journal,* 22/1 (2013) 136.
7. Brian Gorlick, "The Rohingya Refugee Crisis: Rethinking Solutions and Accountability" *Refugee Studies Centre* 131 (2019) 1. Many of the insights presented in the following sections, have been inspired by Gorlick's meticulously researched, analytical study of the situation of the Rohingya, from the point of view of the international community and the U.N.
8. For an overview of Rohingya influx to Bangladesh, See https://reliefweb.int/report/bangladesh/historical-review-rohingya-influx-1978; and C. R. Abrar, "Repatriation of Rohingya Refugees,"http://www.burmalibrary.org/docs/Abrar-repatriation.html, accessed on 10/03/2020;

   Also Refer: Mohfidul Hoque (ed.), *The Rohingya Genocide: Compilation and Analysis of Survivors' Testimonies*, published by the Centre for the Study of Genocide and Justice, Liberation War Museum, September 2018.
9. https://www.right-docs.org/doc/a-hrc-res-34-22/, accessed on 9/03/2020.
10. UN doc ref: A/HRC/39/64, 18 September 2019, accessible via:https://www.ohchr.org/EN/HRBodies/HRC/Pages/NewsDetail.aspx?NewsID=23575&LangID=E, accessed 10/03/2020.
11. See *Sexual and gender-based violence in Myanmar and the gendered impact of its ethnic conflicts* (UN doc ref: A/HRC/42/CRP.4, 22 August 2019) Available at:

    https://www.ohchr.org/EN/HRBodies/HRC/MyanmarFFM/Pages/sexualviolence.aspx; and

    Economic interests of the Myanmar military (A/HRC/42/CRP.3, 5 August 2019) at: https://www.ohchr.org/EN/HRBodies/HRC/MyanmarFFM/Pages/EconomicInterestsMyanmarMilitary.aspx,accessed on 11/03/2020.
12. "UN Independent International Fact-Finding Mission on Myanmar advances accountability and initiates new investigations," https://www.ohchr.org/EN/HRBodies/HRC/Pages/NewsDetail.aspx?NewsID=24334&LangID=E; The FFM Report with key UN resolutions and other authority, official statements, advocacy updates and news is available in the Mission's website at: www.ffmmyanmar.org.
13. A/HRC/42/50, at paragraphs 76 and 85.

14. See Ashley S. Kinseth, "The Trouble of Proving "Genocide Intent: The Modern Rohingya Crisis in Historical and Political Context," J. INT'L L. & POL. ONLINE FORUM, https://nyujilp.org/wp-content/uploads/2019/03/Kinseth_Final-.pdf, accessed on 11/3/2020, for a historically rich analysis of the concept of Genocide and how it could be readily applied to the context of the crimes against the Rohingya, by the agencies of the State in Myanmar, in nexus with other religio-cultural forces, which the international community is failing to take note of and admit, taking refuge in the loopholes in the interpretation of the convention on genocide.
15. U.N. Human Rights Office of the High Commissioner, "UN Independent International Fact-Finding Mission on Myanmar advances accountability and initiates new investigations," https://www.ohchr.org/en/NewsEvents/Pages/DisplayNews.aspx?NewsID=24334&LangID=E, accessed on 12/3/2020.
16. United Nations – General Assembly – Seventy-third Session – Agenda Item 74(C) - Resolution adopted by the General Assembly on 22 December 2018, https://undocs.org/en/A/RES/73/264, accessed on 13/03/2020.
17. Gert Rosenthal, "A Brief and Independent Inquiry into the Involvement of the United Nations in Myanmar from 2010 to 2018," 28 May, 2019, https://www.un.org/sg/sites/www.un.org.sg/files/atoms/files/Myanmar%20Report%20-%20May%202019.pdf, accessed on 12/3/2020.
18. General Assembly Resolution on the 'Situation of Human Rights in Myanmar' highlights this point: "[…] encourages the United Nations system […] to ensure that all engagement with Myanmar takes into account, and addresses, human rights concerns [….]".
19. In the report: "Time to Break Old Habits: Shifting from Complicity to Protection of the Rohingyas in Myanmar," Liam Mahony, Director of Field view Solutions, notes:

    The organisation with the most information about protection realities in Rakhine was UNHCR, resulting from the protection monitoring of various partners that it coordinated, its substantial deployment, its long-term presence and its network of contacts. But few other organisations were benefitting from this information. In many other conflict settings, UNHCR as protection lead manages a protection monitoring process which produces regular public summaries of data on protection incidents and trends to assist all protection cluster members with their planning and advocacy. This was not happening for Rakhine State, and especially not for the north. On the contrary, there was a high-level (UN Resident Coordinator and UNHCR) policy of hiding information, which is part of the reason OCHA (The United Nations ***Office for the Coordination of Humanitarian Affairs***) was constrained from having a presence in the north. Scores of NGO staff gather data on incidents of abuse or other humanitarian protection gaps, and feed this into UNHCR's highly secret data system – a system with many inputs but few outputs. This has been the quietest, most invisible Protection Monitoring System this author has ever encountered (p. 26).

    The report is available at: http://www.fieldviewsolutions.org/fv-publications/Time_to_break_old_habits.pdf, accessed on 13/03/2020.
20. See Ekkehard Strauss, "The UN Secretary-General's Human Rights Up Front (HRUF) Initiative and the Prevention of Genocide: Impact, Potential,

Limitations," *Genocide Studies and Prevention: An International Journal*, 11:3, Article 8, https://scholarcommons.usf.edu/cgi/viewcontent.cgi?article=1504&context=gsp, accessed on 14/03/2020.

21. Mahony, "Time to Break Old Habits: Shifting from Complicity to Protection of the Rohingyas in Myanmar," 6.
22. Mahony, "Time to Break Old Habits: Shifting from Complicity to Protection of the Rohingyas in Myanmar," 6.
23. Rosenthal, "A Brief and Independent Inquiry into the Involvement of the United Nations in Myanmar from 2010 to 2018, 24.
24. See *International State Crime Initiative Report* (London: University of Queen Mary, 2018), http://statecrime.org/data/2018/04/ISCI-Rohingya-Report-II-PUBLISHED-VERSION-revised-compressed.pdf, accessed on 14/03/2020.
25. For an analytical treatment of the vilification and demonisation of the Rohingya, and generalisation of the Rohingya as Islamic extremists, See Md. Ali Siddiquee, "The portrayal of the Rohingya genocide and refugee crisis in the age of post-truth politics," *Asian Journal of Comparative Politics* (2019), 1-15, 3.
26. For a genealogy of the demonisation of the Rohingya as the Other, in the context of the resistance of the Rakhine Buddhists, in spite of the joint resistance of the Rohingya Muslims and the Rakhine Buddhists, against the Bamar Buddhist hegemony, in the past, but in the present context of Islamic geopolitics and the political conditions of Myanmar state, see Faizah Binte Zakaria, "Religion, Mass Violence, and Illiberal Regimes: Recent Research on the Rohingya in Myanmar," *Journal of Current Southeast Asian Affairs* 38/1 (2019) 98-111.
27. C. Christine Fair, "Arakan Rohingya Salvation Army: Not the Jihadis You Might Expect," *Lawfare,* Sunday, December 9, 2018, https://www.lawfareblog.com/arakan-rohingya-salvation-army-not-jihadis-you-might-expect, accessed on 15/3/2020; Nyein Nyein in Interview with Sidney Jones, "No Evidence of Any ARSA Links to ISIS: Terrorism Expert," *The Irrawaddy*, 4 June, 2019, https://www.irrawaddy.com/in-person/interview/no-evidence-arsa-links-isis-terrorism-expert.html, accessed on 15/3/2020.
28. On 18 October 2019 at an *International Conclave on Justice and Accountability for Rohingya* in The Hague, the Minister of Justice of Gambia, HE Abubacarr Marie Tambadou, announced that on 4 October 2019 his government had instructed its law firm to file proceedings before the International Court of Justice concerning Myanmar's obligations under the 1948 *UN Genocide Convention.* On 11 November 2019, Gambia filed its application. See https://twitter.com/Gambia_MOJ;

    https://www.dutchnews.nl/news/businesswire/foley-hoag-leads-the-gambias-legal-team-in-historic-case-to-stop-myanmars-genocide-against-the-rohingya/; https://aawsat.com/english/home/article/1986496/gambia-files-rohingya-genocide-case-against-myanmar-world-court; https://www.theguardian.com/world/2019/nov/11/gambia-rohingya-genocide-myanmar-un-court.
29. See Priya Pillai, "Three Complementary Legal Strategies for Accountability: A Momentous Week for the Rohingya," *Opinio Juris*, http://opiniojuris.org/2019/11/19/three-complimentary-legal-strategies-for-accountability-a-momentous-week-for-the-rohingya, accessed on 16/3/2020.

30. 47 FFM Report, *op cit*, (A/HRC/39/CRP.2, 17 September 2018), para 81, p. 24. Also See Melissa Crouch, *The Constitution of Myanmar: A Contextual Analysis*, Hart Publishing, 2019: https://www.bloomsburyprofessional.com/uk/the-constitution-of-myanmar-9781509927364/.
31. FFM Report, *op cit*, (A/HRC/39/CRP.2, 17 September 2018), para 81, p. 24. Also See Melissa Crouch, *The Constitution of Myanmar: A Contextual Analysis*, Hart Publishing, 2019: https://www.bloomsburyprofessional.com/uk/the-constitution-of-myanmar-9781509927364/
32. See https://theaseanpost.com/article/myanmar-army-warns-against-changing-constitution-0 - A/HRC/42/50, para 95.
33. See Human Rights Council, " Sexual and gender-based violence in Myanmar and the gendered impact of its ethnic conflicts," - A/HRC/42/CRP.4 – Forty Second Session, 9-27 September, 2019, for a detailed and graphic description revealed in the findings of a Independent International Fact Finding Mission, of the sexual violations against the Rohingya and the other minorities, by the Myanmar military and other security agencies, targeting of the civilian population in Rakhine, Kachin and Shan States since 2011.
34. See December 2018 report of the Global Justice Centre, *Beyond Killing: Gender, Genocide and Obligations under International Law*, in particular chapter VI on Genocide and International Organisations. The report is available at: http://www.globaljusticecenter.net/files/Gender-and-Genocide-Whitepaper-FINAL.pdf.
35. Myanmar enjoys a trade surplus with China, and in December 2018 it was reported largely border-area exports from Myanmar to China totalled US$2.4 billion, while imports from China totalled $900 million, https://www.mmtimes.com/news/myanmar-china-border-trade-focus.html, accessed on 16/03/2020.
36. The Global Centre for the Responsibility to Protect - Occasional Paper *If Not Now, When? The Responsibility to Protect, the Fate of the Rohingya and the Future of Human Rights*, Dr Simon Adams, January 2019, at p. 10. The report is available at: http://www.globalr2p.org/media/files/occasionalpaper_rohingyafinal.pdf.

    Being able to seek 'asylum' in Bangladesh arguably satisfies one of the requirements of the R2P regime, as there may be no easier way for the international community to meet its responsibility to protect than providing asylum and other international protection on adequate terms. See 'Embracing the 'Responsibility to Protect': A Repertoire of Measures Including Asylum for Potential Victims', Brian Barbour & Brian Gorlick, *International Journal of Refugee Law (IJRL)*, 20 (4), December 2008, Oxford University Press; *UNHCR New Issues in Refugee Research* paper no. 159 (July 2008), available at: https://www.unhcr.org/research/working/487b619b0/embracing-responsibility-protect-repertoire-measures-including-asylum-potential.html.
37. Human Rights Council resolution: https://reliefweb.int/report/myanmar/situation-human-rights-myanmar-ahrc40l19.
38. Senior Correspondent, "UN resolution on Myanmar: Abstention from voting doesn't mean opposing Bangladesh, Japan says," bdnews24.com, November

19, 2017,https://bdnews24.com/bangladesh/2017/11/19/un-resolution-on-myanmar-abstention-from-voting-doesnt-mean-opposing-bangladesh-japan-says, accessed on 17/3/2020; Amnesty International, "UN: China fails to scupper resolution on Myanmar's persecution of Rohingya," December 5, 2017, https://www.amnesty.org/en/latest/news/2017/12/un-china-fails-to-scupper-resolution-on-myanmars-persecution-of-rohingya/; https://www.hrw.org/news/2019/06/20/japans-cold-blooded-approach-rohingya-crisis, accessed on 17/3/2020.

39. https://www.dhakatribune.com/bangladesh/foreign-affairs/2019/10/05/hasina-modi-for-expediting-efforts-for-sustainable-rohingya-repatriation.
40. SeeTapan Bose, "Rohingyas: Pawns on the Geopolitical Chessboard," *The Rohingya Refugee Crisis: Towards Sustainable Solutions*, Imtiaz Ahmed (ed.), (Bangladesh: University of Dhaka, 2019) Chapter 11.
41. IANS, "Refugee status or deportation for Rohingyas? SC may rule before CJI retires," *Business Standard*, August 16, 2019,https://www.business-standard.com/article/current-affairs/refugee-status-or-deportation-for-rohingyas-sc-may-rule-before-cji-retires-119081600125_1.html, accessed 17/03/2020; Supreme Court Observer: A Living Archive of SCI, "Rohingya Deportation: Mohammad Salimullah v. Union of India – Case No. WP (C) 793/2017, https://ww.scobserver.in/court-case/rohingya-deportation-case, accessed on 17/3/2020.
42. See Nehginpao Kipgen, "The Rohingya Crisis: The Centrality of Identity and Citizenship," *Journal of Muslim Minority Affairs* 39/1 (2019), 61-74, https://doi.org/10.1080/13602004.2019.1575019, accessed on 1/6/ 2020, for an insightful discussion on the how issues of identity and citizenship, lie at the core of the non-effectiveness of the three-stage plan put forth by China as a regional power, on 20 November, 2017 in agreement with Bangladesh and Myanmar, and in consultation with 51 countries, mostly from Asia and Europe. The first phase was to effect a ceasefire on the ground for people to stop fleeing, to restore peace, order and stability. The second phase was for Myanmar and Bangladesh governments to find a mutually acceptable condition for the Rohingya refugees to return. And the third and final phase was to work toward a long-term solution for poverty elevation, that is, to improve the socio-economic conditions of Rakhine state and its people.
43. For a thoughtful discussion on the political considerations of repatriation, See Megan Bradley, "Is Return the Preferred Solution to Refugee Crises? Exploring the Moral Value of the Right of Return", *The Political Philosophy of Refuge*, David Miller and Christine Straehle (eds.), (Cambridge: Cambridge University Press), Chapter 8.
44. See Archana Parashar, Jobair Alam, "The National Laws of Myanmar: Making of Statelessness for the Rohingya,"*International Migration* (2018), can be accessed at: https://onlinelibrary.wiley.com/doi/full/10.1111/imig.12532; and *Tools of Genocide: National Verification Cards and Denial of Citizenship of Rohingya Muslims* published by Fortify Rights on 3 September 2019, in particular pp. 46-48. The report is available at: https://www.fortifyrights.org/publications.html
45. See the March 2019 survey produced by *Xchange – Research on Migration* at: http://xchange.org/reports/TheRohingyaSurvey2019.html

46. See for example, AFP, "84 Rohingya stopped from boat journey to Malaysia," ASEANPLUS NEWS, May 19, 2019, accessed March, 20, https:// www.thestar.com.my/news/regional/2019/05/19/84-rohingya-stopped-from-boat-journey-to-malaysia/ and Reuters, Cox's Bazar, "Police rescue dozens of Malaysia-bound Rohingyas on boat," *The Daily Star*, September 5, 2020, https:/ www.thedailystar.net/backpage/news/police-rescue-dozens-malaysia-bound-rohingyas-boat-1743880, accessed on 20/3/2020.
47. See FFM news release of 5 August 2019: United Nations – Human Rights – Office of the High Commissioner, "UN Fact-Finding Mission on Myanmar exposes military business ties, calls for targeted sanctions and arms embargoes," accessed March 21, https://www.ohchr.org/EN/NewsEvents/Pages/ DisplayNews.aspx? NewsID=24868&LangID=E; FFM report on the economic interests of the Myanmar military (UN doc ref: A/HRC/42/CRP): United Nations – Human Rights Council, "Economic interests of the Myanmar military (16 Sept 2019), accessed March 21, https://www.ohchr.org/EN/HRBodies/HRC/ MyanmarFFM/Pages/EconomicInterestsMyanmarMilitary.aspx
48. See 'Reparations and Refugees' by Bernadette Ludwig, in I Ness (editor) *Encyclopedia of Global Human Migration*, 2013, pp. 2566-2570, Wiley-Blackwell, Hoboken, New Jersey.
49. Rome Statute of the International Criminal Court, http://legal.un.org/icc/statute/ 99_corr/cstatute.htm, accessed on 20/3/2020.
50. See Dinah Shelton, *Remedies in International Human Rights Law* (3rd ed), Oxford University Press, 2015; Steven Ratner, Jason Abrams, James L Bischoff, *Accountability for Human Rights Atrocities in International Law: Beyond the Nuremburg Legacy* (3rd ed), Oxford University Press, 2009; Nina Jorgensen, *The Responsibility of States for International Crimes*, Oxford University Press, 2009, at pp. 192-207; John Murphy, 'Civil Liability for the Commission of International Crimes as an Alternative to Criminal Prosecution', *Harvard Human Rights Law Journal*, Vol. 12, 1999, at pp. 28-56; Christian Tomuschat, 'State Responsibility and the Country of Origin', in Vera Gowland Debbas (editor), *The Problem of Refugees in Light of Contemporary International Law Issues*, Martinus Nijhoff Publishers, 1995; David Matas, *No More: The Battle against Human Rights Violations*, Dundurn Press Limited, Toronto, 1994, chapter 12 on 'Compensation'; Luke Lee, 'The Right to Compensation: Refugees and Countries of Asylum', *American Journal of International Law*, Vol. 80, 1986; Payam Akhavan and Morten Bergsmo, 'The Application of the Doctrine of State Responsibility to Refugee Creating Situations', *Nordic Journal of International Law*, Vol. 58 (3-4), 1989, at pp. 253-254.
51. Michael A Becker, "The Situation of the Rohingya: Is there a role for the International Court of Justice?" https://www.ejiltalk.org/the-situation-of-the-rohingya-is-there-a-role-for-the-international-court-of-justice/, accessed on 20/ 03/2020.
52. Gorlick, "The Rohingya Refugee Crisis," 27.
53. *Ibid.*
54. *Ibid.*, 28.

9

Indigenous Knowledge and Stigma of Marginalisation: Call for a Collaborative Enterprise of Nation Building

— *Prof. Jesurathnam Devarapalli*

Introduction

Growth of civilisation and its complexity is a continuous process and is a clear reflection of the system of knowledge employed in the making of the nation. Human population across the geographical frontiers and timelines in their desperate interaction with nature in conquering their needs accumulate their experience and convert them into a system of knowledge of various frequencies. Especially in a complex society of having divergent ethnic and economic groups the knowledge perceived, acquired and celebrated varies from one social group to another. Basically the knowledge can be categorised as indigenous and non-indigenous owing to the stock of the population that is processing it. As of now every nation state have people belonging to different social and cultural categories, while some considered to be under developed, backward and have least participation in the nation building process when compared to their so called advanced counterparts who generally dominate the growth curve.

However, these two apparently contrasting categories excel in their respective domain of knowledge and complete their life routine. Always a dichotomy is recognised labelled with their know-how and the very approach followed in getting things done. The indigenous knowledge is captioned as traditional and belonging to the marginal groups while the non-indigenous knowledge often called western and is considered to have scientific temperament and is the most preferred. Needless to say a wide gulf is created between the two i.e. the indigenous and the non-indigenous (the modernised). Accordingly the participation of the former is thoroughly restricted not only in the macroscopic development and growth process but even in the matters very pertinent to them at a very microscopic level. In this backdrop it is envisaged here to analyse and understand the indigenous knowledge system and examine how far this can be applicable at macroscopic level in spite of its limitations, and to what extent the marginalised groups be made active partners in the development endeavours with due dignity. By doing so it not only ensures inclusivity but also minimises the owes of developmental tragedies, since every system has its limitations and the human experience in developmental history revealed that integrated efforts have better results as it facilitates for complementary role of diverse streams.

Indigenous Knowledge

It is considered to be the intellectual product of a people who invented it locally without the support or influence of the outer world. As such indigenous knowledge gives a pride recognition which is witnessed not only in traditional societies but also in scientifically advanced communities. However, when we address to indigenous knowledge it is implied to belonging to a localised group like a native population, tribe, aboriginal, autochthon or ethnic group which is not widely spread and in distinction of the colonial people that occupied territory. According to International Labour Organisation indigenous people are - "tribal peoples in independent countries whose social, cultural and economic conditions distinguishing from other sections of the national community and whose status is regarded wholly or partially by their own customs or traditions or by regulations" (ILO,1989). From this perspective it is construed that indigenous knowledge is labelled differently in different places owing to the ethnic category that creates it, as everywhere we can find the native or natural inhabitants. In the recent decades nativity gaining credible importance in socio-economic and psychological point of view due to the constant mixing of the population through migration. As such the cultural milieu of the native, give them their identity inspite whatever acculturation has taken place and they are determined to preserve their identity due to the dominating pressure of recent occupants.

Then what actually is indigenous knowledge? How is it useful? People in their natural habitat keep interacting with the environment over generations creating skills from time to time to tackle mundane needs based on their understanding, developing their own ideologies, philosophies and values around it. The whole gamut of human know how is leading a congenial life in co-existence with nature is designated indigenous knowledge. It is always an integral part of the cultural system and is interconnected with various aspects of individual and social life and hence have an holistic effect. Different terms are in usage codifying this knowledge such as nature's science / knowledge, tribal knowledge, traditional knowledge, local knowledge, local wisdom, traditional ecological knowledge, aboriginal knowledge etc; (Huntington, 2000; Tinnaluck, 2004; Barnhardt and Kawagley, 2005; Reo and Whyte, 2012). In a nutshell this knowledge system is called 'ethnoscience' differentiating from modern science. Different explanations are offered so to define indigenous / traditional knowledge within its functional ambit. Acknowledging several definitions of indigenous knowledge, Ocholla (2007) refers to the use of NRF (National Research Foundation 2003) which say indigenous knowledge is a "complex set of knowledge and technologies existing and developed around specific conditions of populations and communities indigenous to a particular geographic area", making a strong point that it has been suppressed so far and it needs to be integrated into the larger body. As Margaret Bruchac (2014) puts it that, "Traditional indigenous can be defined as a network of knowledge, beliefs and traditions intended to preserve communicate and contextualise indigenous relationships with culture and landscape over time". She further raises the issue of imprecise usage of the related basic concepts like 'knowledge' (factual data), 'belief' (religious concept) and 'tradition' (practice) in describing indigenous epistemologies. All these view-points holds that indigenous knowledge is something indispensable with any people since it is knitted together in their cultural fabric and instrumental in meeting all kinds of social, economic, psychological and emotional needs. This knowledge system is generating from within the group and is never considered a separate field in their social experience unlike the non-indigenous knowledge. Warren (1992) states that indigenous knowledge is "used synonymously with traditional and local knowledge to differentiate the knowledge developed by a given community from the knowledge generated through universities, government research centre and private industry (the international knowledge system, sometimes called the western system)"[cf. Louise Grenier, 1998].

Characteristic Features of Indigenous Knowledge

Characterisation of indigenous knowledge stems from the contradictions it suffers when compared to modern knowledge system. Being the cultural product of a small scale society which is mostly illiterate historically, this knowledge is neither systematically recorded nor codified for the reference and application outside of the society. Since there are no written records, the survival of this knowledge heavily relies on the memory of the individual members who are bearers of it and is spread through oral communication prone to erosion over time. This knowledge is recognised only within a specific culture due to its very origins in it and is valued within this cultural frame. Indigenous knowledge is highly localised and it is not having universal validity as it is experienced and empirical rather than experimented and theorised like modern knowledge. It is constantly changing and reconstructed showing its dynamism in response to the prevailing social and environmental conditions. This is generally scattered in the society across different social parameters like age, gender, shaman, chief etc. Therefore, tapping this knowledge require an intensive participatory study (see; Ellen and Harris,1996 and Ocholla, 2007).

The attitude of looking modernity and indigeneity as polar ends create a big gulf between the two. In fact, they both are instrumental in meeting the survival needs of the respective groups and these people fall back on it in managing the natural resources and in maintaining social harmony. When we think that western knowledge is the present modernity, in fact it has its primordial in its tradition, as how we see the roots of Ayurveda in Indian tradition. Therefore, making a dichotomy of tradition and modernity may not stand logic rather they both are in continuum inter-influencing. This indicate that what is modern today will become tradition tomorrow and the infirmities of tradition being rectified in modernity. That's why Foundation for Revitalisation of Local Health Traditions defines modernity in terms of "Evolving Tradition" (FRLHT, 2013). The knowledge systems either modern or traditional or in a state of fluidity and are prone to face ups and downs. The traditional system when found in a state of "decline does not imply anything fatal or suggest an inability to revive or discount future potential....indigenous revitalisation requires a deep understanding of cultural processes beyond the politics of knowledge and the pressures of a currently mono-cultural globalisation process (Shankar, 2019:32).

Usefulness of Indigenous Knowledge

Though discriminated and discarded by the scientific community, indigenous knowledge was evaluated and advocated by researchers who take interests in the native cultures and their know-how. As a result efforts were made by a number of organisations and even government bodies to rope in indigenous knowledge in the developmental and national building efforts of their respective states. Emilie J. Ens and others have listed five principles for managing NCRM (Natural and Cultural Resource Management) of Australia in a collaborative approach of indigenous and non-indigenous knowledge-

1. Recognise the validity of the both indigenous and non-indigenous environmental philosophies.
2. Create more opportunities for improved cross-cultural respect and collaborations.
3. Involve indigenous people and their knowledge and interests at all stages of the indigenous NCRM project or research (including planning, design, implementation, communication and evaluation).
4. Ensure that time and continuity of effort and resources are available (to undertake participatory processes and for trust - building and innovation).
5. Establish high level political support through legal and policy frameworks to maintain continuity of government commitment to indigenous NCRM.

   [Taken from Emilie J.Ens et al]

These five principles will promote the application of indigenous knowledge in developmental process. The "development efforts that ignore local circumstances, local technologies and resources... many modern technologies, traditional techniques have been tried and tested; are effective, inexpensive, locally available, and culturally appropriate; and in many cases are based on preserving and building on the patterns and processes of nature" (Grenier, 1998). He observed that in order to control termite attack on orchards some farmers of Zimbambwe prefer indigenously prepared ashes or a mix of certain herbs with onions and paraffin instead of chemical pesticides (*ibid*).

Cross-Cultural Application of Indigenous Knowledge

Spreading of modern knowledge in various forms across the geo-social boundaries from the place of their origin is very common, even into the interior secluded tribal areas. But the acceptance of indigenous knowledge across cultural barriers has been a difficult task and is often looked with suspicion. Some authors argue that there are a number of scientists and resource managers who appreciate indigenous knowledge and prefer to work with indigenous people (Ross et al, 2011; Fernandez-Gemenez, 2000). According to Tinnaluck (2004), "In Budapest,UNESCO-ICSU world conference on science stressed the importance of integrating traditional knowledge into science especially in scientific education and research". Nowadays we can see indigenous knowledge being used in many disciplines like development projects, health and medicine, scientific research, technology, environment, and so on.

Indigenous Knowledge in Development and Sustainability

Development is an important process that is not curtailed by time, space and culture in other words every society, everywhere all through history is subjected to progressive change in the direction and the taste of the people concerned so that life becomes easy. But this tendency has also led to rapid destruction of natural resources and critically damaged habitat and environment. Leisurely, it was realised by the so called advanced societies that a variety of resources were lost and were not to available for the future generations. But those societies like tribes that are technologically lacking behind found to keep up a harmonious relation with nature and maintain a balance between the need and supply of the resources ensuring continuity of the resources. Social scientists and development planners are now very conscious of sustainability of development and promote the idea of sustainable development when they design any development programme. The native populations are observed to follow this principle since times immemorial which has been embedded in their very culture. Sustainable development according to Titilola is, "the utilisation, management and conservation of natural resource base and the orientation of technological change to ensure the attainment and continued satisfaction of human needs - such as food, water, shelter, clothing and fuel for present and future generations"(1995:12). From my own fieldwork experience I noticed that as per their custom the Chenchu avoid hunting female prey with the belief that continuation of the species will not be affected in future. Even for firewood they collect the broken dried branches of those trees which are plenty available in the area and they never use the costly wooded and delicate trees like teak, rosewood, red sanders, sandalwood etc. By this practice they are ensuring the biodiversity of the area. Further, Chenchu tribe recognise customary territorial rights where from they collect non-timber forest produce especially gum and this prevents the excessive blazing of gum trees. Even their house construction materials constitute only grass, bamboo and a few variety of hard wood trees which are abundantly grown. All these traditional practices cultivated by them ensure the sustenance of the habitat which in turn provide for their food, shelter and medicine even for future generations.

Indigenous Knowledge in Health and Medicine

Health is a universal concern and people respond to it in umpteen ways whereby evolving out divergent means of treating diseases and provide good health. A number of medical systems are seen across the world that has got international recognition such as *allopathy, homeopathy, accupuncture, unani, siddha, ayurveda* etc. These medical practices are highly institutionalised and validated by both theory and empiricism, however there is internal discrimination among them, especially *allopathy* claim to be the supreme of all others. Coming to the native cultures they do have their own way of meeting the health needs if not by one locally developed practices that have long cultural legacy. They are most commonly called magico-religious practices since the etiology, treatment and recovery are all attributed to the supernatural influences. This kind of practices doesn't rest on any scientific evidence but in many cases proved to be working at the community level. Not only that, among Chenchu they also use pressure application techniques in dealing with sprains, pains etc; which suppose to stimulate concern nerve endings. Added to that they have a rich knowledge of medicinal herbs used to treat a variety of diseases, ailments, organ-system dysfunction by using pills, decoctions, pastes and powders. This shows that Chenchu indigenous knowledge of health is an integrated system of psychotherapy, physiotherapy, administering of drugs drawn from plant and animal products to modern medicine. The logic that prevails here is that a sound health require many things apart from medicine which may include "physical, spiritual, socio-cultural, and psychological well being" (Grenier, 1998).

Indigenous knowledge made significant contributions to modern system of medicine. The important medical systems in India like ayurveda and siddha have evolved out of the native practices of tribes and other groups that used plant and animal products. These systems directly depend on the natural principles where many disease are controlled through food regulations and lifestyle management, and the drugs used are also extracted directly from the nature. Not only that, the indigenous knowledge also helped biomedicine by providing many wonder drugs that have cured many vexed diseases. The cough syrup contains 'Ephedrine' extracted from Ephedra sinica used in Chinese traditional medicine. Tubocurarine an alkaloid extracted from bark of Chondrodendron tomentosum has anaesthetic properties used by hunters of S. America as arrow poison. Digoxin used in treating heart diseases taken from Foxglove plant (Digitalis purpurea) was established by William Withering (Silverman, 1989). The anti-hypertension agent reserpine is identified from Rauwolfia serpentine and malaria drug quinine from Cinchona. All these were used by indigenous populations in different ways, are now figure in the drug list of allopathy medicine. Similarly, Aboyade and Katerere (2019) have listed out a number of plant products used by indigenous people of West Africa are helpful in effective management of diabetes. Their food plants contain secondary metabolites such as phenolic acids, triterpenoids, polyphinols and alkaloids which have an:- diabetic potential.

Indigenous Knowledge Role in Scientific Research

From the above discussion we know that nature provides solutions to most of our problems. There is a decreasing tendency on the cordial dependency on the nature for human needs from the early man to the present day advanced people. When we go back to the indigenous knowledge tapped from different populations especially in the matters of health we can realise the genuine need to subject such a system to scientific screening for authentication and wider utility. Especially in the use of various plants for treating disease, it becomes encouraging to identify the active ingredient for its effective utilisation. Picking up the species directly from nature by scientists has shown only 10% success, but considering the species used in ethno medicine there is double the rate of success. By this we can understand the potential of indigenous knowledge in saving the time, enhancing the success probability and reducing the costs of experimentation, thus encouraging scientific vigour. In Canada, scientists involving the local people extracted their traditional knowledge and developed new techniques in locating and tagging the whales for scientific monitoring and thus indigenous knowledge used to provide baseline data about the environment and the behaviour of whales (Grenier, 1998). The non-timber forest produces that are collected by the tribals of Andhra Pradesh and many other states in India led to many research projects and ultimately ending up in many industries and commercial activities. A variety of gums and resins seasonally used by tribals have been now supporting industries to produce various finished goods from them. In the same way many medicinal herbs have opened doors for pharmaceutical research, honey plants establishment and food processing units. Kani tribe of Agasthiya hills of Western Ghats in Kerala eat the berries of 'Arogyapacha' (Trichopus zeylanicus) when they go into the forest. Dr P. Pushpangadan, then Director of Jawaharlal Nehru Tropical Botanical Garden and Reserch Institute, while leading a team on ethnobotanical expedition in Western Ghats employed Kani tribesmen as guides. These men without eating any thing except munching a few black berries from some of the plants never shown tired while the scientific team suffered fatigue. Seeing their exhaustion Kani men offered them some berries and in no time the team felt full of energy and vitality. This made the team to conduct scientific research on those berries and ultimately produced 'Jeevani' a energy tonic that got now international market. According to FRLHT(2017) "the tribal societies in India still have acess to over 6500 species of ecosystem-specific medicinal plants with enormous health potential" and can promote lot of scientific research on one hand and develop a variety of industries on the other. According to Ellen (2004), the architect of binomial nomenclature and founder of modern biological classification has taken much of classificatory system from the Lapp people of Northern Scandinavia (cf. Green, 2008).

Indigenous knowledge Monitoring Development Impacts

Tribal communities and their habitat happened to be the target of a variety of development or welfare activities as these are the rich zones for resources exploration and exploitation, in addition to that of many welfare activities being commissioned in order to ameliorate the tribes from their sufferings. Development and welfare are insuperable and are inter-influencing. Many developmental projects are commissioned in tribal areas be it hydroelectric projects, mining activities, irrigation dams, railway projects etc. All these activities are usually undertaken without the knowledge of native populations, leave alone their involvement or consent for it. The natives with no formal education can predict the negative impact of these multipurpose projects as perceived with their value system and practice, the local people of Keonjhar district (of Odisha) especially of tribal regions raised strong protest against the upcoming Mittal Steel project raising the issue of environmental degradation and spread of new diseases. Ultimately the project has been winded up half the way, due to the court intervention. The Chenchu tribe recollect the environmental damages that happened due to Srisailam Dam and its subsidary constructions. The Adiya tribe of Wayanad, Kerala complain that the temperatures have raised remarkably over a few decades due to the deforestation taken place for providing space for big structures of RCC roof, and modern agriculture. It is often a failure of many welfare programmes introduced in tribal areas simply because the targeted groups' requirements were not properly understood by the planners and the involvement of tribes in person or their knowledge in planning and implementation stages is not done.

Indigenous Knowledge Provide Environmental Baseline Data

The indigenous populations are more sedentary and lead their entire life over generations in the same place. Either it is forest, desert, mountain, coastal or polar regions, they have a clear understanding of all the natural features of it and well equiped to utilise them or adopted to lead a successful life. Louise Grenier (1998) states that "scientific understanding of Canada's vast eastern Arctic ecosystem remains severely limited. Fortunately, Inuit hunters know the life histories, population dynamics, migration patterns and spatial and temporal distributions of the wildlife". When I have to criss-cross the Nallamalai forest of Andhra Pradesh, for research activities, the Chenchu youth are always my help because they know where the tigers and bears move, which location have what kind of plant and animal resources. That's why many non-tribal medicine men hire Chenchu shamans to extract the best of the medicinal herbs and supply them for pharmaceuticals. They have a very clear understanding of the impact of seasonality on the quality and efficiency of various forest products. Thus, they are a part of the local ecosystem.

Grenier make a reference to the attempts of commercialising the production of edible palm oil from a tree native to Belzian rain forests utterly failed inspite of employing cracking and rendering technologies imported. But at the same time the indigenous people, using a variety of simple local technologies continue to produce oil. In one of the striking boat tragedy in 2019 of Godavari river near Katchileru village in Devipatnam area, in spite of the best of the technological deployment and navy divers press to service it failed to locate the boat leave alone to bring it out having around 50 passengers trapped in it. Finally it is Satyam and his team who are traditional fishermen using normal technology were able to bring the boat to the bank, of course with all passengers dead. Similarly, the 'Marakallu'(local fishermen) of Godavari have a clear knowledge of the water currents, tidal impact and designed a variety of nets to harvest fish ensuring the continuity of species under different natural and dynamic reflections of river everyday and seasonally. They use only manual boats to avoid pollution due to use of diesel thus the native people's understanding of the local environment help them design technology which may be simple but manageable by themselves and strike a balance between nature and human needs, and culturally appropriate.

Marginalisation of Indigenous Knowledge

In this era of globalisation while monoculture is all pervading, the diversities, local wisdom, native technologies and identities are all threatened to vanish. Even in the matters related to the development of vulnerable sections the decisions are taken by someone who doesn't have any knowledge of their affairs. It is a common experience across the globe that those groups that are tradition bound; numerically small with specific localised identities are always ignored, neglected, humiliated and ultimately marginalised. When we try to understand it, "marginalisation is both a condition and a process that prevents individuals and groups from full participation in social, economic, and political life enjoyed by the wider society" (Alakhunova, et al 2015). Most of the indigenous populations are pushed under this category which "refers to exclusion- a state of being left out or insufficient attention to something, for example, indigenous knowledge" (Ocholla, 2007). The classification paradigms show indigenous knowledge and the non- indigenous knowledge as separate entities. Indigenous knowledge is termed as intangible knowledge by Nonaka and Takeuchi (1995) since it is embedded in the particular culture, while the codified or textualised knowledge is called tangible knowledge. They argue that though tangible and intangible knowledge are not different entities, the tangible has flourished due to its accessibility while the intangible diminished though they can supplement each other. Due to its non-application the indigenous knowledge accumulated over generations has gone into oblivion and its further growth and integration has retarded. Moreover, the communities themselves are marginalised, the knowledge system they generated is also marginalised or if at all it is used, it happened without according due to recognition to the creators of that knowledge. This kind of situation has now lead to the question of rights, where many indigenous people across the world are demanding for their right of expression, decision-making and their rights to natural resources (Grenier,1998). In recollecting the awful situation of the marginals it can be better understood in the words of Marie Battiste (2014:2)- "generations of exploitation, violence, marginalisation, powerlessness, and enforced cultural imperialism of aboriginal knowledge and peoples has been a significant and often painful undertaking in the past century". To understand this statement in detail we have to analyse the features attributed to the marginalised as enumerated by Hilary Silver (1994)

- They have physical as well as social attributes that set them apart, and which are objected to, by a predominant group.
- Marginalised people experience separation and subordination.
- They have shared social standards about who belongs, and who does not.
- Social rejection, or social underestimation, is the social impediment and transfer to the edge of society.

In a multicultural society, the efforts towards development should be multipronged rather than implementing a homogenous blueprint across the social groups. It is simply because, that the perceptions and needs are very much interlinked, when perceptions are culturally venerated, the solutions offered should be culturally appropriate otherwise the entire effort goes waste. In the world of colourful and diverse cultural manifestations, "it is sheer arrogance and patently false to believe that there is only one way of knowing nature" (Shankar, 2019). Realising the importance of indigenous knowledge and considering the marginalisation suffered by indigenous population, the United Nations Declaration on the Rights of Indigenous Peoples (UNDRIP) was adopted by the General Assembly on the 13 September 2007 establishing universal framework of minimum standards for the survival, dignity and well being of the indigenous peoples of the world. This is a clear indication of giving significance weightage to indigenous knowledge where it can collaborate with the modern science. For the indigenous people to survive and exercise their human rights and to conserve and propagate their wisdom necessary legal reforms have to be made (Daes, 1993:13).

Prospects of Collaboration

Whatever the epistemological or categorisation differences are visible, knowledge perse is unsegmented. From whatever source we access it whether from texts or directly from cultural system it is existing in the interest of human welfare, made by the humans for themselves. Instead of looking at the flip side of it, we should march in the direction of integrating both the tangible and intangible ends of knowledge. The biased attitude to the intangible can be overcome when indigenous ways of knowing is examined empirically. If indigenous knowledge has some limitations, even western sciences have also been responsible for many destructive effects, and moreover indigenous knowledge can facilitate relationships of human beings to both one anther and to their ecosystem which is notoriously absent in the western science (Kincheloe and Steinberg, 2014). Questioning the copyrights of science for the knowledge, Lesley Green (2008) comments - "There is not, I believe, one universal knowledge to which science is privy and to which all other knowledge traditions must defer". Keeping in view environmental safety, economic viability, human rights, inclusiveness and sustainable development we have to venture into a new era of collaboration between indigenous and non-indigenous knowledge systems which has already started in some sectors.

In my fieldwork among Koya tribe at Kalleru on the banks of Sabari at the confluence of three states of Andhra Pradesh, Odisha and Chhattisgarh, noticed an Ayurveda pharmacy at Motu of Odisha borders. This is actually managed by a non-Koya man who happened to live with the Koya people for some years and learned all their herbal formulae. Later he went back and started his pharmacy clubbing with Ayurvedic techniques, and he is running a flourishing business and at the same time catering to the needs of many patients across the states. As long as this knowledge remained with the Koya it would have not done much except to the Koya themselves. Even in Nallamallai forest area a number of non-tribals approach the Chenchu tribe for identifying and collection of medicinal herbs which in turn they supply to the pharmaceutical companies. But they give no recognisation to Chenchu and moreover this exploitation has led to the depletion of various herbs and they have become scares to the tribals themselves. In the process of rejuvenation of forests from deforestation, the forest departments across country have started aforestation drive promoting only a few commercially valid and quick growing species, ultimately defeating the spirit of reviving the forest. This exercise became successful to some extent only when the local tribals were involved and multispecies saplings are raised which in turn encouraged biodiversity. Because tribals are aware of the plants that are commonly grown in their surroundings and their utility value in their socio-economic life. Hence they take care in protecting them. A good example of collaborative exercise between allopathy with siddha is noticed in Tamil Nadu and Puducherry. When there is rapid increase of Dengue and Swineflu cases, though the patients are treated in allopathy hospitals, they are also allowed to take herbal drinks prepared by the siddha doctors. And this has shown very encouraging results.Therefore, whenever there is an outbreak of these diseases, this herbal drink is offered to all the patients in the government allopathy hospitals and in addition it is also given as a preventive medicine to everyone.

The Government of India in its national health policy 2017 has taken some steps in the direction of collaborative efforts of diverse medical systems to ensure best of healthcare to people. Some of the important policy discussions include-

1. Encourage medical pluralism along with allopathy, giving importance to AYUSH (Ayurveda, Yoga, Unani, Siddha and Homeo).
2. Mainstreaming different healthcare systems and providing cross-referral links.

3. AYUSH doctors are appointed even in urban primary health centers (National Health Policy, 2017).

All these measures are in the right direction of overcoming medical ethnocentrism and ensuring safe and cheap healthcare to all sections of society, by roping in the hitherto neglected indigenous medical systems.

Indigenous Knowledge in Nation Building

People and nation are inseparable as they inter-influence and hence nation building is a continuous ongoing process. People that occupy a territory identified by their language, culture or identities constitute nation professing self rule. So in the process of building the nation the involvement of all sections of the people become very important especially in a multicultural nation. The destiny of the nation need to be decided by its own people and not by any external agency so that sovereignty is ensured. However, if only one section of the population, perhaps a dominant group or a minority, plays the decisive in matters pertaining to national importance, the outcome would be non-representative and would lead to many problems, even to the extent of splitting national unity. The marginalised sections are usually unheard or least considered for any vital decision making, neither their knowledge system is given due consideration. That is the reason why we see many nations confront with civil disobedience and unrest leading to huge causalities and breaking down of nation state into smaller kingdoms as we see in many parts of African continent. Therefore, a collaborative mode is the best option between the dominant and the marginalised groups in a nation to uphold its unity and integrity. Wilful negligence of the marginal's leads to the violation of human rights and jeopardise their prospects of elevating their position and promoting their culture. It is not that they be treated as informants or subjects but should be made equal partners and collaborators in the entire process of growth and development.

Conclusion

From the above discourse it is very clear that knowledge is a human creation aimed to make life easy and keep the world liveable for generations to come. Though epistemological controversies try to categorise knowledge into different systems, but in true sense knowledge is a continuum and a process that transforms in the relation to the time and situation. The dichotomies of indigenous and modern, or traditional and scientific or local and universal have limited value and is more hypothetical as we can enumerate both merits and demerits in either cases. Instead, taking both the ends of it in a complimentary role in addressing the human needs have better advantage than shooting the target with either of them would only encounter with minimum success or even disappointment. Therefore, a collaborative effort is much needed in employing the indigenous and non-indigenous knowledge systems whereby each can play its effective role in fulfilling the task in its entirety. In a multicultural society, it is always healthy to involve the divergent ideologies in making the nation. When certain sections of the people are marginalised and automatically their emotions, ideologies and expectations have no reflection in the portrayal of the nation which we are trying to build up. A collaborative approach in the national building process give due preconisation to all the sections, and treat each group as an equal partner (collaborator) rather than treating them as subjects or informants. This kind of involvement of the marginalised ensure the protection and preservation of indigenous humanity (Battiste, 2014) and indigenous knowledge as you know is the social capital of the poor (Gorjestani, 2000).

References

1. Aboyade, Oluwaseyi M. and David R. Katerere 2019. Tribal and indigenous knowledge in West Africa:The use of food plants in the management of diabetes.In Katerere R. David; Wendy Applequist; Oluwaseyi M.Aboyade and Chamunorwa Togo (Ed) Traditional and indigenous knowledge for the modern era: A natural and applied science perspective. Boca Raton, London, New York: CRC press: Tylor and Francis group.
2. Alakhunova, Niyare; Oumar Daillo; Isabell Martin del Campo and Whitney Tallarico 2015. Defying marginalisation: An assessment tool.The Elliott school of international affairs,The George Washington University. Elliott.gwu.edu/sites/g/files/zaxdzs2141/f/world%20Trade%20organisation.tdf. Accessed on 27/04/2020.
3. Barnhardt, Roy and Kawagley Angayuqaq Oscar 2005. *Anthropology and Education Quarterly,* Vol. 36(1) pp. 8-23.
4. Battiste Marie 2014. Research ethics for protecting indigenous knowledge and heritage: Institutional and research responsibilities. In Norman K. Denzin, Yvonna S. Lincoln and Linda Tuhiwai Smith (Ed) Handbook of critical and indigenous methodologies.Thousand Oaks:Sage publications,inc.print pp. 497-510,online pp. 2-16, Accessed on 16/01/2020.
5. Bruchac, Margaret 2014. Indigenous knowledge and traditional knowledge. In Smith, C (Ed) Encyclopedia of Global Archaeology. New York: Springer, pp. 3814-3824.
6. Daes, Erica Irena 1993. Study on the protection of the cultural and intellectual property rights of indigenous peoples (E/CN.4/Sub.2/1993/28) Geneva, Switzerland: Subcommission on prevention of discrimination and protection of minorities, Commission on Human Rights,United Nations Economic and Social Watch.

7. Ellen, Roy and Holly Harris 1996. Introduction. In Roy Ellen, Peter Parkes and Alan Bicku (Ed) Indigenous environmental knowledge and its transformations: Critical antropological perspective. Australia and Canada: Harwood Academic Publishers.

8. Ellen, Roy 2004. From ethnoscience to science, or "what the indigenous knowledge debate tells us about how scientists define their project. *Journal of Cognition and Culture.*Vol.4(3), pp. 409-450.

9. Ens J. Emilie; Max Finlayson; Karissa Preuss; Sue Jackson and Sarah Holcombe 2012. Australian approaches for managing 'country' using indigenous and non-indigenous knowledge. *Ecological Managemen & Restoration* 13(1), January pp. 100-107.

10. Fernandez-Gimenez M. 2000. The role of Mongolian nomadic pastoralists' ecological knowledge in rangeland management. *Ecological Applications* Vol. 10, pp. 1318-1326.

11. Foundation for Revitalisation of Local Health Traditions Trust (FRLHT) 2013. Towards an integration of traditional knowledge and science, sociological, political and epistemological reflections, an Indian perspective. Bangalore, India: FRLHT.

12. Foundation for Revitalisation of Local Health Traditions Trust (FRLHT) 2017 Database, Trans Disciplinary University, Bangalore.

13. Gorjestani, N. 2000. Indigenous knowledge for development: Opportunities and challenges. Paper presented at UNC-TAD Conference on Traditional knowledge. Geneva. 1 November.

14. Green, Lesley J.F. 2008. 'Indigenous knowledge' and 'Science': Reframing the debate on knowledge diversity. Archaeologies: *Journal of the World Archaeological Congress* Vol. 4(1), April. pp. 144-163.

15. Grenier, Louise 1998. Working with indigenous knowledge: A guide for researchers. International development research centre: Ottawa On, Canada.

16. Huntington P. Henry 2000 Using traditional ecological knowledge in science: Methods and applications. *Ecological Application,* Vol. 10(5), October, pp. 1270-1274.

17. International Labour Organisation (ILO) 1989, Convention on indigenous and tribal peoples in independent countries. (No. 169, 28 I.L.M 1382) Geneva, Switzerland.

18. Kincheloe, Joe L and Shirlay R. Steinberg 2014. Indigenous knowledge in Education: Complexities, dangers and profound benefits. In Norman K. Denzin, Yvonna S. Lincoln and Linda Tuhiwai Smith (Ed) Handbook of critical and indigenous methodologies.Thousand Oaks: Sage publications,inc.print pp. 497-510, online pp. 2-16, Accessed on 16/01/2020.

19. National Health Policy 2017. Ministry of Health and Family Welfare, Governament of India. nhp.gov.in/nhpfiles/national_health_policy_2017.pdf. Accessed on 27/04/2020.

20. National Research Foundation (NRF) 2003. Indigenous knowledge systems. (online) http://www.nrf.ac.za/focusareas/iks/ Acessed on 10/05/2020.

21. Nonaka, I and Takeuchi, H 1995. The knowledge creating company: How Japanese companies create the dynamics of innovation. New York: Oxford University Press.

22. Ocholla, Dennis 2007. Marginalised knowledge : An agenda for indigenous knowledge development and integration with other forms of knowledge. *International Review of Information Ethics,* Vol. 7, September, pp. 1-10.

23. Reo, Nicholas James and Whyte, Kyle Powys 2012. Hunting and morality as elements of traditional ecological knowledge. *Human Ecology*. Vol. 40, pp. 15-27.

24. Ross Anne; Kathlen Pickering Sherman; Jeffrey G. Snodgrass; Henry D. Dekore and Richard Sherman 2011. Indigenous peoples and the collaborative stewardship of nature: Knowledge binds and institutional conflicts. Wallnut Creek, CA:Left coast press.

25. Shankar, Darshan 2019. Contemporizing tribal and indigenous medical knowledge: An Indian perspective. In David R. Katerere et al (Ed) Traditional and indigenous knowledge for the modern era: A national and applied science perspective. Boca Roton: Tylor and Francis.

26. Silver, Hilary 1994. 'Social exclusion and social solidarity: Three paradigms'. *International Labour Review*, Vol. 135, pp. 531-578.

27. Silverman, M.E 1989 Profiles of Cardiology-William Withering and an account of the Foxglove. *Clinical Cardiology,* Vol. 12, pp. 415-418.

28. Tinnaluck, Yuwanuch 2004. Modern science and native knowledge: Collaborative process that opens new perspective for PCST. *Quark* No. 32 April-June, pp. 70-74.

29. Titilola, T. 1995. IKS and sustainable agricultural development in Africa: Essential linkages. Indigenous knowledge and development monitor, Vol. 2(2) online:http://www.nufficcs.n//ciran/ikdm/.

30. Warren, D.M. 1992. A preliminary analysis of indigenous soil classification and management system in four ecozones of Nigeria. NISER:Nigeria.

10

Hidden in Plain Sight: 'Caste'ing the City or Spatial Politics in the Indian Metropolis

— Prof. Amitha Santiago

"The great metaphor of the Leviathan, whose body is formed out of all the bodies of individuals..."

– Giorgio Agamben
Homo Sacer: Sovereign Power and Bare Life[1]

What is ideology without a space to which it refers, a space which it describes, whose vocabulary and links it makes use of, and whose code it embodies?

Henri Lefebvre: The Production of Space[2]

The paradox of the metropolis is made possible by a consistent structuring of formal inequalities publicly denied. The "secret" violations of explicit rules of social equality encoded by the state in democratic institutions and artifacts are deliberately and legitimately hidden in plain sight in India's cities. These violations govern the spatialising of caste hierarchies in urban, globalised, tech savvy cities in India. Caste and class alliances are reinstalled within this rural-urban dialectic that is made to take form and shape in place, so that spatialising the city performs publicly manifested yet institutionally denied caste segregation practices in urban India. The means to access of urban commons follows in its trail.

Needless to say, this is forwarded in the state's sanctioning of spaces for development such that rural geographies are envisioned as under developed and marked for urbanisation. The becoming of the rural into urbanity is anticipated forthrightly by rural migrations to cityscapes.

The city becomes the space of arrival and encounter for in-dignified and self-respect-seeking rural communities from the lower castes. This movement driven by conscientious Dalit self-work in itself must cloak the urban space in raiment of egalitarian and liberative hues suggesting that the Ambedkarite call to the promise of metropolitan anonymity[3] en route to liberation from caste identity has achieved fruition.

Space in urban India had exuded for many the possibility of a secular, non-religious ordering of existence, so much so that caste, erroneously characterised as a pre-modern power grid on which the lives of people were drawn seemed to lose place. However, this losing of place is only in the telling of a fantasy of secular, organised metropolitan space. In the locus of the social real, migrations of Dalits to the city prodded caste dynamics to shape-shift and rearrange itself in terms of clandestine and overt postures of beckoning that on close contact were excluding of lower castes, while playing at charades of inclusion.

The city was drafted to become a technology that was deceptively secular while it delivered caste segregation practices steadily. Those excluded posed a direct threat to the grammar of spatial discriminations hitherto effectively hegemonised in villages. The Dalits excluded thus far began their movement to urbanity that raised flags of democracy and liberation while proffering irresistible dreams of recognition as whole citizens that were withheld by rurality. Urban commons were announced as being available to all. However, the invisible line of control that acted out thwarting of specific kinds, delivered re-packaged dictums and rules of engagement for the migrating Dalit populations.

Publics are opened up for entry by those who were always and already acknowledged as full citizens, and who could be used and managed by the urban economic power players in state and corporate houses to full advantage and towards greater productivity. Dalit migrants who enter this political-economic-social could not be thus managed or used and are identified as threatening to the status quos and so are necessarily incarcerated while seemingly allowed freedoms in all public spheres in the city.[4] So that as Agamben points out: "A space and time which are equal for all living things does not exist."[5]

The cry of the Dalit that travels to the city/town in search of liberation from caste rings through in many a life narrative, including Manoj Byapari's "Itibritte":

> This is the city which from boyhood to youth gave nothing but hunger, humiliation and torture. On several occasions it tried to kill me.

> Closing my eyes I can still see amidst dark recesses of time the assassin's face waiting for me with open dagger. This city is my enemy; there is no question of loving it. But why still my heart aches? Why eyes get filled with tears?[6]

Here it is then, Foucault's bio power hungry technocratic urbanity that must necessarily qualify, measure, appraise as well as hierarchize, rather than simply show itself in all its murderous splendor.[7] The city that is the manifested technology of state power that allows the migrant in on its terms, that marks the urban experience of Dalits in cities with a snarling presence that secures for the upper caste bourgeoisie a tidy inflow of labourers marching into its gates with songs of liberation that will never be in tune with the cities orchestrations.

Joel Lee in his study of odors and segregated spaces in cities, establishes that a continuity of caste discrimination is present, albeit sensorarily. He vividly shows how the lower caste and lower class were given select housing in spaces where dominant class and upper caste groups would not have to see or feel their presence in proximity to theirs. The study Lee makes of sensorial-spatial practices repetitively generated for such organised segregation along caste lines by the municipality is replete with cases of hygiene and sanitation being seen as non-basic to living spaces allotted by the municipality for the under caste/class. As Lee observes:

> Less consistently, but more toxically, than the rural Mehtar *tolâ*, the urban Valmiki *bastî* has come to perform the same referential function vis-à-vis caste ideology: it provides spatial-sensory "evidence," however spurious, of what makes one group unlike another.[8]

Juxtapositioning this narrative with Ratan Kumar Sambharia's "Phulwa" and we find that the two accounts make for the telling of a paradoxical tale of the city. Phulwa is a short story that gives a blow by blow account of Phulwa's rise to economic comfort and caste free living in the city. She employs an upper caste Rajput abandoned by her educated husband as her maid and looks on her as a daughter. When the zamindar's son Rameshwar comes visiting her in the city she leaves no stone unturned showing him how well she lives. In an endorsement of the cities difference from the rural space she declares:

> Our village has thirty-six variations of caste. In the city, however, there are only two castes – the rich and the poor.[9]

While those who have access to education are able to perceive discrimination in cities as class based thereby paying homage to the

Ambedkarite vision of class replacing caste in urban spaces. Ambedkar famously said: "What is a village but a sink of localism, a den of ignorance, narrow-mindedness and communalism?"[10] in opposition to Gandhi's ideal village republics[11]. Ambedkar's call to migrate to cities was hope to those hounded by caste practices for centuries. Ambedkar is famously known to have exhorted oppressed castes to leave the "narrow minded" villages for city life. It also sought out Gandhi's India, which lived in its villages, and tasked it in the direction of introspection and self-critique. If Gandhi's idyllic of a "Ram Rajya" was to be found in "village republics", the city was that imaginative assemblage that held the possibility of replacing caste with class.

Offering the promise of the metropolitan machine, Babasaheb Ambedkar, who grew to iconic status amongst the Dalit masses, seen as the foremost pillar of the Indian Constitution as it came into existence in independent India, as well as Gandhi's openly intellectual and political challenger, described the village in India as "narrow minded" and urged his fellow Dalit sufferers to leave the rigid caste system of the villages behind to migrate to towns and cities where their lives could enter casteless anonymity. Perhaps, it is in keeping with this rhetoric of the urban vs the rural that most Dalit accounts of the city and the village present the transformative potential of the urban setting and the overt aggressive caste practices of the village.

Even if one took a random time period of a decade, from about 2006-2016 alone, to verify if the call that Ambedkar gave had waned in the days long after India gained independence, we would find that an approximate jump of around 40% Dalits were seen choosing to migrate to towns and cities in an effort to extricate themselves from the stranglehold of caste identity in villages. In the case of religious minorities, relocation by choice to cities has been the trend for decades, with the larger numbers being from communities of Dalit Christians and Muslims, looking for opportunities for social mobility in cities. Studies uncover that compared to 29% Hindus living in cities, a good 40% of Muslims and Christians from socially oppressed and disadvantaged circumstances move to cities. Even so, this data alone does not mark urbanity as being imbued with an egalitarian pragmatics.[12]

Imaginatively, however, the city has had the longest history of announcing the demise of inequality and social injustice. Interestingly, one of the earliest equalising city spaces was envisioned by the 15th century poet saint Guru Ravidas in his song "Begumpura". He sings of a "realm with the sorrowless name..." He imagines an urban space "with no pain, no taxes or cares". Ownership of property is not known to exist in this place, nor "wrongdoing, worry, terror or torture..." Ravidas speaks of freedoms from hierarchy here as well as liberation from spatial and labour discriminations:

> Where none are third or second – all are one;
> They do this or that,
> They walk where they wish,
> They stroll through fabled places unchallenged.
> Oh, says Ravidas, a tanner now set free;
> those who walk beside me are my friends."[13]

The poignant longing for such liberation comes through in his signature line.

Gail Ombvedt in her "Seeking Begumpura"[14] speaks of Saint Guru Ravidas of the "untouchable" Chamar community who sang of a fictional city 'Begumpura'. In her words it is "was an expression, in the early modern age, of a utopia, perhaps the first one in Indian literature. In some ways it seems to stand alone, yet it was a harbinger- of the kind of social vision that would underlie all the later struggles and theorising of anti-caste intellectuals. Begumpura was, for Ravidas, an imagined city, without geographical location, without a history; it was to be a later task to build it in space and time." Ombvedt notes that Begumpura is a radical bhakti Utopian envisioning of space where freedom from sorrows and taxes combines with freedom of movement. Similarly, Sant Tukaram speaks of Pandharpur, a city where even the headman labours, and "where time and death 'had no entry'"[15]. So, urban spaces have often been part of a prophetic vision for a radical politics of liberative egalitarian living.

Cutting from the imaginative to the real, a study using ward level data released by the census, recruited by Pranav Sidhwani examines residential segregation along caste lines in the ten most populated cities in India. He finds that far from being egalitarian spaces, cities regenerate the social hierarchies of caste in villages quite efficiently through strategic denial of access to hygienic spaces and basic necessities such as drinking water, sanitation and necessary public - private goods and services.[16]

Gopal Guru's critique of modernity in urban space concurs with this analysis when he points to the inequitable distribution of goods, capital and access to resources and opportunities for social mobility in cities and the mindful repetition of marginalisation of lower caste groups.[17] A caste-free space is only partially attainable within the city as the modern is a creature that cheats on itself to achieve a contradictoriness that sustains the dialectics inbuilt within migration practices.

A number of Dalit writings represent this search for a caste-free space in urban centers, which emerges as a contradictory zone of contact between caste groups. One such life narrative, Baluta, has the protagonist Daya Pawar saying of the city that it:

> "Seemed like a precious stone set in a ring on a rich man's hand. It would gleam an invitation at you, but it never end up on your finger."[18]

Joel Lee in his "Odor an Order: how Caste Is Inscribed in Space and Sensoria"[19] graphically shows how the arrangement of under caste/ class migrants to cities deploys caste polarisations in spatialising practices. There is as it were a sense of inclusion through exclusion. The presence of Dalits in assigned spaces of neglect and disparity is not an oversight by the state but a ploy to appease the upper castes. This technology of deliberate neglect is played out in every city space, so that lower caste groups are often made to feel like outsiders bestowed with a reluctant entry point into urbanity, albeit for the sustenance of the state's economic power. In such a power play the state holds the lower caste labouring community at an unthreatening, safe distance and allowed access to education, products, capital and spaces on its terms. The differences between these segregated communities is kept distinct by way of lack of sanitation and hygiene, jobs offered to them, spaces made accessible to them, an unequal opportunities, which though established are largely contestable. So, while accommodating Dalit migrants into city spaces, spaces are so organised such that the fact of an incarcerated existence becomes an irreducible part of the Dalits' life world and experience of the city. This potently suggests that the Dalit in urban space is a non-citizen or a "not-quite-citizen" who exists in such public spheres as deemed appropriate by the state.

At this point, it is interesting to attend to the critical rethinking of the public sphere presented by K Satyanarayana in his edited volume on Dalit Studies[20]. In a chapter titled "Dalit Reconfigurations in Modernity: Citizens and Castes in the Telugu Public Sphere" he identifies the publishing of Telugu Literature as an urban commons, which needed persistent negotiation by Dalit writers in order to establish their life narratives as legitimate forms of literary practice. He argues that a conceptual shift was necessary in marking the function of Dalit writing. He states that Dalit writers advanced a critique of the self of the modern human citizen which is often understood as male, upper caste and Hindu. In this direction of critique Dalit Telugu literature create a category of the not-quite-citizen figure of the Dalit in cities, attempting to re-contour and rethink public spheres through a process of asserting a new Dalit selfhood in urbanity.

He goes on to point out that Dalit writers have consciously made these assertions and claims as scholars, poets, fiction writers, and critics in order that recognition of their life worlds and lived experiences permeate into the power grid of state controlled spaces in the urban setting. In so doing, he launches a strident and full throated critique of the prominent Telugu literary critic and scholar of languages and culture at the University of Wisconsin-Madison, Vecheru Narayana Rao, who made a drastic intervention in 2002.

In summary, he dismisses Dalit literary writing as being non-literary and asserts that the judgement of what is good poetry should be made only by established poets. Standing against poetry that produced social consciousness, he laments the weakening of "sahitya" by Dalit and Feminist writers in Telugu. He names Virasam writers as "middle-class opportunists" who have no specialised training or qualifications to be recognised as literary figures. He goes on to bemoan publishing houses who "publish whatever they write, as it is". This trend he claims has "blurred the distinctions between literature and society and between the language of addressing problems in society and the language of literary criticism. Therefore, literature has lost its special status."[21]

In his end notes, Satyanarayana cites Sarathi, a Marxist critic, who asserted that Narayana Rao has sadly failed to understand and to recognize the role of the poets and writers in social practice and to be appreciative of the fact that any good literature must first be a literature of the people, that which is both popular with and felt by the people and which can be evaluated therefore judged as good literature. Sarathi confronts the defining of good literature as the task of established writers with the recognition that it is social groups who must have a key role in the definition of what is good literature.[22]

In Satyanarayana's chapter, Sikhamani's poem "An Apology" ("Kshamapana") gives full force to the apology expected from Dalit readers and poets alike for Brahmanical failure to depict Dalit life and problems:

I apologise, dalit!
I am a poet, a rare poet
Why my name,

My background?
I'm a Brahmin
With a glorious lineage
Oh, please accept my apologies, dalit!
Never had the time to write
a line about you
the past thousand years,
so engrossed I was in
amorous and ascetic literary pursuits…[23]

The poem can easily be seen as a tongue-in-cheek critique of Brahmanical literary techniques and themes, but as Satyanarayana points out it is more importantly an outspoken critique of the claim to a secular poetic self that the Telugu literary artist might well seek to assert in modernity. The social movements and activisms that perpetuated changes in literary spheres and publication reinvented both the notion of the poet and the idea of Telugu public spheres.

As we can see, intellectual spaces are typically mobilised as the spatialisation politics of caste in urbanity. The publication of literary writers in cities is a means of representing diverse contexts and identities to a ready, reading, educated audience. And the publication of these texts for schools, colleges and universities is a form of mass production and consumption that is the metropolis' habitual practice. The beginnings of the Dalit movement in literary circles in Karnataka, is a case in point. B. Basavalingappa's "boosa" (chaf /hogwash) statement about the hitherto Brahmanical literature that had been published and read widely across the state launched the critique of print capitalism and publishing houses that was the stronghold of the upper castes in Karnataka. Bangalore's Dalit community and wider Karnataka hailed the "boosa" statement as a long overdue critique of Brahmanical literary dominance and furthered the way for the publication of Dalit writers.[24]

Sengupta's question thus is a relevant one:

> What intervention could be made by the poor migrant Dalits and destitute to understand the evolution of the idea of space? Memory, remembrance and narrativisation of the impossible experience of (un)belonging to the city could be the crux of Dalit intervention to the notion of space.[25]

It is useful at this point to take a leaf out of Agamben's deployment of Foucault's ideas on bio politics. The depreciating value of the human form as subject in terms of simply bodily tasking by modernity is highlighted in Agamben's positing of camps as being the new form that modernity takes in urbanity.[26] That in fact the bare life of a non-citizen subject is allowed to exist in a segregated space alone in any given urban scape, which typically excludes the mass of people slotted as not-quite-citizens. The migration of caste groups to city spaces alerts upper castes to the crisis of spatialising existence within cities. The upper caste counters the Dalit migrations to urban spaces weaponising urban planners and policy-makers into a frenzied spatialisation of caste segregation practices. So that while Gandhi saw the city as being oppressive to rural India[27], urban reality sniggers its way into replicating the rural incarceration of castes in selective quarters/ wards. Gandhi's village thus comes to town and city. State power works for upper caste privilege and Dalit repression to social mobility in this way. The caste system in India's metropolitan centers gains longevity and spread through a deliberate politics of spatialising the city, which deploys spatial exclusions and inclusions that sustain the power grid of caste.

In literary representations by Dalit writers, we find that the urban space holds the potential for engagement and transformation, even if it is an incomplete and contradictory liberative potential. For Dalit communities migrating to the city, the migration means an emerging from the rigid spatial caste normativity of the village to the road that leads to the promise of liberation in the city. While seeming to allow certain equalities the city disfigures these very equalising elements in its resolute sanctioning of planned segregation practices. Dalit literary texts make a case for the city being a space where social, economic and political equality is possible in the entrance of under castes into education, workspaces and enfranchisement.

Some equalising practices come with being in urbanity. "Phulwa"[28] narrativises the class mobility that Phulwa experiences with access to creature comforts and water from a tap rather than a caste well. However, urban spaces, primarily slums, allocated for lower caste dwelling are often places where there is little access to basic amenities, sanitation and connectivity. While literature written by Dalit writers represent the scourge of caste practices as aggressively visible in rural India many narratives suggest the city as a space that markets egalitarian principles, the case of Dalit individuals and their social mobility in cities is seen as potentised by a contradictory trope rather than the ability of the city to embody bold democracy or equality.

The short story by V Hanumanthiah, "Wedding Lamps in Holeya Street"[29] is a graphic representation of the spatial contradictoriness of the city which offers a promise on the one hand and preserves caste sanctions on the other. The poignant and real account of V Hanumanthiah's life as a struggling poet in Bangalore, Tiptur and other small towns in Karnataka are interspersed with liberative events. Yet one sees that the polities of the urban space into which he and Shailaja enter make the process of liberation from caste string together difficulties and cruelties that the city organises with aplomb.

"Bes"[30] another powerful piece of short fiction by Sambharia brings to the fore the ways in which the metropolis organises caste distinctions in terms of attire. When Agani dresses to present herself as a Rajput upper caste girl she subversively enters caste to protect herself from the sexual assaults that are regularly and normatively organised against lower castes on the bodies of women. The highway becomes a minefield of sorts where her Rajput attire alone is her armor against sexual assault by men of every caste, who have been trained to lust after and treat as easily available, any woman of the lower caste.

"Bes" is a powerful comment on the dangers of transiting between the points where the city ends and the rural is anticipated. The fact that this piece of fiction positions the body of the woman in a highway between her village and the city from where she is travelling back home, lays claim to the visible structuring of caste and gender assault that women from the lower castes succumb to and resist through manifold strategic interventions. The subversive use of the upper caste attire embodies subversive praxis in contesting patriarchal huntsmen in search of women's bodies as sites where caste hierarchies can be endorsed. It locates caste on the dangerous mode of transiting along the urban-rural continuum.

These and several other life narratives of Dalit writers call to attention the fact of the lower caste person being in a category of not-quite-citizen or identifiable by the state as non-citizen. The tale told by the state's apparatus of the non-existence of caste in city spaces serves the purposes of silencing voices against caste oppression in order to sustain caste hierarchies in urbanity. In real space and time, the state's secular garb is a case of the emperor's new clothes. It creates a faithful ally in secular dogma that often discounts narratives of Dalit spatial discriminations by way of claiming a lack of vocabulary and language to voice its persistent presence. It is here that the literary voice speaks discontent and resistance to state governance of the public sphere, literary and architectural, calling out the secular urban charade of the emperor in space and time.

References

1. Agambena, Giorgio, 1942. *Homo Sacer. Sovereign Power and Bare Life.* Stanford, Calif. :Stanford University Press, 1998.
2. Lefebvre, Henri, Donald Nicholson-Smith, and David Harvey. *The Production of Space*, 1991. Print.
3. Omvedt, Gail. *Dalits and the Democratic Revolution: Dr. Ambedkar and the Dalit Movement in Colonial India*. New Delhi: Sage Publications, 1994. Print.
4. Sengupta, S.. "Undecidable Spaces: Rethinking Caste and the Technologies of Abandonment in Manoranjan Byapari." (2019).
5. Giorgio Agamben: The Open: Man and Animal. Stanford, CA, Stanford University Press, 2004, p. 40.
6. Byapari, Manoranjan. *Itibritte Chandala Jiban, Vol. 2*. Kolkata: AB Prakashani, 2016. Print.
7. https://caringlabor.wordpress.com/2010/08/06/michel-foucault-right-of-death-and-power-over-life/
8. Lee, Joel. "Odor and Order: How Caste is Inscribed in Space and Sensoria." *Comparative Studies of South Asia, Africa and the Middle East*, Vol. 37, No. 3, 2017, pp. 470-490. *Project MUSE* muse.jhu.edu/article/683279.
9. Sambharia, Ratan Kumar (Trans. Mridul Bhasin). Thunderstorm: Dalit Stories. Hachette: London UK. 2015.
10. https://www.livemint.com/Sundayapp/jcI32BcTZvlS0qWeEPk21O/Ambedkar-and-the-economics-of-segregation.html
11. https://www.yourarticlelibrary.com/society/gandhis-vision-of-the-ideal-society-in-india/38521
12. https://thewire.in/urban/indias-urbanisation-is-dangerously-exclusionary-and-unequal
13. https://Roundtableindia.co.in/lit-blogs
14. Omvedt, Gail. Seeking Begumpura : The Social Vision of Anticaste Intellectuals. New Delhi :Navayana Pub. : Distributed by IPD Alternatives, 2008.
15. *Ibid.*, p. 12.
16. Sidhwani, P. 2015. Spatial Inequalities in Big Indian Cities. Economic and Political Weekly. 50. 55-62.
17. https://roundtableindia.co.in/index.php?option=com_content&view=article&id=4654:modernity-and-its-margins-a-critique&catid=118:thought&Itemid=131.
18. https://migrationaffairs.com/neither-rural-nor-urban-incomplete-migration-in-dalit-life-narratives/
19. Lee, Joel. "Odor an Order: how Caste is Inscribed in Space and Sensoria" *Comparative Studies of South Asia, Africa and the Middle East*, Vol. 37, No. 3, 2017, p. 470-490. *Project MUSE* muse.jhu.edu/article/683279
20. Rawat, Ramnarayan S, and K Satyanarayana. *Dalit Studies*, 2016. Print.
21. Rawat, Ramnarayan S, and K Satyanarayana. *Dalit Studies*, 2016. Print.

22. Sarathi, "Roopavadaniki Tirogaminchina Velcheru," *Andhra Jyothi Dinapatrika*, May 19, 2003, and "Sahityam Sahityam kosam kadu, Prajala Kosam," *Andhra Jyothi Dinapatrika*, July 14, 2003. Cited in Rawat, Ramnarayan S, and K Satyanarayana. *Dalit Studies*, 2016. Print.
23. Rawat, Ramnarayan S, and K Satyanarayana. *Dalit Studies*, 2016. Print. p. 167.
24. Satyananrayana, K and Susie Tharu. Editors. Steel Nibs are Sprouting: New Dalit writing From South India. Dossier II. Kannada and Telugu.Harper Collins. India. 2013. pp. 2-4.
25. Sengupta, S. "Undecidable Spaces: Rethinking Caste and the Technologies of Abandonment in Manoranjan Byapari." 2019.
26. Ek, Richard. "Giorgio Agamben and the Spatialities of the Camp: An Introduction." *Geografiska Annaler. Series B, Human Geography*, Vol. 88, No. 4, 2006, pp. 363–386. *JSTOR*, www.jstor.org/stable/4621535. Accessed 28 Sept. 2020.
27. http://urbanupdate.in/gandhi-city/
28. https://scroll.in/article/802709/how-phulwa-once-a-downtrodden-woman-made-the-zamindars-son-green-with-envy
29. https://it-it.facebook.com/866748356729230/posts/wedding-lamps-on-holeya-streetn-k-hanumanthaiahtranslated-by-s-r-ramakrishnamy-f/1484911731579553/
30. https://caravanmagazine.in/vantage/bes-excerpt-ratan-sambharias-thunderstorm-dalit-stories.

11

Globalisation and Need for Skill Development at Secondary and Senior Secondary levels of Education in India

— Prof. Yazali Josephine

General Introduction

India's transition to a knowledge-based superpower requires a new generation of educated and skilled people. Part of the unemployment problem in India emanates from the mismatch between the skill requirements of employment opportunities and the skill base of the job-seekers. According to the National Knowledge Commission (which advises the Prime Minister's Office on higher education) – Out of the Indians between age group 18 to 24 years, only 13% enter Higher education, and rest of the 87% is entering into the world of work or unemployed. The largest share of new jobs in India is supposed to come from the unorganised sector that employs up to 93% of the national workforce and produces 60% of GDP. Those who are entering into the world of work mostly to the unorganised sector are without any skills. The mismatch is likely to become more acute in the process of rapid structural changes of the economy in the new era. It is, therefore, necessary to reorient the educational and training systems and introduce greater flexibility in the school education and training system. It will enable the economy to quickly respond to labour market. To achieve this, India needs to implement a new flexible school education system: basic education to provide the foundation for learning; secondary, sr. secondary. The school education system must be attuned to the new global environment by promoting creativity and improving the quality of education and training. India is coming into its dividend as an unusually young country in an unusually aging market, a young, fresh-faced nation in a graying world, Nandan Nilekani observed in his book, "Imagining

India: Ideas for the New Century". According to Another observation, by 2025, 25% of the world's workers will be Indians. Developing skilled workers enhances the efficiency and flexibility of the labour market. India must meet aspirations of its youth in 18-25 years (over 150 million) and canalise this vast energy. It is crucial to introduce new policy planning and invest in skill oriented, quality secondary, sr. secondary and vocational education and training (VET). A steady supply of skilled manpower can only be supported by a robust New Policy planning in Post-secondary education. A key issue, then, is what reforms/interventions are needed to improve the effectiveness of the system.

There are five approaches at this level may work out positively:

Our concern at this particular juncture is regarding policy planning at Secondary (class 9-10), and Sr. Secondary (class 11-12). Policy planning and Reforms at Secondary (class 9-10), and Higher Secondary (class 11-12) sector may be at four levels:

A. Planning a Skills Based Curriculum at secondary and sr. secondary level (targeting +2 stage)
B. Development of Vocational Education
C. Upgrade the vocational training institutions to enhance the skill sets required for remote services (targeting secondary dropouts who are entering into world of informal sector)
D. Strengthening the standards of school education to ensure employability by WTO
E. Encourage Public-Private partnership in skill development

Introduction

To contribute effectively to the innovation economy and capitalise on the growing opportunities of globalisation, India's young workforce must develop skills that are more market-driven. Given expanding trade and globalisation, India's workforce must have skills that are aligned with its transforming economy and can support the country's continued economic growth. India's ongoing but incomplete transformation from agriculture- to a manufacturing- and services-based economy requires training a workforce with distinct skills for a market. India's present growth is led by service sector, which has had a boost due to the ICT revolution. India has recently witnessed a big boom in the BPO/KPO sector because of the liberalisation, globalisation. This new window of service sector export led growth in India is not an opportunity that can be frittered away. Similar to export of manufacturing sector service sector also requires a steady supply of highly skilled manpower which can only be supported by a robust New Policy planning in Post-secondary education. There are two approaches at this level may work out positively:

1. Policy planning for Transformation of secondary and senior secondary education (Class 9-10), and Sr. Secondary (Class 11-12) sector into skill oriented education.
2. Policy planning at higher education.

Our concern at this particular juncture is regarding policy planning at Secondary (Class 9-10), and Sr. Secondary (Class 11-12). Policy planning and Reforms at Secondary (Class 9-10), and Higher Secondary (Class 11-12) sector may be at four levels:

A. Planning a Skills Based Curriculum at secondary and sr. secondary level (targeting +2 stage)
B. Development of Vocational education
C. Upgrade the vocational training institutions to enhance the skills required for remote services (targeting secondary dropouts who are entering into world of informal sector)
D. Strengthening of the standard to qualify the skills to ensure employability by WTO

Policy planning for Transformation of secondary and senior secondary education (class 9-10), and Sr. Secondary (Class 11-12) sector into skill oriented education.

Importance of Secondary and Senior Secondary Education for India

India's transition to a knowledge-based economy requires a new generation of educated and skilled people. Its competitive edge will be determined by its people's ability to create, share, and use knowledge effectively. A knowledge economy requires India to develop workers – knowledge workers and knowledge technologists - who are flexible and analytical and who can be the driving force for innovation and growth. To achieve this India needs a flexible education system: basic education to provide the foundation for learning; Secondary, Sr. Secondary and tertiary education to develop core capabilities and core technical skills; and further means of achieving lifelong learning. The education system must be attuned to the new global environment by promoting creativity and improving the quality of education and training at all levels. As a knowledge economy by 2020 India requires to develop knowledge workers. To achieve this India needs a flexible education system: basic education to provide the foundation for learning; secondary's secondary and tertiary education to develop core capabilities and core technical skills; and further means of achieving lifelong learning. In brief:

1. This is part of the vision of India to ensure universal secondary education by 2017, i.e. the end of the 12th Five Year Plan.
2. Whereas the target for GER by the end of the 11th Plan could be fixed at 75% for secondary stage.
3. Ensure 100% enrolment and retention up to Sr.Secondary stage by 2020.
4. According to the National Knowledge Commission (which advises the Prime Minister's Office on higher education) – Out of the Indians between age group 18 to 24 years, only 13% enter Higher Education.
5. For rapid economic growth and employment generation we need to concentrate on the balance 87% of the people.
6. The largest share of new jobs in India is supposed to come from the unorganised sector that employs up to 93% of the national workforce and produces 60% of GDP.
7. India must meet aspirations of its youth in 18-25 years (over 150 million) and canalise this vast energy.
8. In India, the maximum job growth in recent years has taken place in the skilled services and manufacturing sectors.
9. Needs to provide the 12 million young people who join the labour force every year with the necessary knowledge, skills, attitudes and experiences to enable them to access these better-paying jobs.

Present Critical Condition of Secondary and Senior Secondary Education

India is passing a critical stage of educational process at Secondary, and Sr. Secondary level. To address some of the critical issues that school educational system is facing today are six or seven such critical issues which educational planners and administrator must address i.e.:

- Rise and fall in financial support and investment in school education
- Call for better vocationalisation of secondary education
- Demand for Relevant need based teacher training and deployment

- Demand for improvement in the infrastructural and resource support
- Need for improvement of science and technology education and computer literacy
- Need for integrated education for disabled
- addressing to the educational needs of girls, and other weaker sections
- promotion of yoga
- Strengthening culture and values and
- Environmental orientation Emergence of international organisations.

New Policy Planning for secondary and senior secondary education-focus on skill oriented education at secondary and sr. secondary level for employment generation

India is coming into its dividend as an unusually young country in an unusually aging market, a young, fresh-faced nation in a graying world, Nandan Nilekani observed in his book, *Imagining India: Ideas for the New Century.* That's not just another observation, by 2025, 25% of the world's workers will be Indians, The Team Lease report points out three hundred and fifty universities, 18,000 colleges and 6,000 ITIs will continue to churn out five lakh technical graduates, along with around 2.3 million graduates (or maybe more) by 2025. According to the Confederation of Indian Industry (CII) unfortunately, just 10-25% of them will be 'employable', McKinsey says Close to 500 million people, will need to go through skill development by 2020. India has recently witnessed a big boom in the BPO/KPO/LPO/HRO etc sector because of the liberalisation, globalisation. In order to sustain this trend, and to ensure that India does not throw away this key advantage, it is imperative that we continue to produce a critical mass of skilled manpower at an accelerated pace. This new window of service sector export led growth in India is not an opportunity that can be frittered away. The changes in the policy planning in this segment are required for this emerging knowledge economy.

Policy Planning Approaches

- Policy planning for Transformation of secondary and senior secondary education (class 9-10), and Sr. Secondary (class 11-12) sector in the New Era of liberalisation.
- Policy planning at Higher education.

Our concern at this particular juncture is regarding policy planning at Secondary (Class 9-10), and Sr. Secondary (Class 11-12). Policy planning and Reforms at Secondary (Class 9-10), and Higher Secondary (Class 11-12) sector may be at four levels:

- Planning a Skills Based Curriculum at secondary and sr. secondary level (targeting +2 stage)
- Development of Vocational Education
- Upgrade the vocational training institutions to enhance the skill sets required for remote services (targeting secondary dropouts who are entering into world of informal sector)
- Strengthening the standards of school education to ensure employability by WTO

A. Planning a Skills Based Curriculum at Secondary and Sr. Secondary Level

Curriculum can be modified to include skill-based education. By doing so we will not only provide industry with the required skilled labour force but also the young generation decent jobs. This will not put extra burden on the national economy as the resources from conventional education will be diverted to technical education.

B. Development of Vocational Education

Vocational education in India aims to develop skilled manpower through diversified courses to meet the requirements of mainly the unorganised sector and to instill self-employment skills in people through a large number of self employment oriented courses. Vocational education is imparted through Industrial Training Institutes (ITIs) and polytechnics. One of the weaknesses of Indian education system is that it does not gives due importance to vocational education. As a result there is a mismatch between the skilled manpower required and skilled manpower available. The challenge for Indian policy-makers is to ensure that both the supply-side players i.e. the government and the private sector, enter into a symbiotic relationship to battle the perception issue plaguing the demand for vocational education.

C. Upgrade the vocational training institutions to enhance the skill required for remote services (targeting secondary dropouts who are entering into world of informal sector)

Over 90 percent of employment in India is in the so called 'informal' sector, with employees working in relatively low productivity jobs. Provision of appropriate skills may thus be an important intervention to increasing the productivity of this workforce. However, both demand side as well as supply-side constraints has inhibited skills development for this sector. On the demand-side, few employees in the informal sector see the importance of skills training. On the supply side, there are a number of institutions which are trying to provide skills training geared to the needs of the informal sector. These efforts are fairly small, not well coordinated and often do not take into account the holistic needs for training and other support services of informal sector workers.

D. Strengthening of the Standards to Ensure Employability by WTO

In the wake of WTO - GATS negotiations, Indian secondary education cannot be left out unprepared. So let us bring the changes through planning:

- Prepare younger generation with new knowledge, renewed skills for understanding technical know-how, sharpening competencies necessary for human and economic development.
- Redesigning methodology of educational process, curriculum and institutional arrangements in development and dissemination of knowledge.
- Bring infrastructural improvement.
- Public-private partnership in strategic areas.

Conclusion

Changing realities – Globalisation, competitiveness and the knowledge economy India's transition to a knowledge-based economy requires a new generation of educated and skilled people which can only be supported by a robust New Policy planning in education.

12

Globalisation and Mental Health among the High School Students of Kadapa, Andhra Pradesh

— *Dr. N. Sharon Sucharitha Gold*

Introduction

In this era where globalisation is playing a pivotal role in all orb of human life, it is of utmost importance to explore how it affects the psychological well-being of human beings. Though the process of globalisation in India has long historical antecedents, its intensity is felt more in recent times than ever before with the advent of satellite technology, extensive global markets and movements of people and materials across the globe. Its impact has been an important concern for social scientists and other behavioural scientists. In this regard, the psychological issues related to the globalisation have remained largely unexplored till date. In this context, this paper aims to investigate the mental health conditions among the adolescent students in the age group of 13-16 years studying 9th and 10th classes in Kadapa town, Andhra Pradesh. Furthermore, this paper attempts to find out if such relationship exists between processes of globalisation and mental health. The data collected from 537 students about the selected factors such as watching on television, use of internet, social media, going on foreign trips as well as individual experiences with relatives and friends living abroad that constitute a segment of globalisation process, and social factors such as family background are correlated with the mental health scale. The scale developed by Dr. Robert L. Spitzer and his colleagues of Department of Psychiatry, Columbia University, USA is used for this purpose.

The study has found that sixty percent of the students do show symptoms of depression, which is an important component of mental health, but in majority cases (34.1 percent) it is only a minimum depression. Three factors are found to have some statistically significant association with depression, i.e., gender, age and globalisation. In case of globalisation however, association is found to be significant when internet usage is not taken into consideration.

Concepts Employed – Working Definitions

Globalisation: It has a variety of meanings; the general understanding is that it is the process of coming together of individuals, nations and communities on a worldwide level mostly on an economic front where the world itself becomes a market place (Guttal, 2007). And in this perspective, the International Monetary Fund has identified four basic aspects: migration of people, movement of machinery and technology, capital and investment movement and dissemination of knowledge (International Monetary Fund, 2000).

Mental Health: Newman (2017) states, according to Medilexicon's medical dictionary, mental health is:

> Emotional, behavioural, and social maturity or normality; the absence of a mental or behavioural disorder; a state of psychological well-being in which one has achieved a satisfactory integration of one's instinctual drives acceptable to both oneself and one's social milieu; an appropriate balance of love, work, and leisure pursuits. (quoted by Prayoga, 2019)

WHO (World Health Organisation) states about mental health as:

> Mental health is more than the mere lack of mental disorders. The positive dimension of mental health is stressed in WHO's definition of health as contained in its constitution: "Health is a state of complete physical, mental and social well-being and not merely the absence of disease or infirmity." Concepts of mental health include subjective well-being, perceived self-efficacy, autonomy, competence, intergenerational dependence and recognition of the ability to realise one's intellectual and emotional potential. It has also been defined as a state of well-being whereby individuals recognize their abilities, are able to cope with the normal stresses of life, work productively and fruitfully, and make a contribution to their communities (WHO 2003:7).

Multiple factors are responsible for mental health disorders which can be from biological, psychological and socio-cultural background causing a variety of forms with overlapping symptoms. Anxiety disorders, mood disorders, psychotic disorders, personality disorders, impulse control disorders are some of the categories of mental disorders. Depressive disorder is one of the common types among the various mood disorders (Gibson, 1989). Depression is a condition where there are persistent feelings of sadness and hopelessness. The affected individual has marked lack of interest in the things once enjoyed. There are disturbances in eating and sleep patterns. The overall social functioning of the individual is affected. According to the Diagnostic and Statistical Manual of Mental Disorders (Fifth edition), the symptoms must be persistent for more than two weeks in order to be considered as depression (American Psychological Association, 2013). Emil Kraeplin, a German psychiatrist is the one who first used the term 'depression'. It is derived from the Latin verb 'deprimere', meaning 'to press down' or 'bring down' in spirit, referring to different types of melancholia as depressive states (Davison, K, 2006). Meyer worked on emphasising the reactions of a person's life influenced by a mixed social and biological framework in causing the melancholic conditions and hence argued that 'depression' is the term to be used (Lewis, 1934).

Mental Health – A World Scenario: According to WHO, neuropsychiatric conditions account for 13% of Disability Adjusted Life Years (DALYs) while like diabetes is only 1% and others injuries (12%), HIV (6%) etc. And Yearly Lived with Disability (YLD) is 33% of Neuropsychiatric disorders and others constitute the rest (WHO 2003:8). Ages 15-24 are the most important in one's life as these form the crucial period in terms of socio-economic integration. In this regard it may be noted that according to the Mental Health Foundation, UK,

> In 2010, mental health and behavioural problems (e.g. depression, anxiety and drug use) were reported to be the primary drivers of disability worldwide, causing over 40 million years of disability in 20 to 29-year-olds (Mental Health Foundation 2015:17).

Referring to the works of Kessler et al., (2005) and Patel, Flisher et al., (2007) the United Nations has stated that 20 percent the world youth (aged between 15-24) experience some form of mental-health condition (2014:5-6). In UK nearly 1 in 5 people aged 16 and older showed symptoms of anxiety or depression in 2013 (Mental Health Foundation 2015: 5-6),and in the USA, 7 percent of adults suffer from major form of depression in a year and children upto 3 percent and adolescents 8 suffer from the depression (Agency for Healthcare Research and Quality, 2009). The Mental Health Foundation's 2016 reports:

> According to the 2013 Global Burden of Disease study, the predominant mental health problem worldwide is depression, followed by anxiety, schizophrenia and bipolar disorder...

> In 2013, depression was the second leading cause of years lived with disability worldwide, behind lower back pain. In 26 countries, depression was the primary driver of disability(Mental Health Foundation 2016:13).

In this background let me briefly review the literature available on mental health studies outside India and within India.

Review of Literature

Mental Health Studies outside India: As the use of social networking sites increased, there is observed less person to person interaction on a personal level but more connectivity on digital front. It is observed that American adolescents aged 13-18 spent lesser time with peers, partying as well as person to person interaction compared to the previous generations. Increased loneliness is observed among those who had more digital interaction compared to the real-world people interaction (Twenge et al., 2019). As the time spent on social media increased, there is increase in depressive symptoms among adolescents. The causes of depression being decreased self-esteem, decreased sleep levels and increased online harassment (Kelly et al., 2019). Another major factor behind the occurrence of mental health problems is the lack of proper interpersonal relationships in the schools (Li et al., 2020). Another pressing concern related to the presence of mental health disturbances is the occurrence of psychosocial stressors, which is really pitiable as the child or adolescent is directly affected by the circumstances for which they are not responsible in any way. The common psychosocial stressors are, experiences of violence, family history of affective disorders, mothers who were psychologically disturbed either during/after pregnancy etc. (Piechaczek et al., 2020).

Mental Health Studies in India: In developing countries as well as underdeveloped countries, social development is lacking due to poverty and unemployment which influence the psychosocial well-being of an individual (Stout, 2009). India has a population of 1.236 billion out of which more than 434 million are children and adolescents, every 5th person an adolescent between 10-19 years (Census of India, 2011). According to the National Mental Health Survey 2016, nearly 7.6% of Indian adolescents between age groups 13-17 ail with mental disorders without any differentiation between the genders (Govt. of India, 2016). A meta-analysis among Indian adolescent students has shown that mental ill-health is prevalent at a rate of 6.3% of community samples and 23.3% of school samples. It is also found that mortality of such students is mostly due to suicide (Patel V et al., 2012). There has been a steady level of increase in the levels of depression over decades even in India at par with the rest of the world. The recorded increase in the number of cases today might be due to increase in awareness in rural India regarding mental health. Apart from this, in the Indian scenario family economy plays a very major role in everything.

Mental Health and Globalisation: Migration of people across the globe can be termed as cultural flows. This is causing a new problem for the psychologists across the world as they need to understand the cultural background of the individuals of different ethnic groups who are referred to them for psychological services (Tribe and Melluish, 2014). On individual front, even if there is no physical migration or travel of people from one country to another, we can notice that the internet and technology of the present day are a source of increased intercultural encounters as well as contacts enhancing the exchange of cross-cultural ideas and practices. This in some societies may be of concern as it is responsible for xenophobic anxiety of being culturally colonised by the economic powers and losing cultural identity due to infiltration of materialistic and capitalistic culture (Leung, 2013). Mood disorders are becoming more prevalent globally among the children and adolescents especially in the recent 10 years (Rosenberg, 2019). This increase in mental health issues seems concurrent with increased smart phone ownership and internet usage according to some researchers.

Some studies like that of Kraut et al., (1998), Takahira et al., (2008), Rosen et al., (2013) and so on show that the excessive use of internet and social media such as Facebook are associated with increased depression. They decreased communication with family members in the household, declined in the size of the social circle, increased aggression and preference for internet communication tended to use the internet more. But other studies have indicated quite opposite trend of the relationship between higher level engagement with social media and psychological wellbeing. Studies carried out by Pantic et al., (2014) and Jelenchick et al., (2012) show that there is a significant positive statistical correlation between depressive symptoms and time spent on but there is no positive correlation between depressive symptoms and time spent watching television. There is no evidence supporting a relationship between social media use and clinical depression.

Teenagers involved in excess use of social media are less engaged in face to face human interaction but are actively involved in texting and chatting via social media. Cyber bullying, depression and suicidal tendencies are said to stem from excessive use of social media (Twenge et al, 2019). Surveys show that 10-20% of children and adolescents worldwide present with mental health problems. The problems start in the adolescent period and if left untreated, will continue to progress throughout life having an impact on various areas such as education, career, family etc. Depression is a major mental health problem seen today among adolescents and young adults. It is said to be the 4th and anxiety the 9th leading cause of illness and disability of adolescents across the globe (WHO fact sheets). Both these are contributors of social withdrawal which in turn is a prime factor in causing suicides.

The review of literature in India, in this context, indicates that no survey or extensive or intensive study has been undertaken so far with regard to the relationship between mental health and globalisation. The present research is an explorative study basically aiming at the extent of prevalence of depression among the young students and find out possible causative factors including globalisation.

The Study

The present study is conducted among the adolescent students of Kadapa town which is the district headquarter of Y.S.R. District in Andhra Pradesh state having a population of 3,44,893 according to the 2011 Census. The hinterland of the town is essentially rural lacking any industry worth its name. When the Nizam of Hyderabad ceded Anantapur district along with Cuddapah to the British in 1800 AD; the senior collector of the British East India Company, Sir Thomas Munro became its first district collector and he carved out separate Cuddapah district in 1807 AD and made Cuddapah town as its headquarter since 1812 AD under Madras Presidency for which Sir Thomas Munro became its Governor later on. In 1881 AD, there were 182 educational institutions. But now there is a university in Kadapa (spelling changed from Cuddapah to Kadapa) town, and there are more than 50 private Engineering colleges, one medical and a dental college run by the government, 151 colleges of government and several private degree colleges, more than 300 schools of government/local body and several private schools. Thus, there is an enormous growth of education in the town and the district. The literacy rate of 10.08 percent in 1911 has increased to 67.88 percent by 2011.

Objectives

- To find out the mental health condition of the adolescents in Kadapa town with regard to depression.

- To identify gender differences (if any) pertaining to the mental health of the adolescent students of Kadapa.
- To find out if there is a relationship between technological globalisation in the form of using social media sites and internet and occurrence of depression among the students.
- To find out if there is a relationship between international travel and cross-border familial presence and depression among adolescent students of Kadapa.

Methodology

No hypothesis is proposed here as it is an explorative study. A short survey has been conducted among the students of high schools located in Kadapa town during January 2020.The technique of self-assessment has been used with the help of a structured schedule that can be self-administered for this purpose incorporating a scale to measure the depression.

Sample Drawn

Out of a total of 109 high schools of English (62), Telugu (41), Oriental (2) and Urdu (4) media located in rural and urban areas of the city, 13 English medium, 4 Telugu medium and one Urdu medium schools are selected randomly using Kendall and Smith's Random Tables. Data from 537 students from both the genders of these 18 schools in total are collected. Attempt has been made for equal representation of the genders among approximately 30 students from class IX and X in each of these schools.

Tool for Measuring Depression

The general PHQ (Patient Health Questionnaire) has 8 modules for measuring anxiety disorders, major depressive disorders, anorexia nervosa, bulimia, alcoholism etc., and is developed by Dr. Robert J. Spitzer, Dr. Janet B.W. Williams, Dr. Kurt Kroenke, and colleagues from Columbia University. The PHQ-9 is the 9-item module used for measuring depression. The score of the PHQ 9 can vary from 0-27. 0-4 being no depression, 5-9 mild, 10-14 moderate, 15-19 moderately severe and 20-27 severe depression (Kroenke, 2002). If 5 of the 9 symptoms are present for most of the day or nearly every day for a continuous period of two weeks, and the questions 1 and 2 are marked as having little pleasure or interest in doing this, it can be likely major depressive disorder according to DSM-5. PHQ 9 may be used to diagnose major depressive syndrome but for diagnosing major depressive disorder, other clinical methods along with history are to be considered according to DSM-5.

There was a specificity of 94% and sensitivity of 64% in screening for major and minor depression in a study validating the PHQ 9 questionnaire in patients with Diabetes Mellitus in non-communicable disease clinics in Mawai (Udedi et al., 2014). PHQ 9 showed moderate to strong correlation with WHO 5, HADS depression, HADS anxiety and the GAD-7 which shows that there is a convergent validity in measuring depression (Maroufizadeh et al., 2019). In the study. The PHQ-9 Validity of a Brief Depression Severity Measure by Kroenke et al (2001) it is observed that the internal reliability of the PHQ 9 has a Cronbach's á of 0.89 which is remarkable. The test retest reliability also is shown to be excellent. The correlation between the PHQ 9 completed by the patient and telephonic administration by MPH within 48 hrs is found to be 0.84. The time taken to administer and review the responses also is shown to be brief which is advantageous to clinicians. These advantages make PHQ 9 a very valuable tool in diagnosing and assessing the severity of depressive disorders.

Socio-demographic characteristics of the sample

The sample of 537 consists 277 girls and 260 boys. Table 1 shows the sample distribution by age and gender.

Table 1: Sample Distribution by Age and Gender

Sl. No.	*Age*	*Gender*		*Total*
		Boy	*Girl*	
1.	< 14 years	13 (33.3.0 %) 5.00 %	26 (66.7%) 9.40 %	39 (100.0 %) 7.30 %
2.	14-16 years	228 (47.80 %) 87.70 %	249 (52,20 %) 89.90%	477 (100.0%) 88.80%
3.	> 16 years	19 (90.50 %) 7.30 %	2 (9.50 %) 0.70%	21 (100.0 %) 3.90 %
4.	Total	260 (48.40 %) 100.00%	277 (51.60 %) 100.00%	537 (100.0%) 100.0%

The sample distribution shows almost equal distribution of genders. A major portion of the sample is between 14-16 years of age. The representation of girls below 14 years is greater than the boys in that age. The percentage of boys above 16 years is greater than the girls given the fact that the girls dropout of school after menarche.

The characteristics of the sample with respect to community and the medium of study show that majority of the participants of the SC community study in schools where Telugu is the medium of instruction sometimes exclusively and where both the mediums are offered. Majority of the students belonging to OC and OBC category are in English Medium Schools.

Table 2: Sample Distribution by Social Background and Medium of Instruction

Sl. No.	*Medium*	*Background*				*Total*
		OC	*OBC*	*SC*	*ST*	
1.	Telugu[1] and Urdu[2]	12 (8.30%) 7.10%	56 (38.90%) 23.40%	70 (48.60%) 61.90%	6 (4.20%) 40.00%	144 (100.0%) 26.80%
2.	English[3]	158 (40.20%) 92.90%	183 (46.60%) 76.60%	43 (10.90%) 38.10%	9 (2.30%) 60.00%	393 (100.00%) 73.20%
3.	Total	170 (31.70%) 100.0%	239 (44.50%) 100.00%	113 (21.00%) 100.00%	15 (2.80%) 100.00%	537 (100.00%) 100.00%

Table 3. Sample Distribution by Religion and Literacy of the Family

Sl. No.	*Family*	*Religion*				*Total*
		Hindu	*Muslim*	*Christian*	*Any Other*	
1.	Illiterate family	38 (69.1%) 10.8%	14 (25.5%) 11.2%	3 (5.5%) 5.9%	0 (0.0%) 0.0%	55 (100.0%) 10.2%
2.	Semi-literate family	65 (63.7%) 18.4%	27 (26.5%) 21.6%	9 (8.8%) 17.6%	1 (1.0%) 12.5%	102 (100.0%) 19.0%
3.	Literate family	250 (65.8%) 70.8%	84 (22.1%) 67.2%	39 (10.3%) 76.5%	7 (1.8%) 87.5%	380 (100.0%) 70.8%
4.	Total	353 (65.7%) 100.0%	125 (23.3%) 100.0%	51 (9.5%) 100.0%	8 (1.5%) 100.0%	537 (100.0%) 100.0%

Illiterate family= Both the parents illiterate; Semi-literate Family = One parent illiterate and the other literate; Literate = Both the parents literate.

Table 3 reveals that 89.8 % of the families is literate and their percentage is highest among the Christians compared to the families of other religions. A slightly higher percentage of illiterate is found among the Muslims. Further, the percentage of semi-literate families is relatively higher than others among the Muslims. The percentage of illiterate families is least among the Christian families.

Major Findings

The Table 4 reveals the statistical significance of depression with reference to various independent variables considered in this study. The statistical tests carried out include t-test, ANOVA and Pearson's correlation.

The t-tests have been done to compare the difference in the mean of depression occurring between the genders and it is significant with one gender having a mean depression greater than the other. When the means of depression occurring in local and urban residents, have been examined using the t-test, it is found that there is no significant difference between the means. The means of different socio-economic backgrounds and religions are compared with regard to depression using ANOVA; these are found to be not significant. Pearson's correlation, however, is seen significant with respect to age as well as globalisation but not parental education.

Table 4: Statistical Significance between Independent Variables and Depression

Sl. No	*Variable*	*Statistical Tests*			*Significance*
		t-test	*ANOVA*	*Pearson's Correlation*	
1.	Gender	t = 3.183 p = 0.002	-	-	Significant
2.	Age	-	-	r = 0.169	Significant at p = 0.01level
3.	Socio-economic background	-	p = 0.190	-	Not Significant
4.	Religion	-	p = 0.737	-	Not Significant
5.	Parental Education	-	-	r = 0.021	Not Significant
6.	Residence	t = 0.529 p = 0.597	-	-	Not Significant
7.	Globalization without internet use	-	-	r = .116	Significant at 0.01 level
8.	Globalization with internet use	-	-		Not Significant

Globalisation here means 'technological globalisation' as stated above. Now there is a need for examining the statistical significance between globalisation and various independent variables such as family member (s) and friends living abroad, those visited abroad, wish to study abroad, using internet at home.

The Table 5 makes it clear that all the independent variables under globalisation have statistical significance which needs further explanation for collectively they do not show any significant correlation with depression.

Table 5: Statistical Significance of different Variables which are part of Technological Globalisation and Depression

Sl. No	Variable	Statistical Tests			Significance
		t-test	ANOVA	Pearson's Correlation	
1.	Family Abroad	t =19.402 p <0.001	-	-	Significant
2.	Friends Abroad	t =19.667 p <0.001	-	-	Significant
3.	Visit Abroad	t=16.679 p<0.001	-	-	Significant
4.	Wish to Study abroad	t=17.491 p<0.001	-	-	Significant
5.	Internet usage from home	-	-	r =0.775	Significant at p = 0.01 level
6.	Internet usage from cafe	-	-	r =0.752	Significant at p = 0.01 level

Discussion on Depression, Gender, Age and Globalisation

The present discussion is confined to only to Depression and Globalisation and only two variables i.e., gender and social background.

Gender: Table 6 indicates there is a significant difference between the degree of depression among the genders. However, it is not clear whether there is a statistical correlation between depression and genders. Further analysis of the data in this regard is presented in Tables 6, 7 and 8. It may be inferred from the Table 6 that 40% of the respondents have no depression out of which girls with no depression are more in number. We can observe that with the increase in the severity of depression, there is increase in the percentage of presence of depression among the boys and decrease in the

Table 6: Degree of Depression by Gender

Sl. No.	Gender	Degree of Depression					Total
		No Depression	Minimum Depression	Mild Depression	Moderate Depression	Severe Depression	
1.	Boys	90 (34.6%) 16.8%	87 (33.5%) 16.2%	60 (23.1%) 11.2%	18 (6.9%) 3.4%	5 (1.9%) 0.9%	260 (100.0%) 48.4%
2.	Girls	125 (45.1%) 23.3%	96 (34.7%) 17.9%	40 (14.4%) 7.4%	12 (4.3%) 2.2%	4 (1.4%) 0.7%	277 (100.0%) 51.6%
3.	Total	215 (40.0%) 40.0%	183 (34.1%) 34.1%	100 (18.6%) 18.6%	30 (5.6%) 5.6%	9 (1.7%) 1.7%	537 (100.0%) 100.0%

same among the girls. However, minimum depression is slightly higher in case of the girls compared to the boys.

The details of the t-test show that the t-value is significant at t=3.062 and at p=0.05 level. The results of the t-test are presented in Table 7.

Table 7: 't' test for Gender and Degree of Depression

		Levene's Test for Equality of Variances		*t-test for Equality of Means*						
		F	*Sig.*	*T*	*Df*	*Sig. (2-tailed)*	*Mean Difference*	*Std. Error Difference*	*95% Confidence Interval of the Difference*	
									Lower	Upper
Degree of Depression	Equal variances assumed	1.366	0.243	3.069	535	0.002	0.258	0.084	0.093	0.423
	Equal variances not assumed			3.062	524.094	0.002	0.258	0.084	0.092	0.423

Age

Table 8 shows clearly that there is a relationship between the age of the respondent and the depression. Most likely that as the children grow into adolescence their responsibilities also increase particularly in poorer families as they are expected to contribute to the family income and lessen the burden of the parents.

Table 8: Pearson Correlation between Age and Depression

		Age	*Depression*
Age	Pearson Correlation	1	.169**
	Sig. (2-tailed)		.000
	N	537	537
Depression	Pearson Correlation	.169**	1
	Sig. (2-tailed)	.000	
	N	537	537

** Correlation is significant at the 0.01 level (2-tailed)

Given the cultural background of the respondents, grown up children have to manage with their studies and domestic responsibilities. But, they need more time for studies as they move up to higher classes. At the same time, the expectations from the adolescent children are increased from the parents. Further, the students of higher classes get social as well as domestic pressure to study well in the competitive world for getting good marks which would guarantee them admission into good institutions so that admission into professional courses would be made easy. Adolescents are subjected to peer pressure as well as physiological changes which occur particularly at this period of life. It is at this age that how others perceive them becomes a major factor. All these are responsible for increased stress which is a direct cause of depression. This is evident from the Table 9 where we can notice the increase of depression from 14 years onwards.

Table 9: Distribution by Age and Degree of Depression

Sl. No.	*Age*	*Degree of Depression*						*Grand Total*
		No	*Minimum*	*Mild*	*Moderate*	*Severe*	*Total Depression*	
1.	12	1 0.5%	1 0.5%	0 0.0%	0 0.0%	0 0.0%	1 0.3%	2 0.4%
2.	13	19 8.8%	10 5.5%	7 7.0%	0 0.0%	0 0.0%	17 5.3%	36 6.7%
3.	14	84 39.1%	72 39.3%	21 21.0%	7 23.3%	1 11.1%	101 31.4%	185 34.5%
4.	15	81 37.7%	72 39.3%	47 47.0%	12 40.0%	6 66.7%	137 42.5%	218 40.6%
5.	16	26 12.1%	22 12.0%	15 15.0%	9 30.0%	2 22.2%	48 14.9%	74 13.8%
6.	17	3 1.4%	3 1.6%	6 6.0%	2 6.7%	0 0.0%	11 3.4%	14 2.6%
7.	18	1 0.5%	2 1.1%	3 3.0%	0 0.0%	0 0.0%	5 1.6%	6 1.1%
8.	20	0 0.0%	1 0.5%	1 1.0%	0 0.0%	0 0.0%	2 0.6%	2 0.4%
9.	Total	215 100.0%	183 100.0%	100 100.0%	30 100.0%	9 100.0%	322 100.0%	537 100.0%

Globalisation: There is hardly any single measuring scale for measuring globalisation in a given place or community. But for the present, as mentioned earlier the items of technological globalisation, using internet, television, having friends and family abroad as well as foreign trips as accesses to being in contact with the rest of the world are collectively considered for this purpose. It is found that globalisation and depression are correlated when the Pearson's correlation test is performed. Table 10 gives the details of the Pearson's Test. It is interesting to note that there is a significant correlation between age and globalisation as the Table 11 shows.

Table 10: Pearson's Correlation test for Globalisation and Depression

		Globalisation	*Depression*
Globalisation	Pearson Correlation	1	.116**
	Sig. (2-tailed)		.007
	N	537	537
Depression	Pearson Correlation	.116**	1
	Sig. (2-tailed)	.007	
	N	537	537

** Correlation is significant at the 0.01 level (2-tailed).

Table 11: Pearson Correlation between Age and Globalisation

		Globalisation	*Age*
Globalisation	Pearson Correlation	1	-.116**
	Sig. (2-tailed)		.007
	N	536	536
Age	Pearson Correlation	-.116**	1
	Sig. (2-tailed)	.007	
	N	536	537

** Correlation is significant at the 0.01 level (2-tailed).

This confirms the fact that age has an association with the depression for the age has an association with globalisation too which in turn has also an association with depression.

The globalisation has an indirect association with the social background regarding depression unlike the age and depression. The Table 4 shows there is no significant association between social background and depression. However, social background has significant association with globalisation (as shown in Table 12) which has an association with depression (see Table 4). This needs to be explained.

The social background is important in Indian societal context as hierarchical system is also enmeshed with economic status as well as social value. Socially and economically better off families are more exposed to the world outside India and they have strong desire to get benefits out of this. Globalisation in a way enhances the social value of the group, family and individual. On the negative side it could also put pressure on the individual to achieve such values in the competitive world. The Table 12 shows an association between social background and globalisation.

Table 12: ANOVA for social background and globalisation

Technological Globalisation					
	Sum of Squares	*df*	*Mean Square*	*F*	*Sig.*
Between Groups	3097.726	3	1032.575	6.113	.000
Within Groups	89868.272	532	168.925		
Total	92965.998	535			

Thus, it is important to note that as depression is not directly related to social background, but it seems there is a significant association between these two variables through globalisation.

Discussion

The data of the present study show that sixty percent of the adolescent population of Kadapa town appear to be on the higher side as the above mentioned world wide data show; the UN points out 20 percent of youth suffer from depression. The difference perhaps could be due to sampling error. In fact, in the present study, only 25.9 percent of the sample show symptoms ranging from mild to severe form of depression which is closer to other studies. Patel et al., (2012) show 23.3 percent depression in the school data as mentioned earlier.

There is gender difference in having signs and symptoms of depression and there is also a difference in terms of their means. This is similar to other studies which do show a difference between the genders as in case of the study of Kelly et al., (2019). It is interesting to note that mild depression is more common in females and percentage of females affected with moderate and severe depression is low, but it is opposite in the case of males. More male adolescents have presented with severe and moderate forms of depression than the mild form. This is not consistent with an earlier study carried among young professional students of the same area where there is no gender difference (Gold, 2019). This is perhaps due to the fact these professional students are free from the social and domestic pressures unlike others. The present data indicate that though there is occurrence of depression among both the genders, the intensity of depression is varying. It could be due to the fact that young boys perceive or experience stress or problems differently than the females or the fact that females are more prone to sharing stressful facts resulting in lesser levels of depression in this area or there is higher demand from the boys than the girls according to cultural ethos; it needs further research. There is no significant difference among the genders in exposure to globalisation by International travel or technology.

There is also a significant correlation between the age and globalisation. The increased level of depression with age needs to be explored in detail as there are again a number of intermediate factors which play a role such as socio-economic status of the family, cultural boundaries and obligations, academic stress, interpersonal relationships, etc (Li et al., 2020).

India being a country where caste system is the backbone of the cultural setting, differences in the different socioeconomic background also are examined. It is found that the analysis of variance shows no significance between the means of adolescents of different social backgrounds with respect to depression, however, there is a significant difference in the globalisation. Thus, there is indirect association between social background and depression. It is also found that the level of parental education has a significant Pearson's correlation with respect to globalisation. This could be due to the fact that people of certain social backgrounds are more educated than the others resulting in increased job opportunities and in turn more income, resulting in higher economic status. The children of such parents have greater opportunities of being exposed to globalisation. This is supportive of earlier studies which showed that economic background and parental education did play a role in affecting adolescent mental health (for example, Reiss, 2019). As there is vast diversity in religion as well as area of residence, both these were considered and examined and found that neither of them has any significance in depression as well as globalisation.

The different variables which are grouped together for technological globalisation are tested independently for depression. Each variable reveals a significant statistical test result as shown in Table 5. Having friends and family abroad shows a significant difference in the means of having depression. It is found to be the same with visits abroad and desire to study abroad. This might be due to the fact that economic conditions of these adolescents might not have been as good and on the other it may also put pressure on them to achieve the same. This is consistent with the finding regarding parental education and exposure to globalisation. However, when all the variables combined together as technological globalisation are tested for correlation with depression, it is found that there is no significant correlation. In fact, a study like that of Keles, McCarae and Grealish (2020) shows an association of internet use and depression among the youth. It is a review study systematically carried out on internet sources about the subject of social media and depression among youth. It has found 13 eligible studies and the findings reveal significant relationship on the four domains of social media: time spent, activity, investment and addiction. All domains are correlated with depression, anxiety and psychological distress. My earlier study among the students pursing medicine and dentistry in the same town also shows a correlation between using social networks and depression (Gold, 2019).

Conclusion

The study supports the observation by both Indian and International studies that adolescents do have mental health issues which need to be addressed. It specifically attempts to find out the impact of globalisation on the mental health of the adolescents in a small town. Since globalisation is a wide phenomenon, and as there is no any measuring scale for this purpose, the study considered only technological globalisation which is improvised for the present. It includes television and internet usage as well as travelling abroad for economic and educational purpose. It is found that more than half of the sample shows signs of depression. Though there is no difference between the genders in the occurrence of depression, there is difference in the severity. Besides gender, age also seems to have an association with depression. It is found that as age increases, there is increased technological globalisation as well as increased depression. This can be due to the fact that as age increases, there is more exposure to the outside world using internet or social media sites etc., which create a desire to 'fit in' with the higher economic class or increased aspirations causing pressure which may lead to depression. With regard to the association between globalisation and depression, there seems to be an association when internet use not included. Depression and stress have a number of etiological factors which may be responsible for the occurrence. It is concluded that though significant relationships between age, gender, globalisation and depression are found, this is an area which requires a further detailed study as the age we live in is dominated by technology and the world has become much smaller.

References

American Psychiatric Association (2013). *Diagnostic and Statistical Manual of Mental Disorders, Fifth Edition (DSM-5).*

Agency for Healthcare Research and Quality (2009). Mental Health Research Findings. AHRQPub. No. 09-P011, Rockville.https://www.ahrq.gov/sites/default/files/publications/files/mentalhth.pdf accessed on 9.4.2020.

Davison, K (2006). "Historical aspects of mood disorders". *Psychiatry*. 5 (4): 115–18. doi:10.1383/psyt.2006.5.4.115. accessed on 11.3.2020

Gold, N. S. Sucharitha (2019). Social Networking Systems - Mental Health and Depression: A Study among Medical and Dental Students.

Gibson, William (1989). Neuromancer. New York: Berkley Publishing Group. p. 128.

Guttal, Shalmali, (2007). "Globalisation". *Development in Practice*. Vol.17 (4/5):523–531. doi:10.1080/09614520701469492. ISSN 0961-4524. JSTOR 25548249.

International Monetary Fund (2000). *"Globalisation: Threat or Opportunity?"* World Health Organisation (2014, August) "Mental health: strengthening our response" Adolescents and Mental Health.

Jelenchick, L.A,Eickhoff J. C, Moreno, M. A. (2013). Facebook depression?" social networking site use and depression in older adolescents. *J Adolesc Health*; 52(1):128-30. doi: 10.1016/j.jadohealth.2012.05.008. Epub 2012 Jul 7.

Keles, Betul, Niall McCrae and Annmarie Grealish (2020). A systematic review: the influence of social media on depression, anxiety and psychological distress in adolescents. *Journal International Journal of Adolescence and Youth.* Volume 25.1. pp. 79-93. https://doi.org/10.1080/02673843.2019.1590851 accessed on 2.2.2020.

Kelly,Yvonne et al. (2018). Social Media Use and Adolescent Mental Health, *UK Millennium Cohort* V. 6: 59-68. https://doi.org/10.1016/j.eclinm.2018.12.005 accessed on 4.1.2019

Kessler, R., P. Berglund, O. Demler, R. Jin and E. E. Walters (2005). Lifetime prevalence and age-of-onset distributions of DSM-IV disorders in the National Comorbidity Survey Replication. *Archive of General Psychiatry*, Vol. 62:593-602.

Kraut, R., Patterson, M., Lundmark, V., Kiesler, S., Mukophadhyay, T., & Scherlis, W. (1998). Internet paradox: A social technology that reduces social involvement and psychological well-being? *American Psychologist, 53*(9), 1017–1031. https://doi.org/10.1037/0003-066X.53.9.1017

Kroenke, K, Spitzer, RL, Williams, JBW (2001). The PHQ-9 Validity of a Brief Depression Severity Measure. *J G Intern Med* V:16(9): 606–613.doi: 10.1046/j.1525-1497.2001.016009606.x

Kroenke, K; Spitzer, R.L. (2002). "The PHQ-9: A New Depression Diagnostic and Severity Measure" (PDF). *Psychiatric Annals*. **32** (9): 1–7. doi:10.3928/0048-5713-20020901-06.

Leung, L (2013) Generational differences in content generation in social media: The roles of the gratifications sought and of narcissism. *Computers in Human Behavior*.Volume 29, Issue 3, pp. 997-1006. https://doi.org/10.1016/j.chb.2012.12.028

Lewis, AJ (1934). "Melancholia: A historical review". *Journal of Mental Science*. **80** (328): 1–42. doi:10.1192/bjp.80.328.1

Li, Jiyau et al., (2020). Mental health problems and associated school interpersonal relationships among adolescents in China: a cross-sectional study, *Child and Adolescent Psychiatry and Mental Health,* V. 14: No. 12.

Maroufizadeh, Saman et al.,(2019). The reliability and validity of the Patient Health Questionnaire-9 (PHQ-9) and PHQ-2 in patients with infertility. *Reprod Health*; 16: 137.doi: 10.1186/s12978-019-0802-x

Mental Health Foundation (2015). Fundamental Facts About Mental Health 2015. https://www.mentalhealth.org.uk/sites/default/files/fundamental-facts-15.pdf accessed on 9.4.2020

Mental Health Foundation (2016). Fundamental Facts About Mental Health 2016. https://www.mentalhealth.org.uk/sites/default/files/fundamental-facts-about-mental-health-2016.pdf accessed on 10.4.2020

Newman, Tim (2017). What is Mental Health? In Medical NewsToday. Reviewed by Timothy J. Legg. https://www.medicalnewstoday.com/articles/154543 accessed on 31.03.2020.

Pantic, Igore et al., (2014). Online Social Networking and Mental Health. Cyberpsychology, Behavior, and Social Networking, Vol. 17, No. 10 https://doi.org/10.1089/cyber.2014.0070

Patel, V, Ramasundarahettige C, Vijayakumar, L, Thakur, JS, Gajalakshmi, V, Gururaj G, Suraweera, W, Jha, P (2012). Suicide mortality in India: a nationally representative survey. *Lancet* 379:2343–2351.

Patel, V., A., J. Flisher, S. Hetrick and P. McGorry (2007). Mental health of young people: A global public-health challenge. *The Lancet*, Vol. 369, pp. 1302-131.

Piechaczek,Charlotte Elisabeth et al., (2020) Psychosocial stressors and protective factors for major depression in youth: evidence from a case–control study, *Child and Adolescent Psychiatry and Mental Health,* V. 14, No. 6.

Prayoga, Aditya (2019). What is mental health? https://dbtlondon.com/uncategorised/what-is-mental-health/ accessed on 17.4.2020.sa

Reiss Franziska (2019). Socioeconomic status, stressful life situations and mental health problems in children and adolescents: Results of the German BELLA cohort-study. *PLoS One.* 2019; 14(3). doi: 10.1371/journal.pone.0213700.

Rosen, L.D et al., (2013). The Media and Technology Usage and Attitudes Scale: An empirical investigation. Computer Human Behavior.1; 29(6): 2501–2511.PMCID: PMC4338964 NIHMSID: NIHMS658683 PMID: 25722534

Rosenberg, Jamie (2019). Mental Health Issues on the Rise Among Adolescents, Young Adults. The American Journal of Managed Care. In Focus blog. https://www.ajmc.com/focus-of-the-week/mental-health-issues-on-the-rise-among-adolescents-young-adults

Stout, C. E (2009). The Psychological impact of Globalisation. The American Psychological Association.https://www.apa.org/news/press/releases/2009/04/stout

Takahira, Mieko et al. (2008). A panel study with 10- 12 year old children in Japan-DOI: 1504/IJWBC(2008.019191). International Journal of Web based communities 4(3):302-318.

Tribe, Rachel & Steve Melluish (2014). Globalisation, Culture and Mental Health. *International review of Psychiatry.*26(5) DOI: 10.3109/09540261.2014.955086

Twenge, J, Cooper, A, Joiner, T, Duffy, M, Binau, S. Age (2019). Period, and cohort trends in mood disorder indicators and suicide-related outcomes in a nationally representative dataset, 2005-2017. *J Abnorm Psychol*. doi: 10.1037/abn0000410.

Udedi, Michael, Adamson, S. Muula, Robert C. Stewart & Brian, W. Pence (2019). The validity of the patient health Questionnaire-9 to screen for depression in patients with type-2 diabetes mellitus in non-communicable diseases clinics in Malawi, *BMC Psychiatry.* Volume 19, Article Number: 81.

United Nations (2014). Mental Health Matters: Social Inclusion of Youth With Mental Health Conditions. Division for Social Policy and Development Department of Economic and Social Affairs. ST/ESA/352. United Nations Publication. http://undesadspd.org/Youth.aspx accessed on 9.4.2020.

United Nations International Children's Emergency Fund (2013). India: Information by Country. https://www.unicef.org/infobycountry/india_statistics.html.Census of India (2011): http://www.censusindia.gov.in/2011-prov-results/paper2/data_files/ india/Rural_Urban_2011.pdf. accessed on 8.4.2020.

WHO (2003). Investing in Mental Health. Department of Mental Health and Substance Dependence, Noncommunicable Diseases and Mental Health, World Health Organisation: Geneva. https://www.who.int/maternal_child_adolescent/topics/adolescence/mental_health/en/ accessed on 7.4.2020.

13

Globalisation and Culture Change among Marginalised Communities in India: Some Critical Perspectives

— Dr. K. Jose SVD

Introduction

India is a land of cultural diversities since ancient times. Because of global commerce, large scale migration and the ever expanding network of communication, exposure to cultural, ethnic and religious pluralism has become a reality in our land. Our efforts to learn to accept and appreciate diversity and draw out meaning from the multitude of diversities are confronted every day calling for great commitment and perseverance. Yet, in the last one decade and more we have witnessed a drastic change in this scenario. The country was going through turmoil of various sorts. Communal elements have played havoc in the safety and security especially of the minority groups through violence and destruction. This has made the country much polarised with regard to its cultures, languages, people, religions, geographical considerations and government policies. Against this backdrop the theme of globalisation is very relevant.

Today, we live in a world of immense communication technology, global commerce and speedy interaction with people and ideologies. This is an opportunity and a challenge. It is an opportunity because there is a great churning of very vital knowledge taking place and challenge because it opens a huge floodgate of choices which leave one exasperated. This calls for an openness to learn from diversity and encounter various visions and ideologies, cultural pluralism and variety. While everyone welcomes the new opportunities that has emerged out one cannot simply leave a number of negative elements unattended. Therefore, the main task now is to understand, analyze and manage globalisation at best to harness its benefits and keep those negative consequences away (Nayan, 2003).

Ever since the term 'globalisation' appeared for the first time in the second half of twentieth century no other word has meant so many different things to different people and has opened up debates in all spheres, most mentionable are academic, social, political, cultural and economic fronts (Sen, 2005:1). Today, looking at overall health of the economy and growth performance, one opines that India seems to have responded to the concept of globalisation in an enviable way. Certainly, when we consider the immense resource base both natural and human one would even raise the expectations to newer heights. Yet, one would immediately pause a while to ponder whether the effects of globalisation percolated to most of the parts of the country, if not to every nook and corner with special reference to North East India.

Cultural values of a given community are put to test while globalisation is accepted and adopted. On the other hand, a community can also be enriched by globalisation when new ideas and experiences are critically adapted taking into consideration the refinement of the core values of a culture. That is to say globalisation *per se* is not what is good or evil but it has to be considered in the context of a specific community and its accumulated cultural values. Secondly, globalisation is not accepted or rejected merely considering the realm of economic development it offers to the people, because a high income index alone do not contribute to the overall wellbeing of the people in its various ramifications. How has globalisation triggered cultural change in the context of North East India? We shall look at these and other issues in the larger framework of India.

Multicultural Context of India

Indian society is a panorama, which has absorbed diverse languages, cultures, religions and people of different origins at different points of time. However, this society is not simply a conglomeration of various ethnic and regional collectivities, but a synthesis that has made India a unique mosaic of cultures. The Indian ethos has evolved down the centuries, imbibing the cultures of the diverse people of India. This uniqueness of our nation is well recognised by the Indian Constitution. In order to affirm the cultural variety and creativity of this land, it is important to have an in-depth socio-cultural and historical analysis of the present day realities. In India, life has become increasingly multicultural, though far from being infallible. Often they are highly fragile when communal clashes take place and property being destroyed during the time of social tensions. More often than not these tensions are attributed to economic and political reasons. It is important to realise they have been caused by psychological distances between communities and aggravated by cultural differences too (Thio, 1989: 175). Cultures separate people more sharply than political boundaries. That is all the more reason for us to realise that cross-cultural acquaintance with the social institutions, world views, and communication styles of other people is important for persons who intend to make any meaningful engagement in civil society.

Unlike any other time in history, today people of different cultures and continents meet together and live closer at a fast growing pace due to migration, travel and work. We in India belong to a country with over 4000 distinct communities and are being urged forward, pushed around or held back by over 42 political parties that derive strength from regional, caste, ethnic, and cultural loyalties. It can be rightly said that India not only tolerates differences, but protects, fosters and celebrates diversity. This diversity extends to religions, languages, cultural practices, dresses, cuisine, and levels of economic development. One earnestly feels that our reflection and social analysis taking cultural considerations in inter-cultural relationships has been insignificant to say the least. Surely the implications of cultural differences or the need to introduce trans-cultural services did not receive the focus they deserve. Often it is assumed that social groups think and act alike, have similar likes and dislikes and respond to life in more or less the same manner. Yet, nothing could be far from the truth (Menamparampil, 1996:14).

Anthropological knowledge of the people of India reveals that almost all known racial groups have migrated to India at different times with their own language, religion and culture. Since there was plenty of space, they could pass on into the interior without much opposition. The caste system also helped to keep the diverse racial, social and cultural groups apart. In India, multiculturalism is best understood neither as a political doctrine with a programmatic content nor a philosophical school but as a perspective or a way of viewing human life. It has three central insights: first, human beings are culturally embedded in the sense that they grow up and live within a culturally structured world and organise their lives and social relations; second, different cultures represent different systems of meaning and visions of the good life, since each realises a limited range of human capacities and emotions and grasps only a part of the totality of human existence, it needs other cultures to help it understand itself better, and expand its intellectual and moral horizon; and the third, every culture is internally plural reflecting a continuing conversation between its different traditions and strands of thought. This does not mean that it is devoid of coherence and identity, but that its identity is plural, fluid and open. A culture cannot appreciate the value of other unless it appreciates the plurality within itself. A dialogue between cultures requires that each should be willing to open itself and learn from one another.

In India, we see that there are a number of ethnic groups and every ethnic group, be it a racial, a linguistic, a cultural, a religious, or a political one, holds a distinct identity. However, when all these elements stand at loggerheads against one another in their self-interest the entire society remains in chaos. Though, Ethnocentrism is, to some extent, a usual socio-cultural phenomenon that an anthropologist always encounters in the study of other's culture, when it intensifies to an undesirable extent, then one group becomes intolerant to the very existence of another, thereby creating disputes among the groups. This results into conflict and tension between groups. Every ethnic group has its own cultural values, which in turn, is the product of its own ecology, technology, and its subsistence economy.

In this context, Bera (2010) feels that Indian civilisation is characterised with religious diversity. A feeling for the sacredness of life and tolerance for other beliefs make existence of religion in India a welcome reality. This is also based on the evolution of Indian culture and history which is of the fruit of great introspection through the various human sciences like Anthropology, Linguistics, Sociology, Comparative Religion, and Political History and so on. When Tylor devoted his two-volume work on *Primitive Religion* (1877) his purpose was to find out a minimum definition of religion that applies to all religions in different parts of the world and different stages of development. He developed the concept of monotheism from animism in the evolutionary scale and elevated the concept of one God dominating over others. Emile Durkheim's work *The Elementary Forms of Religious Life* (1912) claimed that religion is a collective enterprise that involves a church or community or fellow believers. Some anthropologists have distinguished between two types of religion, a folk religion and an official theological religion (Srinivas, 1952). On the other hand, Bronislaw Kasper Malinowski (1954) asserted that religion gives humans the courage to face challenges for a long duration of time, giving a more positive attitude to life. What is striking about Indian situation is the pluralism affecting every realm of human existence.

Having seen the multicultural context of India we shall now discuss here the issue of globalisation and thereafter the cultural changes caused by these and other factors within the tribal communities of North East India.

Concept of Globalisation

The world events in the past decade have made it clear that we are living in a compressed world. Events in one area of the world, even those that may have appeared to be localised at one point in time, are now echoed repeatedly across the globe. The emerging complex dynamics that connect global and local processes have intensified. In fact, 'globalisation' is not a new process in human history, but something that marks contemporary globalisation as different. Globalisation connotes fundamental social, political, and economic change. The globalisation processes, including neo-liberal economic policies, spread of information and communication technologies, consumption cultures, rapid urbanisation, and transnational migrations, have altered the pattern of human lifestyles and relationships around the globe. The economic and cultural dimensions of globalisation are also partly responsible for increasing social and health problems of individuals and communities (Sarma, 2013). No doubt, globalisation is the expansion and the intensifications of connections and movements of people, goods, capital, ideas, and cultures between countries. It is a process that involves the widening, deepening, speeding up and growing impact of worldwide interconnectedness. While it may be beneficial to world economic development, there is also an equally clear viewpoint that it is a contributing force for an increasing inequality between individuals and nations.

Though many consider globalisation is not a new phenomenon, the intensity and speed with which it interacts and transforms 'simple societies' calls for adequate attention and analysis. Globalisation opens up the floodgates of a multitude of global interactions, ranging from the expansion of cultural influences across borders to the enlargement of economic and business relations throughout the world. For the economist, globalisation is essentially the emergence of a worldwide market. It is a historical process, the result of human innovation and technological progress. It also refers to the increasing integration of economies around the world, particularly through trade and financial flows. For the historian, it is an epoch dominated by global capitalism. Sociologists see globalisation as the celebration of diversity and the convergence of social preferences in matters of lifestyle and social values. To the political scientist, it represents the gradual erosion of State sovereignty. From a multidisciplinary angle, globalisation may be treated as a phenomenon, a philosophy and a process which affect human beings very profoundly (Khan, 2003). There are also broader cultural, political and environmental dimensions of globalisation that are very seldom addressed. While aiming to promote efficiency through competition and the division of labour global markets offer greater opportunity for people to engage with more and larger markets around the world. It means that they can have access to more capital flows, technology, cheaper imports, and larger export markets. But markets do not necessarily ensure that the benefits of increased efficiency are shared by all.

To appreciate this, it is necessary to take a more complex view of the process of globalisation than is often adopted. This more complex and multidimensional conceptualisation views globalisation as a simultaneous and interrelated operating system in the economic, technological, communicational, political and cultural spheres of human life. But the cultural implication, rather less easily accepted by some, is that globalisation involving not the simple enforced distribution of a particular western lifestyle, but a more complicated dissemination of the entire range of institutional features of cultural modernity. And in so far as globalisation distributes the institutional features of modernity across all cultures, globalisation produces 'identity' where none existed. This is the most significant cultural impact of globalisation. Contrary to our thinking, globalisation does not naturally take away our natural tendency to hold fast to our distinct culture and identity. The more our economy globalises the greater importance we do give to our language, culture and cuisine (Naisbitt, 1996). It is our everyday experience that varieties of food items, clothes, medicines, private vehicles and other many consumer items are flooding world markets to cater to every requirement of modern living. Here we would do well to remember that it is increasingly accepted that a cross-cultural involvement with people of various ideologies, communication styles, and religious persuasions pays much dividend for a forward looking community.

Social Sustainability of Globalisation

As years go by there is a shared sense that globalisation is a powerful synergy that has already spread its overarching wings in gently taking away many out of poverty and that, if properly harnessed, could further promote growth and development to the benefit of many more. Yet, for many years people of various categories, for a variety of reasons raised concerns regarding certain effects of globalisation on jobs, wages, and job insecurity. In this context, a number of observers have come to question about the sustainability of globalisation from a social point of view. It is necessary to shed light on the relationship between globalisation on the one hand, and employment, uncertainty and inequality on the other hand. To the extent possible, relevant mechanisms, statistical evidence and policy options have to be formulated to draw pathways for both industrialised *vis-a-vis* developing country perspective.

Globalisation epitomises external influence and in political sphere it stands for spread of democracy, self-rule, civil society and human rights both in individual and collective sense. Therefore, most of the culturally distinct people desirous of protection of identity would take advantage of the global situation and continuously engage in democratic or violent nationalist mobilisation to benefit from the increasing spread of global capital and the urge for the right to self determination. The logic that globalisation transformed the whole world into a supposedly global village / society has paradoxically strengthened the tendency among various peoples towards defining themselves collectively in both primordial and modern nationalist senses. As market is the central institution of globalisation, the people with distinct identities would surely be motivated to obtain a self-ruling space in independent or autonomous nationalist terms so as to get the material benefits and become equal partners in the level playing field of market capitalism. And, the ones with no or amorphous identity will be engaged in constructing a distinct identity to obtain these instrumental and material benefits unleashed by globalisation (Nanda, 2009).

The discussion on globalisation often focus strongly on total employment growth or levels, without considering in any detail whether trade has any implications for structural adjustment. Job turnover and displacements are immediate possible responses to globalisation, when workers may be forced out of jobs. In the longer term, one important implication of globalisation should also be sectoral adjustment in the economy. This is, at least, what traditional trade theory would predict: following an opening up of the economy, some sectors should expand and others contract. There may also be a skill bias, as demand for one type of skill may expand at the expense of another. This calls for a considered opinion on policy implications too. The first policy implication that emerges is that economists and policy-makers need to try and identify the groups of society that win and lose from globalisation. Generally, the high skill *versus* low tech dichotomy has been employed for this, with the latter being the group that may have to expect losses. While we take into account the social sustainability, a new emphasis is being put not only on the question of educational background, but also on the type of tasks an individual performs. To take a simple example, taxi drivers with relatively low educational attainment may not need to fear that their jobs be taken away, while computer programmers with university degrees may see their jobs being relocated, as they can be performed online by similarly skilled people elsewhere.

Globalisation and the North East India

While globalisation has opened the floodgates of free inflow of goods and services, little it has paved the way for the outflow from this region. People have become victims, rather than beneficiaries of globalisation. There is failure on the part of everyone to take advantages of globalisation as number of factors operates retarding proper marketing of indigenous resources. The prevalence of lack of development inadequate governance and prevalence of rampant corruption retard many an initiative by individuals and other organisations. Marketability of indigenous resources, progress and prosperity has become major casualties. Benefits of Government of India's Look East Policy and Thailand's Look West Policy have not trickled down to the common masses, as North East is caught in a myriad of problems. The advocates of globalisation consider it as a wonderful agent of positive change. However, the critics oppose it vociferously calling it an enemy of the underdeveloped economies. There are indicators that globalisation affects the poor though it has in fact extended its hands to poverty reduction (World Bank, 2000). Therefore, globalisation is an ever growing integration of national economies into the international economy through cross-border transactions in goods and services and widespread diffusion of technology. No doubt it has gathered momentum in the last two decades and more.

With the increasing concern of widening of interstate disparities and lack of development, it is highly imperative to assess the effects of globalisation on North East India, a relatively underdeveloped region of the country. It is pertinent to raise the questions: has the region been able to gain from the benefits of globalisation? What are the major issues and challenges confronting or likely to confront in the coming years? What are the unexplored opportunities that can be harnessed? This would require an examination, an examination of the prevalent scenario of the region in the pre and post-globalisation period. In any case, it is observed that globalisation leaves the youth of North East India confused as they encounter new goods and services they are eager to buy paying even a huge price. They are in danger of being swept away by the whirlwind of change and globalisation. However, there is a need to keep some balance, the important thing while changing they should be guided to keep the core values of their culture. Otherwise they will lose their identity with no foothold on the ground. That will make them aliens in their own land, uprooted from the mores of their ancestors. This exactly is taking place among the endangered cultures in North East India as well.

In North East India the tribal societies have experienced radical transformations during a short period of time. They have moved from the preliterate to a modern society, from an animistic belief system to other complex systems of religions, from community oriented social practices to self-centered individualism, or in other words from customary practices to modern and postmodern conditions, the societies have undergone radical transformations. So here we shall delve at some length on tribal systems and see how they impact globalisation and lead to culture change.

Tribal Systems and Globalisation

Tribal systems are most popularly known as indigenous systems and their culture, traditions, social practices, occupational pattern and so forth, grow and get strengthened from their own experiences. But once the outside elements with cultural diversity start penetrating into the tribal system, especially after the influence of neo-liberalisation processes, it undergoes tremendous change both from within and outside.

When we speak of cultural diversity it is usually used to a society with people of different ethnic roots that occur in their language, clothing, art and other traditional practices that are similar or substantially different from group to group. There are also traditional practices which are highly valued and received with great admiration among the people of an ethnic group. There are also areas of similarity in most cultures, so that the people of the region have number of commonalities which make them feel for one another and understand each other. But two things are important: similarities and differences. While the similarities bring in the cultural practices harmony in society and promote peace among them, the differences between the ethnic groups sometimes are used negatively by selfish motives towards creating social unrest and dissensions. So in any society culturally or ethnically diverse mixture should be able to maximise opportunities to promote 'unity in diversity', rather than the manipulation of diversity against the unity of its various businesses, for selfish purposes.

As Archbishop Thomas observed in the one day consultation on priorities in social science research in North East India, organised by *Sanskriti* - NEICR on August 13, 2011:

> "As people are distancing themselves from their own cultures under the impact of globalisation, they are also forgetting their inherited and time tested ethical values, in this way vital social bonds are breaking up, and the sense of community and common belonging is getting lost. The codes of conduct that motivated and guided them are no more respected and thus communities can end up as a bunch of rootless individuals and groups without identities. We are now developing self-imposed limits to our freedom by surrendering our reasoning power to irresponsible media and aggressive ideologies that propagate divisive thinking, he said. He suggested that we intensify our reflection on the problems of violence, corruption, threat to environment and erosion of cultures and communities".

The globalisation of the production and distribution of goods and services is a welcome development for many people in that it offers them access to products that they would not otherwise have. However, some are concerned that the changes brought about by globalisation threaten the viability of locally made products and the people who produce them. For example, the new availability of foreign foods in a market – often at cheaper prices – can displace local farmers who have traditionally earned a living by working in their small plots of family owned land and selling their goods locally. Globalisation, of course, does more than simply increase the availability of foreign made consumer products and disrupt traditional producers. In the context of the tribes of North East, it is feared that globalisation may bring in large scale commoditisation of their cultures and would erase their unique identities that are so far consolidated mostly on the premise of ethnic particularities. The impact of globalisation is tremendous. The question, however, stands as has our tribal societies shown willingness to tap the innumerable possibilities? Has our indigenous products explored the global markets at least on experimentation? Participation in globalisation and management of indigenous resources compel everyone to address these real problems soon so that the people of this region could gain maximum real benefits for the maximum number of people for a prolonged period of time.

It is true that much before the dawning of globalisation there was presence of a far more distinct and well defined, robust and culturally sustaining connection between geographical place and cultural experience. These connections cemented individual identity with communities and thus cultural identity was more coherent. This identity was something that people took it for granted as there was almost a sacrosanct and envious individuality existed, which never intruded in their customary laws, thus their cultural continuity was a treasure house for all eternity. Later when the globalisation invaded in every sphere of life it swept like a devastating tide of voluminous flood – and this made communities wake up to take note of responding to its manifold ramifications. Thus, on the one hand cultural identity is at risk everywhere with the arrival of globalisation, certainly it is also true on the other hand experience would tell us that globalisation, has been perhaps the most significant force in generating and proliferating cultural identity. This story involves a rather different understanding of the idea of broader identity than the somewhat narrower understanding of an individual or community and certainly more complex understanding of globalisation.

Concluding Thoughts

North East India has a tremendous potentiality of natural, material and human resources. The marketability of these is far from wanting due to external and internal factors. For too long, ethnicity has been the focal point of contention and politics in this part of the country has been used and misused by different ethnic groups and 'powers that be' for different purposes. The pertinent question which intrigues everyone is how prepared are the 'simple' communities to make a considered decision which involves responding to the forces of globalisation in their own terms.

Beyond the economic and political debates, it is observed that globalisation is a challenge to cultures, in particular, to marginalised communities and their identities. Interestingly, when we look around us today we find what is specific and the local acquires the object of global desire that the so called global circulates freely, unhindered in the local market. In such a scenario where the local and the global seem to overlap, the discursive articulation of the difference of identities and social and cultural practices become more crucial (Baral, et al., 2004). These have led to underdevelopment and erosion of the capacity of the individual and quality of life. A sense of deprivation has developed particularly among the educated youths of the region.

However, the need for coexistence and space sharing are to be taken up with a more serious note by cultures of the North East India without compromising on traditional values or endangering territorial boundaries. After all, culture and tradition are subject to change with the passing of time. People of North East India have a number of commonalities than differences and this strength will have to be en-cashed to deliver the benefits of globalisation. Leaders of various categories would do well to envision the path of progress in line with the cultural moorings of the people.

Certainly it is time to jump into the wagon of globalisation in order to reap the maximum benefits, with calculated risks, welfare and larger good of the people ever in mind. Globalisation no doubt, has provided glimpses of a global market yet, that does not affirm the larger sharing of wealth and resources but of speeding up of the cultural differences and impoverishment. While a very small number of urban elites have begun to reap the benefits of globalisation, many others will be consistently left out in this race. And that is the challenge North East India needs to address now more than ever before.

References

Alex, T. (1989). *Sociology*. New York: Harper and Collins.

Baral, K. C. and Prafulla, K. (eds,), (2004). *Identities: Local and Global*. Delhi: Pencraft International.

Bera, G. K. (2010). 'Perspectives in Religion and Religious Diversity in India', Agartala: Cfr. *Mother Teresa Memorial Lecture*, 21st August 2010.

Sarma, B. B. (2013). 'Environmental Anthropology: A Discipline with Positive Intentions'. In Gautam Kumar Bera and K. Jose SVD (eds.). *Anthropology in India: Retrospect and Prospect*. New Delhi: Abhijeet Publications.

Chanda, N. (2003). 'What is Globalisation? Coming Together: Globalisation Means Reconnecting the Human Community'. Yale Global Online. http://www.globalenvision.org/library/8/567. accessed on 10th December 2019.

Durkheim, E. (1915). *The Elementary forms of Religious Life*. London: Free Press.

Khan, M. (2003). 'Teaching Globalisation'. *The Globalist*. 28 August 2003.

Malinowski, B. K. (1954). *Magic, Science and Religion and Other Essays*. New York: Doubleday Anchor Books.

Menamparampil, T. (1996). *The Challenge of Cultures*, Bombay: Saint Paul Society.

Menamparampil, T. (2011). 'Key Note Address'. One day consultation on Research Priorities in Social Sciences in North East India, *SANSKRITI* – NEICR, Guwahati: August 13, 2011. *MSS*.

Naisbitt, J. (1996). *Megatrends in Asia*. New York: Simon and Schuster.

Nanda, S. K. (2009). 'Nationalism in Global Era: A Case Study of Northeast India'. Shillong: *The NEHU Journal*. VII (1).

Sen, A. (2005). 'The Three R's of Reforms', *Economic and Political Weekly*. 40(19), p. 1.

Srinivas, M. N. (1952). *Religion and Society among the Coorgs of South India*. Oxford: Clarendon Press.

Tylor, E. B. (1877). *Primitive Culture: Researches into the Development of Mythology, Philosophy, Religion, Language, Art, and Customs*. 2 vols. New York: Henry Holt and Co.

World Bank, (2000). *Poverty in an Age of Globalisation.* Washington, D. C.: World Bank.

14

Cultural Metaphors Interfacing Tradition and Modernity in the Globalised Era

— Dr. G Lazar SVD

Introduction

Every interpretation is guilty. But some interpretations are less innocent than others. Interpreting globalisation in the post-modern era is guided not only by the assumption that there is no such thing as an innocent reading but also that *philosophical reading* reckons with its guilt differently (Althusser and Balibar, 1997:14)[1]. In the post-modern and post-truth era there is a struggle to understand better economic, political and social categories through cultural metaphors. It is one thing to talk of how transformation has taken place in the globalised era, but it is also necessary to see how cultural metaphors work. At one level it is the appropriation of symbols by the superpowers. At another level, the *dalits*, the out-castes also have their own independent, autonomous categories, or what is called the inner cosmology. This is what we learn from Gramsci[2] and Althusser, who talk of cultural hegemony, state apparatus and cultural apparatus, of hegemony by consent, for force.

Althusser and Eric Fromm[3] have tried to give a larger domain to culture which is now looked at as necessary space to construct our ideologies, to construct a space where we can formulate communities, to create a sense of the past, a sense of the tradition. According to them one has to understand culture not as a mere effect of something else, something outside it but as something that even makes us look at the economic and social categories in a different way. But that kind of cultural space becomes more radical, more meaningful in today's world. Human history is passing through an age of extreme fragmentation of theoretical constructs of identities of ideologies. If one has to construct a cosmology of *dalits* will it again be a caste category or a class category? It is to be noted that even among the *dalits* there is plurality and heterogeneity.[4] It is not just a question of resolving it and then creating homogeneity. We have to retain this heterogeneity; and that is where cultural criticism comes into our rescue. The second issue that shapes our ambivalences today is the collapse of all kinds of grand narratives. It may be Marxism, but today we cannot look at any of these ideologies as a totalising explanation of grand narratives. Grand narratives here mean something that explains. For example, the notion of progress shaped by the enlightened theory of development, the kind of Baconian[5] idea of endless progress will completely liberate us.

In the post-truth era of globalisation all these explanatory theories are called into question. The collapse of grand narratives and the recognition of the fragmented self have led to a kind of severe ambivalence mutually opposing thought systems and ideologies. So the result is that because of these two we have now ended up with what we can call the loss of the united self or the unified self. It is this that makes one to understand this category, that makes one feel everything and accommodate all these differences in one unified self. This has led to a loss of roots, loss of nativity, disappearance of a lot of local knowledge because only that which comes to us in the name of science is understood as knowledge.[6]

The structure of the contribution is as follows. We first pay some attention to issues of definition, being aware that the concepts of globalisation and culture need to be unpacked. Then we describe the research design and describe challenges of globalisation and cultural marginalisation. The final sections set out how cultural change may be brought about.

Different Perspectives of Globalisation

Globalisation is the process of interaction and integration among people. Globalisation is multifaceted and encompasses many heterogeneous forces. It is an extremely complex process operating at many different levels and with vastly different resultant effects according to where, why, and how it is happening. Its meaning appears to be variable and therefore difficult to define. Despite this, there is a literature emerging that has dealt with these complexities and has tried to create some conceptual order.

Beerkens (2003) described the world in terms of its reliance on the compartmentalism of economies, cultures, power bases, and identities that a geographical extension toward the global level is almost seen as an absurdity. Furthermore, Van der Wende (2004) articulated the following points of emphasis in defining, in particular, the concepts of globalisation and also brought internationalisation into the picture. Globalisation emphasises an increasing convergence and interdependence across societies. In this context, a blurring role of nation-states is envisaged. Although the nation-state becomes more interconnected and activities across borders are increasing, internationalisation assumes that nation-states continue to play their economic, cultural, and social roles. The liberalisation of international trade and global markets are often viewed as the strongest move towards denationalisation. In higher education, cooperation between nation-states is expanding, and national policies are placing stronger emphasis on regulating or facilitating border-crossing (i.e., international) activities (see also Luijten-Lub, Van der Wende, & Huisman, 2004).

Globalisation and Cultural Marginalisation

The major consequences of globalisation have been the de-location or marginalisation of traditional religions and belief systems, the beginning of the disintegration of the traditional social fabrics and shared norms by consumerism, cyber-culture, post-truth new-age religions and changing work ethics and work rhythms, and the fast spreading of quick-fix cultures. The globalisation destroys local culture and making the world more similar. This is also known as cultural unification. Globalisation also brings new values that are not dear to the native cultures. Now many cultures are able to interact with each other which causes the individuality of that culture to fade.

According to Prof. Ram Dayal Munda (2005), Indian States were reorganised during the mid-fifties along linguistic and cultural lines. However, little thought was given to the existence of tribal languages and culture and tribe majority areas were dissected and distributed over several states making the tribal groups into a minority in whichever state they were in. This happened particularly in the central Indian belt. Thus, the Bhil cultural area was divided into four and distributed over Gujarat, Rajasthan, Madhya Pradesh and Maharashtra; the Gond area was divided and distributed over Madhya Pradesh, Maharashtra and Andhra Pradesh; Jharkhand tribal area was divided and distributed over Bihar, West Bengal, Odisha and Madhya Pradesh; the Nilgiri tribal area was distributed over Karnataka, Kerala and Tamil Nadu; the Naga area between Nagaland, Manipur, Assam, and Arunachal Pradesh and there are Naga tribes even in Burma.[7] The basic issue, as is the case with all tribal/indigenous areas elsewhere, is economic, social and cultural dispossession arising from internal colonialism leading to poverty, malnutrition, illiteracy, unemployment and loss of self-respect among the people of Jharkhand, particularly the Adivasi people.

Furthermore, Ram Dayal Munda (2005:10), puts is very bluntly that the right to life is directly impacted through the practice of sterilisation among vanishing tribal groups and putting tribal persons in confrontational situations in the name of law and order or in the name of controlling Naxalism, destruction in the name of national development is the greatest threat to the Adivasi's right to live. It is painful to know the so-called 'national development' projects in mining, hydro-power and industry have caused disruptions of thousands of communities, and once they have broken up, tribal groups have no chance of survival as individuals with a distinctly tribal identity.

In this increasingly globalised world one witnesses that nation states fail to protect the identities of communities and its cultures. They have become agents in the hands of bigger market forces and the sovereignty of the nations is getting eroded day by day and furthermore, we see a lot of fragmentation, breaking up of nations, breaking up of identity and breaking up of cultures. Every day the human community is fenced off in a state of exile. There is a cultural dislocation of the native cultures. The alien culture, the oppressors' culture completely destroys the local culture. When we feel an acute sense of loss of being into this culture and we cannot go back to what we have lost. There is a kind of perpetual state of exile. This notion of exile creates a kind of ambivalence. The exile constitutes a dislocation that is physical, geographical, cultural and social and, above all psychological. When we examine the history and essence of Marxism, we see that its aim is to establish on the earth a Society of Universal Brotherhood. Hence, for each society, the economic basis will be different. However, when Marxism in the form of the unilinear theory is accepted, it only serves to destroy many societies, all in the name of advancement of the so-called primitive, backward and stagnating ones. In the name of, tribal welfare, the Onges have been destroyed in the Andamans, the original natives of Australia, the natives of Papua New Guinea – the same is the fate of many small societies. That is not socialism but social Darwinism. More and more people will be marginalised and destroyed, all in the name of globalisation.

Socio-Cultural Dimension of Domination

On discussing about culture, Rikowski (2002) stated that cultures, under the influence of globalisation, may either be brought together or appreciated as being different or they may be homogenised. Jones, Steffy, and Bray

(1991) argued that the culture of an organisation is pervasive, permeating all of its activities. It has a profound impact on how it operates, what it achieves, and how those who work in the culture of an organisation is pervasive, permeating all of its activities. It has a profound impact on how it operates, what it achieves, and how those who work in the organisation feel. Culture is hard to describe and is often simplified to mean "the way things happen around here." Culture is the underlying or latent assumptions, values, and philosophies that help explain why things happen the way they do in an organisation (Jones et al., 1991). Hofstede (2001) identified three manifestations of culture that are visible through the following practices:

- rituals (defined as collective activities that are technically unnecessary),
- heroes (defined as people who possess characteristics that are highly prised), and
- symbols (defined as words, gestures, pictures, and objects that carry meanings recognised as such by those who share the culture).

Basically, he contended that culture is about how one expects people to behave. It sets boundaries to what people's drives and personalities would have them do. Each society has different attitudes towards five big issues of social life: collective versus individual identity; hierarchy; aggression and gender roles; otherness and the unknown; and short-term versus long-term gratification of needs (Hofstede, Pederson, & Hofstede, 2002). Such attitudes play a role at the societal and organisational levels. Schein (1996) defined organisational culture as "a set of basic tacit assumptions about how the world is and ought to be that a group of people share and that determines their perceptions, thoughts, feelings and, to some degree, their overt behaviour" (p. 11).

The Indian tribes and Dalits are increasingly marginalised because they worship their ancestors, and have nature spirits, the mountain spirit, river spirit, animal spirits etc. They have their own languages. These people of India often wrongly believed that they are backward and primitive. In the name of up-gradation of lifestyle of poor indigenous tribal people, the market forces have created wealth for their interests at the cost of livelihood and security of these tribes in the areas. The mainstream globalisation model of development promotes the Gross Domestic Product (GDP) neglecting the inclusive growth of economy. According to the World Bank, development projects every year involuntarily displace one million people in the developing countries from their land and homes (World Bank, 1994). In India alone, between 1951 and 1990 around 21.3 million persons were displaced by development projects. Among this number 8.54 million (40 percent) were tribal or indigenous people and only 2.12 million (24.8 percent) were resettled (Government of India, 2002: 458). Therefore, there has been created a major rift between the elites and grass root tribal people. The regions inhabited by tribal people are facing wrath of not only economic exploitation but environmental degradation due to excessive extraction of resources. The process of globalisation and liberalisation has affected the indigenous communities of India, particularly their culture, languages and style of life.[8] The extent of devastation in tribal areas and marginalisation, displacement and pauperisation of the Adivasi people that has already taken place has been pointed out by Dr. B.D. Sharma (1995), Walter Fernandes (1992).

Globalisation has very clearly made us feel the slaughtering of identities, of our native cultures, of our own modes of being. We need to analyse the effects of globalisation on cultural and social categories of marginalised communities. When one master culture comes and subjugates another native culture, when it dominates politically and economically, what actually happens is the most crucial of the dominations; this is the cultural domination. This is where the notion of Gramsci's hegemony comes in. There are two kinds of dominations, he says. One is domination by coercion which is political and economic. In this there is a superior political, economic and social force which coerces, and uses force. On the other hand, there is another hegemony which is hegemony through consent of the oppressed, that we accept that this foreign culture is eminently superior to our culture, and this foreign knowledge is eminently superior to our knowledge. So this is a colonisation of the mind in cultural terms. It is impossible to resist, so this is what has led to the images of the intimate enemies: the enemy is not outside, rather it is within us.

How do we analyse it further? Algerian - Franz Fanon had introduced a cultural metaphor to take this issue further. When we talk of colonisation, we see today that the categories are posed in the binary opposition, of the self and the other, the coloniser and the colonised, man-woman, whites-blacks, Hindus-Dalits, etc. Centre to that is the question of the self and the other. So, when a Hindu Brahmin tries to dominate the Dalit, he completely tries to control the other not just in economic and political terms, but even in cultural terms.

Now how do we salvage this loss of cultural identity which is essential to developing a cosmology and identity? This is a psychological and cultural puzzle, because, the other is now seen as an extension of the self. To cite an example, when British wanted to control or contain the Indians, one of the effective methods they did was to bring education to India. It is a historical fact that English literature was introduced in India education as a subject of study, even before English was introduced in British universities. It was believed by the British that one of the ways to civilise Indians was to give them the best of their literature. Raja Ram Mohan Roy and Rabindranath Tagore are standing examples of who absorbed this and believed that English education was a very important step for our own deliverance.

Contrary to expectations, the Jharkhand state is experiencing great difficulties, despite the promises of creating a super state. The Jharkhand movement for statehood has been seen as a movement of cultural reconstruction. It had a vision of reconstructing a state modeled after an ideal tribal state, as a self-reliant, dignified society based on social equity, economic cooperation, consensual democracy, religious tolerance, cultural coexistence, strong work ethics and collective joy. Yet the achievement of the state in the past 25 years since its formation has been miniscule, for the basic reason of lack of vision. The issues of dispossession from land, water and forests, jal, jangal, jamin, continue; there is a general lack of work culture; corruption is at its peak; there is a serious problem of maintenance of law and order and an unprecedented spread of communalism. The state planning effort demonstrates no sense of prioritisation – it is paying more attention to urban development than to rural development and in doing so it has forgotten its tribal agenda (Ram Dayal Munda, 2005: 15-16).

The Rohingya problem is another case in point. The people who call themselves Rohingya are the Muslims of Mayu Frontier area, present-day Buthidaung and Maungdaw Townships of Arakan (Rakhine) State, an isolated province in the western part of Myanmar across Naaf River as boundary from Bangladesh (Chan, 2005). Najeeb Washaly (2019) would say that Myanmar decision to deny citizenship to Rohingya as well as to oust them from Myanmar has political, ideological, and cultural reasons. Politically, the problem is about identity politics and nationalism. Burmese nationalists argued that the Rohingya would construct themselves politically if they were granted national identity. Unrecognised identity is the major challenge for the Rohingya today. Politically and sociologically identity is linked to power. That is, acknowledging the Rohingya as an ethnic identity means accepting it as a political national identity as well. This is because Myanmar is governed by Buddhist-majority militia, and everything, including major ministries, is under its control. Ideologically, it is due to Islamophobia. The Buddhist monks fear that Islam may prevail and spread to the nearby states. They worry about the assumption that Rakhine state will become an independent Muslim state. Hence, the Buddhist monks seek to make Myanmar totally Buddhist, posing that the establishment of Islamic state in Myanmar may lead to partition as the case of the Indian partition, and will lead to the establishment of East Pakistan. Culturally, the language and culture of Rohingya are completely different from other languages and cultures in Myanmar, and that is why they have been called foreigners or invaders. The Buddhist monks claim that Rohingya as an ethnic group never existed in the cultural history of Myanmar though there are references of the Rohingya ancient history in Myanmar.[9]

Smartphones and the internet gave the Uighurs (autonomous region of Xinjiang in north-west China) a sense of their own identity – but now the Chinese state is using technology to strip them of it. Many Muslims of Uighurs region on arrival from foreign countries are transported to detention centres. These centres have become an important part of what Xi Jinping's government calls the "people's war on terror", a campaign launched in 2014, which focuses on Xinjiang, a region with a population of roughly 25 million people, just under half of whom are Uighur Muslims. As part of this campaign, the Chinese government has come to treat almost all expressions of Uighur Islamic faith as signs of potential religious extremism and ethnic separatism. Since 2017 alone, more than 1 million Turkic Muslims, including Uighurs, Kazakhs, Kyrgyz and others, have moved through detention centres. Most Uighurs in the detention centres are on their way to serving long prison sentences, or to indefinite captivity in a growing network of internment camps, which the Chinese state has described as facilities for "transformation through education". These camps, which function as medium-security prisons and, in some cases, forced-labour factories, attempt to train Uighurs to disavow their Islamic identity and embrace the secular principles of the Chinese state. They forbid the use of the Uighur language and instead offer drills in Mandarin, the language of China's Han majority. Only a handful of detainees who are not Chinese citizens have been fully released from this "re-education" system. China's version of the "war on terror" depends less on drones and strikes by elite military units than facial recognition software and machine learning algorithms. Its targets are not foreigners but domestic minority populations who appear to threaten the Chinese Communist party's rule.

Controlling the Uighurs has also become a test case for marketing Chinese technological prowess around the world. A hundred government agencies and companies from two dozen countries, including the US, France, Israel and the Philippines, now participate in the highly influential annual China-Eurasia Security Expo in Urumqi, the capital of the Uighur region. The ethos at the expo, and in the Chinese techno-security industry as a whole, is that Muslim populations need to be managed and culturally isolated. The government officials, civil servants and tech workers who have come to build, implement and monitor the system don't seem to perceive Uighurs' humanity. The only kind of Uighur life that can be recognised by the state is the one that the computer sees. This makes Uighurs population only as data – code on a screen, numbers in camps. They have adapted their behaviour, and slowly even their thoughts, to the system.[10]

In the same vein we can also talk about the Korean minority that has been stigmatised and excluded from positions of power in the society in Japan.

Furthermore, in the era of globalisation the ideology of nation-state has become a hegemonic ideology for countries in the world. The idea of one-nation-state is subsumed and integrated into one-nation concept isolating the other minority cultures. This idea is extremely aggressive and something that we continue to critique for its mindless power, the Dalits and tribes in India, Rohingya in Myanmar, Koreans in Japan, and Uighurs in China will have to recourse to the State powers. Does it mean that we have a solution in the nation-state model? The ultra-nationalists believe they would return Myanmar to its supposed pre-colonial glory, when a Buddhist order thrived, uncontaminated by foreign influences, and all subjects of king enjoyed an abiding sense of national unity (Wade, 2017). They gave nationalist flavour to this with the slogan 'Burma for the Burmans' while Monks insistently repeating that 'to be Burman is to be Buddhist' (Ullah, 2017). According to Bill Ashcroft et al (2007), nationalism became a national tradition and as a practice that will sustain the entity of dominant powers in communities. This myth of nationhood, masked by ideology, perpetuates nationalism, in which specific identifiers are employed to create exclusive and homogeneous conceptions of national traditions. Such signifiers of homogeneity always fail to represent the diversity of the actual 'national' community for which they purport to speak and, in practice, usually represent and consolidate the interests of the dominant power groups within any national formation (Bill Ashcroft et al, 2007). This paper further explained how nationalism is utilised to create new concepts of a nation-state. For them 'all the instrumentalities of state power are subsumed and legitimised as the 'natural' expressions of a unified national history and culture.' Usually, this is the case because one ethnicity is dominant or in the much greater majority (Ryan, 2010). Likewise, Barker (2004) noted:

> *The representation of identities is a 'political' question because they are intrinsically bound up with questions of power as a form of social*

regulation that is productive of the self and enables some kinds of identities to exist while denying it to others. p. 95.[11]

The other is always seen as the extension of the self. The white man in the case of British to India and the Chinese to Uighurs Muslim minority in China, the Japanese to Korean minority in Japan, and the high castes in India looked at the others as an extension, an inferior category to be brought up.

Mahatma Gandhi viewed this social issue of fighting for equality and difference from a different perspective unlike Franz Fanon of Algeria or Nelson Mandela of South Africa. Gandhian political philosophy of Hind Swaraj was a new reconstruction in the history of post-modern philosophy. Gandhi's politics was situated outside the mainstream enlightenment thought. The correct perspective of understanding the Gandhian ideology as a whole would be to study it in relation to the historical development of elite nationalist past in India. For Gandhism, like Russian populism, was not a direct expression of peasant ideology. It was an ideology conceived as the intervention in the elite nationlist discourse of the time and was formed and shaped by the experience of the specifically national movement. It is only by looking at it in that historical context that it becomes possible to understand the unique achievement of Gandhism, that is, its ability to open up the possibility for achieving perhaps the most important historical task for a successful nationalist revolution in a country like India. Gandhi perceived that there is a cosmology available within the Indian peasantry which was completely harnessed by Gandhian Anthropology.

This above observation makes it clear why Gandhian philosophy makes an appeal from outside the Western epistemology. Gandhi could establish a kind of communion, a symbolic communion with the peasantry, which explains the enormous appeal that Gandhi had on the peasantry. Gandhi proved there is something outside the Western rational thought to which the Indians responded.

The most important question is, how do we bring the hidden forces: the Dalits and Tribes, which were totally marginalised because of the onward march of Globalisation and Liberalisation which tend to explain everything in terms of profit and loss of commercial terms, or cause and effect scientific terms. Is there anything like a non-scientific or non-commercial method with which we can construct our sociology and cosmology. This philosophy we specify not in civilisational terms but in cultural terms.

Rediscovering the Cosmology of the Periphery

We start our discussion from the very issue of Dalits entry into temple, or women entering into Shabarimala temple in Kerala. To make the Dalits or women enter into temples means that one basically accepts the terms laid out by the mainstream Hindu Scriptures – they have sanctified the temple already and you allow the Dalits or women enter into it. We can also quote from Swami Vivekananda who said that you have to open the scriptures for the Dalits. The question that any low caste person has to ask is: why should the Dalits read the Hindu scriptures? Does their emancipation lie only in their reading the so called *Shruti* and *Smruti* revealed to the sages of Hindu tradition? As Leveridge explains, each human being is born the same way and experiences the same stages in life. The difference, however, is the environment in which each individual grows up and the language to which he/she becomes accustomed to. This creates identities of a certain culture and language, differing this person from another. Sivakami's *Grip of Change* makes a solemn attempt to go beyond the manacles of mere casteism by presenting the Dalit cultural and political identities emphatically. According to Soumya Nair (2017:81), Dalit literature is a vital part of the Dalit culture and politics. Dalit writers need to strengthen and disrupt the vain, exaggerated, ritualised and highlighting society that suppresses them. Historically, in Indian classical literature, there is no place for the Dalits moreover they are portrayed by the upper caste writers as bizarre people. Subaltern literature in crux is a gripe literature and it constructs the social identity of the oppressed. The philosophers like Homi Bhabha, Edward Said and Gayatri Spivak bear out to the institution of postcolonial theory and construction of identity in the educational world. Supremacy is a major issue in postmodernism, the subaltern writing is dogmatic and it proclaims the cultural identities of the relegated.[12] However, radical it looks on the outside, like we have to open the scriptures to the Dalits because it was denied to them, the statement that the Dalits should be making is that they do not need the scriptures, because they have their own scriptures. This is to say the Dalits have to construct their own scriptures. Construct means not from nothing, but they have to rediscover them. This is the kind of cosmology we are supposed to work upon (Soumya Nair, 2017:82).

We need to construct a new knowledge system for the Dalits and women in this globalised era because the knowledge systems of those in periphery have been denied. We need to continuously keep moving between what is available within history to us in terms of our scriptures. Dalits and women have to establish their own spiritual traditions. If their spiritual tradition is more non-violent, more cooperative and not very aggressive, then it has the potential not only to emancipate the Dalits, tribes and women but also to emancipate all the other oppressed. In this way the Dalit cosmology could provide us with an alternative.

As the world is caught up with narrow nationalism we do not have a way out in the nation-state model. The problems connected to the suppression of local culture cannot be solved. On the one hand, we cannot endorse the existing structure of the nation-state, nor can we go back to a romantic kind of village set-up. We can take recourse to Gandhian attitude to decentralisation, to no-violence. We cannot be violent to nature and the indigenous culture any more. The existing technologies and patterns of living have become extremely violent. It is the philosophy of living and getting integrated with the native culture and environment which produces a cosmology of its own. We cannot change nature and culture, but it is our understanding of nature that we can and must change. In this globalised era we are made to understand that anthropology itself is undergoing a change. Here it is necessary to turn to oral traditions and oral culture, and to a-historical categories. The big question is do Dalits and Tribes of India try to explore into a non-Brahminical categories? This is what the American Negros did when they rejected Western classics and brought their own cultural forms, especially through jazz. Does such a thing really happen in our country? So it is not between Brahmins or non-Brahmins or high class or Tribes but within this world, we have got so many worlds. So all the Dalits, Tribes, Muslims, Christians, women, and other castes. The low castes or tribes cannot be dumped together. We have to see to what different cosmologies and anthropologies they constitute.

Conclusion

When summing up, while discussing about the issues of globalisation and marginalisation in the context of culture we have to refer to the anxieties and ambivalences, the experiential and theoretical that is faced with in the globalised era. Experiences with the post-truth era constitute one kind of anxiety and our theoretical constitutes another. The marginalised need to turn to their original oral traditions and oral culture and to a-historical categories. The marginalised people have their own cultural identity which they have being focusing for long time in their respective genre, every marginalised group understands the subaltern quest on caste, colour, status, culture language and religion. The Dalits and tribes of India are the true populaces in India and rediscovering the Dalit script gives bigger representation of these marginalised groups who were subverted for centuries. Dalit scripts written in different languages are the sense of wakefulness of injustice towards the caste system as well as the social and political institutions. Thus, the rediscovering of the inner cosmology of the downtrodden prompt the apprehensions, anxieties, desires, and hidden pain of caste struggle. The image of social justice that is presented by the script writers of the Dalit movements has to stimulate the perception in the encounter which will counter all repressive and tyrannical structure.

References

1. Beerkens, E. (2004). Global opportunities and institutional embeddedness. Higher education consortia in Europe and Southeast Asia. Enschede, Netherlands: CHEPS.
2. Beerkens, H. J. J. G. (2003). Globalisation and higher education research. Journal of Studies in International Education, 7, 128-148.
3. Fernandes, Walter (1992). National Development and Tribal Deprivation. New Delhi: Indian Social Institute.
4. Hofstede, G. (2001). Cultures consequences: Company values, behaviours, institutions and organisations across nations. Thousand Oaks, California: Sage.
5. Hofstede, G.J., Pederson, P.B., & Hofstede, G. (2002). Exploring culture: Exercises, stories and synthetic cultures. Boston: Intercultural Press.
6. Jones, J. W., Steffy, B.D., & Bray, D.W. (1991). Applying psychology in business: The handbook for managers and human resource professionals. Lanham, MD: Lexington Books.
7. Luijten-Lub, A., Van der Wende, M., & Huisman, J. (2004). On cooperation and competition: A comparative analysis of national policies for internationalisation of higher education in seven Western European countries. Journal of Studies in International Education, 9, 147-163.
8. Rikowski, G. (2002, January 22). Globalisation and education. A paper prepared for the House of Lords Select Committee on Economic Affairs, Inquiry into the Global Economy. Retrieved September 23, 2009, from Education-Line Web site: http://www.leeds.ac.uk/educol/documents/00001941.htm
9. Schein, E. (1996). Three cultures of management: The key to organisational learning. Sloan Management Review, 38(1), 9-17.
10. Van der Wende, M. (2004). Introduction. In J. Huisman & M. Van der Wende (Eds.), On cooperation and competition. National and European policies for the internationalisation of higher education. Bonn, Germany: Lemmens.
11. Sharma, B.D. (1995). Globalisation: the Tribal Encounter, New Delhi: Vedam Books.
12. Ram Dayal Munda (2005). "Globalisation and the Challenges of Tribal Development", Durghabai Deshmukh Memorial Lecture. DDML. XIV/05/500, July 15, 2005.
13. Barker, C. (2004). The Sage dictionary of cultural studies. Sage.
14. Ashcroft, B., Gareth Griffiths, and Helen T. (2013). Post-colonial studies: The

key concepts. Routledge. p. 135.

15. Ryan, Micheal (2010). Cultural studies a practical introduction. Wiley-Blackwell.
16. Ullah, A. A. (2017). Rohingya Migration: Is It a Function of Persecution. pp. 1-4.
17. Wade, F. (2017). Myanmar's Enemy Within: Buddhist Violence and the Making of a Muslim'other'. Zed Books.
18. Sivakami, P. Palaiyana Kalitalum. Sivakangai: Annam (P) Ltd. 1989.

Notes

1. Althusser, L., and É. Balibar. 1997. Reading "Capital." New York: Verso. [Google Scholar]
2. The Marxist intellectual Antonio Gramsci (1891–1937) developed the theory of cultural hegemony to further the establishment of a working-class intelligentsia.
3. Erich Fromm, (born March 23, 1900, Frankfurt am Main, Germany—died March 18, 1980, Muralto, Switzerland), German-born American psychoanalyst and social philosopher who explored the interaction between psychology and society.
4. For example in Andhra Pradesh, Telangana and Tamil Nadu the Dalits are divided among themselves basing on their own cultural and social background. In Andhra Pradesh and Telengana the Dalits are divided into Maalas and Madigas. Potitically they belong to one category of Dalits yet they would not compromise with each other on inter-caste marriage. Even on political seat sharing they stand apart. Similarly in Tamil Nadu the Dalit community is divided as Parayas and Pallis. Though there is some amount of social interaction between them, yet, emotionally they would not mix with each other.
5. Bacon's philosophy of science is the account of inductive reasoning given in Book II of Novum Organum. The defect of all previous systems of beliefs about nature, he argued, lay in the inadequate treatment of the general propositions from which the deductions were made.
6. This idea is taken from V.S. Sreedhar from his, "Interaction of Tradition and Modernity in the Globalised Context" (1997:78), Published by Visthar, Dodda Gubbi Post, Bangalore.
7. Ram Dayal Munda (2005). "Globalisation and the Challenges of Tribal Development", Durghabai Deshmukh Memorial Lecture. DDML. XIV/05/500, July 15, 2005. pp. 11, 15.
8. Jaysawal, Neelmani and Saha, Sudeshna. "Marginalisation of Tribal Communities due to Globalisation" (July 4, 2014). Indian Journal of Dalit and Tribal Studies, Vol. 2(2), 37-54 (2014). Available at SSRN: https://ssrn.com/abstract=3390699.
9. This idea is expressed more vividly by Najeeb Washaly (2019). "Rohingya: The Identity Crisis" see: https:www.researchgate.net/publication/331286962.
10. As quote and narrated by news reporter Darren Byler in "China's hi-tech war on its Muslim minority" see Google search: uighurs population.com

11. As discussed by Najeeb Washaly (2019). "Rohingya: The identity Crisis", https:www.researchgate.net/publication/331286962

12. Soumya Nair Anoop Kumar. "Language and Cultural Discourse of Indian Dalit Literature from a Subalternist's Perspective", International Journal of Management and Applied Science, ISSN: 2394-7926 Volume-3, Issue-9, Sep.-2017.

15

Marginalisation of Minority Dalits in India and Global Networks

— Dr. James Ponniah

Introduction

We all live in a globalised world wherein the process of globalisation has encompassed almost all spheres of human existence and its influence in our lives is unimaginably inescapable. Against this background, this essay explores how Dalits of India have taken to globalisation. In particular, it examines if and how minority Dalits (i.e., Dalit Muslims and Dalit Christians) exploit the processes of globalisation for their emancipatory agenda. This essay is divided into four sections: First section looks at some of the existing writings that address the question of why Dalits in India embraced the Abrahamic faiths of Islam and Christianity. The second section of the essay describes briefly their experiences of discrimination and exclusion within their respective religious communities. The third section of the essay exposes the nation state's role as an unjust master. The final section is an examination of if and how Dalit Christians and Muslims have appropriated global networks to their advantage.

I. Subaltern Embrace of Non-Indic Faiths To Overcome Marginalisation

Historians of both Islam and Christianity in India as discussed below have argued that it is the practice of untouchability and caste discrimination in India that drove most of the Dalits in India to embrace today's two important minority religions, namely, Islam and Christianity. According to some estimate, 75% of Muslims in India are Dalits. It means that 100 million out of 172 million Muslims who embraced Islam in India are Dalits. Most of the Dalit and most backward castes which practice Islam also have members in Hinduism. Dalit and other depressed castes such as Banjaras, Dhobis, Nats, Lalbegis, Halalkhors, Jogis, Pasis, Mochis, Khatiks, Julahas, Darzis and the Rangrezes in Bihar, for instance consist of both Hindus as well as Muslims. According to Nadeem Hasnain, "overwhelming majority of the Indian Muslim population comes from the lower Hindu castes who have been coming into the fold of Islam to escape from social persecution and the oppressive socio-economic disabilities."[1] According to Ejaz Ali, a Dalit Muslim leader (who founded 'All-India Backward Muslim Morcha'—AIBMM), as Yoginder Sikand notes,[2] Islam played a key role in the emancipation of the Dalits, a role which was forgotten when Islam became the religion of the rulers. For him, Islam took root among the common masses in India primarily through the agency of the Sufis "whose teachings of love, brotherhood and social equality attracted many Dalits to the new faith, shackled as they were by the chains of the caste system and the Brahminical religion. Seeing the early Muslims eating from the same dish and praying together in the same mosque, the Dalits entered the Muslim fold in droves. It was not by the sword but through the love and compassion that the Sufis exhibited in their behaviour towards the poor, principally the Dalits, that large numbers of Hindus converted to Islam."[3]

Just like Islam in India, Indian Christianity is predominantly a Dalit religion as 14 out of 20 million Christians are Dalits.[4] It simply means 70 % of all conversions to Christianity in India took place among the Dalits. Mass movements of conversion to Christianity among Dalits were triggered by various social, economic, cultural, political and religious reasons as studies indicate. According to Webster, by the early twentieth century approximately one million Dalits had converted to Christianity.[5] Mass conversion that took place among Dalit groups included *Chuhras* of Punjab, *Chamars* of North India (Uttar Pradesh, Bihar and Madhya Pradesh), *Vankars* of Gujarat, *Mahars* of central and western India, especially Maharashtra, *Paraiyars* of South India and *Pulayas* of Kerala. But one motif that underlined most of the conversion stories among the Dalit Christians is liberation from discriminatory caste system and an aspiration for self-dignity. Through conversion, Dalit Christians chose for themselves their own new destiny by opting for a religion that promised human dignity and new self-esteem. Contrary to the commonly held view, Christian missionaries did not go all out to convert the Dalits in big numbers to up the Christian population in many instances of conversion. For instance, it was at the initiatives of enlightened Dalit leaders like Yerraguntala Periah that the missionaries converted the Dalits in the Ongole region of Andhra Pradesh to Christianity.[6] As noted by Webster some of these leaders came from known religious backgrounds such as Yogi Nasariah movement or Ramanjua Sect[7] and opted to embrace Christianity for the well-being of their community. Further, it was not merely for the material benefit that they went to seek membership in Christian churches. In fact, some of the missionaries did show hesitation to covert the Dalits suspecting their motif. To quote an instance, when Rev. Clough did not respond very positively to Madiga's request for group conversion as he suspected their motif to be material benefits, some spoke up "we do not want help. By the blisters on our hands we can prove to you that we have worked and we will continue to work. If the next crop fails, we shall die. We want to die as Christians. Baptize us therefore."[8] Further, it was not their illiteracy or ignorance that was capitalised by Christian missionaries to woo them into Christianity. On the contrary, as mentioned above, it was the enlightened Dalit caste leader's desire to know the truth, a truth that is universal and their decision to embrace a religion—that believes in equality, justice, compassion, love and fraternity, a religion that will give them self-respect, a religion that will stand with them in their struggle for human dignity—that pulled them towards Christianity.

II. Discriminated and Disillusioned within: Dalits' Predicament in the New Religion

While Dalits converted to Islam and Christianity as each of this religion professed their faith, rather categorically, in a God who created all humans as His Children and as equals regardless of who they are, their experience of equality, fraternity and human dignity in their respective Muslim and Christian local communities were, more often than not, negative and disappointing as described below.

Islam

Though Islam preaches and believes in social egalitarianism which attracted the erstwhile lowly and the untouchable castes to embrace Islam, the brand of Islam which emerged in the cultural soil of Indian subcontinent is marked by social inequality. It is so because in most of the cases the new converts to Islam relinquished their former religious faith but not their caste-based pedigrees and social status. They brought forward caste-based customs, beliefs and practices to the new socio-religious milieu. In this regard, Hasnain observes: "while Islam may not be having castes or caste-like groupings, the Indian Muslims do have."[9]

As a result, as sociologists of Indian Islam take note of, there are three broad categories of social groupings in Indian Islam, namely, *ashraf* (noble born), *ajlaf* (mean and lowly), and *arzal* (excluded) who are placed on vertical hierarchy in Indian societies. Indian Muslims live as social groups and maintain their identity and distinguish themselves from other Muslim groups in ways which are very similar to those of caste communities among the Hindus. Just like Hindu Varna system, Muslim communities in India too "constitute a hierarchy in which castes are ranked in order of social precedence."[10] However, these three broad categories have their limitations in that they might fail to capture local variants, diversities and specificities and therefore, there cannot be one single pan-Indian social stratification for Indian Muslims. Imtiaz Ahmad, had elsewhere observed that "the real units of social stratification are the caste-analogues, and the day-to-day relationships between different individuals in any local community are determined by their membership of the caste-analogue rather than by the broad categories. In the study of Muslim social stratification, therefore, it is the caste-analogue which constitutes a more significant analytical unit."[11] This caste-analogue is totally dependent on local socio-economic-cultural milieu in which different caste groups are situated.

In order to understand the existing practices of untouchability among Indian Muslims, scholars differentiate between two approaches to Islam, namely, "textual Islam" and "lived Islam." While the former summarily denies any practice of discrimination among Indian Muslims on ideological grounds, the latter have underlined "persisting socioeconomic inequalities between Dalit Muslims and other social groups,"[12] and have documented "sites and instances of untouchability being practised."[13] Dalit Muslims' experience of discrimination both in rural and urban settings include denial of access to water, or maintenance of separate glass/vessel for Dalit Muslims to drink or eat from, segregated hamlets, discriminations in the mosque such as sitting in the last row (to avoid such discrimination, in some places Dalit Muslims have built their own mosques) and separate cemeteries for the Dalit Muslims. The survey done by Prashant K Trivedi, Srinivas Goli, Fahimuddin and Surinder Kumar on more than 7,000 households across 14 districts between October 2014 and April 2015 in the populous northern Indian state of Uttar Pradesh also confirms the existence of discrimination and untouchability in their midst. Almost a third of the survey's respondents stated that they were barred from burying their dead in an "upper-caste" burial ground. They do so either in some other place or in one corner of the main ground. Many Dalit Muslims do not get invited to non-Dalit weddings. Some are seated separately at non-Dalit Muslim feasts and have to eat later than people from dominant castes. Many say they are served food on different plates. While some Dalit Muslim children are seated separately in classrooms and eat separately during lunch breaks. Most of the Muslims offer prayers in the same mosque, but in some places "Dalit Muslims" felt discriminated against in the main mosque. In this regard, one writer observes, "you can try to leave caste in India, but caste refuses to leave you."[14]

Christianity

As in Islam, in Christianity too the key question is "how far the Dalits who converted to Christianity could get rid of caste-based discrimination?" [15] Has Christianity given them true self-dignity? Has it delivered on the promises of a new life it offered? Answers to these questions are complex. But, the complexity in spite of its nuances can be articulated just in one sentence: Caste-discrimination and Dalit exclusion continued even after conversion. Continuation of caste-based occupational patterns among Dalit Christians is one of the important reasons for the continuation of Dalit oppression. The works of Dogar[16] and Wiebe and Peter[17] show that occupational patterns (including manual scavenging) as in case of Dalit Christians in north-west India and those of agricultural workers, daily wage labourers and small cultivators in different part of India are quite similar to those of Dalit Hindus. Most interestingly, as Wiebe and Peter have highlighted, there existed and continues to exist a 'patron-client relationship' between caste Christians and Dalit Christians in several parts of India as it was the case between Hindus and Dalit Hindus. The unequal and hierarchical master-client relationship between caste Christians and Dalits Christians in rural Tamil Nadu lead to the continuation of Dalit Christians' low social status. Since caste-based occupations of Dalit Christians had not changed in many instances after conversion, their social status remained low and subsequently caste-based discriminations too continued.

As in Islam, caste customs and practices are rampant too in lived-Christianity. As Archbishop Casmir of Madras-Mylapore Catholic Archdiocese and Bishop Azariah of CSI diocese, Chennai openly and painfully acknowledged three decades ago, when Hindus became Christians, they brought into Christianity the Hindu social structure of caste system, and continued their caste-based customs. As a result, Church in India suffers from "caste-ridden vestiges of Hinduism."[18] As numerous studies and reports have shown, Dalit Christians, in spite of benefits they have enjoyed through Christianity especially through education and job-opportunities, continue to be discriminated and suffer humiliations in Christian churches. Dalit activists and scholars normally talk about five-fold discrimination of Dalit Christians, namely, discrimination by 1. The State, 2. Caste Hindus, 3. Fellow Hindu Dalits, 4. Upper caste Christians, 5. The sub-groups of Dalit Christians themselves. In this section, we will briefly focus on the last two forms of discriminations.

That Dalit Christiansare treated as second-class citizens in mainline churches is a painful fact. It is so because the upper caste people who embraced Christianity continue their past cultural traditions and customs. It is not uncommon that caste Christians continue to append caste suffix to their names and such caste titles go with their names when they are read out in mass intentions, marriage bans and funeral services. Caste Christians celebrate their life-cycle rituals as per their old caste customs and their dress code and food habits remain the same as those of their Hindu counterparts. These continued practices of caste Christians simply meant the customary rituals of social distance, untouchability and social stratification are reproduced and perpetuated in the lives of Indian Christians too. Through these caste-based customs and traditions, the subordinated social status of Dalit Christians are also constantly played out and reinforced in the minds of local Christian communities. Unfortunately, the rituals of precedence undertaken during Church festivals perform the same function when Dalit Christians are made to undertake the traditionally assigned roles of playing the drums or carrying torches, as they are seen as services assigned to socially subordinated people.

Apart from the cultural traditions, caste-based practices have also unfortunately crept into the very institutional structures and practices of mainline churches. Many studies undertaken for this purpose have indicated the following[19]: 1. The construction of two chapels (one for non-Dalits and another for Dalits), 2. Separate seating arrangements for the Dalits within the same church (either two aisles of the church or the last row of pews given to the Dalits or asked to sit on the floor while high castes are given benches), 3. Two separate cemeteries and two separate hearses to carry dead bodies, 4. Two separate queues for receiving holy communion or Dalits receive after the caste Christians, 5. Dalits forbidden to serve in the altar or be lector at the sacred liturgy. 6. Palm Sunday and corpus-Christi processions not permitted to enter Dalit streets, 7. Dalits not to participate in the washing of the feet ceremony on Sunday, Thursday, 8. Some churches refuse contribution from Dalits for parish patron feast, 9. The Feast of the Patron celebrated separately by the Dalits. Perhaps one of the obvious forms of discrimination of Dalits in mainline churches is the lack of sufficient representation of Dalit Christians in leadership positions as priests, Bishops and cardinals. As it is a topic much talked about, I will not take it up for discussion for lack of space.

Another significant form of caste-discrimination Dalit Christians suffer from is that of inter-caste discrimination between Dalit Christians themselves. Like their Hindu counterparts, Dalit Christians too have caste-system among themselves. They do not inter-dine nor inter-marry and they maintain social distance between themselves. "Notwithstanding conversion, caste-system with all its prejudices is not destroyed but is unfortunately prevalent among the Christian converts also......These Christian converts follow the same usages, customs, manners and habits of life characteristic to each particular caste. Except in the matter of religious belief, there is absolutely no differentiation between the converts and their Hindu brethren."[20]

Even as we refer to the prevalence of caste-discrimination among Dalit Christian themselves, in no way it can justify the existing practices of unequal treatment of Dalits by caste Christians, which is anti-Christian, to say the least. Caste-based practices and differential treatments in Christianity is counter-witness to the very egalitarianism and unconditional love preached by Jesus. But, it is unfortunate that the Church leadership at times did not see it as unchristian. For instance, way back in 1923, the letter of Pope Gregory XV in 1923, allowed the request of the then missionaries "to adjust to certain caste practices"[21] while taking into account the 'difficulties' faced by the upper caste converts.

III. State Marginalisation

Though Dalit Muslims and Christians experience multiple forms of discrimination and humiliations at different levels, the nation state never bothers about them. Nor does it consider them as unconstitutional. It is because both the Dalit Muslims and Dalit Christians lost their legal status as schooled castes by the Indian nation state through the controversial 1950 Presidential order which delisted non-Hindu Dalits from SC status. Affirmative Action for the Dalits (SC's) in India to compensate for the historical injustice done to them owes its origin to the 1935 Government of India Act. "According to this Act a list or schedule was drawn up, containing the names of castes considered to be low in the social hierarchy for whom special facilities were extended in order to partially compensate them for centuries of deprivation and to enable them to advance economically and educationally. Many of these castes had members who claimed different religious affiliation, not all of them being Hindu. Several castes, such as the Banjaras, Dhobis, Nats, Lalbegis, Halalkhors, Jogis, Pasis, Mochis, Khatiks, Julahas, Darzis and the Rangrezes, consisted of both Hindus as well as Muslims."[22]

This law in Article 341 was amended by the Presidential order of 1950 as mentioned earlier to notify that only Hindus could be considered as members of a Scheduled Caste and hence eligible for the special benefits that such castes enjoy. The social and civil life of non-Hindu Dalits drastically altered overnight in 1950 as Sikand writes, "with one stroke of the pen, millions of Muslim, Christian, Sikh and Buddhist Dalits were struck off the Scheduled Caste list."[23] As the presidential order further goes on to state "a non-Hindu Dalit would be considered for such benefits if he or she converted to Hinduism or declared himself or herself to be a Hindu, this itself being a violation of Article 25 (1) of the Indian Constitution, which lays down the right to the free practice of religion,"[24] it is suspected that "increasing Hindu numbers and preventing Dalit conversions to non-Hindu religions seem to be among the probable reasons behind the amendment."[25]

Though Buddhist and Sikh Dalits were later included to the list of SCs with much struggle (Sikhs in 1956 and Buddhists in 1990), Dalit Christians and Dalit Muslims are continued to be derecognised as SC's in spite of repeated appeals and protest marches. As a result, "they are not covered under any compensatory measures such as reservations and special legal safeguards which are otherwise extended to Dalits who belong to Hindu, Sikh and Buddhist Communities,"[26] even though Dalit Muslims and Dalit Christians too face caste-based prejudices as equallyand strongly as their counterparts in other religions on a day-to-day basis both within and outside their respective religious communities. However, the legal safeguards against untouchability, discrimination and atrocities that are normally available to the Dalits in India are not extended to them since they are not in the official category of Scheduled Castes. On government records, Dalit Christians are either considered 'Christians/Indian Christians' or OBCs in most part of India. "The existing legal protections against discrimination and atrocities for SCs under Untouchability (Offences) Act, 1955; the Protection of Civil Rights Act, 1976; the Scheduled Castes and the Scheduled Tribes (Prevention of Atrocities) Act, 1989 and the Scheduled Castes and the Scheduled Tribes (Prevention of Atrocities) Act Rules, 1995 are not applied to Dalit Christians."[27] These Acts seeks "to provide protection against various forms of violence, atrocities and discriminations such as depriving facilities; denial of rights; eviction; economic exploitation including wrongful occupation of land and other properties; personal attack and exploitation including insulting, intimidating harassment and dishonouring and heinous criminal activities including rape, molestation, murder and massacre of SCs and STs."[28] Various reports and studies have clearly shown that discrimination, violence and atrocities being committed on Dalit Christians are mostly on castelines. They are easily committed against Dalit Christians and Muslims with impunity precisely because the latter cannot seek police and legal protection under these laws. Such a situation for the Dalit Muslims and Christians can be easily construed as a deliberate form of religion-based discrimination. Dalit Muslims and Christians suffer these acts of discrimination on account of professing a particular religion. As Article 15 of Indian Constitution disallows any form of discrimination by the state towards its citizens on the basis of religion, race, caste, sex and place of birth, nation state's treatment of Dalit religious minorities seems unfair and discriminatory.

Global Networks, Subaltern Religious Minorities and Voices of Emancipation from Marginalisation

The Dalit Christians, who are the oppressed minorities within Christian minorities, as noted earlier, suffer marginalisation at twin sites, i.e., both in the church and in the larger society. Within the church they face caste discrimination meted out to them by high caste lay Christians, caste-minded Christian leaders, the non-human institutional structures. Likewise, in the larger civil society too, I think that they encounter multiple forms of discrimination and marginalisation mainly from five sources, the high caste non-Christians, Hindu religious leaders, Hindu fundamentalist groups, non-Christian OBCs and the discriminatory State machinery. To overcome the above mentioned range of marginalisation, the Dalit Christians have reached out to international agencies, taken their issues to global platforms and employed geo-political strategies to garner support outside India and to pressure the power centres in India. Their efforts at the global level are two-fold: A. Internationalisation of Dalit Christian Issues within the Church and B. Internationalisation of Dalit Christian Discrimination by the State.

A. Internationalisation of Dalit Christian Issues within the Church

To fight injustice at the ecclesial level, Catholics have appealed to the Vatican and the Protestant Christians have worked in close collaboration with the WCC (World Council of Churches) to obtain support to overcome ecclesial discrimination at three levels, namely, at the individual level, the collective level and structural level. For instance, one of WCC's contribution was the creation of Dalit Solidarity Programme (DSP) in 1992 whose aim was not only to support the Dalit struggle in India by assisting in the transformation of the internal organisation of member churches and facilitating their development programmes for the Dalit Christians, but also to raise awareness of Dalit issues within WCC member churches and to take Dalit issues to the international fora including the United Nations and to the wider international community. To materialise its vision, it supports the participation of Dalit activists in international events such as the World Social Forum, and co-operates with the NCCI (National Council of Churches in India), the Lutheran World Federation and the Christian Conference of Asia to build international support for the Dalit emancipation in India. The concerted efforts of Dalit intellectuals, theologians and church leaders from India made WCC to discuss the problem of Dalit Christians in its World Conference against Racism in Durban in 2001 and later in Seoul Korea. Another important step in the internationalisation of Dalit issues was in making the 'great injustice to Dalits in India and in the Church' as the theme for the Ecumenical week of prayer at the global level for Christian unity in 2013. Initiated in 1968, this annual week of prayer celebrated from 18 to 25 January (in the northern hemisphere) or at Pentecost (in the southern hemisphere) is jointly hosted by the WCC's Faith and Order Commission and by the Pontifical Council for Promoting Christian Unity of the Roman Catholic Church. To mark its centenary, the Student Christian Movement of India (SCMI) was invited to prepare the resources for the Week of Prayer for Christian Unity (WPCU) 2013 in collaboration with the All India Catholic University Federation and the National Council of Churches in India. In this connection, Dalit issues were seen in the Vatican II website which for instance read: "while reflecting on the significance of the WPCU, it was decided that in a context of great injustice to Dalits in India and in the Church, the search for visible unity cannot be disassociated from the dismantling of casteism and the lifting up of contributions to unity by the poorest of the poor."[29] As a result of Dalit Christian's engagement with Dalit issues at the international fora, they were specially invited to the first-ever International Congress of the UN on Discrimination Based on Work and Descent held in New York on 21-23 September, 2019, alongside the UN Climate Summit. This event that discussed the problem of Dalits in India, including that of Dalit Christians, was organised by The Asia Dalit Rights Forum and the National Campaign for Dalit Human Rights in collaboration with other national/international organisations like the

Africa Network on Slavery and Discrimination, Trust Africa, European Roma Grassroots Organisations Network, The Inclusivity Project and the Boston Study Group.

The Dalit Catholic Christians' efforts to internationalise their discrimination in the church had only limited success. Encouraging examples in this regard are the initiatives of Voice of Dalits International (a UK based Christian organisation, established in London in 1999) and its offshoot, Christian Network Against Caste Discrimination (CNACD) (established in 2013). The latter held a two day 2 Day Conference, 'Christian Responsibility to Dalits & Caste Discrimination,' on 9th and 10th May 2017 which was chaired by cardinal Peter Turkson, Prefect of the Dicastery for the Promotion of Integral Human Development in the Vatican. No doubt Dalit Christians' fight against the state has received support from the hierarchy within the Catholic church and its official body, CBCI (the Catholic Bishops' Conference of India) which along the National Council of Churches in India and the National Council of Dalit Christians observes, since 2009, August 10 as the black day, a day in which the controversial presidential order that disqualified non-Hindu Dalits to access the benefits of SC reservations offered by the Indian state for education and jobs came into force. Further, in December 2016 the Catholic Church released a document called "Policy of Dalit Empowerment in the Catholic Church in India". This report had accepted the existence of untouchability and discrimination against Dalits in the Church and calls upon the local churches to remove the discrimination against the Dalits and to take steps to restore their honour and respect in the social milieu. However, Dalit Christian leader's request to the Pope on the eve of Indian bishops' *Ad Limina* visit to Rome (official meeting of the bishops with Pope once in five years) to take up Dalit Christians' problem with the Indian Catholic Bishops and "to take responsibility with accountability to eradicate casteism, untouchability and discrimination of Dalits within the Catholic Church,"[30] was turned down by Vatican. Dalit Christians were disappointed because Pope Francis did not address the issue in any of the meetings. Earlier in 2015, Viduthalai Tamil Puligal Katchi (VTPK) and the Dalit Christian Liberation Movement (DCLM) had complained to secretary-general Ban Ki-Moon of the UNO and several UN bodies against the practice of segregated cemeteries for Dalits in Tamil Nadu and framed it "racial discrimination" within the Church in Tamil Nadu. They demanded that the UN take action against the Holy See, a permanent observer to the UN, whose Churches in Tamil Nadu are indifferent to such discriminatory practices.

B. Internationalisation of Dalit Christians' State-Produced Discrimination

The Dalit Christians of India undergo multiple modes of discrimination and injustice not only in the Churches but more so by the nation state that affect their lives in the larger civil society. To confront the discriminatory policies of the state and its attitude of indifference to existing forms of discrimination in larger society, Dalit Christians of India have taken deliberate and conscious steps to internationalise the discriminatory policies of the State and appeal to the international bodies like the UN to pressure the Indian nation state to protect Dalits and to render justice to them.

Their efforts in this regard are three-fold. First, they would approach various international bodies like United Nations organisation to internationalise Dalit Christian problems in India. Secondly, they drew upon Dalit groups' links with international human rights NGOs, and formed a transnational advocacy network (TAN) and networked with organisation like CSW (Christian Solidarity Worldwide) and ADF (Alliance Defending Freedom). Thirdly, they opened up channels of communication with select foreign governments in the west such as UK, the countries in European union and especially USA which stared pressuring Indian state for action in favour of Dalit Christians.

Let us take the case of violence against Dalit Christian in Kandamal between 2008-09 and see how Dalit Christian's international advocacy and lobbying worked in this context. To internationalise both the violence against Dalit Christians and the discrimination of Dalit Christians by the state as a special human rights issue, they built a strong partnership with international organisations such as Christian Solidarity Worldwide (UK), Dalit Freedom Network (Australia, Canada, Germany, UK and USA), Stefanus Alliance International (Norway) and Release International (UK). One of the articulate Dalit Christian leaders, Ajay Sing, Director of Odisha Forum for Social Action in collaboration with John Dayal played a major role not only in shaping the UN's Special Rapporteur, Ms Asma Jahangir's report on Freedom of Religion or Belief after her mission to India in 2008, but also subsequently did advocacy and lobbing to prepare stake-holders report to the United Nations Human Rights Council for the Universal Periodic Review 2012.[31]

While these efforts of Christians in internationalising the problem of religious freedom in India indicate their lack of confidence in the Government of India in controlling the Hindu radicals and in restoring the situation of religious freedom especially for the Dalits, it also throws light on Dalit Christian's new strategy to engage in international polity. Since India is a signatory to the Universal Declaration of Human Rights and it ratified the ICCPR (International Covenant on Civil and Political Rights), it can be pressurised and made accountable to the international bodies as regards its home-situations of religious freedom and human rights. As Ajay Sing puts "international advocacy is naming and shaming, it does not possess any power or legal status. India awakens only when outside people speak about what is happening here."[32] India's credibility as the one of the largest democracies of the world will erode gradually if the situation of religious freedom worsens. It is this perception that guides India's Dalit Christians as they engage in international lobbing and advocacy.

C. Dalit Muslims in India and International Advocacy

As far as Dalit Muslims are concerned, there is near absence of international advocacy. In spite of all my attempts for a month to gather information in this regard, I could not discover any substantial data that demonstrate Dalit Muslim's efforts to muster international support for their cause. The only related information I could obtain was about an international seminar entitled "Marginalisation of Dalit Muslims with Special Reference to Democracy, Identity and Livelihood" organised in collaboration with Deshkal Society and the Heinrich Boll Foundation.[33] This seminar that took place on 14 July 2002 in Patna played a pivotal role in creating Dalit Muslim consciousness and to realise its identity as a separate class within the Muslim society in India. Apart from this, there is sacristy of data to point to Dalit Muslim's initiative to tap the resources of different global networks to advance their emancipatory agenda. It is so because perhaps, unlike Dalit Christians, Dalit Muslim activism in India is focused more on electoral politics both at the state level as in case of Pasmanda Muslim Mahaz (PMM). Secondly, the Islamic leadership and ordinary Muslims both globally and nationally continue to think of their religious life and their social relations through the prism of Islamic texts. They hardly acknowledge Islam as a social reality and rarely view at as a lived religion that is deeply embedded in the socio-cultural milieu of a place. While this failure continues to dismiss certain aspects of lived Islam as aberrations of pure textual Islam, it not only creates a chasm between text-based Islam and lived Islambut also fails to generate emancipatory consciousness among Muslims in general to overcome the non-egalitarian dimensions of lived Islam and to align it with the egalitarian values of textual Islam. Such an absence of emancipatory consciousness can explain why Dalit Muslims are yet to win the support of good-willed non-Dalit Muslims in their struggle for equality and justice both within and outside Islam. Thirdly, the absence of Dalit Muslim diaspora outside India is one of the major reasons for Dalit's lack of international lobbying and advocacy. In the case of Dalit Christians, it is their diaspora group that lives outside India that is vastly responsible to take the Dalit Christian issues to the international fora including the UN by making use of their connections with international NGO's and human rights organisations. While the presence of Dalit Christian diaspora and their global activism have paved way for internationalising Dalit Christian issues in India and for pressuring both Indian Christian Churches and Indian government to look into the Dalit Christian demands for justice, the non-presence of Dalit Muslim Diaspora as an entity at the international level might account for the lack of international advocacy on the part of Dalit Muslims in India.

Conclusion

This essay has shown that the Dalits among the religious minorities in India (i.e. Dalit Christians and Dalit Muslims) is one of the most discriminated marginalised groups in India as they suffer social discrimination both within their respective faith communities and outside of them in larger civil society. They also suffer biases, discriminations and injustices at the level of institutions both of the faith communities and of the state that continue to be in the hands of the high castes in India. To fight this situations in their respective religious spheres, both the Christian organisations like DCLM and the Muslims organisations like Pasmanda Muslim Mahaz and The All India Backward Muslim Morcha (AIBMM) have undertaken multiple strategies and launched different emancipator projects. While both Dalit Christians and Dalit Muslims converge in political activism to address their grievances with the nation state, they also diverge from each other at least in one respect. While Dalit Muslims have taken the route of electoral politics to find solution to their problems, the Dalit Christians have embraced the path of international advocacy and lobbying not only to remove discriminatory practices within the churches but also to challenge the nation state for its willful complicity with the high caste power centers that discriminate and harass the Dalit religious minorities socially, constitutionally and legally. To overcome these unjust socio-political and religious forces is a herculean task and it certainly requires that Dalit Christians and Dalit Muslims learn from each other and tread each other's hitherto unexplored paths for a hopeful inclusive future.

References

1. Nadeem Hasnain. "Muslims in India: Cast Affinity and Social Boundaries of Backwardness," In Ashfaq Husain Ansari (ed.), *Basic problems of OBC and Dalit Muslims* (New Delhi: Serials Publications, 2007), 32-45, p. 33.
2. Yoginder Sikand. "A New Indian Muslim Agenda: The Dalit Muslims and the All-India Backward Muslim Morcha," *Journal of Muslim Minority Affairs*, 2001, 21:2, 287-296.
3. *Ibid.,* p. 292.
4. S.M. Michael. "Dalit Encounter with Christianity: Continuity and Change" in Rowena Robinson and Joseph Marianus Kujur (eds.) *Margins of Faith: Dalit and Tribal Christianity in India* (New Delhi: Sage Publications, 2010), 51-74, p. 52.
5. John C.B. Webster. The Dalit Christians: A History (Delhi: ISPCK, 2000), 33.
6. *Ibid.,* 41-46.
7. *Ibid.,* p. 43.
8. Duncan B. Forrester. *Caste and Christianity: Attitudes and Policies on Caste of Anglo-Saxon Protestant Missions in India (* London: Curzon Press, 1980), p. 77.
9. Hasnain, *Ibid.,* p. 33.
10. Imtiaz Ahmad. "Can There Be a Category Called Dalit Muslims?" in Kira Hall (ed.), *Studies in Inequality and Social Justice: Essays in Honour of Ved Prakash Vatuk* (Meerut: Archana, 2009), 64-81, p. 64.
11. Imtiaz Ahmad. 'The Ashraf and Ajilaf Categories in Indo-Muslim Society,' *Economic and Political Weekly*, 1967, May 13, 887-890, p. 890.
12. Prashant K Trivedi, Srinivas Goli, Fahimuddin, Surinder Kumar. "Does Untouchability Exist among Muslims? Evidence from Uttar Pradesh" *Economic & Political Weekly*, April 9, 2016, Vol. LI, No. 15, 32-36, p. 33.
13. *Ibid.*
14. Soutik Biswas, "Why are many Indian Muslims seen as untouchable?" 10, May 2016, https://www.bbc.com/news/world-asia-india-36220329(Accessed June 30, 2020)
15. Sobin George. "Dalit Christians in India: Discrimination, Development Deficit and the Question for Group-Specific Policies," *Working Papers Series, Indian Institute of Dalit Studies*, Vol. 6, No. 2, 2012, p. 5.
16. Vidya Sagar Dogar. '*Rural Christian Community in North West India*', (New Delhi: CISRS and ISPCK, 2000).
17. Paul D. Wiebe and John S. Peter. 'The Catholic Church and Caste in Rural Tamil Nadu', in Harjinder Singh (ed.), *Caste among Non-Hindus in India* (New Delhi: National Publishing House, 1977), pp. 37–49.
18. S.M. Michael, *Ibid.*
19. S.M. Michael, *Ibid.,* p. 59.
20. *Ibid.*, p. 62.

21. Cited in Louis, Prakash. 'Caste-based Discrimination and Atrocities on Dalit Christians and the Need for Reservations', *Working Paper Series*, II(04) (New Delhi: Indian Institute of Dalit Studies, 2007).
22. Sikand, *ibid.*, p. 290.
23. Sikand, *ibid.*, p. 291.
24. *Ibid.*
25. *Ibid.*
26. Sobin George, *ibid.*, p. 5.
27. *Ibid.*, p. 16.
28. *Ibid.*
29. http://www.vatican.va/roman_curia/pontifical_councils/chrstuni/weeks-prayer-doc/rc_pc_chrstuni_doc_20120611_week-prayer-2013_en.html (accessed Jan 15, 2020)
30. https://mattersindia.com/2019/09/pope-urged-to-discuss-dalit-christians-with-indian-bishophops-on-plight-of-dalit-christians/ (Accessed on Jan 15, 2020)
31. *Freedom of Religion in India: A Report to the United Nations Human Rights Council for the Universal Periodic Review 2012* (Bhubaneshwar: Odisha Forum for Social Action, 2012.
32. Interview with Ajay Sing in Bhubaneshwar on 28 May 2013 (11.30 a.m—1.00. p.m).
33. Mamjur Ali. "Politics of 'Pasmanda' Muslims : A Case Study of Bihar" *History and Sociology of South Asia,* 2010, 4 (2): 129-144, p. 139.

16

From Casteist-Capitalist Systems Towards Trajectories of Dalit Emancipation

— Prof. A. Maria Arul Raja SJ

Dalit World with its Assertive Struggles

The term "Dalit" is at once a realistic portrayal of victimhood, assertive claim of subjecthood, and articulate voice of communityhood of the victims of untouchability. It stands for resisting every form of degraded hierarchy and for promoting radical spirit of egalitarianism. On the other hand, the system of capitalist mind-set in collusion with corporatisation and casteism stands for systemic evil of mindless oppression for profiteering purposes at any cost. In other words, the Dalit sensibilities run counter to the capital-centred culture of accumulating the greed-triggered profit, and caste-oriented pride. One cannot naively claim that the upward mobility by the Dalits with decent salary, higher education, or political placement can automatically annihilate casteism.

Dalits are expected by the Manuvada prescription not to own up personal assets or collective resources. Their products are not readily bought by the caste-minded people especially the food materials and milk products for fear of untouchability. That is why, Ambedkar, the great stalwart of the struggles of the untouchables, believed in strengthening the anti-caste movement for paving the way for social revolution and Dalit emancipation. He did not opt for mere accommodation of the Dalits by the ruling elite with mere tokenism of offering some pittance. What is essential for him was the absolute insistence of human dignity and freedom of Dalits. Mere right to vote on the political plane during the election drama[1] even with the policy of affirmative action like reservations for the Dalit candidates have not yielded desirable results of Dalit emancipation. Neither the choice of the candidates, nor the conduct of the elections is under the Dalit supervision. After the elections the winners do not incorporate the Dalit aspirations into their priorities, policies, or statutes. All the claims of the programmes of the development of the Dalits, in the last analysis, seem to ultimately uproot the Dalits from their aspirations of cherishing dignified rights ensuring their life and livelihood.

In this brief paper, the first part analyses the multiple disabilities imposed on by the nexus between casteism and capitalism. The second part deals with some proposals of the trajectories of Dalit empowerment.

Dalits Imprisoned within the Casteist-Capitalist Systems

In the context of the global neo-liberal capitalism and the local systems of casteism, Dalits do not have the purchasing powers. They cannot afford to influence the capitalist economy or the corporatisation of the economic activities. The fruit of their labour is not assured with appropriate remuneration. Their contribution to the national economy is conveniently eclipsed with aggressive capitalist- casteist settings in India. In other words, the Dalits are progressively pauperised. In the Indian capitalist-casteist system of political economy, a good number of well-off Dalits have not realised even their dream- homes and the wretched among them live under thatched roofs or tiled ceiling called houses. Their participation in evolving economic policies, political process, educational opportunities and employment programmes are severely restricted and manipulated. But the new image of Dalit capitalist set afloat by the capitalist discourses "is a creation of the dominant castes to diffuse the potential risk of Dalit rebellion against capitalism. It is a clever plot to lure the oppressed class into the promises of capitalist dreams".[2] One has to realise that even the richest Dalits, with their negligible presence and beggarly profits, are nowhere in the caste—capital schemes of the economic order. Even the emerging Dalit entrepreneurs are quickly orphaned and abandoned by the caste lobbyists resulting in the death of networking with other colleagues in the business world.

Nexus between Casteism and Capitalism

It is claimed by some people that capitalism could uproot the rigidity of casteism with opportunities, competitiveness and profits open to all. But in the Indian soil, it has solidified the heinous crime of unbending casteism. Perhaps, that is why Ambedkar envisioned a sort of state socialism to look into the needs of the control of industrial and agricultural sectors for monitoring the flow of capital with the production of the surplus for ensuring the welfare of the marginalised lots. But the neo-liberal system of economy while pretending to offer some pittance for the Dalits with patronage in terms of some employment opportunities or miniscule income, seeks to drive them away from claiming their due share. "The bland promises of the neo-liberal regime seem unable to surmount the caste hegemony. Growing wage gaps and loosening of state control over public capital put marginalised sections like Dalits at the threshold of insecurity. Neo-liberalism has failed the Dalit enterprise." In the economic history of India, the feudalist, state capitalist, state socialist and neo-liberal systems of economy has consistently and effectively have been depriving the Dalits of their rights with the all-pervading culture of corruption.

In front of the mega structures of the oppressive caste capitalism, the miniscule capital[3] of the Dalits cannot negotiate any business deal or capital enterprise. But with reservation policies, liberation of economy, and growing critical awareness, and educational opportunities, merely a handful Dalits have their own houses, private vehicles, and some consume goods. But their attitudes and aspirations are very much along the lines of simulating the behaviours of the self-elevated caste groups like exploiting the less fortunate Dalits and dismissing their voice of dissent and cry for human rights. The growing hunger for unbridled consumerism, rampant greed, and oppressive market principles of the Dalit elite will turn out to be handy instruments in the hands of casteist-capitalist powers for exploiting the marginalised from among the Dalits.

The process of Sanskritisation is followed by some of the Dalits with the belief of getting an upward movement in the caste ladder. Sometimes even with some moderate earnings or abysmal impoverishment, they seek to imitate the typical rites, rituals, choice of the deities, scriptural traditions, food habits, particular dress code, or linguistic specialism counted to be idealised brahminical values. Deep down there is a discontentment of their own long cherished traditions and ways of life, while following them in a clandestine or less conspicuous manners. But they are frequently sought after by the caste people for menial jobs or services attached to minimum wages attached with stigma like scavenging or without that like simple clerical assignments. Often times, the caste ways of treating the Dalits are with disdainful mockery or disparaging hatred.

Neither the acquired upward economic mobility, nor the blind imitation of the caste behaviour by Dalits has assured them of a respectful treatment in the eyes of the caste-minded majority of the Indians. When the Dalits claim their legitimate positions and promotions, they are pushed down with derogatory remarks by the caste communities. In case of Dalit achievement of success due to their brilliant efficaciousness in the political realms or employment situations, it is belittled by non-Dalits with baseless deviant labelling or contemptuous remarks.

When the Dalit community is fragmented as the capitalist segment and the proletariat one, the agenda of annihilation of the systemic evil of caste system cannot be achieved. The proletariat segment will be burdened with the struggles against the capitalist casteist groups and capitalist Dalit group. The presence of multi-layered classes among the Dalits will dampen the collective spirit of breaking the shackles of casteism and slow down the process of Dalit emancipation.

In India, the caste structure of the society keeps on excluding the Dalits with multi-layered exclusion. It determines the economy, controls the polity, influences the judiciary, conditions the executive, dominates the legislature, prejudices the media, grips up the civil society, and governs the culture. Accordingly the Dalits are treated by them with mild or wild expression of violence. The prevailing culture of hostile distance from the caste society directly and indirectly in the strategically vantage positions of democratic institutions, policy making, budget allocations, media sphere, business world, IT sector, educational centres, or non-government organisations from top to bottom. Even with such antagonistic attitudes, when a couple of Dalits try proving their mettle in these sectors, these efforts are nipped in the bud. If they further assert themselves, they are dealt with temporary 'unfavourable inclusion',[4] eventually forcing them to sell their human dignity and labour for a throw-away prize leading them to helpless resignation, acute depression, and self-hatred.

Trajectories of Dalit Emancipation

Dalit struggle against their oppression is as old as the origin of casteism. Their voice of dissent against capitalism is as young as the beginning of the cultures of accumulation of the capital. Against the background of this organised and on-going dehumanisation of the Dalits by the immoral alliance between the systemic evils of capitalism and casteism, they have been evolving some intuitive measures for confronting them. By way of giving a face-lift to an organised Dalit struggle against the casteist-capitalist systems, let us propose the following trajectories in view of accelerating their empowerment:

- The discourse on Dalit suffering and struggle has to be related to the suffering of other subaltern groups struggling to remove the systemic evils of discriminatory hierarchy at the global level. For instance, Ambedkar was primarily engaged in the critical re-reading of the negative impact of the growing global capitalism upon the Dalits rather that the short-sighted national movements waging a war against the British imperialism.
- Accordingly the Dalit struggles are to be geared towards fighting against capitalist forms of governance, accumulative ethos of culture, and consumerist patterns of productivity in view of breaking the backbone of fossilised caste structures. Private capital and caste-based ownership of land perpetuate inequality at all levels running counter to the welfare of community of untouchables. But these very evils are unfortunately bequeathed to the caste-minded Indian ruling elite by the British imperialism.[5]
- Propertied individuals from among the Dalits, without the vision of annihilation of Casteism, are turn out to be stooges in the hands of casteist-capitalist forces. They become agents of fragmentation blocking the progress of Dalit emancipation. Such individuals are to be continuously educated with the integral vision of Dalit emancipation.
- The process of Sanskritisation consciously or unconsciously practiced by the Shudras and Dalits becomes an easy tool in the hands of the communal forces to segregate the Dalits as the inimical others. This process helps casteism to be increasingly solidified. Hardened. Hence both the Dalits and Shudras are to be alerted to consciously shy away from imitating the cultural practices of the so-called high caste people. Instead they have to identify and practice the ethical traditions, egalitarian ethos, aesthetics of solidarity and from their own cultural soil as well as from other groups of people across for their empowerment.
- The stories of their ancestors promoting these supreme values and universal principles of communitarian humanisation with personal dignity are to be excavated from out of the collective consciousness of the Dalits. They need to be professionally documented for research purposes and popular discourses. Re-reading such stories from the location of Dalit hermeneutical sensibilities could help them to construct new paradigms for challenging casteism and capitalism in the contemporary scenario.

- The memories of multiple forms of violence against the Dalits and the proactive response by their forefathers and foremothers are to be revisited with the perspectives of critical historical consciousness.
- The inter-textual and comparative reading of both the texts of the Law of Manu and Indian Constitution are to be undertaken in the realm of scholarly probe. The research findings of such efforts are to be popularised with appropriate people-friendly expressions.
- The dubious roles of religions in the politico-cultural realms are to be exposed. Both the official religious prescriptions by the pundits and the popular religious practices by the subalterns are at once deployed for the purposes of the legitimation of the oppression and interrogation of the same. While religions cannot be totally dismissed with iconoclastic blindness, the possibilities of creatively making use of the religious energies for Dalit empowerment cannot be ruled out. When the religious practices, be they official or subaltern, stand the test of promoting the ethics of egalitarianism, aesthetics of solidarity, and empowerment with humanisation, then they could be incorporated into the Dalit liberative discourses. If not so, such burdensome anti-human religious traditions are to be dismissed.

Notes

1. We come across many apprehensions about the integrity of the executives entrusted with the duty of managing the democratic process of exercising the citizens' franchise with paper ballots or EVMs. Even after winning the elections, a large number of Dalit candidates are not free from the intimidation or incentives from the caste forces for making choices of their own conscience of serving the marginalised.
2. Suraj Yengde, *Caste Matters,* (Gurgaon: Penguin Random House, 2019), p. 212.
3. It is very rare to see shop owners, petty contractors, small scale money lenders, and salaried people with or without landed properties from the Dalit communities becoming entrepreneurs at the regional or national levels.
4. Cf. https://www.adb.org/sites/default/files/publication/29778/social-exclusion.pdf accessed on 12 January 2020.
5. Even the Nehruvian mixed economy is gradually camouflaged by the neo-liberal policies favoured by the successive governments from 1990-s onwards. They have developed them into crony capitalism at this moment of history.

17

Globalisation and its Impact on Education of Dalits

— *Dr. Wesly Kumar V S J*

Introduction

Globalisation has brought with it several debates and one of the most debated issues is education. Education acts as an instrument for the emancipation of humankind. The major function of education is the transformation of society with norms and values. Indian nation has acknowledged the critical role of education and has given utmost importance to it. This paper aims at understanding the concept of globalisation and to assess its impact on the education Dalits.

Globalisation

Globalisation is the term used to describe the growing interdependence of the world's economy, culture, and population, brought about by across the countries in business, goods and services, technology, investment, people, and information. But the term gained popularity in the early 1990s, as such arrangements shaped modern in everyday life.

Globalisation is also a connection of different parts of the world resulting in the expansion of international cultural, economic, and political activities. It is an integration of goods and people among different countries. This process has effects on the environment, culture, political system, economic development and on people around the world (Kolb, 2019).

In simple terms, globalisation is the process by which people and goods move easily across borders. Even though it is an economic concept, it has cultural element, as ideas and traditions are traded and assimilated. Globalisation has brought many benefits to many people, but not to everyone.

Effective education system is the foundation of opportunities to lead a decent life, ensuring all the children have adequate access to education irrespective of their income level. The exclusion from education is one of the basic causes of global inequality. People can only contribute and benefit from globalisation if they are endowed with knowledge, skills, values, with the capabilities and rights.

Globalisation is a boon for some and a curse for others. The boon factor of globalisation is for rich, business persons, industrialists, real estate personnel, capitalists, entrepreneurs, software companies to mention only a few. The curse factor is for labour, employees of middle income group, part-time workers, oppressed and exploited people such as scheduled castes, scheduled tribes, other backward castes and Muslim minorities to mention a few.

The impact of globalisation on education is a major concern, and it has affecting the socio-economic conditions of Dalits in terms of education, employment, access to land, poverty and other welfare programmes.

Globalisation further led to marginalisation of the marginalised sections of the society. In other words, globalisation severely affects the Dalits and other underprivileged sections, who are deprived in accessing education, employment, housing, food, healthcare etc. such a way globalisation affects the lives of Dalits differs significantly from non-Dalits.

Globalisation is a process in which societies, politics, culture and economic situation have, in some sense, come closer together. The purpose of this article is to examine the impact of the reforms on the Dalits. The study confines itself to the most predominant dimension of education.

Education of Dalits

Education is the most important pre-requisite for achieving the goals of personal, social, political, economic and cultural development, and it is the most effective instrument for meeting the challenges the Dalits are facing, in their day to day life. Historical evidences in this regard indicate that Dalits were excluded from the education since centuries. Although Article 21A of the Indian Constitution stipulates that the State shall provide free and compulsory education to all children of the age of six to fourteen years it still remains an elusive. However, owing to reservation and affirmative action in the arena of education, substantial progress has been made in the education of Dalits, during few decades.

Table: Gender-wise Literacy trend among Dalits (SCs) and Total population

(Figures in percentage)

Year	*All*			*Scheduled Castes*		
	Male	*Female*	*Total*	*Male*	*Female*	*Total*
1961	34.44	12.95	24.02	16.96	3.29	10.3
1971	39.45	39.45	29.46	22.36	6.44	14. 7
1981	65.60	65.50	43.67	31.12	10.93	21.4
1991	64.13	64.13	52.21	49.91	23.76	37.4
2001	75.30	53.70	64.84	66.64	41.90	54.7
2011	80.90	64.60	73.00	75.20	56.50	66.1

Source: National Commission for S.C's and ST's, 5th report, 1998-99, Vol. I; Census Report, 2001; Report of National literacy mission at http://www.nlm.nic.in; censusmp.nic.in/censusmp/AllPDF/6Literacy21.12,www.scdd.kerala.gov.in/images/Sc_Census%20_2011.ppt, accessed on 12th August 2014.

The above Table demonstrates that the Dalits attained comparatively better literacy rate in the last four decades. Literacy rate of the Dalits improved considerably from 10.3 in 1961 to 66.1 in 2011. This trend indicates positive movement among the Dalits marking the proportional to the rhetoric of special provisions made for the weaker chapters. Despite the provisions, the growth of Dalit education was very slow to the literacy level of general population. The socio-economic conditions were also responsible for educational growth. The Government of India had confessed that the officials of educational departments were displaying a hostile attitude towards the education of the Dalits. However, the consciousness of the education is being generated among the Dalits (Yagati, 2003). The data shows the variation in the literacy rates among Dalits and general population. In the general population, female literacy rate is poor and the position of Dalit female is worse (5th report of National Commission for SCs, 1998-99). When we compare the literacy levels of Dalits and other castes, still this community is lagging behind in educational achievements which highlight the significance of their deprivation. It is a known fact that without education other constitutional safeguards, reservation would be of no use. It would also be hard for Dalits to send their children to private schools. But it is to be kept in mind that the enrolment alone does not give any substantial amount of educational achievement when the rate of drop out is also substantially high among the Dalits. Despite several kinds of State assistance, the dropout rate is also alarming at the primary, middle and secondary stages of education in respect of Dalits. In spite of that the sphere of primary and elementary education could not remain unaffected from globalisation.

The Dalits and their children kept on torment from different types of social disabilities as well as economic deprivation, and education. The drop-out percentage among Dalit students demonstrates the status of their educational development. Around 33.58 percent of Dalit children are dropped out from classes I to V, 64.83 percent in classes I to VIII, and 70.39 percent in classes I to X in amid 2004-05. This demonstrates the issue turns out to be more awful at the higher levels of schooling. The educational status of the Dalits keeps on being much lower than that of others, as figures indicates that they hold low literacy percentages and there is an increasing gap between the educational status of the Dalits and others. Further, the educational status of Dalit girls is also very low compared to the total female literacy of indicating a very wide gap. Though 34.40 percent of Dalit girls of classes' I-V drop out from school, the rate increases in higher classes by 72.59 percent. The enrolment of children of Dalits has increased considerably at the primary stage because of the educational policies, but the participation more or less in proportion to their share in population at the primary level. Notwithstanding the way that the dropouts declining, the gender disparity still exits. The Dalits are vulnerable as a result of related effects of low budgetary status, and lower parental capability percentages. From the data on school dropouts of Dalits in Andhra Pradesh, we can understand the factors accountable for children being pushed out of schools and relentless illuminations for dropouts, for instance, desperation, nature of education, and lack of interest in education and examination failure. It locates the explanation in terms of an absence of the social norm which promotes a child's right to education.

Commercialisation of education is continuously increasing. The system of primary and elementary education in rural and urban settings has been subverted almost totally as the rich upper castes send their children to private/convent schools, the government schools have been reduced into dysfunctional. Dalit children do not have access or the opportunity to attend high-cost and presumably 'good-quality' private schools. And the tuition fees are also high in those schools, they were compelled to send their children to government schools. Even today, the importance of the English language has been increased everywhere and is very difficult for most of Dalit children, educated in vernacular medium, to compete with their counterparts (Teltumbde, 1997). It is observed that the majority of the Dalit students are enrolled in Arts and humanities, and it becomes difficult for them to meet the job requirements of the multinational companies. Higher education is also severely affected by globalisation.

The free market ethos has entered in the educational sphere in a big way. So commercialisation of education is no more a mere rhetoric; it is now a big reality. In other words, corporate sector has entered into this area, transforming the education into an enterprise for profits. In the present day private educational institutions are more commonly known as education industry (George, 2013).

At present, large number of medical, engineering, management and technological institutions have been established under private management, for which the entry is with a large amount of money, known as capitation fees, and those are highly expensive and inaccessible to the Dalits. The emerging areas of software, bio-technology, and bio-informatics are almost beyond the reach of the Dalits. Many elite institutions like IIMs, IITs are not affordable for the Dalits. In a true spirit of globalisation many foreign universities are invading the educational spheres through hitherto unfamiliar strategic alliances with the commercial agencies, of course, at hefty dollar equivalent prices (Teltumbde, 1997). If wealth becomes the main criterion for admission, the children of Dalits may not get any chance of entry into these educational institutions.

Their chances of acquiring jobs in the high-tech industry as well as in the multinational corporations have been getting curtailed since the beginning of the process of globalisation in India. The system of primary and elementary education has been subverted almost totally. Since, majority of the rich upper caste send their children to the private/convent/public schools, government schools have been reduced into dysfunctional. Such government schools, does not have hardly any infrastructure and teachers and unable to compete with prestigious private sector schools. Further, majority of Dalit are undergraduates in Arts and Humanities, it becomes difficult for them to meet the job requirements of the multinational corporations. Even if some of the Dalits aspire to compete in the technology driven new job market, it would be, perhaps, out of their reach to acquire the requisite qualifications at exorbitant rates from various engineering and management institutes. It is precisely due to these reasons that Dalits are rarely to be found in the prestigious management schools all over the country (Mandal, 2009).

The globalisation has created a new situation where *Dalits* are pushed to a state of anxiety. This paper seeks to investigate the implications of globalisation in the arena of education, from a *Dalit* perspective.

Impact of globalisation

Even to the globalisation, the Dalit are still out of the mainstream of the society, because of their poverty, backwardness in education, lack of technological advancement etc,. They are unable to get their share out of the advantages of globalisation, as a result a huge gap is created between the rich and the poor.

Beck (2000) focuses on globalisation with regard to society, economics, politics and culture Giddens, and McGrew (1990). And Lewis (1992) sees globalisation as an increase in global social relationships. In this context, Jogdand (2000) addresses the Structural Adjustment Programme (SAP), sponsored by the World Bank and the IMF.

The Macroeconomic Policy Framework supports the elimination of state involvement in the social sectors. This volume represents the first critical assessment, in particular, of the likely impact of the Dalits. It offers comprehensive coverage of all issues arising from the current process of globalisation in India and the manner in which it impacts Dalits day-to-day lives.

Thorat (1997) studied the effect on Dalits. According to him, Dalits suffered from discrimination on the basis of caste and untouchability in the private labour market. The writings of Teltumbde (2001) and Rai (2002) provide a detailed theoretical and empirical account of the implementation of structural reforms, based on evidence from the international community.

These studies conclude that the reforms will hit the Dalits in a very crude manner and that these policies will accentuate their deprivation. Mungekar (2001) sees these reforms as a gradual withdrawal of the state from economic activity and doubts that the benefits of prospective economic growth would be brought down to the poor Dalits in the process of economic growth.

Maikkel (1999) examines the impact of economic reforms on Dalits and its implications for the nation. It analyzes the effect of recent liberalising and privatising trends and the consequent withdrawal of the state on Dalits, in particular in the sense of employment opportunities and the policy of reservation.

Shah (2002) argues that the role of the interventionist in bringing about social change is required to be performed by the Indian State under the Directives of the Constitution. Dalits, the socially and economically most marginalised in Indian society, see the state not only as providing equal opportunities but also as creating positive conditions for improving their socio-economic condition.

Galanter (1984) provides analysis of the methods by which India has addressed the problems of marginalised. It contains an incisive examination of the interaction of legislature, administration and judiciary in carrying out national policy. He examines the implementation of the formal processes for improving the substantive condition of suppressed people.

Dushkin's (1972) study endeavors a survey of the basis, history and highlights of the defensive segregation framework itself as the official approach toward the 'Untouchables'. The activity of a crucialpart of the framework ensured political portrayal and she looks at certain ramifications, outcomes of the framework as far as positions of authority, general supposition and possibilities for future.

Sheth (1987) contends that the polarisation of the electorate caste lines and the going with danger of brutality have prompted the scrutinizing of positive discrimination. The critique supportsthe use of financial criteria for distinguishing the recipients of the program and keep up that the present procedure has fortified caste identity.

Gaikwad (1999) and Mitra, (1990) contend that, whatever changes have occurred among the Dalits in the sphere of education and occupation are because of the reservations. The arrangement is not implemented in true spirit and its advantages have not permeated into the less fortunate strata of the Dalits.

Different reservations are provided for various categories of the beneficiaries. Reservations for Dalits have educational, governmental jobs, legislative and economic spheres. Mishra and Kaur (1990) feel that the target of the policy was a more equitable distribution of economic resources and worthwhile sharing of power at different levels within the running of the state affairs. Consistent with them, the policy has did not realize its objectives and has resulted within the formation of an elite class with vested interests during this section. Masani (1990) argues that reservations increase inefficiency and deliberate merit. Regarding the utilisation of the scholarships provided for the SC students,

Oommen (1977) observed to that value the actual beneficiaries have been now not the poorest yet the most deserving amongst the SCs but those everyone had been meanwhile economically better off among them. Sachchidananda (1974), Chitnis (1977) Kirpal (1978) and Kaul (1993) came equal to comparable conclusion. They argue that the economically better off among the SCs had been able to avail the new opportunities that came in the wake of reservations, but few managed to gain advantage of higher education or even professional education. Similarly economic benefits had failed to percolate down to the poor Dalits. It is the better off from among them who had mainly benefited from the various programmes like IRDP (Bandopadhyay,1984; Aiyar, 1985).

Public Report on Basic Education in India (PROBE, 1999), and Nambissan (1996) examine the distinct historical experiences of Dalit communities in the context of education and assert that equity in education was not consciously practiced in formal schooling system. In the overall context of inadequate public resources for schooling, greater privatisation of qualitative education for the elite, and the search for non-formal alternatives for the educationally-backward they observe, it is likely that socially and economically vulnerable groups will suffer greater neglect. One of the profound changes in contemporary Indian society has been the emergence of a new sense of identity among the Dalits.

Parvathamma (1989) argues that the Dalits, socially and economically the most oppressed section of Indian society, look upon the State not only to provide equal opportunities but also to create positive conditions for improving their socio-economic conditions. There are very few studies on Dalits in the context of globalisation.

Mahesh (2000) feel that under globalisation there will be a frontal assault on pollution, impurity and untouchability. He feels that globalisation has set into motion an intricate interplay of continuity and change in the social order. At the same time the globalisation has increased insecurity, inequity, displacement, and brought about a situation of 'end of employment', while widening the gap between the rich and poor.

With regards to reforms, each country should decide about the nature and extent of globalisation that can be constructively introduced in their socio-economic and educational systems. While it is difficult to resist the temptation of falling in line with the international trade, it is necessary that while doing so, national interests should be kept in view. This is more so in the field of education, which is intimately concerned with the development of human capital. Ultimately, any hasty involvement in the global educational market can end up in harming the vital interests of students, and particularly of poor and downtrodden for generations to come.

Education sector in India is facing serious concerns and encounters. While there is a pressure to prepare global citizens who are ready to squatter the highly competitive world, the grassroots realties present a similar image. The vital aim of education is to enable children develop their potentials, pinpoint and pursue a meaningful purpose and recognise the right of others to do the same. However, current research has reflected the need for availability as well as upgradation of physical infrastructure and remoter deployment of resources to enhance the quality of schooling. On one hand, most private schools are seen utilising resources to enable their pupils to express themselves, exploring their natural and social milieu; government schools due to the legalistic hurdles and lack of physical infrastructure are unable to cater to the demands of education. This comes as an irony since the government policies and documents unmistakably focus on responding to the physical, psychosocial and emotional needs of children with the purpose of holistic minutiae of their personalities. The priority snooping for the country remains particularly with improving the quality of education and making education effective, enjoyable and relevant to the children. Schools have to aim at providing children fruitful experiences that enable them to realise fully their innate talents, develop capacities and empower all children in their learning, wideness differences of castes, religion, gender and disability. It's only when the country will be worldly-wise to provide quality education to the children wideness the socio-cultural milieu; it will be worldly-wise to truly unzip the potentials of a globalised world (Baird, 2009).

Conclusion

Globalisation has many effects on education, and it facilitates the transition from an industrial-based society to an information-based. At the same time, there is another side to globalisation. While the rich grow richer, the poor are becoming poorer. Thus, the education gap between the rich and the poor are widening. Poverty, lack of education and social status have caused a moral crisis, damaging many Dalit families, resulting in increasing unemployment, suicide, violence, racism and drug abuse and anti-social behaviour. In the 21st century, education systems faces the challenges of equipping students with the new knowledge, skills and values needed to be competitive in a global market while at the same time producing graduates who are responsible citizens of the country.

The studies reveal that the globalisation has a positive impact on Dalits in the context of education. The globalisation creates awareness about importance of education and the parents are more concerned about their children's future, thus admit them in good schools, even to their poor economic conditions, by keeping their mind on their children to secure good job and settle in the future. It is pertinent to mention that a majority of the parents are interested in English medium private schools, but their financial condition did not allow them to bear the expenses of these schools. However, the globalisation has resulted in downsizing the staff in government sector. Due to reservations in education, the Dalits are being educated. But there are no government jobs. If some jobs are available, the same are under contract or temporary basis. There is lot of insecurity.Under the globalisation, the socioeconomic conditions of the vast majority of the Dalits are going from bad to worse, rather than improving. Hence the governmentshould ensure good quality primary education for all and enforce the reservation policy in private sector also for the benefit of Dalits. Under the present situation the role of the state becomes crucial for the empowerment of Dalits as the state cannot deny socio-economic justice to the Dalits still. This essay concludes with the assertion that the issues concerning socio-economic justice of the Dalits need to be addressed seriously.

References

Aiyar, S.S. (1985). Reforming IRDP: Unsuccessful attack on poverty, *Indian Express,* August 19.

Baird, R. (2009). Private Schools for the Poor Development, Provision, and Choice in India.Gray Matters Capital. (http://dise.in/Downloads/Use%20of%20Dise%20 Data/Ross%20Baird.pdf).

Bandyopadhayay, D (1984). An Evaluation of Policies and Programmes for the Alleviation of Rural Poverty in India, *Quality of Work Life*, January-April, 1(1-2).

Béteille, A. (1987). *Essays in comparative sociology*.USA:Oxford University Press.

Chitnis, S. and Aikara, J.(1977). The Scheduled Castes and College Education: A study of Drop-Out and the Situation of the Scheduled Caste Students of Bombay, *ICSSR Research Quarterly* 6 (326), 1.

Dushkin, L (1972). Scheduled Caste Politics' in J M Mahar (ed), The Untouchables in Contemporary India, Tuscon: University of Arizona Press.

Gaikwad, S. L (1999). Protective Discrimination Policy and Social Change, New Delhi: Rawat Publications.

Galanter Marc (1984). Competing Equalities, Delhi: Oxford Press.

Geetha, B. Nambissan (1996). Exclusion and Discrimination in Schools: Experiences of Dalit Children, Working Paper Series, New Delhi: Indian Institute of Dalit Studies and UNICEF.

George Goldy M. (2013). Human Rights, Dalits and the Politics of Exclusion, *Afro Asian Journal of Social Sciences*, Vol. 4, No. 4.1 Quarter 1, 1-24.

Giddens, Anthony (1990, The Consequences of Modernity, Stanford: Stanford University Press.

Jogdand, P.G. (2002). Globalisation and Dalits, Social Action, Volume 52, No. 1.

Kaul, R. (2001). Accessing primary education: Going beyond the classroom, *Economic and Political Weekly*, 155-162.

Kirpal, V (1978). Higher Education for the SC's and ST's, *Economic and Political Weekly,* 13: 165-169.

Kolb, Melina (2019). What is globalisation? Devasahayam Madonna, Helen Hillebrand, and Steven R. Weisman (eds), Washington: Peterson Institute for International Economics.

Lewis, P (1992), 1945-1992. Global politics: Globalisation and the Nation- State, UK: Polity Press.

Mahesh Rangarajan (2009). Environmental Issues in India: A Reader.

Maikkel, E. E. (1999). Untouchable: Dalits in Modern India. Lynne Rienner Publishers.

Mandal Bankim Chandra, (2009). "Dalits and Reservations in the Private Sector", *Voice of Dalits*, Vol. 2, No.1 January – June, 45-57.

Masani, Minoo (1990). Abolish reservations: promote meritocracy. *Mainstream*' 28 (1): 6.

Mishra, R. G., & Kaur, G. (1990). Reservation Policy and Personnel Selection. New Delhi: M.D. Publications Pvt. Ltd.

Mungekar, B.L., (2001). State, Market and the Dalits : Analytics of the New Economic Policy, in Michael, S.M., (ed.), Dalits in Modern India: Vision and Values, New Delhi: Vistaar Publications.

National Commission for SC's (1998- 99) report, New Delhi: NCSC.

Oommen, T K (1990). Protest and Change - Studies in Social Movements, New Delhi: Sage.

Parvathamma, C. 1989. Scheduled Castes at the Cross Road, New Delhi: Asish Publishers.

PROBE (1999). Public Report on Basic Education in India. New Delhi: Oxford University Press.

Rai, Sheela (2002). Social and conceptual background to policy of reservation, *Economic and Political Weekly* 37(42).

Sachidananda (1974). Education among the Scheduled Castes and Scheduled Tribes in Bihar, Patna: Institute of Social Studies.

Shah, Ghanshyam ed.(2002). Social movements and the state (Readings in Indian government and politics, vol. 4). New Delhi: Sage Publications.

Sheth, D. L. (1987). Reservations Policy Revisited. *Economic and Political Weekly*, 1957-1962.

Teltumbde, Anand (2001). 'Globalisation and Dalits', Nagpur: Sanket Prakashan.

Teltumbde, Anand, (1997). Impact of New Economic Reforms on Dalits in India, Department Sociology, University of Pune, Pune.

Thorat, S (1997). Social security in unorganised sector in India: How secure are the Scheduled Castes, *The Indian Journal of Labour Economics* 42(3).

Ulrich, Beck (2000). Risk Society: Towards a New Modernity, London: Sage.

Yagati, C.R. (2003). Dalits' Struggle for Identity: Andhra and Hyderabad 1900-1950, New Delhi: Kanishka Publishers.

18

Changes in Socio-Economic Status of Erstwhile Andhra Pradesh: Post-Independence Period

— Dr. G Jagadeesh & C. Amara Rao

Introduction

This paper attempts to examine the status of the marginalised and excluded social groups in terms of Access to Land, Occupational Distribution, Education, and Poverty in undivided Andhra Pradesh with a special reference to Scheduled Castes (Dalits) and Scheduled Tribes (Adivasis). The analysis points out that these disadvantaged people lag behind other Social Groups in terms of Land Holding, Monthly Consumption and Expenditure, and Poverty despite visible progress on all fronts of Development Indicators. The study unearths alarming escalation of atrocities against Scheduled Castes (Dalits) and Scheduled Tribes (Adivasis) in connivance with the Politicised Corporate and Corporatised Political powers of all hues and allegiance and the tacit support of the Government Machinery and Bureaucracy in the digital era.

Agriculture and Dalits

Andhra Pradesh has a sizeable Scheduled Caste (SC) and Scheduled Tribe population (ST). The SC population in 1961 was 4.9 million constituting 13.8% of the total population in the state. The ST population was 1.3 million, accounted for 3.7% of the state population. The latest census (2011) specifies a three-fold increase in the number of SCs and four-fold increase of STs in the state during the last five decades vis-à-vis between 1961 and 2011 (Table 1). In 2011, population of SC and ST is about 13.9 and 5 million comprising 16.4% and 5.6% respectively of the total population in the state. Andhra Pradesh accounts for about 6.9% of total population of SCs, and 6.0% of the total STs in India. As compared to all-India, the percentage of SCs in the total population is marginally lower and that of ST population is nearly 2 % lower in the state. The share of the state with respect to the population of the country appears to be declining. Although proportion of the SC/ST population has increased over time in the state as well as all-India, rate of increase in the state seems to be relatively lower than all-India average.

Table 1: Distribution of SC/ST population in Andhra Pradesh and India

Year	*Andhra Pradesh*					*All India*					*% of AP in India*		
	Population (in M)			*% in T P*		*Population (in M)*			*% in T P*				
	SC	*ST*	*All*	*SC*	*ST*	*SC*	*ST*	*All*	*SC*	*ST*	*SC*	*ST*	*All*
1961	4.9	1.3	35.9	13.8	3.7	64.4	29.9	439.2	14.7	6.9	7.7	4.4	8.2
1971	5.8	1.6	43.5	13.3	3.8	80	38	548.2	14.6	6.9	7.2	4.4	7.9
1981	7.9	3.1	53.5	14.9	5.9	104.8	51.6	683.3	15.8	7.8	7.6	6.2	7.8
1991	10.6	4.2	66.5	15.9	6.3	138.2	67.8	846	16.5	8.1	7.7	6.2	7.9
2001	12.3	5	76.2	16.2	6.6	166.6	84.3	1028.6	16.2	8.2	7.4	6	7.4
2011	13.9	5.9	84.5	16.4	7	201.4	104.3	1210.2	16.6	8.6	6.9	5.7	7

Note: 1. TP – Total Population; SC – Scheduled Castes; ST – Scheduled Tribes
Source: Census of India.

It also needs to be mentioned that the SC and ST communities in Andhra Pradesh as well as in the country are not homogeneous groups, there are a number of sub-castes/groups within each groups. Particularly in Andhra Pradesh, there are about 59 sub-castes in SCs. The important ones are ***mala, madiga, relli, and adi andhra***. Within the ***mala*** **and** ***madiga,*** there are about 25 and 18 sub-caste groups respectively. Similarly, there are about 33 sub-tribes among STs in the state. Important ones among them are ***Gonds, Koyas, Konda Reddies,*** **Baghathas, Chenchus, Jathapus, and** ***Savaras***. We have mentioned that there is an increase in numbers among the Scheduled Tribes. This sharp rise in the state particularly during the 1970s is due to the inclusion of a community called *Lambada /Sugali*, which mostly lives in the plains. Another major reason is- when *Government has notified Lambadas* as Scheduled Tribes in Andhra Pradesh, many *lambadas* from the neighbouring states of Maharashtra and Karnataka have migrated to Andhra Pradesh to claim ST status. Therefore, the *lambadas* stand out as the single largest tribal group and constitute about 40 percent of the total ST population in the state (Venkatanarayana, 2006).

Access to Land

Land has been and is one of the essential factors of any economic activity and is one of the fundamental natural resources that produce food and non-food products. For ages in India, land has been serving the people as one of the greater sources to generate income, more specifically, rural population since our Indian Economy is agriculture dominated. The productivity and ownership of land besides serving as the engine of economic growth, as well determines the level of social equality and inequality in the society. During the British rule, land was resourceful golden goose and land revenue formed and contributed major income to the exchequer. Perhaps, for this reason marginal and small farmers and tenants experienced dehumanising exploitation of the rulers and intermediaries associated with the collection of land revenue. Ownership of land formed the basis for the classification of the social groups into Zamindars, Mahalwars, and Ryots, which resulted in class and status distinctions and sowed the seed of rivalry to claim leadership and thus dominance and abuse got perpetuated in the society. Such struggle for power and dominance resulted in skewed distribution of land. Invariably it is associated with the caste system which is essentially a ladder in nature and function. Obviously, the Land is mostly in the hands of the upper and the dominant peasant castes and willfully excluded the Scheduled Castes. Thus, there emerged two distinct categories in the casteist society of India vis-à-vis: those who own the land and those who do not own any significant amount of land. Landowning farmers hence enjoyed and wielded higher status and hegemony over the latter. The concentration of ownership holdings in a small number of households, who own 80 percent of cultivating area, left three-fourth of the total rural households economically poor, physically weak, and psychologically down. To reduce inequalities India has initiated and attempted land reforms. Unfortunately, such initiatives have not brought expected and required relief and status to the most vulnerable sections in the society like the landless labour and small tenets. Instead, the land holding in few hands continue to persist in different forms on *binami* names. The present paper inspects not only the distribution of landholding pattern in general but also in particular among the Schedule Castes and Schedule Tribes of undivided Andhra Pradesh. For the simple reason that Andhra Pradesh is one of the leading States which has commenced several land legislations to augment the production and to reduce the inequalities in the distribution of land, productivity of land and generation of income. The most notable legislations among them are as follows:

1. Andhra Pradesh (Andhra Area) Estates Land (Reduction of Rent) Act, 1947: The major objective of this Act was to provide for reduction of rents payable to ryots in Estates approximate to the

level of assessment levied on lands in Ryotwari area in the neighbourhood.

2. The Madras Estate (Abolition and Conversion into Ryotwari) Act, 1948: It provided for the repeal of the permanent settlement, the acquisition of the rights of land-holders in permanently settled and certain other estates in the province of Andhra and the introduction of the Ryotwari settlement in such estates. "Estate" means Zamindarior under-tenure or an Inam Estate. This act extends to the whole state of Andhra.
3. The Andhra Pradesh (Telangana Area) Tenancy and Agricultural Lands Act, 1950. The major objectives of this Act are (1) to regulate the relations of landlords and tenants of agricultural lands, (2) to regulate alienations of land, (3) to prevent excessive sub-division of agricultural holdings, (4) to provide for the legislation of co-operative farm and (5) to empower government to assume in certain circumstances management of agricultural lands.
4. Andhra Inams (Abolition and Conversion into Ryotwari) Act, 1956 to abolish and convert certain Inam lands into Ryotwari lands. It extends to the whole of the state of Andhra but applies only to Inam lands.
5. Andhra Tenancy Act of 1956 provides for the payment of fair rent by cultivating tenants and for fixing the minimum period of agricultural leases in the State.
6. The Andhra Pradesh ceiling on Agricultural Holdings Act, 1961 provides for the imposition of ceiling on agricultural holdings ranging from 27 acres to 324 acres depending upon the class of land.
7. The Andhra Pradesh Land Reform (ceiling on Agricultural Holdings) Act, 1972, which provides for a ceiling area of one standard holding ranging from 4.05 hectares (10 acres) to 10.93 hectares (about 27 acres) in the case of wetland and from 14-16 hectares (35 acres) to 21-85 hectares (54 acres) in case of dry land.

Despite the above stringent land legislations and enforcement of the same, even today it is interesting to note that the concentration of land is still in the hands of few high caste politically influential and powerful households in Andhra Pradesh.

Undivided Andhra Pradesh has a sizeable Scheduled Castes and Scheduled Tribes population. According to census, the Scheduled Castes population in 1991 was 10.6 million constituting 15.9 percent of the total population of the state. The Scheduled Tribes population was 4.2 million constituting 6.3 percent of the total population. The Scheduled Castes are distributed throughout the state, whereas the Scheduled Tribes are in the hilly and forest areas of Srikakulam, Vizianagaram, Visakhapatnam, East Godavari, West Godavari, Khammam, Warangal, and Adilabad districts and the Nallamala forest interiors. The 2001 census specify an increase in both number and percentage of SCs and STs in undivided Andhra Pradesh. In 2001, there were about 12.3 and 5 million SCs and STs comprising16.2 and 6.6 percent of the total population in undivided Andhra Pradesh correspondingly. As per 2011 census, population of SCs and STs is about 13.9 and 5 million comprising 16.4% and 5.6% respectively of the total population in the state. We shall now consider the changes in land holding distribution among the Scheduled Caste and the Scheduled Tribes.

Table 2: Percentage distribution of operational holdings and operated area different social groups in undivided Andhra Pradesh

Year		*Category*			
		SC	*ST*	*Others*	*Total*
1976-77	Nos	13.4	6.3	80.3	100
	Area	6.9	6.2	86.9	100
1980-81	Nos	12.6	6.4	81	100
	Area	6.9	6.3	86.8	100
1990-91	Nos	12.73	6.88	80.39	100
	Area	7.48	7.23	85.29	100
1995-96	Nos	12.12	7.11	80.77	100
	Area	7.42	7.56	85.02	100
2000-01	Nos	11.85	7.47	80.66	100
	Area	7.86	8.23	83.91	100
2005-06	Nos	11.8	7.69	80.49	100
	Area	7.84	8.36	83.8	100
2010-11	Nos	11.1	8.0	80.9	100
	Area	7.7	8.7	83.6	100

Source: 1. various issues of Report on SC/ST Land Holdings
2. Agricultural census, 2012.

Table 2 explains the operational holdings and area operated by different groups since 1976-77 to 2010-11 in undivided Andhra Pradesh. In 1976-77, SC, households constituted about 13.4 percent of total holdings but controlled only 6.9 percent of the area, while others constitute about

80.3 percent of the total holdings but controlled 87 percent of total operated area. By 2000-01 the percentage of SC holdings declined to about 11.85 percent and their controlling area share slightly increased to 7.86 percent. Whereas the percentage of others' holdings remained the same, i.e. 80.7 percent and their operated area share slightly declined to 84 percent of total operated area. In 1976-77, ST operational holdings constituted 6.3 percent of total holdings and controlled 6.2 percent of the total operated area. By 2000-01, their holdings increased to more than 7 percent while their share in area also increased to 8.23 percent. During 2005-06, we notice, both increasing trend, in terms of operational holding and operated area. However, in 2010-11, SC operational holdings registered 11.1 percent and they controlled only 7 percent of area out of the total operated area at the same time STs operational holding was 8 percent and controlled 8.8 percent of total operated area. On the other hand, the rest of the social groups owned the other 80.8 percent of operational holding and controlled 83.6 percent of total operated area.

Table 3: Percentage distribution of operational holdings and area Operated by scheduled castes in undivided Andhra Pradesh

Year		*Different Size group*					
		Marginal	*Small*	*Semi medium*	*Medium*	*Large*	*All groups*
1976-77	Nos	64.8	19	11.5	4.1	0.6	100
	Area	22.3	23.1	26	21.5	7.1	100
1980-81	Nos	67.7	18.9	10.2	2.9	0.3	100
	Area	27.6	26.2	25.2	15.2	5.5	100
1990-91	Nos	70.67	18.43	8.7	2.03	0.17	100
	Area	31.98	28.28	24.4	12.38	2.96	100
1995-96	Nos	73.46	17.75	7.39	1.32	0.08	100
	Area	37.15	29.74	22.51	8.82	1.78	100
2000-01	Nos	73.84	17.64	6.98	1.42	0.12	100
	Area	36.45	29.53	21.33	9.36	3.33	100
2005-06	Nos	74.59	17.42	6.63	1.27	0.09	100
	Area	38.32	30.21	20.9	8.64	1.93	100
20010-11	Nos	76.2	17	5.74	0.99	0.06	100
	Area	41.44	31.1	19.03	7.04	1.38	100

Source: 1. Various issues of Report on SC/ST Land Holdings.
2. Agricultural census, 2012.

The percentage distribution of operational holdings and area operated by Scheduled Castes in Andhra Pradesh is presented in Table 3. From above Table 3, it is noted that, most of the SCs are small or marginal farmers. According to 1976-77, 83 percent of SCs are both marginal and smallholding farmers, controlling nearly 46 percent of total operated area of SCs.

Their percentage tremendously increased to about 91.5 percent controlling nearly 66 percent of total operated area in 2000-01, on the other hand medium and large holdings declined from 4.7 percent (controlling nearly 29 percent of total operated area) to 1.4 percent (controlling nearly 12 percent of total operated area). In 2010-11, both marginal and small together accounted for 93.2 percent of operational holding only controlling 72.54 percent of operated area. On the other hand, both medium and large together accounted for 1.05 percent of operational holding and they control 8.43 percent of operated area.

Table 4: Average size of the holdings operated by Scheduled Castes (in hectares)

Year	*Size groups*					
	Marginal	*Small*	*Semi medium*	*Medium*	*Large*	*All groups*
1976-77	0.41	1.45	2.69	6.21	14.65	1.19
1980-81	0.43	1.46	2.62	5.66	16.48	1.06
1986-87	0.41	1.4	2.56	5.59	14.41	0.95
1990-91	0.41	1.4	2.56	5.58	16	0.91
1995-96	0.42	1.39	2.53	5.53	19	0.83
2000-01	0.41	1.39	2.54	5.47	21.88	0.83
2005-06	0.41	1.38	2.52	5.44	16.49	0.8
2010-11	0.41	1.38	2.51	5.36	16.5	0.41

Source: 1. Various issues of Report on SC/ST Land Holdings.
2. Agricultural census, 2011.

Table 4 presents average size of the holdings operated by Scheduled Castes during 1976-77 to 2010-11. The trend among the marginal, small, and semi-medium has not changed remarkably. However, medium farmers average size of holdings showed the decreasing trend from 6.21 percent in 1976-77 to 5.37 percent in 2010-11 and large farmers average size of holding registered increasing trend from 14.65 percent in 1976-77 to 16.5 percent in 2010-11.

Occupational Distribution

Having scrutinised the landholding distribution pattern among SCs and STs in erstwhile Andhra Pradesh, we now move to the status of the occupation distribution in erstwhile Andhra Pradesh with reference to SC/ST.

Economic conditions of people in one or the other way are governed by the occupational structure of the household. Most of the SCs and STs continue to be in their traditional hereditary occupations, and agriculture stands out as the principal source of livelihood.The changes in the occupational distribution among different social groups during 1971-2011 in undivided Andhra Pradesh state is in the Table 5. It is evident from the table that during 1971 to 1981 there was an increase in the percentage of SC agricultural labourers as cultivators from 14.66% to 17.41% while percentage of SC agricultural labourers declined from 73.04% to 68.24%. In case of general workers, the percentage of cultivators declined from 34.43% to 32.73% and percentage of agricultural labourers also declined from 38.24% to 36.78% during the same period. Regarding the non-farming workers, it increased from 12.3% to 14.35% in case of SC workers and very same trend carried on among the general workers from 27.3% to 30.49%. Thus, there is some marginal improvement in the SC workers as cultivators and non-farming workers. These statistics point to some upward economic mobility of SC workers. This may be attributed to redistribution of wasteland and surplus land under 20-point programme in 1970s (Nancharaiah, G. 2000). During 2001-2011 in case of SC cultivators it declined from 11.59 % to 7.94% and in case of STs, the decline was from 41.01 % to 29.70%. Of course, in the case of general workers the percentage of cultivators too declined from 25.47% to 18.42%. In case of SC agricultural labourers, the trend remains the same during 2001-11, whereas ST agricultural labourers have recorded increasing trend.

It is important to note that during 1981-2011, the percentage of cultivators in all the categories has declined and percentage of non-farm workers increased significantly. Land owned by the dominant cultivating castes had declined because they were moving out of rural areas and agricultural activities to the urban areas and the non-agricultural activities. Further, the data explains that despite land redistribution in several phases most of the Dalits remained as landless agricultural labourers. Therefore, there is an urgent need to probe into the reasons and causes for the failure and economic and social backwardness of Dalits and Adivasis despite several stringent land reforms in erstwhile Andhra Pradesh.

Table 5: Occupational Distributions among Different Social Groups in Andhra Pradesh

Category	*Percentage in Total Main workers of SCs*				*Percentage in Total Main workers of STs*				*Percentage in Total Main workers general population*			
	1971	*1981*	*2001*	*2011*	*1971*	*1981*	*2001*	*2011*	*1971*	*1981*	*2001*	*2011*
Cultivators	14.66	17.41	11.59	7.94	37.05	43.21	41.01	29.70	32.45	32.73	25.47	18.42
Ag.Labourers	73.04	68.24	64.21	64.35	50.40	43.72	41.86	52.75	38.24	36.78	33.83	39.96
Non-farming workers	12.3	14.35	24.20	27.71	12.55	13.07	17.13	17.55	29.31	30.49	40.30	41.62

Source: Statistical Abstract of Andhra Pradesh, 1971, 1981, 1991, 2001and 2011.

MPCE and Poverty

After examining the occupational distribution in erstwhile Andhra Pradesh with reference to SCs and STs, we will survey the status of the monthly per capita consumption expenditure and poverty.

Income poverty is only one of the multiple deprivations that the SCs and STs have suffered continuously, even after nearly six decades of development planning. Across social groups, the percentage of population living below the poverty line is significant and it is the highest among the ST and SC communities when compared with others.

The mean consumption expenditure based on NSS Consumption Expenditure Survey data clearly points out differences in the level of consumption expenditure across social groups. Table 6 evidently presents the glaring gap between SCs/STs and other social groups. Furthermore, the gap in terms of mean consumption expenditure between SCs and STs and the 'other' social groups is alarmingly on an increase over a period of time, evidently confirming economic inequalities across social groups.

Table 6: Average Monthly Per Capita Consumption Expenditure (MPCE) across Social Groups in Andhra Pradesh (in Rs.) – Nominal Prices

Year	*Rural*					*Urban*				
	ST	*SC*	*OBC*	*Others*	*All*	*ST*	*SC*	*OBC*	*Others*	*All*
1983	129	131	-	159	156	129	131	-	159	156
1993-94	263	230	-	308	289	358	347	-	416	409
2004-05	431	495	581	722 (629)	586	698	829	908	1245 (1063)	1019
2009-10	753	962	959	1313	1020	1776	1647	1755	2322	1982

Note: 1. Based on URP (Uniform Reference Period); 2. The 'others' for 1983 and 1993-94 includes OBC category, figures in ( ) for 2004-05 are comparable with 'others' in 1993-94 and 1983.

Source: Venkatanarayana Motkuri, 2013.

The head count ratio of poverty measured using NSS Consumption Expenditure Survey data also shows that the percentage of poor was much higher among the SCs and STs and lower among the 'others', indicating wide disparities across social groups in the state (Table 7). Moreover, the disparity in terms of level of poverty has increased especially between STs and 'other' categories. Although, the overall poverty ratio and the ratio among SCs and the other social groups had declined, the head count ratio of poverty (HCR) among STs in both the rural and urban areas had increased during 1993-94 and 2004-05. Whereas, the recent estimates during

2009-10 in poverty ratio among the STs has declining trend. Most of the increase/decrease in the poverty ratio among STs was due to the increase/decrease of poverty ratio among agricultural labourers belonging to ST community. It points out the failure of state in effectively carrying out and reaching the policy initiatives and programmes to marginalised sections like STs and SCs. Had the Government Machinery ensured foolproof implementation and execution surely in erstwhile Andhra Pradesh we would have registered further declining trends in poverty among SCs and STs.

Table 7: Poverty Ratio (HCR) among Different Social Groups in undivided Andhra Pradesh

Year	*Rural*					*Urban*				
	ST	*SC*	*OBC*	*Others*	*All*	*ST*	*SC*	*OBC*	*Others*	*All*
1993-94	58.4	64.4	-	42.4	48.1	43.9	45.5	-	34	35.2
2004-05	60.3	41.8	31.6	16.1 (26.4)	32.3	50.1	35	23.8	16.5 (20.4)	23.4
2009-10	40.2	25.7	24.3	10.3	22.7	21.2	19.8	19.7	14.7	17.7

Note: 1. ***Tendulkar Committee Methodology*** is based on MRP (Mixed Reference Period); **2**. For the year 2009-10 state poverty line is updated based on price indices of CPIAL and CPIIW.

Source: Venkatanarayana Motkuri, 2013.

Atrocities against SCs/STs

We shall now move to the ground reality about the safety and security of SCs and STs. In spite of reaching to the skies and claiming to be one of the biggest democracies in the world it is very disturbing and unfortunate to know after seven decades of Independence SCs and STs do not enjoy freedom and their due rights enshrined in the constitutions.

Table 8: Atrocities against Scheduled Caste in Erstwhile Andhra Pradesh

Crime	*2005*	*2006*	*2007*	*2008*	*2009*	*2010*	*2011*	*2012*	*2013*	*2014*	*2015*
Protection of Civil Rights Act, 1955	61	93	122	123	39	50	10	9	6	9	0
Murder	37	52	46	48	35	43	64	54	53	34	23
Attempt to commit Murder	-	-	-	-	-	-	-	-	-	21	29
Rape	74	97	105	88	99	100	131	104	114	61	104
Attempt to commit Rape	-	-	-	-	-	-	-	-	-	2	5
Assault on women with intent to outrage her Modesty	-	-	-	-	-	-	-	-	-	116	153
Insult to the Modesty of Women	-	-	-	-	-	-	-	-	-	25	31
Kidnapping & Abduction	21	12	25	18	19	18	19	11	14	12	10
Dacoity	0	3	0	0	1	0	1	0	3	0	0
Robbery	0	5	0	0	4	1	0	1	1	1	1

(Contd...)

Arson	9	13	17	5	12	17	14	7	5	9	7
Grievous Hurt	459	657	541	651	722	709	708	626	659	34	3
Riots	-	-	-	-	-	-	-	-	-	28	23
Other IPC Crimes	1212	1445	1327	1682	1836	1874	1630	1444	1720	1191	1283
Total	1873	2377	2183	2615	2767	2812	2577	2256	2575	1543	1672

Source: Crimes in india. 2015, NCRB.

Table 8 presents the Atrocities against Scheduled Castes in Erstwhile Andhra Pradesh. In 2015, a total of 1672 cases of crime against SCs were reported in the state as compared to 1543 cases in 2014, showing an undeniable increasing trend. It is important to note that highest numbers of victims are women. The intention behind Rapes and Assaults on women is to outrage their Modesty and indirectly inflict sense of subordination among the SC men. Even though, an SC headed the Constitutional Drafting Committee, the intended outcome and fruits are still elusive to the SCs and STs. It is very clear from the statistical data during 2005-15. It is very atrocious and shameful in 21st century too the crimes against SCs are greater than ever. ***The reasons for atrocities are plenty and invariably related to domination, hegemony and exclusion and some of them are land disputes, land alienation, bonded labour, indebtedness, non-payment of minimum wages as well as non-economic causes such as caste prejudices and practice of untouchability, deep-rooted social resentment, political factions on caste lines and refusal to perform (formerly traditional) services like digging burial pits, arranging cremations, removal of the carcasses of dead animals and beating of drum, etc.*** Another valid reason for this growing trend is that the educated SCs have become aware of

Table 9: Atrocities against Scheduled Tribes in Erstwhile Andhra Pradesh

Crime Head	*2005*	*2006*	*2007*	*2008*	*2009*	*2010*	*2011*	*2012*	*2013*	*2014*	*2015*
Protection of Civil Rights Act, 1955	0	12	3	5	2	4	3	0	0	1	0
Murder	12	8	11	7	4	7	9	16	9	5	4
Attempt to commit Murder	0	0	0	0	0	0	0	0	0	7	5
Rape	34	60	44	37	37	41	46	42	37	17	21
Attempt to commit Rape	0	0	0	0	0	0	0	0	0	1	2
Assault on women with intent to outrage her Modesty	0	0	0	0	0	0	0	0	0	29	29
Insult to the Modesty of Women	0	0	0	0	0	0	0	0	0	4	4
Kidnapping & Abduction	2	4	10	2	1	1	5	0	2	10	4
Dacoity	0	0	0	0	0	0	0	0	0	0	0
Robbery	1	0	0	0	0	0	0	1	0	0	0
Arson	1	2	4	2	0	2	0	2	1	1	2
Grievous Hurt	70	118	87	123	130	102	112	132	82	3	0
Riots	0	0	0	0	0	0	0	0	0	4	1
Other IPC Crimes	199	291	291	316	330	425	397	346	415	239	198
Total	319	495	450	492	504	582	572	539	546	321	270

Source: Crimes in india. 2015, NCRB.

Constitutional Rights and asserting them and refusing to be submissive to the high caste hegemony. Whatever, atrocities on SCs even in today's digital and virtual world is unfortunate, inhuman and cold-blooded. To divert the attention of the enlightened SCs from the increasing atrocities and denying the rightful access to socio-economic and political power, the hegemonic castes in connivance with the political and economic powers have successfully sown the seed of division among the SCs sub-castes leaving them to fight among themselves and never allowing them to be together. One of the best examples is the fierce support and opposition for the ABCD categorisation of SCs (open rivalry and hatred among Malas and Madigas).

Historical Perspective of Caste conflicts in AP: Karamchedu to Garagaparru via Tsundur

Karamchedu Incident-1985

Karamchedu is a rural village in the Parchuru Assembly segment of Andhra Pradesh. On 17 July 1985, the upper caste landlords brutally murdered six Dalits and grievously injured twenty more. After a long legal battle that went up to the Supreme Court, only one person was given life imprisonment and thirty more were sentenced to a three years of prison term. The main accused and mastermind behind this carnage was Mr. Daggubati Chenchu Ramaiah, father of then-MLA of Parchur, Mr. Daggubati Venkateswara Rao. Daggubati Chenchu Ramaiah was a very close relative of TDP founder N. T. Rama Rao (NTR) because of marriage. His son, Daggubati Venkateswara Rao, was married to NTR's beloved daughter Purandeswari.

These landlords raised cash crops like cotton, tobacco, and red chillies besides traditional crops. They are one of the few richest farmers in Andhra Pradesh and are into cinema industry and money lending (call money). They have monopolised the village economy and social life. Along with these landlords in the outskirts of Karamchedu, Malas, Madigas, and Yerukulas too were living side by side. They depended on the landlords for livelihood. Invariably these marginalised had affinity to landlords' political association obviously for livelihood reasons laced with ignorance and age old submissiveness that has evolved into socio-biological reality. In other words, upper caste wielded social, economic, and political power. Traditionally all the landlords, upper caste and the marginalised were staunch Congress Party loyalists. *Whenever* political power had to be in the hands of the marginalised due to caste wise rotation, Landlords tacitly always exercised *politics of accommodation to ensure the continuity of the dominance of upper caste. Also applied process of vicarious participation*

(G. Ram Reddy 1989) on a dummy leader of the marginalised community projecting a symbolic prestige to the whole community and thus incapacitating the potential social capital (the ability of people to work together for a common purpose) of the marginalised community. Some educated Dalits who came in touch with Christianity and Radical Left thinkers desisted the tactics of landlords and asserted their due rights. It was not that palatable to the landlords and the upper caste. They were waiting for an opportune time to annihilate the upcoming Dalit youth leadership by hook or crook. Meanwhile matinee icon NT Rama Rao launched a political party by name Telugu Desam, almost all the landlords and upper caste who are Kammas jumped into Telugu Desam and switched their loyalties. However, Dalits chose to remain in the Congress Party. This irked the upper caste and added an insult to their social status and dominance. To their luck, during the elections, Mr. Daggubati Venkateswara Rao son of landlord Chenchu Ramaiah and son-in-law of NTR became Member of Legislative Assembly (MLA) from Parchur. Around this time two Kamma youth, Potina Seenu and Rayineedu Prasad took their buffaloes to the drinking water tank in Madigapalle. They fed the buffaloes with washings of rice in buckets. While they were washing the dirty buckets in the tank, Katti Chandraiah, a Dalit boy, objected to it. His courage angered Seenu and Prasad. They were about to beat up Chandraiah, fortunately Munnangi Suvaartha, a Madiga woman happened to come there to fetch drinking water from the tank. She tried to protect the boy from the attack. Dalit woman's courage and boldness deeply hurt the upper caste ego. The upper caste which was itching to teach the rising Dalit leadership used the trivial occasion for a ghastly attack on Madigas. Duddu Moshe, Duddu Ramesh, Tella Yehoshua, Tella Moshe, Tella Muthaiah, and Duddu Abraham lost their precious life at the hands of upper caste brutality in collusion with politico-bureaucratic power.

Neerukonda Incident-1987

In July 1987 at Neerukonda, a village in Guntur District of Andhra Pradesh this time Malas were massacred by once again upper caste landlords for the same reasons as was in case of Karamchedu.

Tsundur Incident-1991

Tsundur is a coast village of Guntur District along Chennai-Kolkata railway line. There are 1665 households with a population of about 5,800. Another upper caste called Reddy is the most dominant community. They are around 450 families. There are 400 Dalit families, of which 300 are Malas and

100 are Madigas. Also about 225 Telaga, 25 Brahmin, about 15 Vysya families and 50 other backward caste families co-exist. Actually, in Guntur district most of the landlords and political leaders are from Kamma community, hence are aggressive and hegemonic. Interestingly in Tsundur and surrounding eight villages, we see Reddy landlords. They are by virtue of their numbers not so aggressive. Of 2,420 acres of cultivable land, the Reddys own 1, 220 acres and only a meager 78 acres belongs to the Dalits. On the other hand, Brahmins own 110 acres, Vysyas 26 acres, Telagas 250 acres and the rest is owned by other intermediary castes. Though most of the land is in possession of the upper castes, there are no big landlords. Most of the land is in the form of holdings that are less than one hectare and is owned by as many as 1044 persons. 253 households own plots that measure between 2.5 and 5 acres and 84 households have holdings of more than five acres each. On an average, each household owns about 12 acres. The land is fertile and irrigated by Krishna canal and yield three crops a year. No Dalit however owns more than a hectare.

There are about 200 matriculates among Dalits. There are 10 to 15 postgraduates and none among the Reddys. Very interestingly, Guntur district has the largest number of postgraduate Dalits in Andhra Pradesh. This is attributed to the presence of Christian Missionaries among the Dalits. Relatively the Dalits of Tsundur are economically independent. Nearly 500 Dalits work with the railways as fitters, maintenance men, and gang workers. A few of them work in the telephone department as well. Dalits are numerically strong and educationally sound in this region. Continuous supply of River Krishna water coupled with Green Revolution farming in this region has become very remunerative and fetching. Hence, round the clock throughout the year generating farmers were busy with agricultural activities. Farming community enjoyed surplus and labourers especially Dalits continuous uninterrupted employment. Dalits too have begun to see money in their hands. In addition, good many abler Dalits have moved out to nearby town Tenali to do petty jobs. They in turn have come in touch with Itha Nagar Dalits of Tenali Town who are educated and socially well informed and assertive of their rights.

In Guntur district, usually Dalits resist all kinds of dominance of upper caste community in the town. It is very visible during Assembly and Parliament, Municipal and College elections. Reddys, Telagas, Brahmins, and other Backward caste communities align with Dalits consequently to counter Kamma domination. Dalits are well built and daring, other upper caste politicians to oppose Kammas utilise therefore their muscle power. For this reason, customarily Kammas are identified with Telugu Desam

Political Party and Dalits and other caste communities are associated with Congress Party. Usually Reddys are very friendly with Dalits. In case of Tsundur, Reddy Community was very different. They were feudal and hegemonic. Though the agrarian relations slowly acquired Capitalist mode due to ever-increasing surplus in agriculture, there was no significant change in cultural and political values of the dominant Reddy community. This we call 'Capitalist Culture' without Capital. Simultaneously Reddy community was showing its dirty authoritative power over Dalits whenever their Community member from Congress party was a Chief Minister. Concurrently Dalit Community with its steady income flow from regular agricultural labour, association with Itha Nagar enlightened Dalits they have realised the value of independence, self-assertion, self-respect and human dignity. They made sure that one of their men was elected as Mandal Praja Parishath President on the same Congress Party Ticket as that of Tsundur Reddy Community. On one side economic growth and on another side political power like railway tracks parallely began to empower the Dalits. In addition, educated youth have come in touch with post-Karamchedu Dalit movement and cultivated radical student politics. This was unpalatable to the feudal Reddys. Inevitable as it were, slowly under the carpet conflicts and tensions were brewing between hegemonic Reddys and Self-asserting and Self-respective Dalits.

This conflict reached its boiling point on 6 August 1991 when seven dalits were cruelly killed by Reddy with tacit of Telaga Community. It was a well-orchestrated caste raid by the Reddys of Tsundur in collusion with the nearby village Reddys and local Telaga Community. The police who are supposed to be the protectors of the poor and ensurers of law and order forced Dalits to run away from Dalitwada since they were sold to and had hand in glove with Reddys. Around 400 upper caste people ganged together divided themselves into two groups. Armed with traditional weapons went killing spree dalits whomsoever they met on their way. They systematically packed the dead bodies in gunny bags and threw into the nearby Tungabhadra drain. Biased media, which is in the hands of upper caste, presented the gruesome massacre as sequel to the past existing conflicts between the Reddy and Dalit Communities.

Partly media version is true. Dalits by installing Ambedkar Statue along with Subhash Chandra Bose and Potti Sreeramulu in the centre of the village questioned symbolically the hegemony of Reddys and sent a strong message that they included in all matters of the village. This did not go well with the upper caste. During Dussera Dalit Youth attempted to watch Chintamani Play along with upper caste. This irritated and amounted to demean the supremacy of the Reddy and Telaga Community. Therefore, upper caste members were nurturing grouse against Dalits. They were also unhappy with claim of Dalit Youth for inclusion and equal treatment in public places. It looked as though they were waiting for an opportunity to avenge the enlightened Dalit youth. To their unfortunate luck Dalit youth touching upper caste person with leg in the cinema theatre did not stop with intense arguments but fuelled their ire and resulted in massacre. They beat the Dalit youth mercilessly. As if it were not enough, they manhandled his father who happened to be a School teacher. He could not digest the insult and decided to leave the village. The rest of the Dalits of Tsundur consoled him and persuaded him to stay back. They advised him to lodge complaint with the police against the Reddys who beat him for no fault. The village Dalit elders even fined the teacher with Rs. 25 for having not complied with their unanimous decision. Later the teacher registered complaint with the police. This did not go well with the Reddys. On 9 July 1991, they called for a meeting under the leadership of Reddy Sarpanch and decided to impose Social Boycott on the Dalits.

Incidentally, the Tsundur Dalit Massacre is government supported and government machinery assisted day light murder. Media tacitly ignored the actual facts. Politicians shed crocodile to ensure and protect their vote bank. One thing is clear- Neither the Rulers who eulogize equality and inclusion, nor the Government Machinery which claims to draw inspiration from the Constitutions and goes by rulebook to protect the rights of the Dalits, Politicians who blare in public and pledge to promote the marginalised in their party and Upper caste who wield political, money and muscle power have same single agenda that is Dalits are to be subservient even if they are educated, employed, land owners, politicians, judiciary and bureaucrats.

Lakshmipeta Massacre-2012

Lakshmipeta a small village of Vangara Block, in North Coastal District of Srikakulam near Madduvalasa Reservoir became open altar to sacrifice Dalits. On 12 June 2012, the blood thirsty landlords hacked four Dalits to death and critically injured about 30 men and women this time surprisingly backward caste politically upcoming hegemonic community called Turpu Kapu. They have sankritised themselves and become vanguards of brahmanical ideology. These forces in a well-orchestrated manner targeted 60 Dalit Families and attacked them with crude and brutal weapons like country bombs, sickles, hatchets, and axes. They enjoyed patronisation of ruling Congress Party leaders of the region. The following died in the blood bath: Burada Sundara Rao (45), Chitri Appadu (35), Nivarti Venkati (65) and Nivarti Sangameshu (40) died in the bloodbath. Bodduru Papaiah died in King George Hospital, Vishakhapatnam on 20 June while receiving treatment. Thus five innocent Dalits were sacrificed their lives.

The reason for this blood bath was none other than Agricultural Land. Government constructed huge reservoir at Madduvalsa to harvest water of River Nagavali tributaries: Suvarnamukhi and Vegavathi. Nearly 15000 acres of land was acquired and thousands of people were mercilessly displaced. Lakshmipeta villagers too have lost their farmland. Lakshmipeta has 250 families. Out of which 190 are Turpu Kapus and the rest of 60 are Dalits. Dalits are landless agricultural labourers. When land was, acquired government compensated the owners with two lakhs of rupees per acre, *pucca* house, and job for one of the family members. Since the Dalits did not own land, though they were settled about seven kilometers from the reservoir, they received neither compensation nor a job except four Dalit families who lost assigned land got Rs.40000 towards compensation. Only 40 Turpu Kapu families were employed in the water depart of reservoir office in addition to compensation. Fortunately, all 250 families settled in *pucca* houses built by the government. When the reservoir levels are low nearly 240 acres of land intermittently comes out of submergence. This land is very fertile with silt and conducive for various crops. For the past five years, this land has been cultivated. Everyone has been enjoying good profits. Having been deprived of land for centuries, the Dalits of Lakshimpeta, as in most other cases, aspired to take over the unaffected land under the project and they have been asserting their rights over the land, which now is in the control of the government. By the way, 60 Dalit families desired to cultivate in only 60 acres of land claiming for one acre each. The rest of the 180 acres was left to the Turpu Kapus. However, the Turpu Kapus did not receive the proposal very well. They asserted that it was theirs even though they handed over to government and received compensation. Dalits questioned the claims and emphasised that the government is the owner and they have right to cultivate as much as they have. The matter reached local administration and unfortunately, they maintained steady silence fearing pressure from government as these Turpu Kapus are supported by powerful lobbies within the ruling party from bloc level to state. Since no agreeable decision was forth coming both the sides approached court for justice. As usual, our courts ordered both the parties to stay away from cultivation until the final verdict was passed. This infuriated Turpu Kapu Community leaders. They began to blame squarely Dalits for the court order even though both the parties simultaneously approached the court. Tensions in the village were mounting, hence government in order to ward off untoward incidents posted police picket instead of resolving it once and for all.

As the frustrations were reaching the peak, the former local bloc president and active member of Congress Party, Botsa Vasudevanaidu instigated the Kapus against the Dalit people with the active encouragement from the then PCC Chief, Botsa Satyanarayana. Other Congress leader, Dharmana Prasada Rao (Minister for Roads and Buildings in Andhra Pradesh Government) from same district who was instrumental and powerful agent of land grab in the region for thermal power plants, industrial corridor projects, and mining tacitly supported. His benamies were land mafia and acquired thousands of acres of level for their own families. They were responsible for the police firings and state-sponsored killings of the people, who protested against land grab in the region. His powerful political leadership and representation of the adverse globalisation, which directly justifies displacement and land grabbing by hook or crook, emboldened Turpu Kapus to indulge in blood bath of Lakshmipeta Dalits.

Though government knew that anything could happen in the absence of police, still on 12 June 2012 police patrolling the village were sent out for election duty without replacing enough police personnel. Taking advantage of the police absence and drawing strength from the ruling party politicians, Turpu Kapus of Lakshmipeta consciously organised themselves under the leadership of Botsa Vasudeva Naidu and avenged unprepared innocent Dalits. All the victims were main bead-winners of the families.

The infuriated Dalits of Lakshimpeta refused to bury the dead for the next three days as the government did not arrest the culprits, their abettors, the kingpins in the massacre and the ruling party leaders who had hand in glove. The Dalit people protested the government's inaction placing the dead bodies of their kith and kin in front of the village. However, the administration did not use SC and ST Atrocities Act against the culprits and their abettors till all Dalit and democratic forces raised their voices in protest. A week after when the law was evoked, it was used against small insignificant elements among the culprits, leaving out safely the main abettors and political leaders like Botsa Vasudeva Naidu, Botsa Satyanarayana and other local politicians.

The political leaders of all ruling parties hovered over the surviving victims of Dalit families pouring out their crocodile tears and false promises of jobs, lakhs of compensation and distribution of land. People have seen through the cunningness of these leaders as well as the empty rhetoric of their false promises. The upper caste brahmanical forces would never allow land to come into the hands of Dalits, as it is both symbolically and in real sense economic and political power. Further, it will nullify all the coercive methods of surplus maximisation of the landed through the forced rendering of the Dalits landless thus; indirectly all forces both small and big join hands to perpetuate the upper caste hegemony and dependence of the Dalits for their survival.

Garagaparru Inccident 2017

Dalits were socially boycotted by the upper caste landlords in Garagaparru village of Palakoderu Mandal, West-Godavari District, Andhra Pradesh for having dared to install statue of Dr. B.R. Ambedkar on the banks of village pond along with Gandhi, Alluri Seetha Rama Raju and Potti Sree Ramulu. It is near to Bhimavaram town, which is known for aqua culture. There are 1500 families in the village of which 400 are Dalits. All of them belong to Mala Caste.

On April 23, when Dalits of this village installed a statue of Dr. B R Ambedkar on the village tank bund, as on par with other national leaders, that very night miscreants from the village removed it from there and placed it near panchayat store, without the consent or any information to the Dalits. It was only with the initiative of officials, the statue was again installed at Panchayat Bhavan. Since then i.e., from 5th May onwards village upper caste landlords decided to boycott Dalits from all social activities. All lands that leased to Dalits were cancelled. All Dalit Tractor drivers, domestic maids, and helpers too were removed from their employment. Dalit labourers were forbidden to work in the upper caste lands. Even one RMP doctor who has been treating Dalits had to vacate his clinic. Heavy penalty was levied on those who violated the sanctions. This time social media, Human Rights Activists and Dalit leaders united and pressurised the government and administration to arrest the culprits before the demand snow balled into a massive movement. The three culprits were arrested and remanded for fifteen days.

Conclusion

Dalits particularly SCs and STs mostly are rustic and agricultural labourers heavily depending on farm works for their livelihood. Even after 65 years of Independence good many dalits live abysmal life without even having few cents of land to have decent home and burial when they die after intensely labouring for the society in general and landlords in particular.

As per the latest statistics, more than 40% of below poverty line people are from SCs. Of these 80% are in villages and depending on farm works where caste atrocities, discriminations and exclusions are in vogue. Failure of land reforms in reducing the inequalities in the distribution of land in the post-Green Revolution is one of the principle reasons for high incidence of poverty among Dalits. To protect the interests of the tenants a few reforms have been initiated they too have not produced desired and expected results in post-independent India. Nonetheless, Land Reforms successfully have largely removed intermediaries like Jamindars, Jagirdars, and Inamdars and reduced incidence of tenancy significantly. However, land concentration persists in the hands of few upper caste landlords and upper caste tenants who have become owner cultivators. The marginal farmers, small-scale farmers, and agricultural labourers who are from socially disadvantaged sections such as Dalits are either becoming agricultural labourers or non-farm workers. From mid-sixties onwards Andhra Pradesh agriculture has been exposed to new technology, which is popularly known as Green Revolution. As a result, the agricultural growth rate increased substantially, particularly, food production, but incidence of poverty continues to be high in the State particularly among SCs and STs, despite high growth rate of food production. The fruits of Green Revolution have not reached agricultural labourers since they are landless. The findings of monthly consumption expenditure between SCs and STs and the 'other' communities are alarming. The gap is on an increase pointing to swelling economic inequalities across social groups. Globalisation, which has brought in Individualism and Consumerism, is further perpetuating this inequality and gap resulting in social hierarchies in consumption too. As per the poverty is concerned, the percentage of poor is much higher among the SCs and STs and lower among the 'others', indicating wide disparities across social groups in the state. The disparity in terms of poverty among STs and other social groups is enormous.

Since Dalits are landless, they have neither identity nor dignity nor economic nor political nor social power. This is very evident from the above incidents of atrocities on Dalits. In all the examples quoted, the perpetrators are peasant landlords. They enjoy induced patronised protection of the government machinery vis-à-vis police, revenue, and bureaucracy. Often times they remain silent and encourage bloody mayhem to teach lessons to asserting Dalits at the behest of ruling parties and their political leadership. Such stooping inhuman government machinery is mostly from the same social fabric. It will not be farfetched to state that the atrocities on Dalits are state sponsored, monitored, and implemented whenever the powers sense threat to brahmanical fascism emerging from the SCs. The hand in glove of rustic landlords with the politicians, the police, bureaucracy, and even corporate is obvious from the above. Unfortunately, of late media too has become a partner of this unholy nexus.

Though, the ruling powers and forces claim credit for having elevated one of the Dalit leaders to Presidential position in democratic India, they feign ignorance when it comes to the social exclusions, social boycotts, and planned atrocities on the Dalits. If the Dalit atrocities, boycotts reach alarming levels then for namesake the rulers shed crocodile tears and condemn them from the rooftops only to bury it in the cellar until another disturbance springs forth. Even after seven decades of independence, the dream of Dr. Ambedkar and the Constitutional provisions have not been realised and actualised in the lives of Dalits. Surely, land reforms have been initiated, social welfare schemes have been planned and implemented, educational institutions have been opened, jobs in the government machinery have been created, bureaucratic opportunities to involve actively in the empowerment of Dalits and Adivasis have been provided, and political leadership has been exclusively reserved always with a rider that ladder social system be not disturbed and the hegemony and power be left to the upper castes. When the supremacy of upper caste is at stake either they slow down the implementation of land reforms, or indirectly prompt their cronies to file public litigation writs to maintain status quo knowing pretty well our courts have bottlenecks while dealing with such cases. If they do not wish to recruit SCs into particular department, office, or position they state that no suitable candidate has applied or even if applied not qualified, thus they will enlarge the backlog. Politically devise divisive modules to contain effectively the surging Dalit assertion (has it not happened in Garagaparru? Four Madiga families are isolated from Malas). On set of Information Technology and Internet Revolution effectively castrated and cocooned the Middle Class, Dalit, Adivasi, and Backward Class intellectuals from indulging in active socio-economic, cultural, and political issues. Unless these people awake and come out of hibernation, we will be lost in the mirage of world-class upcoming smart capital that plainly and doubtlessly serves the partners and perpetrators of Dalit atrocities.

References

1. Dharma Kumar (1992). Land and caste in south India. Manohar publication, New Delhi.
2. Radha Krishna (2004). Agriculture Growth, Employment and Poverty, 43rd conference of Indian Society of Labour Economics, Bangalore.

3. Nancharaiah. G (1987). Land legislation and changing agrarian structure; A case study of a deltaic village, Andhra Pradesh economic association, fifth annual conference, Department of Economics, Sri Krishna Devaraya University, Ananthapur District, Andhra Pradesh.
4. *Ibid,* pp. 65-66.
5. Reddy Pratap. K and K. Hanumantha Rao, (2004). "Land Use Pattern in Andhra Pradesh- Trends and Relationships" inG. Gopal Reddy (2004) Institutional Policy Options for Sustainable Agricultural Development, National Seminar organised by Dept. of Economics, Pre Conference Volume, Osmania University, 2004, pp. 61-71.
6. *Ibid,* pp. 65-66.
7. Sanyal, S.K. (1976). 'A review of the conceptual frame work of land holdings survey', *Indian Journal of Agriculture Economics*, July-September, pp. 26-27.
8. Krishna Rao, Y.V. (2005). 'Globalisation: Neo-Liberal Economic Policies and small Farmers Development, in R. Radhakrishna (2005) India In A Globalizing World, Academic Foundation, New Delhi and CESS, Hyderabad, 2005, pp. 391-407.

10 Kripashankar (1988). "Land Transfer in Uttar Pradesh", *Economic & Political Weekly*, (July 23).

19

Some Aspects of Globalisation in the Realm of Philosophical Perspectives and Current Socio-Cultural Changing Phenomena

— Dr. Paul Roche

Ludwig Josef Johann Wittgenstein's first sentence in his only published work called "Tractatus Logico-Philosophicus" states, ***"Die Welt ist alles was der Fall ist."*** It means that 'The world is everything that is the case.' "Everything that is the case" here could mean everything that is current, that is happening, and that is evident or true.[1] Even Bertrand Russel, his teacher and predecessor in Cambridge, England, wrote that "Wittgenstein's Logico-Philosophicus, whether or not it prove (s) to give the ultimate truth on the matters with which it deals, certainly deserves, by its breadth and scope and profundity, to be considered an important event in the philosophical world."

Bertrand Russel uses the word 'profundity'[2] on purpose. When we analyse the life of Wittgenstein, we might come to grips with his achievements. Born on April 26th 1889 in Vienna, Austria, he was 'a charismatic enigma.'

Photo 1: Ludwig Wittgenstein

An attempt is made to connect some ideas of philosophy as expounded by Wittgenstein. When he says that the world is 'everything that is the case', he refers to a concept of globalisation. He does not say cosmos or universe, but the world. Globalisation is a fact as he has inferred already in his *Tractatus.*

A Short Note on Wittgenstein's Life

Born to a wealthy family in Vienna, Austria, on 26th April 1889. He was tutored privately at home until he was 14. He studied in the *Technische Hochschule* in Berlin and later went to Victoria University in Manchester, England for his Ph.D., but did not complete it then. In Trinity College, Cambridge, he did complete his doctorate under Bertrand Russel in 1929.

He was the youngest of 8 children of Karl and Leopoldine Wittgenstein, one of the wealthiest families in the Austro-Hungarian Empire. He was interested in mechanics, and already at the age of 8, he made a sewing machine which functioned perfectly. He started studies in the *Realschule* (a type of Secondary School) in Linz, Upper Austria, where he was looked upon as shy, strange and not very normal. Due to his interest in mechanics, he went to Berlin in 1906. But he left it to study under Russell.

After one year of training, in 1920 he took up the post of elementary school teacher in Trattenbach, in Lower Austria, which was a small farming village. Later he taught in Puchberg am Schneeberg and Otterthal. In Trattenbach, he slept in the school kitchen.

Photo 2: Wittgenstein (5th from right) with his elementary school pupils in Trattenbach, Austria, in 1920.[3]

He went to Skjolden in Norway, where under complete isolation, he conceived his ideas of *Tractatus*. During the Second World War, he wrote most of his points for his *Tractatus*. Returning to Austria, when he gave away his portion of sizeable inheritance, mostly to his family members and to Poets Georg Trackle and Rainer Maria Rilke[4].

There are various reports about what Wittgenstein did with his inheritance, but one interesting statement that he made was that he did not earn that money on his own and that was the reason why he gave it all away.

Wittgenstein and Globalisation

One might wonder what Wittgenstein has to do with globalisation. According to him, only in isolation can you conceive creative and profound thoughts in the mind. He visited his hut in Norway several times for short periods of time, and once for 13 months. He wrote his *Philosophical Investigations* and part of his *Tractatus* in this hut. His concepts and his articles have reached a wide research audience in England and Europe. It is estimated that over 6000 Ph.D. theses have already been published based on Wittgenstein's works, his family, his living abodes in Vienna, rural Austria, Rural Norway and Cambridge in England. It is fascinating to study

Photo 3: Wittgenstein Volksschule, (Primary School) in Trattenbach, Lower Austria.[5]

Illustration 4: Wittgenstein Dictionary for Primary Schools[6]

his *Tractatus* and its original thinking, which have captured the intellects of most philosophers of the 20th century, including those studying the current philosophical contexts. "The limits of my language are the limits of my world", he said famously, and books are written about it.[7] We shall return to Wittgenstein at the end of this paper.

Example of Jallikattu as part of globalisation

The random picking of an English newspaper shows the Headline, "One killed in Pudukottai *Jallikattu*" "A 30-year-old (man) was gored to death by a bull during a *Jallikattu* event at Vadamalapur, in Pudukottai district, while a six-year-old girl was injured…near Manapparai in Trichy district on Saturday."[8]

"The death was unfortunate. It happened in spite of elaborate arrangements to ensure the safety of all. We were keen on avoiding casualties," Pudukottai Collector P. Uma Maheshwari told *The Hindu*. When Jallikattu was forbidden by Animal Activists, the Tamil Nadu government took up the case. Opposing the ban on Jallikattu, over two hundred thousand people had thronged in Marina beach of Chennai to protest against the ban. (See Photo 5.)

Photo 5: Crowds that had assembled to protest against the Jallikattu ban

The communication outreach is very noticeable and proven to be effective in the case of Jallikattu, when Tamil communities around the world, including children, protested against its restrictions and the government and the legal system had to give in to allow it albeit with some stringent restrictions and amendments.

Photo 6: Jallikattu in progress

In the pictures shown here, only young men, mostly from registered Jallikattu clubs, plan and conduct the event and enter the arena. Most spectators now are aware of the dangers of being even a distant spectator during the event. Many visitors, even those who are at a safe distance, may be gored to death by run-away bulls, some of which have been fed alcohol to become more ferocious. Although it is forbidden, some bull breeders do not heed these restrictions imposed on them by animal activists.

Photo 7: Jallikattu in progress near Madurai

Bullfight in Spain

Now let us move on to an international arena. Bullfights are popular events in Spain. When this author went to see a Bullfight in the town of Estella in Spain in 1984, almost all the townspeople had gathered there and all the schoolboys and girls were present there too. When the bullfighter/matador gored the bull with multiple spikes, and finally the bull fell down when its heart was pierced with precision by the matador, all the spectators clapped their hands, and many threw leather pouches filled with wine for the matador. When the bull fell to the ground, dead, the girls near me all turned away and were sobbing in tears. I asked the girls sitting next to me, "Hi, why do you come here if you don't want to see the bull getting killed?" They said, "It is our culture. We have to come as a whole community" said the two girls who spoke a bit of English.

Photo 8: Bullfight in progress in Estella, Navarra, Spain

Photo 9: Matador thrown over by the Bull

But Spain's bullfighting season, which begins in earnest after the Feria, is off to a controversial start. A famous matador's artistic flourish cast an international shadow over the activity insiders consider more ritual than sport, and has further divided Spaniards over bullfighting's place in society.

For instance, the Bullfighter knocked down by the bull here (Photo 10), after he had killed 2 bulls, was himself gored to death by the third bull in Estella, Spain.

Photo 10: This matador killed two bulls, but tragically, the third one killed him

Similarly, despite the dangers, people do come in large numbers for Jallikattu events, including foreign tourists, who come to Aranganallur near Madurai in South India, which is the most famous Jallikattu centre.

Globalisation of food items

For example, potato chips of all types, sweet and sour, especially by "Lae" company, have conquered the taste buds of most Indian youngsters, since it is sold for five rupees, and it has become the accepted snack of most schoolchildren. Some schools have snack shops, selling these chips during lunch time.

International franchises of fast-food companies like MacDonalds, Kentucky Fried Chicken (KFCs) and Pizza Huts have already come to occupy upscale eatery centres in big towns and cities. It has become the "conspicuous consumption". More often than not, if you are able to afford going to these above-mentioned restaurants, you most probably belong to a high income bracket group. The lengthening queues in front of these fast-food joints in Chennai are a tell-tale sign of being well-to-do, and of course, it is related to globalisation.

The field of education

If you are attending a vernacular school, you are not considered equal to an English-medium school pupil. This is indeed contentious. Students in the vernacular schools are extremely smart, too. But parents do spend a great deal of money to send their children to English-medium schools, in order to ensure a bright future for them.

Of course, the ability to speak English fluently and flawlessly, along with a degree to go with it, assures most students of a great career in life. Globalisation has taken roots, and students with higher qualifications in English, French, Spanish and German can and do get attractive jobs with lucrative salaries.

Once this author was travelling from Toronto to London, and the neighbour in the first class[9] seat was a computer techie, earning big sums and travelling throughout the world. I asked him, "If you had a choice, in which country would you settle in?" He being an Indian, I was quite surprised by his reply. He said, "Spain." This was 15 years ago, when the situation there was relatively prosperous.

Mobile Phone Use and its global impact

According to a survey by e-Marketer in 2015, it was estimated that India would have over 800 million mobile phone users in 2019. When I asked Google (or, when I "googled" it) how many people use cell phones in India, the answer came in 1.18 seconds, giving "About 3,46,00,00,000 results" (3,460 million results). Apart from the impact of data-gathering speed of our internet service providers, what is amazing is the great advancement in computing skills, usage and availability. Nowadays using cell phones starts from the time they are babies. They play with it, talk through it and have conversations with it, real or imagined. Does it affect people? Yes, it does.

Are mobile phones killing its intense users?

"Keep Your Phone Out of Your Pocket" says a study published last year in the *Journal of Craniofacial Surgery* that linked cell phone radiation to decreased bone density in the pelvis, and a 2008 study conducted by the Cleveland Clinic found that it lowers fertility in men."[10] (I'm not commenting on that!).

Modern cell phones have already started killing people by hundreds according to a recent news report, and soon, it would kill millions. What is going to stop the unhindered march and expansion of this development?

Smartphone Addiction Definition

"The official name for smartphone addiction is Nomophobia which is defined as having a fear of not being with your phone. Cell phones have been around for years though, so why the sudden increase in personal dependence? Well, quite simply, its defined by the nature of the content on the device… we're talking internet, social networks, apps, video, music and so on."[11]

Globalisation: Impact and Future Scenarios

As Angel Gurría, the Secretary General of the OECD said:

> "A close look at globalisation reveals a major positive force which provides key contributions to global progress and prosperity. During the past decades, globalisation has: raised productivity and employment; helped lift millions out of poverty; revolutionised communications; fostered competition; boosted global economic growth and interdependencies through trade and FDI (Foreign Direct Investment) flows; and facilitated scientific discoveries which will help us lead longer and healthier lives."

The Benefits of Globalisation are: more International Trade; more goods & services; generally available at lower prices; more wealth in the world; lower cost and higher standard of Living; Waste Reduction from greater Economic Efficiency.

Globalisation aims to benefit individual economies around the world by making markets more efficient, increasing competition, limiting military conflicts, and spreading wealth more equally.

Globalisation Benefits World Economies

The Milken Institute's "Globalisation of the World Economy" report of 2003 highlighted many of the benefits associated with globalisation while outlining some of the associated risks that governments and investors should consider, and the principles of this report remain relevant.

Some disadvantages of globalisation include:

- **Interdependence:** Interdependence between nations can cause regional or global instabilities if local economic fluctuations end up impacting a large number of countries relying on them.
- **National Sovereignty:** Some see the rise of nation-states, multinational or global firms, and other international organisations as a threat to sovereignty. Ultimately, this could cause some leaders to become nationalistic or xenophobic.
- **Equity Distribution:** The benefits of globalisation can be unfairly skewed towards rich nations or individuals, creating greater economic inequalities.

Writing in the quarterly *Milken Institute Review* in late 2017, Dani Rodrik, author of "Straight Talk on Trade: Ideas for a Sane World Economy," argued that a rebalancing of globalisation is necessary to restore more voice to labour and its needs for job and income stability while focusing attention globally on where the biggest economic gains can be made.

Stop Press!

At the time of going to press, news has emerged that Corona Virus has become a pandemic.

It has affected over 390,000 people and killed over 17,150 persons worldwide.[12] As we are talking about globalisation, the global impact of Corona Virus and its negative effect on financial markets and share prices indicate a harrowing trend of huge losses and the disaster to the world economy.

The New York Times reports that 158 million people are asked to stay home.[13] Over 195 countries and territories are already affected. Globalisation's worst effects can be gauged by the closure of all schools, colleges and educational institutions for at least two weeks, till the 31st of March 2020. Will it continue further? No one knows. I have taken 24th of March 2020 as the cut-off point before going to the press.

Concluding Remarks

In the end, let us return to where we started. Ludwig Wittgenstein, in his last, and concluding paragraph of his Tractatus Logico-Philosophicus, states: *Wovon man nicht sprechen kann, darüber muss man schweigen.*

Translated, it means: ***Whereof one cannot speak, thereof one must be silent. (7)***

Also: About what one cannot speak, one must remain silent. (7) *Remain silent*, is a passive translation. More active would be, "Keep quiet", or sharper still, would be, "*Shut up*." And that's what I'm going to do now.

References

1. Monk, Ray, 1990, *Ludwig Wittgenstein: The Duty of Genius*, New York: Macmillan.
2. Hacker, Peter, 15 February 2018, *Wittgenstein's Legacy: The Principles of the Private Language Arguments,* https://doi.org/10.1111/phin.12186
3. *Tractatus Logico-Philosophicus (TLP)*, 1922, C. K. Ogden (trans.), London: Routledge & Kegan Paul. Originally published as "Logisch-Philosophische Abhandlung", in *Annalen der Naturphilosophische*, XIV (3/4), 1921.
4. Robins, Spencer, 2015, Wittgenstein, Schoolteacher, What the Philosopher learned from his time in elementary-school classrooms, in Paris Review (www.theparisreview.org)
5. Weber, Desiree, Wittgenstein Initiative: Wittgenstein's Dictionary for Elementary Schools (Wittgenstein's Woerterbuch) (https://wittgenstein-initiative.com)
6. Biesenbach, Hans, 2011, Anspielungen und Zitate im Werk Ludwig Wittgensteins, Bergen: The Wittgenstein Archives at the University of Bergen.
7. Sluga, Hans D., *University of California, Berkeley*, and Stern, David G., *University of Iowa*, eds. 2006, The Cambridge Companion to Wittgenstein, Cambridge University Press, https://doi.org/10.1017/CCOL0521460255
8. Flowers III, F.A. and Ian Ground, 1999, Portraits of Wittgenstein, Abridged Edition, Bloomsbury Academic, London.
9. Oxaal, Ivar, 2011, On the Trail to Wittgenstein's Hut: The Historical Background to Tractatus Logico-Philosophicus, Transaction Publishers, New Brunswick (USA) and London (UK).
10. *The Hindu*, dated January 19, 2020, p. 7.[14]
11. Kanterian, Edward, (2007) Ludwig Wittgenstein, Published by Reaktion Books Ltd., London, UK, www.reaktionbooks.co.uk

Notes

1. The German word *Fall* has five different meanings and eight phrasal expressions. Wittgenstein uses then interchangeably, and hence he said that his book *Tractatus Logico-Philosophicus* should have both the original German and the corresponding English translation.
2. Bertrand Russell's use of the word "profundity" with reference to Wittgenstein's book implies great depth of insight or knowledge, or intensity of a state, quality, or emotion. All these are embedded in his book.
3. https://www.theparisreview.org/blog/2015/03/05/wittgenstein-schoolteacher/
4. René Karl Wilhelm Johann Josef Maria Rilke, better known as Rainer Maria Rilke, was a Bohemian-Austrian poet and novelist (Born in Prague in 1875, an died in 1926 in Switzerland).

5. Photo credits: © *Désirée Weber*© 2020 Wittgenstein Initiative, Kriehubergasse 15/23, 1050 Wien, Austria.
6. *Ibid.*
7. See the webpage: Norwegische Spurensuche nach Ludwig Wittgenstein, Østerrike über dem Fjord: In einem Kaff in Norwegen schrieb der große Philosoph einige seiner wichtigsten Texte, REPORTAGE, Klaus Taschwer, 2. Juni 2017. (Article in German)
8. The Hindu English Newspaper, dated Sunday, January 19, 2020.
9. My family and I were upgraded to First Class because our Airline had overbooked…sometimes they do it just in case there are last minute cancellations.
10. Read more: http://www.oprah.com/health/dr-oz-explains-cell-phone-dangers-and-how-to-avoid-them#ixzz6CETMySOG
11. *Source:* https://www.bankmycell.com/blog/smartphone-addiction/#chapter1
12. www.worldometers.info
13. www.nytimes.com
14. Jaisankar, G. The Hindu, Sunday 19th January 2020, p.7.

20

The Gentiles as the Marginalised People of the New Testament Era Through the Eyes of Saint Paul

— Dr. Arockiasamy Savarirayan, SVD

Introduction

Saint Paul in the New Testament and in the history of early Christianity was known as the Apostle to the Gentiles. He went down in the history of the infant Church in her emerging days as a very significant champion of the Gentiles in an effort to establish and stabilise their social and religious rights. In more ways than one, Paul fulfilled the plan of God the Almighty and Jesus, the Son of God in opening the doors of the universal economy of salvation to the non-Jewish population while the Jews claimed monopoly over it. The topic that I intend to unravel here is "The Gentiles as the Marginalised People of the New Testament Era: Through the Eyes of Saint Paul".

There are many concepts that need clarification here for the type of readers of this volume. Unless we know who, this Saint Paul is, his provenance and his ministry, we will not be able to appreciate him. Similarly, there is a need to identify who these Gentiles were and why they were considered a marginalised community, in order to get into their shoes. Therefore, a brief and concise attempt will be made at the outset to address a few basic concerns and then propose St. Paul as someone who brought about the necessary changes and dragged the Gentiles from the periphery to the centre and recognised them as the people of God and for whom Jesus Christ shed his precious blood. We will also propose St. Paul as one of the models for the modern-day champion liberators who work for those in the margins of every society. Thus, together with St. Paul, we will arrive at the point that the Jews and the Gentiles are partakers of God's salvation and no one in the world is to be pushed to the periphery based on their religious and caste identity or based on money, muscle and political power.

This article is divided into three parts. The first part portrays Paul as a marginalised Jew and an Apostle. As a person who was pushed to the periphery, he could have very well behaved like numerous paranoids who suffered in their childhood and went on to persecute the people through gruesome genocides down the centuries.[1] Paul was a marginalised warrior who fought for the marginalised people. The second part identifies the Gentiles at the backdrop of the New Testament era and their relationship with Paul while the third part will delve into the courageous movement of the Gentiles from the margin to the centre that was made possible by Paul in an effort to achieve the plan of God while cooperating with the programme of Jesus the Master. The article will end with a few action plans in terms of practical application. We will look at the whole issue through the eyes of St. Paul and that will help us focus better on the issue under investigation.

Part - I

Saint Paul: A Marginalised Jew and an Apostle

1. Saint Paul, a Marginalised Jew

Biblical sources on Saint Paul could be classified as primary sources[2] and secondary sources.[3] There is also a third source which bears the name of Paul but contains the interpretation of Pauline message by the chosen leaders of the Second Generation Christians in the context of the later part of the 1st Century CE and the early part of the 2nd Century CE.[4] Saint Paul was a diaspora Jew. He didn't live in the confines of the Jewish territories where Jesus was born, concentrated his ministry, died and rose from the dead. Perhaps, he didn't also use the TaNaK[5] which was used in Palestine although one surmises that he could have learnt it while in Jerusalem under the feet of Gamaliel, the Rabbi. He could have read, interpreted, prayed, meditated upon Septuagint[6] that was available to him. These were enough reasons for him to be kept at the periphery.

We come to know of his geographical origins only from the secondary sources. The Lord Jesus himself introduced Paul to Ananias, a disciple of Jesus at Damascus, as "a man of Tarsus" (Acts 9:11). After his encounter with the Lord, Paul went to Jerusalem and tried to join the disciples there. Barnabas introduced him to the Apostles in Jerusalem. His presence and the arguments with the Hellenists challenged them even to the extent of making many efforts to kill him. But when the believers came to know of this, they saved him by sending him off to Tarsus (cf. Acts 9:26-30). Later, "Barnabas went to Tarsus to look for Saul" (Acts 11:25). It was at later stages that Paul himself revealed his whereabouts and that too in the context of his arrest in the temple of Jerusalem and as part of his defence on the steps of the fortress Antonia (cf. Acts 21:27-38[7]). Paul said, "I am a Jew, from Tarsus of Cilicia, a citizen of an important city" (Acts 21:39). Thus, Paul was very proud of his origins.[8] Yet, in the eyes of the Jews of Judea, he was outside the margins of the Jewish land, religion and culture and naturally he was despised. Although belonged to the same ancestral Jewish religion, Paul's geographical provenance and the modes and expressions of his faith became causes of suffering marginalisation and even expulsion from the temple as we will explain below.

Acts 21:27 says that certain Jews from Asia could not tolerate Paul's entry into the temple of Jerusalem. In spite of being a Jew, born of Hebrew parents from the chosen Israelite race and an ardent Pharisaic believer and practitioner who "advanced in Judaism beyond many among (his) people of the same age, ... far more zealous for the traditions of (his) ancestors" (Gal 1:14), Paul was denied entry into the temple. We may infer that it is also because of his association with the Gentiles and what he taught to them as we will discuss at a later stage.

2. Saint Paul, a Marginalised Apostle

2.1 Based on the Secondary Sources: For the sake of continuity and proper comprehension, let me continue with the information available in the secondary sources. Upon arriving in Jerusalem, Paul met with James, the bishop of Jerusalem and recounted all the things that "God had done among the Gentiles through his ministry" (Acts 21:19). The authorities in Jerusalem were happy with Paul but they feared that Paul's association with the Gentiles and his insistence on not performing circumcision did not go well with them. They suggested a few ways and means to please the people and impress them positively. Thus, they persuaded Paul to join four men who were under a vow to go through the rite of purification and also meet the expenses of shaving their heads. Paul obliged these suggestions wholeheartedly. In spite of this, when Paul entered the temple, they caught him and dragged him out and even went to the extent of trying to kill him. Thanks to the tribune who acted promptly and went down town with soldiers and centurions (cf. Acts 21:20-38) and saved the man whose story will soon reach Rome, the centre of the Roman Empire.

2.2 Based on the Primary Sources: Paul could not be counted among the apostles of Jesus as he did not qualify himself based on the characteristics earmarked by Saint Peter. Quoting Ps 109:8, Peter in Acts 1:20 says that someone has to take the place of Judas Iscariot who betrayed Jesus and became one of the causes of his death but the one who takes place should have the following qualifications: (i) One who accompanied Jesus in the company of the Twelve; (ii) His stay with Jesus should have been from the day John the Baptizer began his ministry till the ascension of Jesus and (iii) A witness to the resurrection of Jesus together with the Twelve (cf. Acts 1:20-22).

Although Saints James, Cephas and John, the acknowledged pillars of the Church in Jerusalem recognised the grace received by Paul and extended the right hand of fellowship and agreed that Paul should go to the Gentiles, not many accepted him as an apostle (cf. Gal 2:9). Many doubted and questioned his apostleship either because he didn't marry or take along a believing sister during the missionary journey or because he refused to accept honorarium for the ministry (cf. 1 Cor 9:5-6) and sustained himself with mean and hard labour despised by many people (1 Thess 2:9[9]; 1 Cor 4:11-12[10]; 9:15[11]). He was accused of mellowing down the Gospel message to please human persons (cf. Gal 1:10). Being pushed to the wall, Paul had to many times defend his apostleship. For example, he would question the Corinthians using rhetoric, if he was not an apostle (cf. 1 Cor 9:1) and challenge the Corinthians that they "are the seal of (his) apostleship in the Lord" (1 Cor 9:2). He presents 1 Cor 9 as a chapter of self-defense.[12] He claims that the Lord Jesus appeared to him. Although he humbly accepts that he is not worthy to be called an apostle because he persecuted the Church but by the grace of God, he is one (cf. 1 Cor 15:8-10).

Part - II

Saint Paul and the Gentiles

2.1 The Identity of the Gentiles

Who were these Gentiles? The term 'Gentiles' in the Bible was applied to all the non-Jewish people or 'nations other than Israel'. The synonyms for the word 'Gentiles' are 'heathens' and 'nations'. They were also addressed as 'God-Fearers' and 'pagan Christians'. The corresponding Hebrew words are '*Goy*' or '*Goi*'[13] and the Greek word is '*ethnos*'. The Gentiles enjoyed lots of hospitality and fraternity with the Jews barring a few wars in the Old Testament times while it is not the same in the New Testament era.

H. Porter speaks about extreme aversion, scorn and hatred the Israelites of Jesus' time expressed to their Gentile neighbours. We are aware of the language of hatred the Jews and the Gentiles had for each other. The writings of Cicero, Seneca and Tacitus also bear witness to this fact.[14] We read in Luke 9:52 that when Jesus sent messengers ahead of him to Jerusalem, they entered a Samaritan village and the natives did not welcome them. James and John, two of the beloved disciples of Jesus requested him permission that they "may command fire to come down from heaven and consume them" (Luke 9:54). Matthean Jesus has been a bit harsh on them although this instruction has to be seen in the light of the entire motive of the Gospel, "Go nowhere among the Gentiles, and enter no town of the Samaritans" (Matt 10:5). Let also not forget that an entire Samaritan village believed in Jesus (cf. John 4).

2.2 God's Love for the Gentiles

Simeon Peter's speech at the Jerusalem Council is a proof that God had always "looked favourably on the Gentiles" (Acts 15:14). Paul, in his turn, was convinced that God of Israel did not reject the Gentiles. He is also the God of the Gentiles. He will justify both the Israelites and the Gentiles based on faith. That is why in Rom 3:29b-30, "Paul seeks to explain how the Gentiles of Rome have entered into Israel's story, a story intended for the restoration of the whole creation".[15] He claims that it is God's grace and plan that he had "to be a minister of Christ Jesus to the Gentiles in the priestly service of the gospel of God, so that the offering of the Gentiles may be acceptable, sanctified by the Holy Spirit" (Rom 15:16).Thus, Paul is seen promoting "God's openness to Gentiles".[16]

2.3 The Gentiles in the Post-Jesus Era

The Gentiles showed lots of eagerness to embrace Christ and join the Way. On the day of the first ever Pentecost, "Parthians, Medes, Elamites, and residents of Mesopotamia, Judea and Cappadocia, Pontus and Asia, Phrygia and Pamphylia, Egypt and the parts of Libya belonging to Cyrene, and visitors from Rome, both Jews and proselytes, Cretans and Arabs" (Acts 2:9-11) and thus all kinds of people were there. Acts 11:1 reports that "the apostles and the believers who were in Judea heard that the Gentiles had also accepted the word of God". When Peter reported how the household of Cornelius received the Holy Spirit, the Church authorities in Jerusalem were silenced and praised God for giving the Gentiles a heart to repent (cf. Acts 11:18).

2.4 Paul Set Apart for the Gentiles

The Lord chose Paul to bring the name of Jesus before three groups of people among whom the Gentiles occupy the primary slot while the second and third positions go to kings and the people of Israel (cf. Acts 9:15). Paul's primary goal and mission were directed towards the Gentiles. That reflected in the action of both Paul and Barnabas when they made a bold, deliberate and conscious choice to turn to the Gentiles once they were rejected by the Jews. Their response to this clarion call was highly encouraging (cf. Acts 13:48) and historical but more importantly it was indeed the will of the one who chose him. Paul's job description was indeed twofold: "to be a light for the Gentiles" and to "bring salvation to the ends of the earth" (Acts 13:47). Acts 13:48 confirms that the Gentiles were so glad about it and praised the Word of the Lord. Paul would reiterate this secondary source in his Letter to the Romans 11:13 when he says, "Now I am speaking to you Gentiles. Inasmuch then as I am an apostle to the Gentiles, I glorify my ministry".

Paul himself testified that he "received grace and apostleship to bring about the obedience of faith among all the Gentiles for the sake of his (Jesus') name" (Rom 1:5). Paul would repeat the same message towards the end of his Letter to the Romans with more intensity, "For I will not venture to speak of anything except what Christ has accomplished through me to win obedience from the Gentiles, by word and deed" (Rom 15:18). Thus, Paul never hesitated to admit and declare that primarily he was set apart to proclaim Jesus among the Gentiles (cf. Gal 1:16; 2:2, 8-9). Quite interestingly, Paul's words in Gal 2:8-9 confirms the decision of the First Jerusalem Council that took place in 49/50 CE that Peter will concentrate his ministry among the circumcised while Paul would look after the Gentiles.[17] One may surmise that the hard work of Paul and other early missionaries bore abundant fruit that "... by the end of the first century CE the membership of the Church was primarily Gentile and its communities were located mainly outside of Palestine".[18]

2.5 Paul Carried Forward Jesus' Vision and Mission

As the apostle of the Gentiles, Paul did not achieve anything new and great, rather I strongly believe that through his Gentile mission, Paul was just carrying forward Jesus' own vision and mission for the universe. For Jesus not only went after the non-Jewish population (cf. John 4; Mark 7:24-30) but he also instructed his disciples to go after the lost sheep of Israel (cf. Matt 10:6), and he never shied away from attending to their needs and never hesitated to appreciate them for their unique gratitude or outstanding faith (cf. Matt 8:5-13; Luke 7:1-10; 10:25-37; 17:11-17). Even though it is widely believed that the Gospel of Matthew is written to the Jewish Christians, one can see Jesus in the 15th chapter of this gospel reaching out to the Canaanite woman in exorcising and delivering her daughter (vv. 21-28), curing the people affected by numerous diseases (vv. 29-31) and feeding the four thousand in the Gentile territory (vv. 32-39). If Jesus didn't go around seeking the non-Jewish people in his life and ministry, his movement with the band of disciples would have just remained as Michael Peppard says, "a regional Jewish sect" or as "Galileans" or "Nazarenes" just "like the Essenes" in the history of Israel. It is "openness to God's elective grace"[19] to the Gentiles that made all the difference. When Paul looked at the life of Jesus, he had a set programme and a paradigm. A major shift in the paradigm came when Paul took the mission to outside Palestine (Asia Minor, the islands in the Mediterranean Sea and the European countries).

2.6 Paul's Conflict with Peter: A War for the Gentiles

The Antiochian episode (cf. Gal 2:11-16) is at the centre of our discussion here. James Dunn calls this event as "one of the most tantalizing episodes in the whole of the NT".[20] It was a time of crisis between someone who trod the path of legalism and orthodoxy and someone who believed in his gospel (cf. Gal 1:11; 2:2) and in a progressive position regarding circumcision (cf. Rom 2:28-29; 1 Cor 7:18-19; Gal 5:6; 6:15; Phil 3:3) and Jewish dietary laws (cf. 1 Cor 8:8, 13). We don't have any systematic report on this historical incident. What we do have, is just a partial account from St. Paul (cf. Gal 2:11-16) and there is no way that we can hear anything from St. Peter or even Barnabas regarding their own description of the affair. We admit that there are also many ambiguous chronological issues regarding the arrival of Peter, Barnabas and Paul to Antioch and when this event took place. We are also not in a position to know why Paul was so indignant with Peter but let Barnabas go free.[21] Since these are matters beyond the scope of this study, we shall concentrate on the event and Paul's take on it.

2.6.1 The City of Antioch

The crisis in question took place in Syrian Antioch, "the citadel of Gentile Christianity"[22] and not in Antioch which is in Pisidia. The Acts of the Apostles 11:19-27 reports that the church in Antioch was born immediately after the death of Stephen when the Christians were scattered following a persecution in Jerusalem. They went as far as Phoenicia, Cyprus, Cyrene and Antioch. A few unknown missionaries from Cyprus and Cyrene began to preach the Gospel in Antioch.[23] A great number of people turned to the Lord and became believers. Upon hearing this good news, the authorities in Jerusalem sent Barnabas to take care of these new believers and brought many more people to the Lord. Later Barnabas went to Tarsus to look for Saul and brought him to Antioch and both of them served the Antiochian community for a year. It is noteworthy that it was in Antioch that the followers were baptized as Christians[24] although they maintained the distinction such as Jewish Christians and Gentile Christians in many ways and that too in spite of eucharistic fellowship which ended in dining together.

2.6.2 The Sequence of the Event

St. Peter was there in Antioch although we don't exactly know when he had come to this place. Paul and Barnabas too were there at that time as we have just seen above. With an open spirit and defying the existing traditionalist view, the Christian community consisting of both the Jews and the non-Jews created occasions of communion, eating together and surprisingly Peter too joined them regularly. For reasons only known to him, Peter withdrew from this fellowship[25] the moment[26] he saw certain men coming from the circumcision faction from Jerusalem (cf. Acts 15:1). Paul was shocked to see the Jewish Christians and even Barnabas[27] joining Peter and he was furious about it. He didn't hesitate to call it a moment of hypocrisy and he was not ready to take it lying down (cf. Gal 2:12). Paul could sense that the Gentile Christians were being marginalised based on the ritual of circumcision and the Levitical law of diet[28]. Both were of major import as we know.

2.6.3 Paul's Preferential Love for the Gentiles

Paul's outright willingness to fight with Peter face to face demonstrated his preferential love, care and sensitivity for the marginalised Gentile Christians. He didn't want to be a stumbling block to the new Christians. Did Paul think of Peter as a weathercock?[29] Paul himself was someone who wished to "become all things to all people" (1 Cor 9:22b). Paul labelled Peter and the Jewish Christians as people who did not act "consistently with the truth of the gospel" and condemned Peter as someone who behaved like a Gentile in spite of being a Jew. And therefore, he had no right to compel the Gentiles to live like Jews (cf. Gal 2:14). No wonder why Paul "opposed[30] him face to face" and considered him "self-condemned" (Gal 2:11). Peter's action misled the Jewish Christians and even Barnabas.

Paul could have thought that the damage is irreversible as the Gentile Christians were an integral part of the Christian flock and the city of Antioch was of great significance in many ways.[31] It is quite possible that Peter acted inconsistently "not only against his conscience and against the revelation that he had received in Acts X, but also against his whole past tradition and custom".[32] But that did not matter to Paul at all as "it was disastrous for the cause of the gospel, for the Gentile Christians would have had to become Jews for full acceptance within the church".[33] Or rather "Paul saw their (Peter and Barnabas) action as a threat to gospel liberty for Gentiles" ... and "Peter's action ... amounted to forcing Gentiles to adopt the Jewish way of life".[34] It was something totally unacceptable to Paul as he wanted to reach the Gospel to all and wished for the unity of the Church.

2.6 The Jerusalem Council (cf. Acts 15:1-29)

This Council, the first of its kind, turned out to be an epoch making milestone for the Church as it was the first ever bold, concrete step the leaders of the early Church took to sort out many basic issues faced by them. We could even call it the mother of all the Councils. It is also called the 'turning-point,' 'centre-piece,' and 'watershed' of the Book of the Acts.[35] As the church began to expand, there arose many questions regarding the relationship between the Jewish Christians and their Gentile counterparts. One was not very sure whether the Gentiles who embraced Christianity should circumcise themselves and follow the Jewish dietary laws given by Moses although the Jews who abandoned Judaism to follow Christ continued to cling on to their Jewish roots. We know that the Jewish Christians struggled, in the first place, to accept the fact that even the Gentiles could become Christians and be saved through their faith in the Lord Jesus. In this background, they posed two vital questions: (i) what is the status of the Gentile Christians? And (ii) how can the Jewish Christians dine together or have fellowship meal with the ritually unclean Gentile Christians who did not bother to fulfil the expectations of the former.

2.6.1 The Run-up to the First Apostolic Council

The Acts 15:1-5 presents that some men who came from Judea to Antioch told the Gentile Christians that they should circumcise themselves in order to be saved. Paul and Barnabas entered into an argument with them and finally Christians at Antioch decided to take the matter to the apostles and elders in Jerusalem. They found Paul and Barnabas as trustworthy envoys who could represent them and their demands. On their way, the apostles dropped in at Phoenicia and Samaria. Their visit caused great joy to the

Gentile brethren there. In Jerusalem, they reported all their experiences to the so-called 'super apostles' and elders who received them well but a few members of the Pharisee party insisted that the Gentile Christians observe the two basic tenets of Judaism. As a whole, it is nice to see that the Gentile Christians here act in a highly illuminated way and help us conclude that the Antiochian episode could have been one of the causes and consequences of this Council.[36]

2.6.2 The Interventions of Peter and James at the Council (cf. Acts 15:6-21)

When Peter spoke at the Council, he highlighted his role in bringing the Gentiles to follow Jesus and expressed his belief that all would be saved through the grace of the Lord Jesus (vv. 7-11). Peter's experience in the house of the Roman Centurion Cornelius (cf. Acts Chs. 10-11) would have been very fresh and inspiring in his mind. In spite of that experience, if Peter had spoken from Jewish perspective that should not surprise us as Peter was aware that he was set apart to preach to the circumcised and that he had struggled to build upon his involvement with Cornelius. Yet, he came up with a revealing statement: "according to God's will, the Gentiles should receive the Gospel as Gentiles".[37] He is seen as "the bridge-builder among the apostles".[38] The speech of Peter was welcomed with a silence while the intervention of James on the other hand settled the matter straightaway. "The Gentile Christians, who had to live alongside these Jewish Christians must accept a few rules, and these were to be written down and sent to them".[39] The issue of circumcision was totally neglected and a few basic dietary laws were given. One sentence that could have silenced the assembly is, "Now therefore why are you putting God to the test by placing on the neck of the disciples a yoke that neither our ancestors nor we have been able to bear?" (Acts 15:10).

2.6.3 Paul's Role in the Apostolic Council and After

Paul together with Barnabas was chosen to participate in the council in order to challenge the position held by the rank and file of the Church in Jerusalem and establish freedom for the Gentile Christians from the Mosaic law.[40] It was a challenging task. Paul was found worthy of being a committed, knowledgeable negotiator. His initiative made the council focus on "vital theological issues (vv. 6-18) before providing practical guidelines for 'the Gentiles who are turning to God' (vv. 19-21)".[41] Paul and Barnabas were given a few chosen men such as Judas (called Barsabbas) and Silas who is called Silvanus to convey the decision of the Council, known as the Apostolic Decree, to the churches in Antioch, Syria and Cilicia besides all the churches Paul evangelised during his first missionary journey (cf. Acts 16:1-4).[42] Thus one can see that Paul could succeed in his effort to convince the leaders at Jerusalem regarding the status of the Gentile Christians.

2.7 The Case of the Weak and the Strong in Corinth (1 Cor 8:1-13)

Who marginalizes whom and what does a champion liberator do in such a situation? Chapter 8 of Paul's First Letter to the Corinthians deals with the issue of food offered to idols, its consumption by one section of the community and its consequent scandal to the other which causes yet another form of marginalisation. This matter was an uphill task for the apostle Paul as he was caught up between two groups of people: the Jewish and Gentile Christians. The party that consumes the food is called the Strong, namely the Jewish Christians while the scandalised and subsequently marginalised group is named as the Weak. They are the Gentile followers of Christ. They have scruples about eating meat offered to idols. It is quite normal for the new entrants into the faith, anyway.[43] The Strong, on the other hand, does not seem to have any concern for their fellow believers who are misled because of their participation at temple meals.[44] The Strong legitimized the eating of idol-meat while serious reservations were expressed by the Weak.[45] It is because of the apparent misinterpretation of their freedom for their own selfish interests, the Strong failed to see the negative and disastrous consequences for the Corinthian community. Paul instead insists on the imperative of restricting one's freedom for the sake of the 'other' that is, for the common good. Paul does it for the sake of the Gospel and its proclamation and in order to win as many people as possible as it is clear from 1 Cor 9:12, 16, 18, 23.[46] Paul tries out an inclusive approach for the common good!

2.7.1 Paul's Take on this Highly Sensitive Issue

Paul couldn't tolerate the fact that a group of people were being marginalised because of their food habits and lack of knowledge. He deemed it right to employ deliberative discourse to deal with it as it permits him to use many rhetorical arguments, strategies and proofs to persuade the Strong to refrain themselves and move closer to the Weak.[47] Paul deliberately distances himself from the Strong[48] as the behaviour of the Strong has not only displeased the Weak but it has also wounded and defiled them.[49] He dares to make his mind clear in 1 Cor 8:11 where he mentions the adverse effects of the behaviour of the Strong ("So by your knowledge those weak believers for whom Christ died are destroyed"). This language of Paul demonstrates that he does fear the adverse effects of the conduct of the Strong, namely the wrong exercise of their authority. He is sure that it will destroy the Weak for whom Christ died. Otherwise he would not have used the imperative 'watch out' (1 Cor 8:9) to address the Strong.[50]

2.7.2 The Guiding Principle of Paul

Paul's concern is not how to exercise his freedom, knowledge and authority but rather love and that too Christ-like love.[51] He applies the principle of 'love' taking neither side but asking both the groups to exercise certain restraints and respect while he distanced himself from eating meat at all cost. Led by love, Paul expects the Strong to abandon their inflated view of the laws while the Weak must escape their meticulous legalistic approach. Both are expected to learn to be sensitive to each other.[52] The key message of Paul to the Strong is one of sensitivity, caution and the practice of Christian charity toward the Weak so that they might not stumble (8:9-13). That Paul is highly sensitive, cautious and charitable is clear from his approach. "When Paul was asked for a ruling on eating the flesh of animals which had been "sacrificed to idols" (cf. 1Cor 8:1-11:1), the last thing that would have occurred to him would be to quote the decision of the Jerusalem church as binding on Gentile Christians. When faced with such questions he argues from the order of creation and the ethical implications of a law-free gospel."[53] Mark D. Nanos appreciates Paul's sensitivity taking it to another level. He says that Paul coined the oblique labels 'weak' and 'strong' in Rom 14:1-15:13 in order to avoid paying attention to any ethnic or cultural distinctions[54] as Jews and Gentiles.

The Pauline perspective has been perfectly pictured by F. F. Bruce:

> But in matters (like food) which were religiously and ethically neutral, he refused to lay down the law. No food, he maintained, was "common or unclean" per se – not even if it had been forbidden by the law of Moses, not even if it came from an animal that had been sacrificed to a pagan divinity. It was human beings that mattered, not food; if a Christian was considering whether or not to eat this or that kind of food, the decision should depend on the effect which the taking or leaving it would have on the conscience of a fellow-Christian.[55]

Taking a leaf out of Paul's life and ministry, all those who fight for the emancipation and the basic rights of the marginalised people have to help those who marginalise examine their knowledge, principles and questions in order that they may be compassionate and charitable to the marginalised and bring them to the centre.

Part - III

A Courageous Movement from Margin to the Centre

3.1 Who Draws the Margin?

Generally, the mighty or the strong dominate and consequently marginalise a particular people or society either based on religion or language or caste or money or muscle or political power. Once a group occupies the topmost position in the hierarchy, the rest of the people are kept in the margins of that particular society. It is also possible that even among the marginalised lot, there could be a different type of hierarchy that is at work. Those of us who know the *Varnashrama Dharma* of the Indian society, would certainly agree that even among the Brahmins who claim to occupy the top spot, there are so many types based on their family of birth, place of birth, money power and the amount of knowledge of the Vedas while the same, unfortunately, applies also to the Shudras who are marginalised and continue to marginalise a few other groups among them, may be with less intensity. The tribal communities that I know vouch for a similar hierarchy created based on how large and how mighty one tribe is.

Countries where Christians are a majority, the minorities suffer ignominy. For example, the Muslims in Pakistan create endless troubles to the Hindus there because they are a minority while the Muslims who live in the Indonesian Islands torture the Christians for the same reason. Most of us are aware of the century old political rivalry that existed between the Irish and the British and painted a religious picture for all the enmity that existed between the Catholics and the Protestants.

The followers of Christ are not very different in this regard. The Catholics would place their Church above all the other denominations either because of their structure or the kind of belief system or the type of rituals they possess. The Orthodox churches may despise the Latin churches in those countries they are a majority and vice versa. The Jews despised the Samaritans based on their race (pure race versus mixed race). The pure race seemed to have won the race against the mixed race. While the story could go on in this manner, we may conclude that the Jewish Christians kept the Gentile Christians at the periphery just because they considered the non-Jews and eventually non-Jewish Christians as unequal.

3.2 The Marginalised Marginalise Others

In his article on "The Jewish Context of the Gentile Audience Addressed in Paul's Letter to the Romans," Mark D. Nanos argues that Paul wrote his letter to the Romans mainly to address the Gentile Christians who could have dominated the Jewish Christians in Rome. These Gentiles would have mixed rather well with the Jews and frequented their synagogues in Rome. In all probability, Paul could have expected that his ministry among the Gentiles would be both known and acknowledged among the Jews. Therefore, Nanos concludes that Paul, his ministry, and those he was seeking to persuade in Rome, could have functioned within the context and jurisdiction of Jewish communities.[56] This argument of Nanos makes us believe that the marginalised Gentile Christians despised the Jewish Christians in Rome at the time of Paul.

3.3 The Image of Body and its Parts (1 Cor 12:12-31): An Inclusive Approach

Paul is well known for using diverse, common and contemporary metaphors and imageries in his missives. He speaks the language of an engineer (cf. 1 Cor 3:10-17), an athlete (cf. 1 Cor 9:24-27) and a physical trainer (cf. Phil 3:12-14). In 1 Cor 12:12-31, he sounds like a physician dealing with human anatomy and its significance in the context of a divided Corinthian Christian community (cf. 1 Cor 1:10). This "exhortation to the Christian assembly at Corinth is the classic Christian use of the metaphor of the body as a symbol of social unity (cf. Rom 12:4-5; cf. Eph 1:23; 2:16; 3:6; 4:1-16; Col 1:18-24; 2:17-19; 3:15)".[57] In line with many renowned "rhetoricians, philosophers, moralists, and historians contemporary with Paul …, He used the traditional topos in the context of an extended plea for unity … to advocate the interdependence of all bodily members (vv. 21, 25-26)"[58] in a conflict-ridden Corinth. The conclusion that Paul draws is crucial to the believers at Corinth, "Now you are the body of Christ and individually members of it" (1 Cor 12:27) and therefore the Corinthians can neither divide the society nor can they afford to despise or marginalise anyone anymore.

We take note of what Paul writes in 1 Cor 12:12-13, "For just as the body is one and has many members, and all the members of the body, though many, are one body, so it is with Christ. For in the one Spirit we were all baptized into one body — Jews or Greeks, slaves or free — and we were all made to drink of one Spirit". This text argues for equal rights to all the parts of the body, however diverse they are. "Christ exists as a body, the parts of which are all the Christians".[59] As a result of the personification, it is understood then that "If one member suffers, all suffer together with it; if one member is honoured, all rejoice together with it. Now you are the body of Christ and individually members of it" (1 Cor 12:26-27). Therefore, it is the responsibility of every member to make sure that no one suffers or rather all enjoy wellbeing. As Gordon D. Fee says, "all members are necessary if there is to be a body" and "If all the parts were of one kind," then we may have only "a monstrosity".[60]

3.3.1 No One Harms his/her Own Body

One can clearly see that Paul's target is the "social body of Jesus-group members" and he goes on to argue that these members "through being dipped in the Spirit (Sacrament of Baptism) include Judean and Hellenistic Israelites, both those enslaved and those who are fee or freed". Making a case for "unity in diversity," Paul further wishes that "just as God arranged the human body as he chose, so too the social body of Christ at Corinth".[61] Therefore, as noted above, there is no room to despise or marginalise anyone. An injury to any part of one's body affects the entire physique so too any attempt to marginalise one member is an insult and scorn to the person him/herself.

3.3.2 Invitation to Clothe Oneself with Christ

In Gal 3:27-28, Paul repeats what he wrote to the Corinthians (cf. 1 Cor 12:12-31) adding an invitation to the Christians at Galatian Churches to clothe themselves with Christ at the time of receiving the Sacrament of Baptism. Then they will realise that "There is no longer Jew or Greek, there is no longer slave or free, there is no longer male and female; for all of you are one in Christ Jesus". All become one in Christ. As it is evident, 1 Cor 12:12-13 is amplified and very well explained in Gal 3:27-28.

3.3.3 Invitation to Follow One's Conscience

In the context in which this seminar is organised, one may question the relevance of receiving the Sacrament of Baptism (thus becoming a Christian) or clothing oneself with Christ (embracing Christ). Paul anticipated this and other related queries two thousand years ago while writing to the Romans (2:14-15): "When Gentiles, who do not possess the law, do instinctively what the law requires, ... are a law to themselves. They show that what the law requires is written on their hearts, to which their own conscience also bears witness; and their conflicting thoughts will accuse or perhaps excuse them". Paul does not mind citing his own example to validate this point. In spite of being a believer, close follower and an apostle of the Lord Jesus and his Father, Paul says that following his conscience he "behaved in the world with frankness and godly sincerity, not by earthly wisdom but by the grace of God" (2 Cor 1:12). All of us, whether we are believers and followers of the Lord Jesus or not, following one's conscience will always keep us on the track and in good stead.

4. Practical Application

4.1 Land of Origin and Religious Affiliation

Paul was marginalised primarily because of the land of origin and his religious belonging. He was a diaspora Jew. His Bible, the Book of his life was the Septuagint. After all it was a translation from the original TaNaK with an extra later unofficial addition which was an *anathema sit* for the Jews of Judea. He practised a Judaism which was not approved by the authorities in Jerusalem. As we have already seen, certain Jews from Asia could not tolerate his entry into the Temple of Jerusalem. Even when he became a staunch believer and preacher of Christ, the Church leaders, ironically in Jerusalem doubted Paul seriously. It is time for every believer and follower of Jesus Christ to shun every form of marginalisation of the other at all levels, to begin with someone's place of origin by way of regionalism based on one's language or caste. At a larger level, marginalisation based on one's creed has to be condemned. The issue of 'rites' is disturbing the conscience of the Church in India as silent voices of dissension is growing. Not many are interested to talk about it while the Laity has strong objections to the way they are divided.

4.2 The Role of the Liberated Victims

The parable of the Unforgiving Servant in Matt 18:23-35 pictures a slave who owes ten thousand talents[62] to his master. During the time of reckoning the servant falls at the feet of the master and cries for mercy. As one would rightly expect, the master forgives him of his entire debt. A man who enjoyed great clemency comes across his fellow servant who owed him a meagre sum of a hundred denarii.[63] Instead of replicating the compassionate attitude of his master, this unruly servant seizes him by the throat and throws his fellow servant into prison (cf. Matt 18:28-30). This is what happens to many people who have experienced many kinds of emancipation from various forms of slavery and oppression. They seem to forget their plight as a thing of the past and enjoy tyrannizing the other or do not make any effort towards their deliverance.

4.3 Association and Disassociation

Paul's association with the Gentiles was misunderstood by both the 'super apostles' and the Jews. They wanted Paul to embrace a tactic of caution. They expected him to soften his approach on circumcision and Jewish dietary laws. They even persuaded him to undergo the rite of purification. As it happened with Paul, many times, even the so-called 'good souls' are caught between two tight corners not knowing whether to associate or disassociate with certain people or groups for fear of being ostracised. One has to learn to walk the tight rope of faith and trust in God and listen to the inner voice which will never mislead us.

4.4 Re-defining Relationships in the Context of Jesus and his Gospel

Nicklas T. and Schlögel, H. opine that those people who accepted Jesus as their Messiah had an identity crisis. They had to redefine their relationship radically and enter into a decisive vertical relationship with God and Christ and through them create a meaningful and conducive horizontal relationship with their neighbours.[64] It has been a difficult proposition for Christians in India whose schools, hospitals and social work centres are high in demand but Christians are branded as foreigners and their wings are clipped in order to suppress them from carrying out their ministries. It is praiseworthy that Mr. Arvind Kejriwal the Chief Minister of Delhi acknowledged that his success as an administrator is attributed to Jesus Christ and his teachings. The Chief Minister of Maharashtra Mr. Uddhav Thackeray reached out to the Christians with a request to pray that the people of India may be safeguarded from the deadly novel Corona Virus.

4.5 The Ordinary Becomes the Extraordinary: An Attitude of Welcoming One Another

Paul begins Romans chapter 14 with an issue of how to accommodate the weak in faith when it comes to the matter of what to eat and what to avoid: "Welcome those who are weak in faith, but not for the purpose of quarreling over opinions. Some believe in eating anything, while the weak eat only vegetables. Those who eat must not despise those who abstain, and those who abstain must not pass judgment on those who eat; for God has welcomed them" (14:1-3). After speaking about the weak, he turns to the strong in chapter 15, "We who are strong ought to put up with the failings of the weak, and not to please ourselves. Each of us must please our neighbour for the good purpose of building up the neighbour. For Christ did not please himself" (vv. 1-3a). As Mark D. Nanos rightly points out the issues in Rom 14:1-15:13, "are unmistakably marked by lines of purity, by what is proper to eat, do and say in the service of Christ that will be both acceptable to God and approved by men" but it is important to note that "Paul concludes this argument by calling both Gentiles and Jews to welcome one another even as God has welcomed both. This echoes the Shema's call for unity of voice of both the circumcised and uncircumcised in glorifying the one God".[65]

4.6 A Lesson from the Covenantal Code of the Israelites

A. John Baptist[66] in his article on "Evolution and Sustaining of Covenant Community in Pentateuch and Historical Books" writes:

> The Covenantal Code treated all the members of the covenantal community as equals. There was no favoured one and hated one. All of them had their rights, privileges and duties. They have to follow the law, as expected of them. Every tribe too had equal footing before God and in respect to other tribes. The Indian society, which is caste ridden for centuries, does not accept the equality of humans. Human beings are not considered as brothers and sisters striving for one ideal egalitarian society. So, the ecclesial community should emphasise this value of equality and be a model for an egalitarian society. It is interesting to note that the Israelite community was called to treat even the aliens living among them as equals. The reason given was that they knew 'the heart of the alien' because they were aliens themselves in Egypt. So, national boundaries and NRCs are human-made. But for God's people there are no such boundaries.

Conclusion

Humanity has always and everywhere kept a small group of people on the top of the hierarchy while the largest were forced to languish at the bottom. A few have continuously remained at the centre of the circle while a vast majority remained at the periphery. It is time to realise that those who marginalise injure humanity and insult God the Creator. Paying due honour to God's creation is in fact an honour to God Himself. Right from the lap of the mother, children have to be taught to respect the other who hails from a different geographical area, speaks a diverse language, worships a dissimilar God, and at times may even have a different value system and appear in diverse attires. It is because any disrespect to the other amounts to distortion.

Saint Paul who was born a Jew in Asia Minor, in today's Turkey and was educated both in Jerusalem (studies related to his religion) and in Tarsus (philosophy and rhetoric) met Jesus Christ whom he tormented and surrendered his entire life to him. The rest of his life was spent on the road and sea voyages in countries around the Mediterranean Sea and in Europe preaching the Gospel of the same Jesus Christ. His last journey to Jerusalem and all the events that occurred over there brought him to Rome where he faced martyrdom but not before introducing the God of Israel to a group of people who were kept at the periphery for no fault of their own. Unless the human race embraces this mission of Paul and puts into practice, racism and oppressive structures will continue to hurt and haunt all of us.

Notes

1. We have numerous examples in Adolf Hitler, Idi-Amin (Idi Amin Dada Oumee was a Ugandan military officer. He was the President of Uganda from 1971-1979. He was popularly known as the "Butcher of Uganda"), Saddam Hussein Abd al-Majid al-Tikriti, the 5th President of Iraq (28th April 1937-30th December 2006) and many others of the same nature.
2. They are the seven genuinely authentic letters of Paul. They are the letters to Romans, Corinthians, Galatians, Philippians, Thessalonians and Philemon.
3. They consist of Acts of the Apostles written by Saint Luke whose main preoccupation was the extensive growth of the Early Church rather than describing a secular history of the Church of the New Testament Era.
4. These are a group letters which are widely known as Deutero-Pauline Letters. They are the Second Letter to the Thessalonians, Ephesians and Colossians besides the two letters written to Bishop Timothy and the one letter to Bishop Titus.
5. The acronym TaNaK stands for the Hebrew Bible (T=Torah, the Law or the First five books of the Bible, also called Pentateuch in Greek; N = Nebi'im, the Prophets, classified as Pre-historical prophets, Major prophets and Minor prophets and K = Kethubim, the Wisdom writings. They contain 39 books).
6. Septuagint is the Greek translation of the Hebrew Bible with the later addition of the seven Deutero-Canonical Books. This translation took place at the end of 3rd Century BCE. Thanks to the Egyptian King Ptolemy II of Philadelphus, for his love for the diaspora Jews, his interest in building up a library and the desire to preserve the Holy Book of the people of Israel among many other books. The Catholics consider these books as additions made at the secondary stage while the Protestants call them as false books and eventually not inspired.
7. Terms such as castle and military barracks could indicate a fortress where the Roman soldiers stayed.
8. Paul's self-description in Phil 3:5-6, "circumcised on the eighth day, a member of the people of Israel, of the tribe of Benjamin, a Hebrew born of Hebrews; as to the law, a Pharisee; as to zeal, a persecutor of the church; as to righteousness under the law, blameless". This information is from the primary source.

9. Paul did not want to depend on anyone for his survival. Neither did he wish to burden anyone. Therefore, he told the Thessalonians, "You remember our labour and toil, brothers and sisters; we worked night and day, so that we might not burden any of you while we proclaimed to you the gospel of God".
10. Paul paints the picture of an apostle who relies on the providence of God and goes through numerous physical and psychological stress in the process of reaching out the Gospel of Jesus as he expresses his views to the Christians at Corinth, "To the present hour we are hungry and thirsty, we are poorly clothed and beaten and homeless, and we grow weary from the work of our own hands. When reviled, we bless; when persecuted, we endure".
11. Paul did not want to take any remuneration lest he becomes a client-apostle and thus the practice becomes a hurdle on the way of the Gospel. His honest feelings come to the fore when defended his apostleship in his First Letter to the Corinthians, "But I have made no use of any of these rights, nor am I writing this so that they may be applied in my case. Indeed, I would rather die than that— no one will deprive me of my ground for boasting!"
12. Cf. P. W. Gooch, "For and Against Accommodation: 1 Cor 9:19-23," in his *Partial Knowledge: Philosophical Studies in Paul*, Notre Dame, Indiana 1987, 124.
13. The Hebrew word *'am'* and the Greek '*laos*' are used to denote the people of Israel in the Old Testament and New Testament respectively. King James Version translates the Greek word '*Hellenes*' as Gentiles while RSV renders it as 'Greeks'.
14. https://www.biblestudytools.com/dictionary/gentiles/ as on 2nd April 2020 at 16.07.
15. Mark D. Nanos, "The Jewish Context of Gentile Audience Addressed in Paul's Letter to the Romans," in The Catholic Biblical Quarterly (61, 1999), 291.
16. Michael Peppard, "Paul Would Be Proud: The New Testament and Jewish-Gentile Respect," *Theological Studies*, Vol. 76(2) 2015, 260.
17. Cf. Arockiasamy Savarirayan, Life in Christ: Gain or Loss? An Exegetical-Theological Study of 1 Cor 9:19-23 and Phil 3:7-11, Unpublished Doctoral Thesis, Rome 2011, 89, says that any "reference to the Apostolic Council's decision that Peter is the apostle of the Jews while Paul is the apostle of the Gentiles (Gal 2:9) would lead us nowhere, as the competence of the Apostolic Council is under scrutiny. Such a decision on the division of labour did not appear in the official minutes of the Council".
18. George, W. E. Nickelsburg, "The Jewish Context of the New Testament," in *The New Interpreter's Bible*, Vol. VIII, Abingdon Press, Nashville 1994, 40.
19. Michael Peppard, "Paul Would Be Proud: The New Testament and Jewish-Gentile Respect," *Theological Studies*, Vol. 76(2) 2015, 262.
20. Richard N. Longenecker, *Galatians*, Word Biblical Commentary, Vol. 41, Word Books Publisher, Dallas-Texas 1990, 64.
21. It is important to know that Paul owes a lot to Barnabas in spite of the many personal struggles they had. It was Barnabas who introduced Paul to the Apostles and the Church in Jerusalem (cf. Acts 9:27) and later went to Tarsus and looked for Paul and brought him to the church at Antioch (cf. Acts 11:25-26). In many

ways, Barnabas was Paul's advocate, mentor and an esteemed colleague in the first missionary journey (cf. Acts 13:2-14:26).

22. F. F. Bruce, *The Book of the Acts*, The New International Commentary on the New Testament, Revised, William B. Eerdmans Publishing Company, Grand Rapids, Michigan 1988, 285 as taken from J. D. G. Dunn, Unity and Diversity in the New Testament, London 1977, 285.
23. Cf. Richard N. Longenecker, *Galatians*, 70, identifies these missionaries as Hellenistic Jewish Christians.
24. *Ibid.*, 70 defines Christians as "Christ Followers" or "People of Christ" as against the previous name "Those of the Way".
25. Cf. R. Alan Cole, *The Epistle of Paul to the Galatians: An Introduction and Commentary*, Tyndale New Testament Commentaries, Grand Rapids, Michigan 1984, 74-75. The circumstances make us believe that Peter could have avoided not only the common fellowship meal but also and more importantly the Eucharistic Table Fellowship/The Lord's Supper. In any case, Peter's action would have infuriated or at least insulted and set a wrong precedence to the newly born Gentile Christians.
26. Cf. Donald Guthrie, *Galatians*, The New Century Bible Commentary, W. B. Eerdman Publ. Co., Grand Rapids 1984, 85, says that it is not just once Peter withdrew from the fellowship meal but rather it could have been a gradual process as denoted by Paul's use of the imperfect tense in the verbs. Peter could have gone through a tedious and painful process from vacillation of mind to yielding to the circumcision party. Richard N. Longenecker, *Galatians*, 73 opines that it is a repeated or habitual eating.
27. Cf. Richard N. Longenecker, *Galatians*, 76, calls the defection of Barnabas as a "blow of great personal magnitude" and Paul "was crushed" the way Barnabas behaved.
28. Cf. Richard N. Longenecker, *Galatians*, 75, says, "...there could be no real fellowship between Jewish believers and Gentile believers in Jesus unless the latter observed the dietary laws of the former. Such a tenet, of course, would have serious implications for the proclamation of the gospel to Gentiles and for a doctrine of the oneness of the body of Christ".
29. Cf. R. Alan Cole, *The Epistle of Paul to the Galatians: An Introduction and Commentary*, 73. We are of the opinion that Peter had the first exposure with the Gentiles in Acts 10:1-11:18 when he visited the house of the Roman Centurion Cornelius and witnessed the descending of the Holy Spirit on Cornelius and his household. One wonders if Peter came under the pressure of James and his men or the so-called circumcision party.
30. Cf. Richard N. Longenecker, *Galatians*, 72, interprets the verb 'opposed' as "Paul's initiative and active opposition (cf. Mark 3:26; Acts 6:9)".
31. Richard N. Longenecker, *Galatians*, 70. We have to take note that Syrian Antioch was the 3rd most important city of the Roman Empire and it was the first Gentile city that accepted Christianity. It was the home-base of Paul's missionary activities as all the three missionary journeys began from here.
32. R. Alan Cole, *The Epistle of Paul to the Galatians*, 74.
33. Richard N. Longenecker, *Galatians*, 78.

34. F. F. Bruce, *The Book of the Acts*, The New International Commentary on the New Testament, Revised, William B. Eerdmans Publishing Company, Grand Rapids, Michigan 1988, 285 as taken from J. D. G. Dunn, Unity and Diversity in the New Testament, London 1977, 284.
35. Cf. David G. Peterson, *The Acts of the Apostles*, The Pillar New Testament Commentary, William B. Eerdmans Publishing Company, Grand Rapids, Michigan 2009, 417.
36. Richard N. Longenecker, *Galatians*, 71.
37. Johannes Munck, *The Acts of the Apostles: A New Translations with Introduction and Commentary*, The Anchor Bible, Vol. 31, Doubleday, New York 1986, 140.
38. F. F. Bruce, *The Book of the Acts*, The New International Commentary on the New Testament, Revised, William B. Eerdmans Publishing Company, Grand Rapids, Michigan 1988, 285 as taken from J. D. G. Dunn, Unity and Diversity in the New Testament, London 1977, 285.
39. Johannes Munck, *The Acts of the Apostles*, 141.
40. Cf. David G. Peterson, *The Acts of the Apostles*, 419.
41. David G. Peterson, *The Acts of the Apostles*, 423.
42. Cf. David G. Peterson, *The Acts of the Apostles*, 437.
43. Cf. B. Hall, "All Things to all People: A Study of 1 Corinthians," in The Conversation Continues: Studies in Paul and John, eds. R. T. Fortna – B. R. Gaventa, Nashville 1990, 139.
44. J. L. Sumney, "The Place of 1 Corinthians 9:24-27 in Paul's Argument," *JBL* 119 (2, 2000), 332.
45. Cf. E. C. III. Still, "Paul's Aim Regarding EIDWLOQUTA: A New Proposal for Interpreting 1 Corinthians 8:1-11:1," 339.
46. S. C. Barton, "'All Things to All People' Paul and the Law in the Light of 1 Corinthians 9:19-23," in *Paul and the Mosaic Law*, ed., J. D. G. Dunn, Cambridge 2001, 278.
47. J. FOTOPOULOS, *Food Offered to Idols in Roman Corinth: A Socio-Rhetorical Reconsideration of 1 Corinthians 8:1-11:1*, Tübingen 2003, 261.
48. Cf. P. D. Gardner, The Gifts of God and the Authentication of a Christian: An Exegetical Study of 1 Corinthians 8-11:1, New York-London 1994.
49. Cf. *Ibid.*, 117.
50. Cf. D. HORRELL, "Theological principle or Christological Praxis? Pauline Ethics in 1 Corinthians 8:1-11:1, *JSNT* 67 (1997), 89.
51. Cf. *Ibid.*, 95.
52. Cf. G. D. Fee, "Eivdwloqu,ta Once Again: An Interpretation of 1 Corinthians 8-10," *Biblica* 61 (1980), 175.
53. F. F. Bruce, *The Book of the Acts*, 285.
54. Mark D. Nanos, "The Jewish Context of Gentile Audience Addressed in Paul's Letter to the Romans," in The Catholic Biblical Quarterly (61, 1999), footnote 30, 291.
55. F. F. Bruce, *The Book of the Acts*, The New International Commentary on the New Testament, Revised, William B. Eerdmans Publishing Company, Grand

Rapids, Michigan 1988, 285 as taken from J. D. G. Dunn, Unity and Diversity in the New Testament, London 1977, 285, quoting Rom 14:14-23.

56. Mark D. Nanos, "The Jewish Context of Gentile Audience Addressed in Paul's Letter to the Romans," in *The Catholic Biblical Quarterly* (61, 1999), 303.
57. Raymond F. Collins, *First Corinthians*, Sacra Pagina, Vol. 7, The Liturgical Press, Collegeville, Minnesota 1999, 460.
58. Raymond F. Collins, *First Corinthians*, 460.
59. William F. Orr and James Arthur Walther, *1 Corinthians: A New Translation with a Study of the Life of Paul, Notes and Commentary*, The Anchor Bible, Doubleday, New York 1976, 285.
60. Gordon G. Fee, *The First Epistle to the Corinthians, The New International Commentary on the New Testament*, William B. Eerdmans Publishing Company, Grand Rapids, Michigan 1987, 609, 611.
61. Bruce J. Malina and John J. Pilch, *Social-Science Commentary on the Letters of Paul*, Fortress Press, Minneapolis 2006, 115.
62. A talent was worth more than fifteen years' wages of a labourer.
63. The denarius was the usual day's wage for a labourer.
64. Cf. Tobias Nicklas & Herbert Schlögel, "Mission to the Gentiles: The construction of Christian identity and its relationship with ethics according to Paul," AOSIS Open Journals, 1-2, from http://www. hts.org.za. doi: 10.4102/ hts.V68i1.1217
65. Mark D. Nanos, "The Jewish Context of Gentile Audience Addressed in Paul's Letter to the Romans," in The Catholic Biblical Quarterly (61, 1999), 292-293.
66. A. John Baptist, "Evolution and Sustaining of Covenant Community in Pentateuch and Historical Books," 9.

21

Higher Education and the Minority Christian Communities in the Globalised Era

— Prof. Victoria A. Masih

Introduction

Human development of any nation rests on the importance it has bestowed on education and its imparting institutions. To impart the necessary knowledge and skills to the population to contribute actively to the design of reforms of structures and processes of educational management which are favourable to the realisation of the Education 2030 Goal it is necessary to *"Ensure inclusive and equitable quality education and promote lifelong learning opportunities for all"*.

Education enhances the human capital to harness the physical and other resources of the nation. In the Indian context which is a developing economy and showcases vibrant socio-cultural variance, importance of education is paramount. But the question remains that with multilayered

Table 1: Religious Composition of Indian Population

Religious Composition	*Population**	*(per cent)*	*State majority**
Hindus	827,578,868	80.5	28
Muslims	138,188,240	13.4	2
Christians	24,080,016	2.3	4
Sikhs	19,215,730	1.9	1
Buddhists	7,955,207	0.8	-
Jains	4,225,053	0.4	-
Other Religions & Persuasions	6,639,626	0.6	-
Religion not stated	727,588	0.1	-
Total *	1,028,610,328	100.0	35

Source: Census of India: 2011, Government of India

Note: * shows the no. of states with religious majority

generic socio-cultural and linguistic patterns of India, it is important that we take due cognizance of the varying needs of these heterogeneous societies and cater to the issue to bring about a par playing ground. In this context the Indian constitution framers played a vital role.

The religious composition of the population is an integral component of the Indian population. The demographic and religious distribution of Indian population shows that it is a land dominated by Hinduism. As a religious group Hinduism, a religion practiced for thousands of years. Its origin is difficult to map out and it is believed to have evolved out of the diverse Indian ways of life, so different and yet in some elusive way integrated.

Table 2: Population Trends for Major Religious Groups in India (1951–2011)

Religious group	*Population % 1951*	*Population % 1961*	*Population % 1971*	*Population % 1981*	*Population % 1991*	*Population % 2001*	*Population % 2011*
Hinduism	84.1	83.45	82.73	82.30	81.53	80.46	79.80
Islam	9.8	10.69	11.21	11.75	12.61	13.43	14.23
Christianity	2.3	2.44	2.60	2.44	2.32	2.34	2.30
Sikhism	1.79	1.79	1.89	1.92	1.94	1.87	1.72
Buddhism	0.74	0.74	0.70	0.70	0.77	0.77	0.70
Jainism	0.46	0.46	0.48	0.47	0.40	0.41	0.37
Zoroastrianism	0.13	0.09	0.09	0.09	0.08	0.06	n/a
Other religions / No religion	0.43	0.43	0.41	0.42	0.44	0.72	0.9

Source: "Population by religious community – 2011". 2011 Census of India. Office of the Registrar General & Census Commissioner. Archived from the original 25th August 2015.

Table 3: Demographic Characteristics of Religious Groups of India

Religious group	**Population (2011) %**	**Growth (2001–2011)**	**Sex Ratio (2011) (total)**	**Sex ratio (2011) (juvenile)**	**Literacy (2011) (%)**	**Work Participation (2011) (%)**
Hinduism	79.80	16.8	939	913	73.3	41.0
Islam	14.23	24.6	951	943	68.5	32.6
Christianity	2.30	15.5	1023	958	84.5	41.9
Sikhism	1.72	8.4	903	828	75.4	36.3
Buddhism	0.70	6.1	965	933	81.3	43.1
Jainism	0.37	5.4	954	889	94.9	35.5
Others/Religion not specified	0.90	n/a	959	974	n/a	n/a

Source: "Population by religious community – 2011". 2011 Census of India. Office of the Registrar General & Census Commissioner. Archived from the original 25th August 2015.

India is the second most populated country in the world with nearly a one-fifth of the world's total population. The revision of the World Population Prospects, 2017, shows that the population stood at 1,324,171,354.

The Census 2011 was unique in its attempt to introduce for the first time a category of "No religion" in which about 2.87 million people were

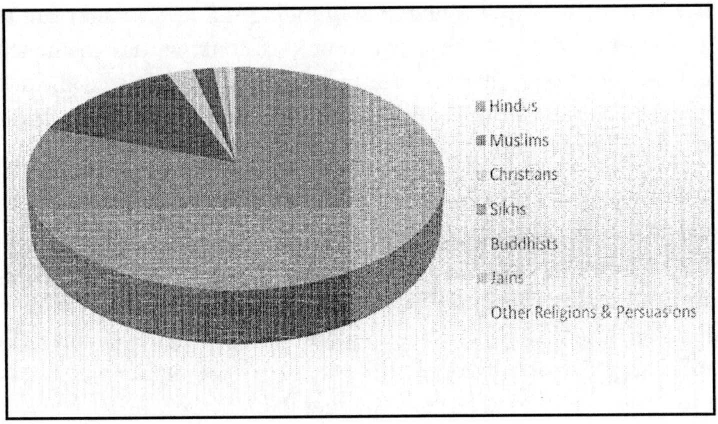

Source: Census 2011, Government of India.

Chart No. 1: Distribution of Population by Religious Categories.

classified. Table 2 shows the decadal composition of population by religious classification. Six major religions have been recognised in the "National Minority" status i.e. the Muslims, Christians, Sikhs, Jains, Buddhists and Parsis have been shown in the table. The different sub-categories of the Islamic population by Sunnis, Shias, Bohras, Agakhanis and Ahmadiyas have been identified as sects of Islam in India. As per 2011 census, six major faiths- Hindus, Muslims, Christians, Sikhs, Buddhists, Jains in total account for over 99.4 percent of India's population, while the rest incorporates the "other religions, persuasions" (ORP). The followers of Other Religious Practices comprised of six faiths of which 49.57 lakhs belonged to strong Sarna, 10.26 lakhs to strong Gond, 5.06 lakhs to strong Sari, Doni Polo (3.02 lakh) in Arunachal Pradesh, Sanamahi (2.22 lakh) in Manipur, Khasi (1.38 lakh) in Meghalaya dominate. The state of Maharashtra recorded the highest number of atheists with 9,652 population in this category followed by Meghalaya (9,089) and Kerala.

The religious composition of the Indian population has undergone massive changes as a result of varied factors. The spatial distribution of varied religious communities underwent massive changes as a result of large scale migration consequent upon the partition of India in 1947. This partition brought a sea change in the distribution and relative dominance of different religious faith in Northern, North-Western and North-Eastern India.

According to 1941 census Hindus accounted for 66.5 percent of the population of the Subcontinent and Muslim's 23.7 percent. Consequent upon partition huge number of Muslims migrated from India to Pakistan and Bangladesh and Hindus migrated to India from these countries. As a result, the percentage of these two religious communities in the total population underwent changes. This was evidently visible in the 1951 Census, as the percentage of Hindus rose to 84.1 percent and that of Muslims fell to 9.8 percent in India.

The Table 3 shows the decadal growth of population by different religious categories. As per the 2011 Census the sex ratio for total population stood at 943 females against 1,000 males. Among the Hindus, 939 females against 1,000 males, Muslims 951 females, Christians 1,023 females, Sikhs 903 females, Buddhists 965 females and Jains 954 females against 1,000 males. Though the absolute proportion of Hindus is higher and forms a majority but the rate of growth shows that the followers of Islam i.e. the Muslim population shows the highest growth rate by 24.6 percent and the lowest is Jainism. The same has been shown in the Chart 4.2 for the decade 2001 to 2011.

Similarly the sex ratio of the population by religious categories shows that Christianity had the highest female and juvenile sex ratio whereas the population from the Sikh community showed the worst performance in terms of sex ratio. Similarly the literacy rate amongst the followers of Jainism followed by Christianity superseded others. It could be deduced that the reflection of education on the preference for girls.

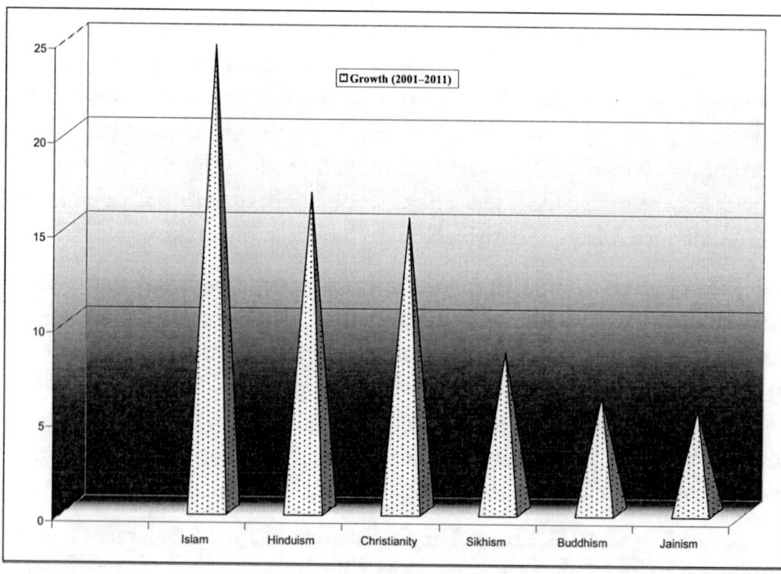

Chart 2: Growth in Population by Religious Composition 2001-2011.

Minority Rights for Higher Education and its Justification

The constitution of the country guarantees to all its citizens the access to education on the grounds of merit. The State is bound by law to initiate necessary steps to ensure that merit based admission takes place and that the demands of the vulnerable sections of the community including minorities. Despite plethora of judicial pronouncements and legislative attempts, the Indicas to determine minority and minority educational institutions and the attempts to regulate admission in the minority educational institutions there still prevails issues of contention that have been discussed at large in the following chapters.

The federal structure and varied culture is the magnitude of India's diversity which on one hand presents the generic beauty of our Indian constitution while on the other it also provides challenges from time to time and necessitates amendments to ensure protection and security of this vividity. The intent behind conferring special rights to minorities is not to discriminate the dominant and the minor group but to establish equality and security of the minorities.

India is a land of 22 official languages and 8 major religions. It is thereby, pertinent to retain the essence of this heterogeneity of the cultural fabric along with ensuring equality. Therefore, the study becomes important as it tries to analyze the existing constitutional provisions, acts and laws and also the judicial orders from time to time with respect to their efficacy in addressing the specific minority issues. In this research work I focus on the Minority Educational Institutions and their management and administrative rights.

Keeping in view the vast population of India which comprises of the minorities it is important that the incorporation of these minority groups holistically in the development process is well envisaged. Education that is understood as the panacea for eradicating all developmental hurdles; it is pertinent to pave the path of the development of the minorities via special impetus on equal opportunity to education. In this move, it is important that the state takes a lead role in framing laws, rules, regulations and methods for the smooth proliferation and functioning of minority educational institutions. The legislative intent as reflected in the Constitution of India through its fundamental rights, directive principles of state policy and amendments made from time to time shows that there has been an ongoing and conscious effort on the part of the state to ensure that the rights of the minorities is ensured. The apex judicial institution, the Supreme Court of India also from time to time has been providing guidelines and judgments for functioning of the minorities educational institutions. A critical analysis is intended to be undertaken to study the fact whether the present Management & Administrative rights of the Minority educational Institution are in concurrence with the intent of their framing.

Religious Heterogeneity and Education

India is conglomeration of many ethnic, religious, caste and linguistic minorities associated with distinct faiths, sub-cultures and genres specific to regions. The amalgam or mix of these heterogeneous communities varying in proportions to main population has been among the central issues of concern of the Indian government and its constitutional framework since inception. Religion in India is marked by its diverse religious beliefs and practices. By the 42nd Amendment to the Constitution India was declared as a 'secular state' in the year 1976. Secularism ensures that all religions are treated equally by the state. The Indian subcontinent is the origin of world's four major religions, Hinduism, Buddhism, Jainism, and Sikhism. India is distinct with its religious diversity and religious tolerance that is ensured also by the laws and customs of the Constitution of India.

As per the Census 2011, 79.8 percent of the population of India practiced Hinduism followed by 14.2 percent Islam, and the remaining 6 percent belonging to other religions including Christianity, Buddhism, Sikhism, Jainism and various native cultural beliefs. Thus, after Islam, Christianity is the 3rd largest religion in India. It is noteworthy that the diverse cultural composition of the land encompasses world's largest population of people adhering Zoroastrianism (i.e. Parsis and Iranis) and Baha'i' Faith, though these communities do not originate from India. Also India is home to third largest Shia population in the world, and also 2 million Ahmadi Muslims. (Census 2011, Government of India)

Indian Constitution and Minority Education

The entire debate in the Constituent Assembly encircled around the question: What rights could or should be conceded to minorities? It was the Article 23 of the Draft Constitution that was shaped as the present Articles 29 and 30. The original draft of the fundamental rights submitted to the Constituent Assembly on April 16, 1947 by the Sub-Committee on Fundamental Rights along with its report did not contain the provisions corresponding to Article 30(1). It did not even refer to the word minority.

The Drafting Committee, sought to make distinction between the rights of any section of the citizen to conserve its language, script or culture and the right of the minorities based on religion or language to set up and administer educational institutions of their choice. For this the committee removed the word 'minority' in the previous part of the draft Article 23 corresponding to Article 29, while it retained the word in the latter part of the draft Article 23 which now forms part of the present Article 30(1).

Exhibit 1

Article 29 Protection of interest of minorities

(1) *Any section of the citizens residing in the territory of India or any part thereof having a distinct language, script or culture of its own shall have the right to conserve the same.*

(2) No citizens shall be denied admission into any educational institution maintained by the State or receiving aid out of State fund on ground only of religion, race, caste, language or any of them.

Article 30- Right of Minorities to establish and administer educational institution:

(1) All minorities, whether based on religion or language shall have the right to establish and administer educational institution of their choice

[(1A) In making any law providing for the compulsory acquisition of any property of and educational institution established and administered by a majority, referred to in clause

(1) The State shall ensure that the amount fixed by or determined under such law for the acquisition of such property is such as would not restrict or abrogate the right guaranteed under the clause]

(2) The State shall not, in granting aid to educational institutions, discriminate against any educational institution on the ground that it is under the management of minority whether based on religion or language.

Articles 15 and 16 *-prohibit the state from making any discrimination on the grounds only of religion, race, caste, sex, descent, place of birth, residence or any of them either generally i.e., every kind of state action in relation to citizens (Article 15) or in matters relating to employment or appointment to any office under the state (Article 16).*

Source: https://www.india.gov.in/sites/upload_files/npi/files/coi_part_full.pdf

International Guidelines

- The Universal Declaration of Human Rights, 1948 and its two International Covenants of 1966 i.e. International Covenant on Economic, Social & Cultural Rights and International Covenant on Civil & Political Rights, declare that "all human beings are equal in dignity and rights" and prohibit all kinds of discrimination–racial, religious, etc.
- The United Nations Declaration on the elimination of all forms of intolerance & of discrimination based on Religion or Beliefs passed in 1981 outlaws all kinds of religion-based discrimination.
- The United Nations Declaration on the Rights of persons belonging to National, Ethnic, Religious and Linguistic Minorities, passed on December 18, 1992 intended to strengthen the rights of the minorities. It enjoins the states to protect the existence and

identity of minorities within their respective territories. It called upon the States to encourage the promotion of national and ethnic, cultural, religious & linguistic minorities; ensure that persons belonging to minorities fully and effectively exercise human rights and fundamental freedoms without any discrimination and equality; create positive conditions to facilitate minorities to articulate their distinctiveness and develop their culture, language, religion, traditions and customs; plan and execute national policy and programmes to address the legitimate interests of minorities; etc.

- The U.N. Sub-Commission on Prevention of Discrimination and Protection of Minorities defined minority (Report of the Sub-Commission on Prevention of Discrimination and Protection of Minorities on its 46th Session, U.N. Doc. E/CN.4/Sub.2/1994/56 (1994).

Judicial Interpretations

- The judiciary took the preliminary step while answering the first question that was made, eight years after the constitution was adopted, in Kerala Education Bill, 1958, where Chief Justice S. R. Das held that a minority means an "community which is numerically less than 50 percent" of the total population. Thus, suggesting the technique of arithmetical tabulation. "Bohra opines that on consideration of 'minority', a numerically minor group in a defined area, some stress on certain characteristics commonly possessed by them and, to them, and that these characteristics serve as objective features of distinction. In this sense the term used to cover "racial, religious or linguistic sections of the population within a State which differ in these respects from the majority of the population." (Bohra Saroj, 2014)
- The Supreme Court in its historic order in its decision in D.A.V. College v. State of Punjab (AIR 1971 SC 173) held that what constituted a linguistic or religious minority must be judged in specificity to the State and its composition and not in relation to whole of India. "Minority' requires being determined only in relation to the particular legislation which is being confronted. If a State Law extending to the whole of the state is in question, the minority must be determined with reference to the entire State population. In such a case, any community, linguistic or religious, which is numerically less than 50 percent of the entire

State population, will be a Minority for purposes of Article 30 (1). (DAV)

- The Supreme Court (TMA Pai Foundation & Ors v. State of Karnataka & Ors, (2002) (SCC 481) held that for the purpose of Article 30 a minority, whether linguistic or religious, is determinable with reference to a state and not by taking into account the entire population of the country as a whole
- The State Minorities Commission Acts usually empower the local governments to identify minorities e.g., Bihar Minorities Commission Act, 1991, Section 2(c); Karnataka Minorities Commission Act, 1994, Section 2(d); Uttar Pradesh Minorities Commission Act 1994, Section 2(d); West Bengal Minorities Commission Act 1996, Section 2(c); Andhra Pradesh Minorities Commission Act 1998, Section 2(d). The Madhya Pradesh (1996) and Delhi (1999) Minorities Commission Acts however rely on the government's notification issued under the National Commission for Minorities Act 1992 to be applicable in this regard. In the states of Himachal Pradesh, Jharkhand, Madhya Pradesh, Maharashtra, Uttar Pradesh and Uttarakhand), Jains have been recognised as a minority. As such the Jain community approached the Supreme Court to seek equivalent and relevant direction suggesting that the central government should provide for a similar recognition at the national level and their demand was addressed by the National Commission for Minorities But the Apex Court did not issue the desired direction, leaving it to the central government to decide the issue. (Bal Patil vs. Union of India, 2005) In a later ruling however, another bench of the Supreme Court upheld the Uttar Pradesh law recognizing Jains as a minority. (Bal Vidya case, 2006)
- Our review suggests that India has been known for its lack of institutional memory. Commissions and committees are formed but their recommendations are rarely adhered. For example, the Kothari Commission recommended for 6 percent allocation of 6 percent of GDP. This was a policy recommendation endorsed by the National Policy of Education, two decades later in 1986 points Prof. Protiva Kundu. In a paper presented jointly by the Centre for Budget and Governance Accountability (CBGA) and CRY for the RTE Forum, says, "After the implementation of RTE in 2010, the school education expenditure has increased just

by 0.2 percent (from 2.5 percent of GDP in 2009-10 to 2.7 percent of GDP in 2015-16)." (Sabrang India, July 24, 2017)

- The total allocation for education is expected to be lower for 2017-18 as the share of Union Government in total spending has decreased from 0.8 percent in 2013-14 to 0.47 percent of GDP in 2017-18. Prof Kundu, further states that, that the per student spending on education is Rs 13,974 per year "India is the only country which is paying less attention on right to education despite it being a fundamental right." Even the former foreign secretary Muchkund Dubey raised his concern citing a recent CAG audit report that shows that the SSA(Sarv Siksha Abhiyaan) budget for 2014-15 had been reduced by Rs 5256 crore, against the budgeted provision of Rs 27,575 crore, due to lower collection of education cess."

Higher Education: A Panacea for Development of Christian Minorities

Education holds the key for the development of minorities in India, there is a need for systematic transformation of the thinking process and the resulting behaviour through proper education. Given the importance of a knowledge economy, the establishment of educational institutions of global standards ought to become the priority of minority communities. Internationalism in higher education needed to be promoted. The development of self-respect, a strong sense of ethics and inter-faith understanding through education were perhaps the most important mission of educational institutions

Religion has been a crucial determinant of the socio-cultural and political rhythm of the masses shaping both intra-national and international politics even today. Besides the fact that it is a part of a person's identity, it is also "a certain variety of communication" (Beyer, 1994, p. 5). At least in some parts of the world, religion's role would be long lasting in terms of certain food habits, and even with regard to cultivation of some crops and raising of some animals (Jordon and Rowntree, 1976, p. 250). For instance, reverence for the cow and prohibition on beef eating among Hindus, and prohibition on pork in the Muslim countries would continue to be there with its own implications for the lives of these animals. In the same way, religious prohibition on tobacco smoking in the Sikh culture does not allow for the cultivation of tobacco in the state of Punjab where Sikh dominates by population. Also, the places of religious worship of varied religions bear their distinct impact on the physical as well as intellectual milieu.

The issues concerning the minorities has been inbuilt and given to our constitution framers. It was rooted by the British by the principle of "Divide and Rule Policy." Everybody has experience of the partition of the country and the "hide and seek game" of the British. The division of the country on the basis of religion and declaration of an Islamic State in Pakistan were the result of the long treacherous British rule. Loot, murder, plunder and wholesale destruction of opposite community at the time of partition of our nation were the scars on the bloody politics of India at the dawn of Independence. (D.S. Prakash Rao, "Protection of minorities rights: Need of the hour", Legal Journal Quest for Justice, Vol. II, No. 1, 2006-07. pp. 63-64)

Even though the separate state was formed for Muslim, a considerable section of Muslims remained in India. There were Indian Christian, Anglo Indian and some Europeans who opted India as their homeland. The framers of the Indian Constitution were keenly aware of the fact that these religious minorities need to be assured "Liberty of thought, belief, faith and worship."

To decipher the term minority in the Indian context, historical documents such as the Motilal Nehru Report (1928), The Sapru Report (1945) and the extracts of the Constituent Assembly of India as the primary source portraying the intent of our founding fathers regarding the term minority. These historical documents do shed light on the term minority but it's only the judgments delivered by the honourable courts of India, which clarify the terminology and the rights which are adjunct to it. It was done for the first time in 1958, eight years after the Nation had a written and adopted Constitution that the Judiciary initiated the primary steps in Kerala Education Bill to decipher the term 'minority'. The honourable court defined the expression 'minority' as a "community which is numerically less than 50 percent" of the total population. Thus, suggesting the technique of arithmetical tabulation. "Thus, while considering 'minority', a numerically smaller group, as against the majority in a defined area, some place emphasis upon certain characteristics commonly possessed by the members constituting the minority and, to them, these characteristics serves as objective factors of distinction. In this sense the term used to cover "racial, religious or linguistic sections of the population within a State which differ in these respects from the majority of the population." (Bohra Saroj, 2014)

Concluding Remarks

When I delve to understand the discrepancies prevalent in education I reach at 4 major categories of inequities. First being the inequality based on gender, second inequality based on geographical location or regional inequality, third is the minority-majority based on inequity and the last inequity based on economic category. In this research I have confine to the minority issue. i.e. the third component. The Indian Constitution guarantees equal right and opportunities to education through its fundamental rights and directive principles of state policy. Minority-majority based inequity is evidently observable in higher education. In the Chapter Two of the research work I have detailed the constitutional provisions. Despite the positive legislative intent of the framer of the constitution the Sachaar Committee presented a skewed imbalance in the educational attainments of the Muslims. Whenever a society or civilisation marks a transition from former authoritative or dominated regime to a more accommodative and democratic regime it tends to welcome challenges and resistance. Drawing the same corollary I understand the situation of accommodating minority rights in our Indian democracy. In the entire debate presented in the Chapters Two and Four of the thesis I deduce that though the constitution provides for the protection, and development of the minorities through guarantee of fundamental rights yet the judicial interpretations, from to time seem to have their own ways of interpreting and directing the laws. Not only have these, from time to time contradicting amendments to the existing Articles on minority rights tend to create contentions and doubts. The picture still remains hazy as of the constitution still fails to provide a clear concept of 'minority' that could be uniformly used.

Thus, after adoption of democracy, India has taken a quantum leap. It is widely understood that it confronts complex, multi-layered competing political, social and economic challenges. It is vital to put the institutional architecture of democracy in place to promote and develop democratic values and principles within our society. The metaphor "bricks and mortar" stands true to define these values and principles that lay a strong foundation in the long run. Experience reveal that the strong functioning of the democratic ethos lies in adherence (in both theory and practice) of the elemental principles of equity, justice and inclusion regardless of caste, creed, gender, age, able-bodied and disabled, and race. The long-term sustainability of democracy faces the challenges of promoting actual equity, justice and inclusivity.

To conclude, I reiterate our concern on importance of autonomy and freedom to be given to Minority Educational Institutions as ensured by the

Constitution with respect to their management and administrative rights. It is pertinent to refer to a research conducted by Nilima Chandiramani, which got published in the Mainstream, Vol. LIV, No. 45 New Delhi. October 29, 2016 on the unwarranted infringements on the rights of minorities from time to time by the legislative as well as the executive to the judiciary bodies of the country. She makes reference to the following observations of their lordships in this context-

> *"...............In conclusion, we hold that if any entity is once declared as minority entitling to the rights envisaged under Article 30(1) of the Constitution of India, unless there is fundamental change of circumstances or suppression of facts the Government has no power to take away that cherished constitutional right which is a fundamental right and that too, by an ordinary letter without being preceded by a fair hearing in conformity with the principles of natural justice."*

22

Status of Hindu SC Vs Christian SC (CSCO) in the Globalised Era

— *Prof. V. Joachim*

Introduction

Caste discrimination is an unacceptable anti-social practice with religious sanction. In a subtle manner discrimination is observed and practiced even among the Christians in the Church and outside. In many Villages there are separate cremation grounds, cemeteries for high caste and low caste. It is a very unchristian practice. Though God created all people equals, men have differentiated and discriminated them as high caste and low caste for their own advantages and to assert their superiority and power over others.

The above scenario prompted the author to undertake a project study on the socio-economic condition of the scheduled caste Christians. This research paper examines how the low caste suffer from social discrimination within the church by Christian Community and in the outside world by other caste people. It's an eye-opener for many social scientists and religious leaders.

Rationale for undertaking the Research

The researcher Prof. V. Joachim (retired) is a repatriate from Myanmar. Born and brought up in Burma to Tamil parents, he migrated to India in the year 1965 when he was 20 years old. After schooling and graduation he pursued his post-graduation in social work and took up a carrier as Assistant Professor in Loyola College in the Department of Social Work in the year 1978.

While in Burma during his school days and later, the general practice observed is, people differentiate and discriminate between Indian Tamils and Burmese and within the Tamils Hindus and Christians. The social discrimination based on caste within the same religion and with people of other religion was not a common practice. All the Tamils living in the same locality had a good understanding, co-operation and unity and all of them identify themselves as Indians of Tamil origin. Caste was not a dominant factor for social discrimination though some elderly people were aware of the different castes among the Tamils, among the youth and the youngsters it made no difference and they closely relate and associate with all the Tamils in Burma without any form of discrimination.

When the researcher came to India, the most shocking and surprising observation noticed by him was the social discriminatory practice among the human beings based on the caste hierarchical system. It is unacceptable anti-social practice with religious sanction. In a subtle manner discrimination is observed and practiced even among the Christians in the Church and outside. In many villages there are separate cremation grounds, cemeteries for high caste and low caste. It is a very unchristian practice. Though God created all people equals, men have differentiated and discriminated them as high caste and low caste for their own advantages and to assert their superiority and power over others.

The above scenario prompted the research to undertake a project study on the socio-economic condition of the scheduled caste Christians. The study revealed that their socio-economic conditions are very poor and they suffer from social discrimination within the church by Christian Community and in the outside world by other caste people.

Another important factor from the Indian constitution is consequent to the Presidential order No. 19 of 1950, paragraph No. 3, the right of SC status is denied to the SC Christians (Christians of scheduled caste origin – (CSCO)

The SC community in general is subjected to various types of disabilities and they suffered suppression, oppression and exploitations. In order to mitigate their sufferings and to develop their lot socially, economically and educationally, the Government of India made special provisions, concession and privileges to the underprivileged SC but the CSCO are not entitled for such facilities as the result of embracing Christian faith.

The CSCO were once SC Hindus but embraced Christianity some generation back due to which they are denied SC status and the privileges that follows that, therefore the objective of the study was to compare the status of SC and that of the CSCO. It is mainly to ascertain the present status of these two communities. In other words whether conversion to Christianity has brought about socio-economic, educational and cultural changes among the CSCO compared to the SC. Social isolation and discrimination being the main cause for considering a Community as SC, having embraced Christianity a few generations ago has it reduced or removed the social discrimination among the CSCO. Because, according to Christian doctrine, faith and believe all human beings are created by god and they are equal in all aspects. What is the reality in practice is the question to be answered.

The general assumption of learned people is that the SC by converting themselves to Christianity will overcome their caste discrimination which is strongly believed and practiced by Hindus and it is alien to Christian doctrine value and practice.

In this study an attempt is made to compare the status of the CSCO with the Hindu SCs with regard the social discrimination, economic conditions, educational level and cultural differences that prevail in the present day. The study of this nature is the vital need of the hour.

Discrimination in Indian Society

Human society is classified, grouped and discriminated on the basis of race (Dravidians and Aryans), colour (whites and blacks of America), language (German and French), and religion (Christian and Hindu). These forms of discrimination/classification are quite natural to human society. Therefore, the society in general is divided and discriminated on the basis of nativity, religion, race, language, etc. Paradoxically within the same community, Indian society, people are further divided and discriminated on the basis of socio-economic, political, religious, language and cultural considerations which are even detrimental to the growth of every individual in the society.

The inhuman form of discrimination universally applicable to India is discrimination on the basis of Caste-Untouchability and social ostracism practiced against Scheduled Castes in India are limiting and restricting their association and inter-relationship with the other castes. Even their habitats are physically separated from the others in rural areas. Hindu society is a caste-ridden society and it is divided into as many as 3000 to 5000 castes (Das-in Mossey Ed. 1994). Caste is based on birth and ascribed status with varying degrees of respectability and circles of social intercourse.

According to orthodox Hindus, the original castes were four in number, based on Varnas, Brahmins or priestly class, Kshatriyas or warrior class, Vaishyas or mercantile and agricultural class and Shudras or peasants and service class created from the different parts of Purusha, Brahma, the cosmic person. Those belonging to these four grades of people can only be Hindus and the untouchables (Scheduled Castes) are outside this four-fold caste system and therefore they do not belong to any caste and are called outcasts. They are casteless, Non-Hindu, Non-Aryan called as Chandalas, Anti-Shudras, Avarnas and Panchamas. Dr. Ambedkar calls them "Protestant Hindus".

During the British period, the 'Avarnas' were first designated as 'Depressed Classes' later 'Exterior Castes' and finally as 'Scheduled Castes'. They suffered from social, economic and religious disabilities. Socially they were isolated and ostracized and considered to be lepers. Economically they were deprived of all means of production and highly exploited and lived a life worse than that of a slave. Religiously they were restricted to the place of worship. Culturally they were not allowed to wear dresses and ornaments they wished and were not permitted to wear chapels and walk in the caste villages. Their dead were not allowed to be buried in the common cremation grounds. Politically they were denied of their rights and privileges.

The Scheduled Castes were subjected to various types of disabilities and they suffered suppression, oppression and exploitations. In order to mitigate their sufferings and develop their lot socially, economically and educationally, the Government of India made special provisions and concessions in the constitution. The idea of offering protective discrimination to the Scheduled Castes and the underprivileged in societies is intended at maintaining a balanced socio-economic development of the Indian Society so that no portion of the society remains weak. *With a view to translating into reality the aims and objectives of the constitution, the Government of India by a resolution of March 15, 1950 has set up a Planning Commission which has been entrusted with the task of achieving all round economic development with emphasis on social justice.* In spite of four decades of planning the status of the Scheduled Castes improved only marginally. A small portion of them get the benefits and have improved their status to some extent but a vast majority still suffer deprivation, poverty, slavery and social discrimination to the core. Real emancipation/liberation is only a dream.

The Indian Government has further discriminated the Scheduled Castes on the basis of religion denying them the constitutional privileges as per the *Presidential Order No. 19 of 1950, according to which the converted Christians - Christians of Scheduled Caste Origin (CSCO) - are not entitled to the benefits and concessions extended to Hindu SCs,* though their socio-economic conditions are not much different from their counterpart SCs.

Overall scenario of SC & CSCO

The contemporary Indian society with a democratic constitution stands for quality, freedom and justice to all citizens. These constitutional guarantees however, are not translated into action and therefore, there is inequality in practice. In fact, the Indian society is characterised by graded inequality and it is rooted in the Indian caste system, which has acquired religious sanctity. The extreme case of inequality is exemplified by the existence of a group of people identified as untouchables. Though untouchability is constitutionally abolished, constitutional guarantees are not translated into action and its practice still continues and so social inequality persists.

The Scheduled Caste list runs in hundreds and in Tamil Nadu there are 76 communities listed in the SC list and they occupy the bottom of the social hierarchical ladder. The socio-economic condition of the SCs even after 60 years of planning is deplorable. The various provisions made in the constitution to bring about the economic benefits have touched only the fringe. Almost 65 percent of the total SC workers are agricultural labourers. They form 33 percent of total agricultural labour force. As they are scattered least organised, they have little bargaining power.

Only 8 percent of SC workers are engaged in cultivation and their size of land holding in most of the cases is less than 2.5 acres. Their major problems are poverty and indebtedness.

Indebtedness is a very common problem among the SCs. Krishnaiah Chetty (1991) states that 62 percent of rural households and 47 percent of urban households among the SCs are indebted. They hardly possess any assets. They form very high percentage among the leather workers and scavengers. They earn very meagre income and live inperpetual poverty. On the social dimensions the SCs are never integrated into the society, their residential areas being segregated from the caste people's houses in the same village. They generally have separate sources of water.

The interaction of the SCs with the caste people is limited to discharging menial jobs to the caste people. They are treated as outcasts.

Education, a vital instrument for social mobility and status of a person, is not to the advantage of the SCs. Educationally the SCs are the most backward because due to their socio-economic handicap they have not benefitted to the expected level. Literacy rate in Tamil Nadu for the entire population as per 1991 census is 62.66%. But for the SCs it is 46.74% only, Enrolment of the SC children in the schools is low and their dropout rate is the highest.

The problems of the SC community in general is presented above, but the problems of a special community, who belonged to the SC community originally are not now considered SC due to their option to follow a religion of their choice other than Hinduism, namely Christianity. As the result of embracing Christian faith, consequent to the Presidential Order No.19 of 1950, paragraph no. 3, the right of SC status is denied to the CSCO though Article 15 (1) the constitution states, *"They shall not discriminate against any citizen on grounds only of religion, race, caste, sex, place of birth or any of them". Presidential Order No. 19 of 1950, Para No. 3 states, "No person who professes religion different from the Hindu or Sikh religion shall be deemed to a member of Scheduled Caste."*

It is the contradiction between the Secular nature of Indian Constitution and the Hindu religious bias in the functioning of the Indian Democracy, especially with regard to the CSCO.

The above consideration raises two fundamental questions: (a) Does person lose his caste membership while joining a sect or another religion Christianity? (b) Given the Hindu based caste ridden milieu and ethos in which one lives, does conversion to Christianity by a Scheduled Caste remove one's social disabilities, economic deprivation and political suppression?

The CSCO are part of the same Indian social fabric, affected by the same social structure and forces, and they are not isolated from these because of their religion. *Srinivas (1997) states that caste cuts across all religions, Dr. Ambedkar (Vol. V) states, conversion has not brought about any change in the social status of the untouchable convert.* In Mandal Commission's opinion (Para 12. 11) though caste system is peculiar to Hindu society, *yet in actual practice, it also pervades the non-Hindu communities in India in varying degrees.* Therefore, whatever faith one may proclaim, if he is an Indian, also proclaims in that faith the practice of caste system, because every Indian believes in caste system and caste system is part of the social system from which he cannot escape.

The focus before the researcher, therefore, was to compare the two communities, the SC and the CSCO, assess the prevalence of casteisms/ social discrimination and economic deprivation among them and arrive at the conclusion as to whether there are differences in their socio-economic life as the result of conversion or in spite of their conversion to Christianity the CSCO live in the same plight as their counterpart SC or whether their condition is better or worse in comparison to the SCs.

The main objectives of the study

The main objectives are as follows:

(1) To assess the general background, educational profile, housing condition and occupation of the SC, and the CSCO.

(2) To find out the economic condition and related factors.

(3) To analyse the social relationship of the respondents with the caste Hindus (CH) and the caste Christian (CC) and their mutual social relationship.

(4) Compare the overall status of the CSCO compared to the SC.

(5) Finally to suggest the role the Govt. and the Catholic Church has to play to mitigate problems of the SCs and the CSCO.

Field Settings

Four villages, namely, Eraiyur, Viriyur, Konankuppam and Kovilanur, all falling under South Arcot District and coming under Pondicherry Diocese (Catholic Church jurisdiction under a Bishop), were selected for the study. All the villages have a parish (a church and a resident priest in the proximity) for more than 100 years. In all the villages, the Caste Christians, Caste Hindus, the SC and the CSCO are living in close proximity. All the respondents belong to "Paraiyar" community.

Total No. of families & No. of families selected

Villages	*Total No. of families*		*No. of families selected*	
	SC	*CSCO*	*SC*	*CSCO*
Eraiyur	119	155	48	60
Viriyur	85	72	33	26
Konankuppam	126	88	51	33
Kovilanur	57	104	28	41
Total	**387**	**419**	**160**	**160**

Main findings of the Study

The most relevant and salient findings to the subject matter are presented below:

- Among the elders 88% of men and 93% of women were illiterate. Among the youngsters almost 50% are literate and the percentage of boys is marginally higher than the girls. Very few had studied beyond the secondary level of education. Almost 80% of children are dropout of the secondary level. Very few children 4% of the SC and 9% of the CSCO have benefitted from Institutionalised educational services. The CSCO are marginally better than the SC therefore the hypothesis "*higher is the literacy level of the CSCO compared to the SC is accepted.*
- A vast majority 68% to live in nuclear families and 75% of the elders are agricultural labourers in both the categories. Self-employed, skilled workers and govt. servants are very few they account for only 5 % of the total.
- A vast majority in both the categories have low and medium level of general awareness regarding their life governance. *Compared to the SC the CSCO have a higher level of general awareness and it is hypothetically established.*
- A vast majority (80% of the SC and 75% of the CSCO) live in thatched mud houses. Thirteen percent of the SC and 7% of the CSCO have received government support for constructing their houses. Besides 12% of the CSCO have received church support to construct their houses. Taking various factors into consideration regarding the facilities and condition of houses, the houses were classified into good, bad and worse. A vast majority of the houses (85% of the SC and 68% of the CSCO) fall under the category of bad housing condition and the rest are classified as worse.
- Vast majority, i.e., 95% is non-Vegetarians and up to 92% eat beef and pork. Almost 80% admit that they eat dead animal especially beef. Fruits, eggs and milk are consumed rarely.
- Seventy percent of them have five and more children in their families. Knowledge about immunisation was very low and only 23% had administered it to all their children. Sixty one percent of the SC and 24% of the CSCO only had adopted family planning norms. *"The food habits and health condition of the CSCO and the SC do not differ". The Family Planning practice is higher among the SC compared to the CSCO is proved.*

- Seventy percent confessed that they consume liquor and 50% have the habit of smoking. Pan and tobacco chewing are in practice among 35% of the respondents. *There is no significant difference in the personal habits of the SC and the CSCO.* About 20 to 25% of their monthly income is spent on the personal habits, majority of the woman have the habit of going for movies. Their leisure time activities are gossiping TV viewing and sleeping.
- The findings reveal that both the communities have affiliation to the political parties and support them. SC have greater affiliation and participation in politics compared to the CSCO. It is because the *SC have an opportunity to contest in the Reserved constituency which is denied to the CSCO.*
- In both the categories men play the dominant role in the decision-making process in the family. Women play a secondary role and they receive low recognition in both the communities.
- Belief in evil spirit, superstition and being possessed by demon were acknowledged and accepted by majority of the respondents belonging to Christians and Hindus. Ear boring ceremony, Tonsuring of children and adult and ritual for the dead and tying thali (yellow thread around the neck of the bride by the bridegroom as a sign of marriage) which are the common practices followed by the Hindus are also observed by majority of the CSCO.
- The primary occupation in majority of cases 75% is agricultural labour. Only the rest (25%) are engaged in farming,self-employment, government jobs, skilled labour etc. Agricultural labourers work only 180 to 220 days in a year. In both the categories their monthly earning is low and majority of them are economically below poverty level. Seventy percent do not possess any land.
- A vast majority of them 80% are indebted. The level of indebtedness is slightly higher among the SC compared to the CSCO. Almost cent percent of the indebted members had borrowed money from non-institutional sources paying a very high rate of interest up to 60% per annum. *The mean income in both the categories is low and their economical level is below poverty line.*
- About 60% of the members from both the categories affirm that they have positive good relationship with the caste Hindu (CH) and caste Christians (CC) the rest have either indifferent or bad / negative relationship. *The relationship of the SC and the CSCO with the CH and CC does not differ substantially.*

- Majority of the respondents from both the categories affirmed that they are rarely invited by the cast, people to attend functions in their families, rather, they are called to carry out some work at the function and they are given second class treatment after the caste people. The trend reveals that the CC prefer to invite CSCO and CH prefer the SC to work at their functions.
- Caste Christians and CH do not wholeheartedly participate in the family functions of the SC and CSCO. If at all they come it is just for the formality sake.
- *The SC and the CSCO have good mutual relationship among themselves. Though they belong to different religions, religion is not a bar to their social relation and interaction. They freely invite each other for social functions and take part wholehearted in all functions.*
- *Both the CSCO and SC are treated equally as low and discriminated without any difference by CH and CC.*
- Majority of the CSCO have been Christians for four generations and more. Except 11% the rest have got married as per church regulations. Majority have baptised all their children and only 50% have received confirmation. To a great extend the CSCO believe and practice Christian Life.
- *A vast majority did admit that the CC practice discrimination against the CSCO and 75 percent affirmed that social discriminatory attitude does exist in the church and church related activities.*

Suggestions

- As the literacy and educational level is low among CSCO & SC, both the Central Govt, State Govt, the church establishment and NGOs should motivate and support the cause of educations for the SC & CSCO. All the educational assistance and concessions extended to the SC should also be provided to the CSCO as their plight is not much different from that of their counterpart. Institutionalised educational services will reduce the dropout rate. It should be given priority.
- Housing is a major requirement. The government could utilise the NGOs and have a long term plan to construct a decent habitat for all with the peoples' participation and contribution.
- Paucity of non-agricultural jobs and lack of skill among the people is the cause for poverty. All efforts must be taken to create

alternative employment opportunities in rural areas and skill training must be imparted among the youth to improve their lot.

- All the government, non-government and foreign projects should focus on the socio-cultural, environmental and behavioural development of the SC & CSCO. It will do a great deal of good for their future lasting development. Dependency on the caste people must be reduced through self-sustainable project that is holistic in nature.
- The social discriminatory practice is the external manifestation of the hierarchical caste system being in force. Slowly but steadily, to eradicate such practice the government must initiate various programmes to bring about integration of the caste people and the low castes. An attitude of equality must be instilled in the minds of children and youth right from the initial school days and common programmes such as celebration of festivals both national and religious must be organised where all can freely participate. Common drinking water source, cemetery and cremation ground must be encouraged. In whichever village there are signs of greater integration, special privileges and programmes must be sanctioned as a motivating factor.
- The three suggestions offered by the SC Community to improve their condition as per the priority are:
  (1) The government must create and offer employment for all.
  (2) Provide land for cultivation.
  (3) Provide house and other basic facilities.
- Three suggestions given by CSCO are:
  (1) The government should consider the CSCO as equal to the SCs and offer all concessions to them as applicable to the SCs.
  (2) Create employment opportunity for all.
  (3) Provide land for cultivation and other basic facilities.
- The CSCO have affirmed that discriminatory practices do exist in the Christian community in the church related activities and in the society. *Church authorities/hierarchies should realise that human dignity and equality are the basic tenets of Christianity and therefore they must aim to bring about a real cultural revolution of change of vision, values and behaviour with regard to caste discrimination. Church should attempt to transform the attitude*

of the people of the high castes to accept the SC and the CSCO as their equals in all respects. The abolition of caste among Christians and the integration of the CSCO in the mainstream as equals should be the top priority of the Church in India.

Conclusions

- It is baffling to observe the caste based discrimination in Indian Society and it is shocking to notice the same discrimination percolating into Christians of Indian origin.
- This being the situation, paradoxically the Presidential Order No. 19 of 1950 denies all privileges entitled to the SCs to the CSCO.
- The socio-economic condition which mainly determines the status of a person does not differ among the SC & the CSCO.
- Caste Christians and caste Hindus maintain social distance from SC & CSCO and discriminate both the groups equally.
- The findings are nothing new. Various commission reports support and affirm that there is prevalence of caste practice within the Christian community and the CSCO are the worst affected. Let us recall the words of Gandhiji who said, *"He may change his garb and call himself a Catholic Harijan, or a Muslim Harijan or Neo-Muslim or Neo-Sikh but his untouchability will haunt him during his lifetime."* Dr. Ambedkar stated, *"Conversion has not brought any change in the social status of the untouchable convert. To the general mass of the Hindus, the untouchable remains an untouchable even though he becomes a Christian."*
- The study confirms to the views of Gandhiji and Dr. Ambedkar. The CSCO are subject to the same disabilities of social, economic, political, educational and cultural status and the disabilities do exist in their oppressive severity in the new environment as the SCs. *Hence it is right and proper that in a secular and democratic country, due to religious conversion, the CSCO should not be denied the privileges and concessions entitled to them.*
- The Church meant to be the proclaimer of the good news to the poor, oppressed and the weak has to play an active role to liberate the CSCO from the clutches of caste and socio-economic disabilities and social discrimination within the church related activities.
- Let us hope the governmental efforts and the initiatives of the church brings solace to the CSCO.

23

Role of Globalisation in Inclusive Education

— Bhargavi Das and Prof. Raja Mohan Rao

Introduction

World Health Organisation (WHO) reports that with a count of around 15% of total world's population, Persons with Disability (PwD) are the largest marginalised group in the world. In other words, it can be estimated that nearly 1 billion people in the world live with one or the other kind of disability. The number of disabled population is considerably higher in developing countries as compared to the developed ones. These sections of population are generally excluded from the mainstream society when it comes to their education, employment, rehabilitation, healthcare etc.

As per Census 2011, in India, out of the 121 crore population, about 2.68 crore persons are 'disabled' which is 2.21% of the total population out of whom the highest number is found in the age group of 10-19 years. This age is basically considered to be the major part of one's life in attending the educational institution. Education is an inherent right for every child irrespective of their caste, class, status, religion etc. Article 26 of the Universal Declaration of Human Rights (UDHR) enumerates that everyone has the right to education and it shall be directed to the full development of the human personality and to the strengthening of respect for human rights and fundamental freedoms. Since 1948 many international covenants and treaties have enumerated the provision of right to education in it. Article 13 of the International Covenant on Economic, Social and Cultural Rights (ICESCR) outlines the responsibility of states to recognize, respect, and uphold the right to education for everyone. Article 28 of Convention on the Rights of the Child (CRC) provides that all children should have a right to free primary education. UNESCO Convention against

Discrimination in Education, the International Covenant on the Elimination of All Forms of Racial Discrimination, the Convention on the Elimination of All Forms of Discrimination against Women, the Convention on the Protection of the Rights of All Migrant Workers and Members of their Families, and the Convention on the Rights of Persons with Disabilities are some of the major international covenants on right to education. Article 45 of the Indian constitution also affirms free and compulsory education for all children until they complete the age of fourteen years.

Though there are numerous national and international policies and programmes for educating a child, but when it comes to education of a PwD, it becomes a very challenging task for the parents, schools as well as the teachers. It was in June 1994, when the Salamanca Statement for the first time paved the way for the approach towards inclusive education in the World Conference on Special Needs Education, held in Salamanca, Spain. It put forward the concept of 'inclusion' as:

> *every child has unique characteristics, interests, abilities and learning needs, education system should be designed and educational programmes implemented to take into account the wide diversity of these characteristics and needs, regular schools with this inclusive orientation are the most effective means of combating discriminatory attitudes, creating welcoming communities, building an inclusive society and achieving education for all. (source: http://www.unesco.org/education/pdf/SALAMA_E.PD, retrieved on june9, 2018)*

Till then these large section of school going children with disability (CwD) were mostly segregated in the special schools, with no or insignificant contact with the 'normal schooling' or with their 'normal peers'. The statement was endorsed by 92 governments and 25 key international organisations who were working towards the principle of 'school for all' with special attention to the CwD.

This was the adjacent period when the process of globalisation started in India. Since the early 90's the Indian government started the policy of Liberalisation, Privatisation and Globalisation (LPG). The Indian Society has witnessed a drastic change after the globalisation along with urbanisation brought in a huge change in the different domains of life (Naidu, 2006). At the most broad level, globalisation refers to the interaction and interconnectedness among the people from all over the globe, free flow of goods, services, information as well as technologies. This in turn leads to people adapting to the changes around them. Globalisation simply doesn't relate to political or economical agreements among the governments but also signifies that everyone is a part of the global system (Shaikh and Ahmed, 2017).

What is inclusive education?

"IE is concerned with removing all barriers to learning, and with participation of all learners vulnerable to exclusion and marginalisation. It is a strategic approach designed to facilitate learning success for all children. It addresses the common goals of decreasing and overcoming all exclusion from human rights to education, at least at the elementary level, and enhancing access, participation and learning success in quality basic education for all. (*Source:* Education for All 2000 Bulletin, UNESCO, No. 32, 1998).

Though with the onset of globalisation, the schools in the Indian set up also began to develop an inclusive schooling, the outcomes were bound to differ in developing countries from their developed counterparts.

Role of Globalisation in Inclusive Education

There have been considerable changes in the field of education globally as well as in India before the evolution of the concept of IE. In the Third wave (Toffler, 1983, as cited in *Milenovic,* 2011) mentioned about three different waves of civilisation i.e. First wave-pre-industrial stage, second wave- industrial age and the third wave-the post-industrial age. The role of the teachers and students changed continuously in each of these stages. In the second wave the teachers were mainly the producers and the students were considered to be the raw materials. The duty of the teachers was mainly to give lectures and instructions to the students so that they can be ready for future competition and be a responsible citizen. This model was considered to be a factory model where teachers' job was mainly to produce the products (students). But in the third stage it changed into the concept of *community learning* where the community consists of the teachers, students, parents, management and all others who shared the same goal and objective-*'learning'*. The learning process in this stage involved development of the critical thinking abilities, problem solving as well as providing a quality education to the students.

There are no nooks and corners in the society left untouched by the impact of globalisation. Globalisation has radically transformed the world in every aspect. The process of this globalised world has both positive and negative outcome on different spheres of life. Education is one such domain which is extensively impacted by the process of globalisation. India being still a developing country, globalisation has both positive and negative implications on the practice of inclusive education.

Globalisation helped the international curricula to reach the Indian schools which helped the students to opt for different curricula available for them. It also eased the availability of various teaching aids required for the CwD in inclusive schools. Global education upgrades the capacity of students to get to evaluate, embrace and apply information to think freely to practice suitable judgment and to work together with others to comprehend new circumstances. Moreover it creates an expanded amount of experimentally and in fact prepared people.

The potential fallback of globalisation IE can be the increased technological gaps and digital divides between advanced countries and less developed countries. Since the early 90's, there has been a mushrooming of schooling which claims to be inclusive only on the paper and not really in practice. Globalisation has led to the privatisation of schools which has eventually increased the burden of educational expenses for the parents of CwD.

Thus, this paper tries to consider the opinions and attitudes of the teachers and parents of CwD about the role of globalisation on inclusive education.

Methodological research concept

This paper is an attempt to study inclusive education as one of the consequences of globalisation.

Aim of the research is to understand the parents attitudes and opinions on inclusive education as a consequence of globalisation.

The objective of the research is to define whether there is a statistic difference in attitudes and opinions of the parents of the CwD on inclusive education as a consequence of globalisation.

Population is composed of parents of the CwD in the territory of the City of Guwahati during May and June 2018 when the research was conducted. A sample of 126 respondents was covered by the research. Among them 35% were the parents of Visually impaired (VI), 50% represented the hearing and speech impaired children, 9% were the parents of children with intellectual disability (ID) and 6% represented the children who had locomotors disability.

For the data collection a five point Likert scale was applied where the respondent mainly had to respond to 10 claims; choosing the options i.e. (a) strongly disagree, (b) disagree, (c) neutral, (d) agree and (e) strongly agree. Microsoft excel is used for data analysis.

Analysis and discussion

Table 1: Data analysis of the six point likert scale

Claims	*Strongly disagree (%)*	*Disagree (%)*	*Neutral (%)*	*Agree (%)*	*Strongly agree (%)*	*Total respondents*
Inclusive education is a consequence of globalization	0	1	24	47	28	**100%**
Inclusive education is needed for a global education	0	0	36	55	9	**100%**
Inclusive education always has a positive outcome	0	8	18	72	2	**100%**
Globalization has improved the quality of education	1	10	4	81	4	**100%**
Globalisation has brought educational reforms	2	7	2	72	17	**100%**
Globalization has made education an expensive task	1	2	23	11	63	**100%**
Inclusive education is needed for a holistic development	0	2	23	71	4	**100%**
CwD are included in normal schools irrespective of any disability	36	20	9	31	4	**100%**
Globalisation has led to exclusion of CwD from Normal schools	2	17	0	60	21	**100%**
Inclusive education is a need of the modern society	0	1	10	87	2	**100%**

Source: Field data.

Note: Figures in parenthesis refer to percentage.

Table 1 shows the data analysis of the responses of the respondents obtained from five point likert scale.

28% and 47% of the respondents strongly agreed and agreed respectively that IE is a consequence of globalisation. 24% gave a neutral answer whereas only 1% of the respondents disagreed to the claim.

36% of the respondents were neutral on the claim that IE is needed for a global education. 55% and 9% of respondents agreed and strongly agreed to the claim respectively. It was noted that no respondents disagreed.

The claim that IE always has a positive outcome was agreed by a large section of the respondents with 72%. Only 2% of them strongly agreed to it. 18% were neutral and only 8% of them disagreed to the claim.

A majority of the respondents (81%) agreed that globalisation has improved the quality of education. Whereas 4% strongly agreed and were also neutral to this. 10% and 1% of the respondents disagreed and strongly disagreed to the claim respectively

72 % and 17% of the respondents agreed and strongly agreed that globalisation has brought educational reforms. Whereas 2% of them where neutral and also strongly disagreed to it. 7% of the respondents disagreed.

A greater part of the respondents with 63% and 11% strongly agreed and agreed to the claim that globalisation has made education an expensive task for the parents of CwD. 23% were neutral to this claim and only 1% and 2% strongly disagreed and disagreed to it respectively.

The claim that IE is needed for a holistic development was agreed to by 71% of the respondents, 4% strongly agreed, 23% were neutral and 2 % disagreed to it.

A considerable fraction of the respondents strongly disagreed and disagreed to the claim that CwD are included in normal schools irrespective of any disability with 36% and 20% respectively. Whereas it is also contrasting that 31% and 4% of respondents respectively agreed and strongly agreed to this. 9% were neutral to this claim.

A majority of the respondents with 60% and 21%respectively agreed and strongly agreed that globalisation has led to exclusion of CwD from normal schools. Nobody gave a neutral answer to this. But 17% and 2% of the respondents disagreed and strongly disagreed respectively to this claim.

87% of the respondents agreed to the claim that IE is a need of the modern society. 2% strongly agreed, 10% were neutral and only 1% disagreed to it.

As a result it can be seen that though there are difference in the opinions and attitudes of the parents of the CwD regarding the role of globalisation in inclusive education it can also be noted that there were few claims where the majority of them had similar views and opinions.

Conclusion and Suggestions

From the data collected and literature reviewed for this study it can be stated that though globalisation has impacted the lives of all the living beings in the planet through one or the other way it wouldn't be wrong to judge that globalisation has both positive and negative outcome. A development for one may not be a development for the other. Whereas it might be on the cost of others' destruction or exclusion. Level of inclusion and the quality of education of the CwD also are bound to be at variance from the developed to developing nations.

In India, the concept as well as the practice of inclusive education is considered to be consequence of globalisation which is very much needed for opening the doors for global education. Though IE is considered to have a positive outcome in learning but many at times it couldn't be afforded by the parents for educating a CwD becomes an expensive as well as challenging task. Despite the fact that globalisation brought many educational reforms with it but still CwD find it difficult to get included in a normal school setting and often face social exclusion.

However, as education is an inherent right of all the children and they must be provided with a quality education without any discrimination, the following suggestion are made to make inclusive education more productive and eliminate the negative consequences of globalisation on IE:

(a) Information and communication technology (ICT) should be used to the fullest extent for the proper inclusion of the CwD in a normal school setting.

(b) Government should look into the schools' fee structures and make it affordable for all the sections of the society.

(c) Exclusion or discrimination of the CwD in any form in the school should be strictly looked after by the government.

(d) The school should make available all the teaching aids required for different types of disability in their schools for better inclusion of the children.

(e) The school managements should review their policies from time to time as with the changing time there might be required changes in the policies.

(f) Interaction and student exchange with foreign universities should be encouraged by the government among the CwD.

To conclude, the empiric research has indicated that IE is an inevitable aspect of social inclusion which enables the CwD regardless of their differences to enjoy their right to education, develop their potential to the fullest extent and furthermore that has been one of the various consequences of globalisation seen as a goal and unconstrained overall procedure, covering a wide scope of economic, political and social spheres in today's world.

References

Mariga, L., McConkey, R. and Myezwa, H. (2014). *Inclusive Education in Low-Income Countries: A resource book for teacher educators, parent trainers and community development workers.* Cape Town: Atlas Alliance and Disability Innovations Africa.

Mônica Pereira Dos Santos (2001). Special Education, Inclusion and Globalisation: A few considerations inspired in the Brazilian case, Disability & Society, 16:2, 311-325, DOI: 10.1080/09687590120035861 http://dx.doi.org/10.1080/09687590120035861 [accessed on May 23, 2020]

Shaikh, Prof. Mumtaz, and Shaikh Bushra Vazir Ahmed. "Role of Globalisation in Inclusive Education." *Scholarly Research Journal for Interdisciplinary Studies*, Vol. 32, No. 4, 2017, www.srjis.com/pages/pdfFiles/15014082138.%20mumtaz % 20shaikh.pdf. [accessed on May 21, 2020]

UN Commission on Human Rights, *Convention on the Rights of the Child*, 7 March 1990, E/CN.4/RES/1990/74, https://www.refworld.org/docid/3b00f03d30.html [accessed on 12 August 2020]

"Universal Declaration of Human Rights." *United Nations*, United Nations, www.un.org/en/universal-declaration-human-rights/. [accessed on May 23, 2020]

UN General Assembly, *International Covenant on Economic, Social and Cultural Rights*, 16 December 1966, United Nations, Treaty Series, Vol. 993, p. 3, https://www.refworld.org/docid/3ae6b36c0.html [accessed 12 August 2020]

"World Report on Disability." *World Health Organisation*, 16 Oct. 2018, www.who.int/disabilities/world_report/2011/report/en/. [accessed on 12 March, 2020]

"2011 Census Data." *Census of India Website : Office of the Registrar General & Census Commissioner, India*, www.censusindia.gov.in/2011-common/censusdata2011.html. [accessed on 12 March, 2020]

24

Impact of Globalisation on Education among the Under Represented Groups in India: A Case Study in Telangana State

— Thomas K. J.

Introduction

We are living in the era of globalisation. The process of education also is influenced or affected by the multidimensional and international aspects of globalisation. The term Globalisation has been used in academic literature to describe a process, a condition, a system, a force and an age[1]. It usually refers to a set of social processes that may transform our present social condition into one of globality. There is dynamism in this process of transformation. But at times globalisation can also create new forms of inequality and exclusion, as it is an ongoing social process in this postmodern era. Anthony Giddens defined globalisation as the intensification of worldwide social relations which link distant localities in such a way that local happenings are shaped by events occurring many miles away and vice versa. Fredric Jameson summarised the concept of globalisation as a consequence of enlargement of world communication and world market. As for David Held globalisation is a process of transformation in social relations and transactions having transcontinental interactions. Roland Robertson suggests that globalisation compresses the world and intensifies the consciousness of the world. James Mittelman holds the view that globalisation compresses the time and space aspects of social relations[2]. According to Manfred Steger globalisation refers to a multidimensional set of social processes that create, multiply, stretch, and intensify worldwide social interdependencies and exchanges while at the same time fostering in people a growing awareness of deepening connections between the local and the distant[3].

Globalisation has brought in complex and multiple trajectories in the avenue of education in every nation. Nations have become interdependent in sharing the advancement in technology and education. Education ceases to be a service sector in the modern era. It has turned out to be a commodity that has to be purchased and sold in the international competitive markets.

Education has been considered the vital propeller for balanced and healthy human development at all times in the history of human beings. But in recent times, education at all levels is impacted by globalisation. The introduction of information and communication technology has paved the way for e-learning and the basic structure of educational system is undergoing immense changes. Access to education is greatly increased due to this kind of new methods of teaching and learning especially in developing countries like India. Education has become a commodity of international trade on a global scale. The globalisation in education helps the society to incorporate itself to the technologically dominated economy and knowledge society at large. Education system in Telangana also is influenced by these new trends during the last few decades, exhibiting the influences of globalisation. Private sector in Telangana has introduced various types of curriculum from Nursery to Secondary level.

However, educational developments influenced by globalisation, needs to sustain the present generation in every aspect of their life, while paving the way for the development of the future generation. Over use of the present resources for the gratification of certain section of the society, may jeopardise the development of the marginalised groups in Indian society. Education with moral values, equity and justice enables one to achieve sustainable development for oneself and also for the society in a globalised economy.

Education plays the most important role in the realisation of the 2030 Agenda for sustainable development, as proposed by the UN Conferences. Attainment of inclusive and equitable quality education is one of the major goals of sustainable development. The United Nations Conference on Sustainable Development was held in 2012 in Rio de Janeiro, Brazil. The UN Conference on Environment and Development held in Rio de Janeiro in 1992 had set the objectives of sustainable development. It was to achieve economic, environmental and social development to meet the needs of the present without compromising the ability of the future generations to meet their own needs[4]. The UN Conference of 1992 brought out the famous Agenda 21 which helped in the formation of UN Commission on Sustainable Development. This commission is under the UN Economic and Social Council.

Part I

1.1 Impact of globalisation on Indian education system

Globalisation in education is seen as westernisation in education by some scholars[5]. But the agents of globalisation are not exclusively western. The present phenomenon of globalisation in education is increasing inequality and instability within the country as well as between the countries in the field of education at different levels. India is not an exception to this phenomenon.

Sustainable Development in education is development that meets the educational needs of the present without compromising the ability of future generations to meet their own needs in education.[6] India has its national development plans and agenda monitored by the National Institution for Transforming India (NITI Aayog). The National Institution for Transforming India (NITI Aayog), with the Prime Minister as its chairperson, coordinates the development plans in very systematic way. India's development mantra is "Sabka Saath Sabka Vikas" (Collective Effort, Inclusive Development). As a developing economy, India has developmental plans to eradicate poverty by increasing the accessibility and quality of education. High level of economic growth, infrastructure development and industrialisation are given priority by the National Institute for Transforming India. The strategy to alleviate poverty includes social inclusion and empowerment of the poor, especially through quality education. The national development goals of India give importance to implement educational goals with equity and inclusiveness.

Development in the area of education is given importance after the economic reforms in India. India began to achieve very fast growth rate for its economy following the economic reforms initiated in 1991.The intensity of poverty also began to decline after the economic reforms and it has helped India to achieve growth in education sector. But the recent economic measures introduced by the central government have adversely affected the growth of the economy. It has adversely affected marginalised groups in the society. Globalisation of education also has increased the literacy gap among the socially and economically marginalised groups when compared to the general population in India.

1.2 Right to Education Act and globalisation

Globalisation does not always help in inclusiveness and equity in educational sector. In spite of the influence of globalisation in educational sector, there is a national commitment towards equitable and inclusive education in India. The Right of Children to Free and Compulsory Education Act 2009 made elementary education a fundamental right for every child in India between six and 14 years of age. However, universal primary education by 2015 was not realised in India. In spite of that, India has committed itself to the Sustainable Development Goals, whereby it has to universalise education up to the secondary level. In order to achieve this the RTE Act has to be revised to include free and compulsory education up to the secondary level.

When we analyse the implementation of RTE, we find that there is wide range of gap at various levels. It is reported that only 9.54 percent of schools in India have complied by this Act. Almost a million teachers are still untrained in our schools. The vacant posts for school teachers are more than half a million in India. The contractual teachers, who are untrained, are employed in many schools across the country, whose number may be more than 4.5 lakhs. According to the Census of 2011, more than 8.4 crore children are out of school, though the same is counted as six million by the Ministry of Human Resource Development. In spite of all the commitment to improve the infrastructural facilities in the schools, more than one lakh schools are closed down during 2015- 2016 period. More than one million schools are having only a single teacher in this country. It is frightening to observe that more than 49 percent of children dropped from schools before they completed their elementary education, in India.[7] All these situations reveal the fact that RTE Act is not implemented in an efficient way to achieve the goals of universalising education at school level.

When a school in the neighbourhood is closed down, like that has happened in Telangana, parents hesitate to send the girl children to a school which is situated far from their villages. The girl children have to face unsafe environment as they have to walk a long distance to reach the school. Thus, the RTE has not achieved its goals as it is facing multiple challenges due to inadequate resources, improper funding, lack of infrastructure, and unavailability of trained teachers in many states, like that in Telangana. Sometimes, text books are not distributed on time to the students and the quality of the books are also deplorable in many cases. The pre-school education in the age group of 3-6 years also was neglected, though the responsibility was entrusted through Integrated Child Development Scheme.

The pre-school education should have been included under the RTE to give it enforceability. It also helps to prepare children for the further levels of education. Implementation of pre-school education is necessary to fulfil the target 4.2 of the sustainable development goal-4, which reiterates that by 2030 ensure that all girls and boys have access to quality early childhood development, care and pre-primary education so that they are ready for primary education.

Proper financing of school education has not happened in the history of modern India. There were strong recommendations by Kothari Commission to increase the spending in education sector to 6 percent of the GDP. It is sad to note that so far, no government has allotted 6 percent of GDP towards the development of the education sector in India, after the Independence. The flagship programme, Sarva Shiksha Abhiyan was entrusted with the duty of implementation of the provisions of RTE in various states. But the devolution of fund to various states through this scheme did not increase the expenditure on school education. Very low per cent of the total Union budget is provided for the expenditure for school education. It was only 2.43 percent in 2014-15, 2.44 in 2015-16, and 2.9 in 2016-17. Even in 2017-18 the budget allocation has not changed much for the education sector[8]. Educationists feel that a law must be enacted to provide a certain percent of the budgetary expenditure on education both at the centre as well as at the state level, in India.

There is insufficient allotment of fund for ICDS, Mid-Day Meal Scheme, and Integrated Child Protection Scheme during the 2017-18 Union Budget. Only 0.05 percent of total allocation in the Union Budget is for Integrated Child Protection Scheme. On the other hand, the National Commission for Protection of Child Rights focuses on the protection of all children in the 0 to 18 years of age group, and has received only an amount of Rs 19 crores during the same period. This is an indication that the schemes that help in implementing the RTE and other redressal forums are not able to function due to lack of allocation of fund by the Union government. It is reported that more than 6.3 million children are undergoing child labour in India. All these data directly manifest that all children in India are not able to have access to basic education during their life.

There is the scarcity of more than half a million trained teachers in the government schools, according to the report of the committee for evolution of new education policy 2016. Thus, many schools are appointing more than 20 percent of untrained teachers in to their schools. Many teachers are burdened with non-academic duties and other administrative work, due to lack of supportive staff. The salaries of the teachers are not paid on time by many schools. And more than 10 percent schools are single teacher schools in some states in this country. The closure of government schools in tribal areas and economically backward areas have triggered the mushrooming of private schools. Children from marginalised background are forced out of the educational sectors when commercialisation of education takes upper hand. Girl children belonging to the tribal communities in Odisha and Telangana are also are denied of basic education whenever a school is closed by the respective state government. Many girl children hesitate to go to schools as there is no usable toilets and clean drinking water available for them in some schools.

Elementary education is going into the hands of private agencies in India due to the influence of globalisation and competition. This is a denial of free education for the children from economically backward areas, as they cannot afford to go to private schools where they have to pay heavy amount towards tuition fees. The principle of equity and justice is compromised when privatisation of schools is unhindered. It is reported that some state like Andhra Pradesh is partnering with profit making international companies to start fee-paying schools for the children. It is going to affect the children of marginalised communities of the state. In many of the schools the School Management Committees are not functioning, though some names are written in the records. A properly constituted and active management committee can positively assert their right to recommend changes in the functioning and monitoring of the school to bring about equity and quality in education. But very often, it does not take place in many schools.

In most of the states Aadhar Card is mandatory to obtain an admission as well as to receive any kind of scholarship at the school level. The No Detention Policy recommended by the RTE is being made optional and left to the discretion of the states, probably from the next academic year. Unaided minority schools are exempted from reserving the seats for children from economically backward classes. Though the deadline for in-service teacher training for the untrained teachers ended by 31 March 2019, there are many teachers who are still not gone for in-service training. Political commitment is needed for the proper implementation of RTE Act to attain educational equity in this country. Allotment of additional resources is an urgent need in every aspect of school education, especially for child protection. Free and compulsory education should be extended up to higher secondary stage and it should be brought under the purview of RTE for implementation. This condition is an unavoidable step to implement Target 4.1 of the sustainable development Goal – 4, where it states that by 2030, ensure that all girls and boys complete free, equitable and quality primary and secondary education leading to relevant and effective outcomes. There is a need for evolving effective evaluation system in schools. The present evaluation system like Continuous Comprehensive Evaluation, is not producing the desired effective learning outcome. The innovative evaluation methods suggested through the draft national policy on education 2019, are not yet approved or implemented in India.

1.3 Literacy in India and the influence of globalisation

Globalisation has not helped in reducing the number of illiterates in India. The number of illiterates aged seven and above in India as per the provisional population totals of Census 2011 is 272,950,015 which constitutes 26 percent of the total population. Thus, the effective literacy rate for India in Census 2011 turns out to be 74.04 percent. For the males the literacy rate is 82.14 and for the females the effective literacy rate is 65.46. Thus, it is very evident that there is a gap of 16.68 percent between male literacy and female literacy rate in India in 2011. Equal opportunity for education is guaranteed in the Indian Constitution. But there are lots of negative factors like globalisation that affect the education of woman in this country. A section on education for equity has been incorporated in the National Policy on Education 1986. It was meant for removing the disparities against women in the field of educational opportunities. The Programme of Action formulated by the Government of India as a follow up of national policy on education 1986 also was aimed at eradicating illiteracy among women by 1995. Education of women in India plays a very important role in the overall development of the country. Though the overall literacy rate in India is 74.04 percent, for the Scheduled Tribes it is 59 percent only. Gender disparity in literacy and education need to be eliminated at all levels. Thus, the Census data reveals that 41 percent of tribal population is still illiterate in India even after 71 years of Independence[9]. It shows that a substantial number of men and women have not achieved literacy in India.

1.4 Access to Education by the Marginalised Groups

Though globalisation has brought with it the advantages of information-communication technology, the marginalised groups in India are not able to attain the goals of education. They have not attained equal literacy rates like the other people in India. Many of their children dropout from school at various stages. Economic poverty forces their children to engage in child labour.

Tribals are the most exploited and deprived section of the population in the Indian society. Though many tribal welfare programmes and policies are formulated in India, tribals still remain excluded from many of the indicators of development. When tribal land and forest are taken away from them, in the name of development programmes, their source of life support itself is taken away. Many of the tribes have experienced geographical, social and cultural isolation for many years. They were alienated from the land and are exploited by the non-tribes in many situations.

Tribal Sub Plan was introduced in India during the Fifth Five Year Plan, together with integrated tribal development projects. Educational development of tribals were taken up as part of social development. Some of the important schemes that helped to improve education of the tribal children include: residential schools, vocational education, scholarships, book grants, free uniforms and mid-day meal programme. However, the enrolment of tribal children is far below the other groups. The dropout rate of tribal children is the most serious reason that affects the educational development. Tribal children are not able to cope up with the curriculum and syllabus. Lessons are not taught in their mother tongues. Often, the teachers themselves are not familiar with the tribal languages, to clarify the doubts of tribal children.

Till the colonial rule, there was no tradition of formal reading and writing in a traditional tribal society. Christian missionaries played the pioneer role in introducing modern system of education in tribal societies. Those who became literates from the tribal societies took up various occupations other than agriculture and became the corner stones of the modern middle class among the tribals. In spite of the safety promised through various Acts in Indian Constitution, tribal population continue to be excluded in development process in India.[10]

Educational planning for the marginalised needs special attention as it is an important component of human resource development. Education should help the marginalised groups to improve their skills which would lead to increased level of productivity. Education is an agent of social change in a globalised world. Technical and vocational education helps the people in securing employment and increases their levels of income, consumption and socio-economic status, especially in a globalised society. However, various sources indicate that the literacy rates of Scheduled Caste and Scheduled Tribe have not achieved the expected growth as shown in Table 1.

Table 1: Literacy Rates of SC/ST from 1961 to 2011

Year	*General*			*Scheduled Castes*			*Scheduled Tribes*		
	Males	*Females*	*Persons*	*Males*	*Females*	*Persons*	*Males*	*Females*	*Persons*
1961	34.44	12.95	24.02	17	3.29	10.27	13.83	3.16	8.53
1971	39.45	18.7	29.45	22.4	6.44	14.67	17.63	4.85	11.3
1981	46.89	24.82	36.23	31.1	10.93	21.38	24.52	8.04	16.35
1991	52.74	32.17	42.84	40.24	19.03	30.07	32.5	14.5	23.63
2001	63.24	45.15	54.51	55.1	34.62	45.2	48.23	28.36	38.41
2011	80.9	64.6	73	75.2	56.5	66.1	68.5	49.4	59

Source: Educational Statistics at a Glance, Government of India, Ministry of Human Resource Development Bureau of Planning, Monitoring & Statistics, New Delhi, 2014.

It is seen from the above Table 1 that the literacy rate of Scheduled Castes increased from 10.27 in 1961 to 66.1 in 2011, while literacy rates of Scheduled Tribes increased from 8.53 percent to 59.0 percent during the same period. It is to be noted from the above table that the percentage of literacy rates of SC/ST are always lower when compared with the literacy percentage of general population. Although the literacy rate of SC/STs has increased considerably, during 1961 to 2011, still there is significant gap between literacy rate of other population and that of SC/STs. There is a literacy gap of 6.9 between SCs and others and 14.0 between STs and others.

The school drop-out rate is a crucial indicator of lack of educational development of the marginalised groups. The dropout rates of SC children are still very high at 32.7 percent in Class I to V, 55.2 percent in class I to VIII, and 69.1 percent in Class I to X during the year 2004-05. The educational gap between the SC population and the general category at higher levels of schooling is always greater, as shown in Table 4.

Table 4: Dropout Rates, 2004-05 and 2012-13 - SC/ST (Provisional)

Category	*Class I-V*			*Class I-VIII*			*Class I-X*		
2004-05	*All*	*Boys*	*Girls*	*All*	*Boys*	*Girls*	*All*	*Boys*	*Girls*
General	31.47	33.74	28.57	52.32	52.92	52.92	62.69	60.98	64.94
SC	32.7	36.1	34.2	55.2	57.3	57.3	69.1	74.2	71.3
ST									
2012-13									
General	21.2	18.3	19.8	39.2	32.9	36.3	48.1	46.7	47.4
SC	17.7	15.4	16.6	42.4	34.4	38.8	51.8	48	50.1
ST	31.9	30.7	31.3	49.8	46.4	48.2	63.2	61.4	62.4

Source: Government of India, XI Five Year Plan, 2007-2012, Vol. I, p. 105. Educational Statistics at a Glance, Government of India, Ministry of Human Resource Development Bureau of Planning, Monitoring & Statistics, New Delhi, 2014, pp. 17.

Part II

1.1 Challenges of Primary Education in Telangana State in the light of globalisation

Telangana Movement for separate statehood is a long and tragic one.[11] As the Congress lead coalition party was ruling at the centre, after a long period of confusion, the Congress Working Committee decided on 30 July 2013 to request the Government of India to create the state of Telangana. The bill was placed in the parliament in February 2014 and the Andhra Pradesh Reorganisation Act 2014 was passed by the Parliament of India. The bill received the assent of the President and later on, Telangana State was officially formed on 2 June 2014.

The government of Telangana has taken a number of steps towards the improvement of primary education and universalisation of elementary education in the state. During 2013-14 there were 43,293 schools functioning under various types of managements with a total enrolment of 61.78 lakh students. Enrolment of boys were more than that of girls. The percent of enrolment of girls in primary level is only 48.7, which indicates a gender gap in enrolment at primary level, in Telangana state, during 2013-14. The state had employed 2.3 lakh teachers and the teacher-pupil ratio during this year was 26.[12] During the same period 56.4 percent of primary teachers in Telangana state were women. The information on the schools reveals that 68.5 percent of the primary schools in Telangana state belong to Mandal Praja Parishad or Zilla Praja Parishad. Quality improvement programmes at primary level need to be focused on MPP and ZPP schools in Telangana state.

However, the facilities available in the government primary and upper primary schools were not satisfactory. The number of upper primary schools without drinking water facilities were 677, in Telangana state, in 2010. In some of the educationally backward district like, Medak (now divided into Medak, Sidhipet and Sangareddy), 508 primary schools were without drinking water. And there were 124 upper primary schools without drinking water facility during 2010.[13] Lack of provisions for drinking water also affects the enrolment and retention of students in such schools of Telangana, leading to very high rate of drop-out in the state.

According to a survey conducted by ASER (2014) around three percent of the children between the age of six and 14 were out of school in the Telangana region during 2013. The percent of out of school children is high in some districts like Adilabad which is more than 6.5 percent whereas it is 5.7 percent for Mahabubnagar under the united Andhra Pradesh. Almost 90 percent of children in age group of 6-17 years in Telangana attend school (91% in urban areas and 88% in rural areas). School attendance is almost universal (96%) in the age group 6-14 years, but it drops to 78 percent in the age group 15-17 years. There is no gender disparity in school attendance in the age group 6-14 years. However, in the age group 15-17 years, a higher proportion of boys (81%) than girls (76%) are attending school.

According to another survey conducted by the Ministry of Health and Family Welfare (2015) of Telangana state, 65 percent of women aged between 15-49 and 83 percent of men aged between 15-49 are literate. In Telangana, 33 percent of women and 17 percent of men aged between 15-49 have never been to school and only 24 percent of women and 31 percent of men aged between 15-49 have completed 12 or more years of schooling.

Telangana has taken a right based approach to primary education with the introduction of RTE Act. This has helped in accelerating access and enrolment at primary school level in Telangana state. This is reflected in the educational programmes like Sarva Shiksha Abhiyan which is implemented in the state of Telangana through Rajeev Vidya Mission. In spite of all these efforts, there is lack of infrastructural facilities and trained teachers in many of the government aided primary schools. Many of the rural primary schools do not have compound-wall, play-ground, drinking water and toilet facilities in Telangana state.

There are serious concerns regarding the quality of education in Telangana. Some studies reveal that there is huge difference in the performance of students of class V in mathematics and languages when it is compared between urban and rural private and government school children in Telangana. Majority of students in primary classes in rural areas of the state do not have the ability to read, write and solve simple numerical problems. The school atmosphere needs to be upgraded with quality infrastructure, proper training for the teachers and very effective monitoring by the government authorities and the community where the school is located. Telangana state has also proposed an agenda for universalisation of secondary education. There are some areas very difficult to reach where some communities live. People who live in inter-state borders need to be specially targeted to ensure universal access to quality education. Children with special needs and children from tribal communities, children on streets and children of migratory communities should be provided with universal access to quality education in Telangana. According to the assessment of the Telangana governmental authorities 100 percent net enrolment rates would have been achieved by 2017. However, it is not achieved so far. The National Literacy Mission is once again re-introduced to improve female literacy. It is also aimed at reducing gender disparities. However, there is gender gap among socially disadvantaged groups at primary and secondary level of education in Telangana. Enrolment has not improved much in rural areas. In order to improve the quality of education, village education committees need to be formed and monitored. It is noticed that enrolment in secondary and tertiary levels of education is low in tribal areas. There is the need to build many more ashram schools for girls in the tribal areas. Child marriages are hindering the education of young girls in different parts of Telangana. Many girls are keeping away from the schools, due to migration or spending time for the care of the siblings. There are no effective educational programmes to take care of the educational needs of the children from vulnerable backgrounds in Telangana[14].

Conclusion

There is no country in the world which is not affected by the effect of globalisation. Education sector of India is impacted in complex and contradicting ways due to globalisation. Educational development in India should consider the educational development of every segment of the society, including the marginalised, the SCs, STs and the minorities. Globalisation is unifying the curriculum, methodology and knowledge systems of different economies under a common platform. The proponents of new economics of education opine that investment in the field of education is guided by profitability aimed at getting maximum returns from it[15]. But the profit motive in educational investment will sideline the marginalised groups in India, who cannot access educational facilities without special legislative protections.

The quality of basic education is the key to a nation's capability to attain development in every sector. It is this capability that helps a nation to improve agricultural productivity, enhances the status of women, reduces population growth rates and enhances environmental protection and raises the standard of living. As no economy is totally self-sufficient, the best educational practices of the other developed nations can be adapted by developing economies like India.

A combination of higher education and research and lifelong learning is necessary for a nation to construct knowledge and information based developing economy through innovative technologies. Only an inclusive and equitable quality education at all levels will help India to attain its educational developmental goals. The educational status of the marginalised groups should be brought in par with the other groups to attain equity in education and societal development. An inclusive educational approach with quality education augments the balanced growth and development of economy, and the society at large, without hindering the educational development of the marginalised groups in India.

References

Amritpal Singh, Puneet Bansal and Rupani Garg. 2013. *Impact of Globalisation on Indian Education System*. International Journal of Engineering Research &Technology, Vol. 2, Issue 12, Dec. 2013.

Bhagat, L.N. and Oraon, Ashok. 2006. Education for Sustainable Development: A Study of Actions, Achievements and Challenges with reference to School Education in India.

Leggett, Jane A. and Carter, Nicole T. 2012. Rio+20: The United Nations Conference on Sustainable Development, *Congressional Research Service*, June 2012.

MHRD. 2001. Selected Educational Statistics, 1999-2000, Department of Education, Govt. of India, New Delhi.

Mukhi, Bhawya Sachdeva and Robin Anand. 2015. Globalisation and its Impact on Indian Education System, International Journal of Engineering Technology, Management and Applied Sciences, Vol. 3, Special Issue, ISSN 2349-4476.

Sing, Amritpal, Puneet Bansal and Rupani Garg. 2013. *Impact of Globalisation on Indian Education System,*International Journal of Engineering Research & Technology, Vol. 2, Issue. 12.

Steger, Manfred B. 2003. Globalisation: A very short Introduction. Oxford University Press.

Thakran, Suman. 2015. Education for Sustainable Development. *Educational Quest: An Int. J. of Education and Applied Social Sciences,* Vol. 6, Issue 1, pp. 55-60.

UN. 2012. The Future We Want. Outcome Document of the United Nations Conference on Sustainable Development, Rio de Janeiro, Brazil, 20-22 June 2012.

UNESCO. 2015. Unpacking Sustainable Development Goal 4: Education 2030.

Wada Na Todo Abhiyan. Sustainable Development Goals: Agenda 2030. A Civil Society Report.

Xaxa, Virginius. 2011. *The Status of Tribal Children in India: A historical perspective,* IHD-UNICEF Working Papers Series: Children of India: Rights and Opportunities, Working Paper No. 7, Institute for Human Development, New Delhi.

Notes

1. Manfred B.Steger.2003. Globalisation: A very short introduction. Oxford University Press.

2. *Ibid.*
3. *Ibid.*
4. Jane A. Legget and Nicole T.Carter. 2012. Rio+20: The United Nations Conference on Sustainable Development. Congressional Research Service, p. 1.
5. Amritpal Singh, Puneet Bansal and Rupani Garg. 2013. Impact of Globalisation on Indian Education System. International Journal of Engineering Research &Technology, Vol. 2, Issue 12, Dec. 2013.
6. World Commission on Environment and Development. 1987. p. 43.
7. DISE 2015-2016.
8. Wada Na Todo Abhiyan. 2017. Sustainable Development Goals: Agenda 2030. A Civil Society Report, p. 32.
9. Census of India 2011.
10. Virginius Xaxa. 2011. The Status of Tribal Children in India: A historical perspective, UNICEF, New Delhi, pp. 1-24.
11. Gautam Pingle. 2009. The Telangana Tragedy – A lesson in Integration and Disintegration, Journal of Indian School of Political Economy, Vol. 21, No. 14, pp. 1-27.
12. Government of Telangana. 2015. Statistical Year Book. Telangana State Portal, Directorate of Economics and Statistics, Hyderabad, pp.1-466.
13. Government of India. 2011. Status of Literacy. Provisional Population Totals, Registrar General, Ministry of Human Affairs, New Delhi, India, pp. 123-159.
14. Sustainable Development Goals: The Way Forward. 2016. Socio Economic Outlook, 2016. pp. 107-120.
15. Bhawya Sachdeva Mukhi and Robin Anand. 2015. Globalisation and its impact on Indian Education System. International Journal of Engineering Technology, Management and Applied Sciences, Vol. 3, Special Issue, pp. 216-220.

25

Adoption of Modern Information and Communication Technology by Marginalised Communities in the Globalised Era: An Empirical Study

— Dr. S. Janet Mary

Introduction

In the Post-Modern era, Information and Communication Technology (ICT) has become indispensable tools to enable communities to access information and other services in the world. However, in the increasingly globalised world most marginalised communities do not get the opportunity to use Information and Communication Technology as they lack access to information relevant to their living. Moreover, despite the vast advances that are being made in the spheres of science and technology, information and communication technology (ICT), medicine, capital mobility, etc., income disparities are ever widening. The trends in poverty reduction have recently worsened. It has been estimated that over 700 million of the world's poor live in Asia-Pacific region i.e., those who earn $1 or less a day. Nearly one of three Asians is poor. The population growth in the developing countries is also adding to absolute number of poor. According to Indian Census 2011, almost 70% of India's population still lives in rural areas, spread across 600,000-plus villages. Overcoming poverty among the marginalised communities therefore, remains the single most important challenge facing those involved in the development activities. Today's communications media are excellent vehicles for any development work. Hi-tech based internet and digital technologies are not only becoming a lot smarter, they are growing more user-friendly and can help marginalised communities in fighting discrimination and poverty by arming them with information, knowledge and technologies. On the one hand, the affluent part of the world is hit by unprecedented overflow of information which is fast increasing day by day. On the other hand, millions of people in developing countries have absolutely no effective communication links to the outside world. There is therefore an urgent need to ensure access to ICT in rural areas or disadvantaged communities to disseminate simple, practical knowledge which will save lives, increase awareness and stimulate development. This research is based on the assumption that media can help reduce the conflict and strengthen organisation. It can help reduce poverty through providing information on how people of their type somewhere else are handling their situation. The marginalised communities have inadequate access to information, technology, expertise, and resources.

It is a historical fact that these poor or in other words the marginalised communities around the world have lived for years without Information and Communication Technology. Therefore, when these technologies are introduced for the first time, adoption becomes a complex problem. Furthermore, in the Post-Modern world where individuals have become independent and so they are diverse in their social and economic life, the way they accept and adopt innovation is also different. These differences are influenced by a number of factors that determine how each individual adopts a new idea. In this study, three independent variables have been identified as having an effect on how individuals adopt modern information and communication technology especially among marginalised communities. These are education, gender and age. The research reported here discusses and describes issues that affect and slow the adoption process. It investigates the problems different groups of people in Puducherry coastal area encounter when getting acquainted with social media use. The study also looks at the challenges that might cause discontinuation and resistance towards ICT use. In addition, the study examines the various stages of new technology adoption. It aims to answer the following question: How do individuals in the marginalised communities with different levels of education, from different age groups and gender adopt social media?

Innovation Theory

There are a lot of issues to be considered when technologies are being introduced in areas where there has never been any form of technology before. For example, who are the possible adopters? Do they have substantial reasons to adopt the innovation? Would the community perceive the need to adopt the innovation? These are some of the questions that need to be asked (Nedevschi et al. 2006). According to Rogers, diffusion is a process whereby a product meant to bring innovation spreads within a population, reaching a number of adopters (1995)[1]. The process begins with the introduction of the innovation to the population and ends when the population fully adopts it. A product or service of innovation can be disseminated and adopted at 100 percent or less (Rogers, 1995). Rogers differentiates diffusion from adoption in that the diffusion process occurs within a society to all different groups, whereas adoption has to do with the individual's feelings and needs (Rogers, 1995).

Stages of Adoption

The adoption of innovation is made up of a number of stages that are usually followed by adopters. These stages assist in understanding how an individual adopts innovation. According to Rogers (1995), these stages can be broken down into five as follows:

Awareness: The innovation is introduced to a person who does not have sufficient knowledge about the product or service. Because of this lack of information the individual does not feel the need to go out and look for more information, and also does not consider buying or using the product or service;

Interest: One decides to find out more about the innovation/product, but does not really know how or if it can be useful in their own life. That is when the individual decides to access information and more knowledge about the product so as to decide whether or not to adopt;

Evaluation: The individual starts making decisions about the innovation. The individual asks questions concerning the use of the product, whether it is really worth buying, whether it would make a difference, etc. These are the types of questions that individuals ask themselves during the evaluation stage. If the innovation appears to be useful to their life, they will try it out;

Trial Stage: This is a stage whereby the product/innovation is used to a limited extent. That was when people attended the training in their own respective places to assess the project's usefulness.

Adoption of ICTs in a Marginalised Area of Puducherry could become advantageous to their needs. After that, they came up with suggestions on how it could be used for the benefit of the whole community; and

Adoption Stage: The individuals use the information they gathered in the interest and evaluation stages and with the results of the trial stage to make a decision to adopt the innovation. At this point, individuals consider a lot of opportunities concerning the innovation. It is adopted with ideas on how it will be used for improvement in their lives. However, due to various reasons, individuals might reject the innovation after they have adopted it (Rogers 1995).[2]

It is believed that an individual might reject an innovation at any time during or after the adoption process. Abrahamson examined this process critically by posing questions such as: How do technically inefficient innovations diffuse and what impedes technically efficient innovations from catching on? Abrahamson makes suggestions for how organisational scientists can more comprehensively evaluate the spread of innovations[3]. In later editions of *Diffusion of Innovation*, Rogers changes his terminology of the five stages to: knowledge, persuasion, decision, implementation, and confirmation. However, the descriptions of the categories have remained similar throughout the editions.

Marginalised communities adopt social media differently from urban populations. Findings from Pierson's study (2002) on ICT adoption and use by self-employed persons and micro-enterprises in Flanders (Belgium) suggest that people living in marginalised areas are more likely to adopt social media for personal and work related reasons. People living in urban areas were more likely to adopt modern information technology for personal reasons. These include online shopping, viewing holiday destinations, communicating with people from other countries, etc. (Pierson, 2002). This is due to different information and communication needs and motivations (Shields and Samarajiva, 1993; LaRose and Mettler, 1989; Patterson and Kavanaugh, 1994). For example, Patterson and Kavanaugh (1994) found that marginalised residents in Australia were more interested in telecommunication services that facilitated interaction with people and events in their local area. Attempts to understand and improve the effectiveness of ICT adoption for agriculture have also been noted ever since ICTs became available for agricultural management and production. Information technology adoption for agriculture and rural development remains a major national and international concern.

According to Osborn (2005), successful development projects connect and balance local skills and knowledge rather than trying to change people into having the skills they need. Much of people's cultural and indigenous knowledge, especially in rural areas, is enclosed within and is expressed through their local languages. Limiting people to the use of ICTs in a foreign language tends to intensify the digital divide. In the process, it makes it difficult for people to quickly adopt ICTs and, in fact, it generates fear. As a result, ICTs are perceived as tools for educated people only (Osborn, 2005).

Variables Identified in the Adoption Process

There are three variables identified as having an effect on the way communities in Puducherry adopted ICTs. Education was found to be a fundamental variable in the adoption process. It proved to have a major role in creating some misunderstandings between different groups in the community. Age and gender were also identified as having an impact on the adoption process.

Education

According to the research, education plays one independent variable that played a fundamental role in information technological adoption in Puducherry coast land. It had positive and negative impacts. Teachers adopted ICTs in order to enhance their teaching skills, to teach learners and community members and also for their own personal benefits such as reading newspapers, shopping online, internet banking, applying for education and maybe other employment opportunities. This showed that teachers had clear ideas on how to use computers, as compared to community members who did not have formal education. Most young people received some high school education but could not complete their studies. Some community members who showed interest in information technology use had completed high school education but could not further their studies. The stagnant state of rural education itself has been a major concern for educational policymakers in India. Pratham's Annual Status of Education Report (ASER) 2016 revealed that despite increased enrolment, a significant proportion of children in Classes 1 to 8 in government and rural private schools could not read text suitable for Class 2 students or do simple arithmetic their age-group may be expected to do (Mody, 2017). The high rate of dropouts—nearly 50% by age 14—compounds this problem. Hence, for the vast majority of rural students who attend government schools, the acquisition of ICT skill-sets and facilities remains a distant dream.

Education also affected ICT adoption in the sense that community members felt inferior to the teachers. This affected community discussions on the project. Lack of education implied that most people in the community depended on teachers; for example, it was difficult for individuals to use computers if teachers were not available. Community members who needed to use computers on weekends and during vacations could not express their needs during community meetings. Some nurses from village clinics also showed interest in ICT adoption. Young people were encouraged by their parents to attend the training. Arts and craft makers were keen on advertising their products online; however, they showed reluctance in the practical use of computers. India's National Policy on Education 1986, modified in 1992, stressed the need for educational technology to improve access, quality and governance of education, with the focus on effective implementation of ICT schemes and programmes, including technical education. Effective implementation would mean overcoming the following challenges:

Gender

4.1 Introduction about the analysis

Two hundred fifty participants within the age limit of 17 and 25 participated in the questionnaire. The data was collected and formed into the tables using formula method. Pie-chart is used for comparing segments of the study. A pie chart helps us in making comparative analysis and shows relative sizes of the data. The main aim of the data collection is to analyze and interpret the results to prove the hypothesis.

4.2 Results of the demographic analysis

4.2.1 Frequency distribution of E-mail users based on their gender

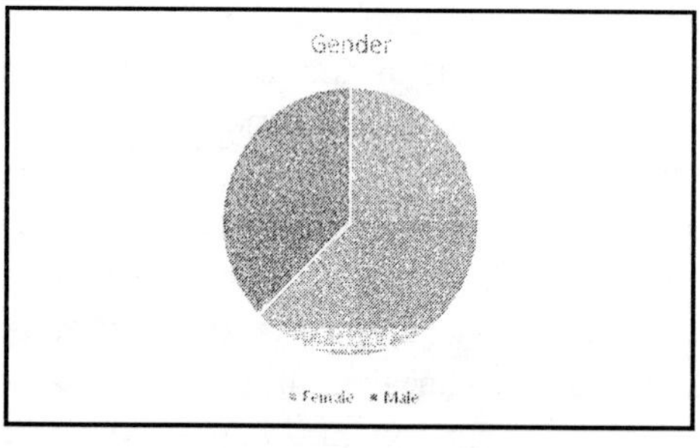

Pie chart 4.2.1 showing the percentage of men and women using You Tube

Gender	*Frequency*	*Per cent*
Male	93	37
Female	157	63
Total	250	100

The Table 4.2.1 highlights the distribution of gender of You Tube users.

From the information given in the pie chart, out of 250 participants, 63% were male (93) and 63% were females (157). This shows that women spend more time with You Tube compared to men. This can be due to the heavy influence of education and peer-support. The application is a clear indication of gender bias as the content available is most likely to be liked by women. A mainstream You Tube user will look up for content relating to conventional information and knowledge. This acts as a magnet for updating with new information and correspondence. Not just that, a lot of features You Tube are designed in such a way that particularly fits the requirement of women.

Gender also played a role in the adoption of social media in the coast lands of Puducherry. The general assumption is that men pay greater attention to technology. Puducherry villages proved that women willingly adopted You Tube App and became skilled in ICT use. Our findings showed that men were slow to adopt ICTs, with the exception of teachers in the schools. Women showed greater interest in attending computer training programmes in the community. Some men explained: 'We do not see the necessity to attend the training because we do not wish to use smart phones.' Some men said they would like to attend the training but could not do so because of their commitment to other jobs in the village. A few young men mentioned that 'we have been away; and when we got back we saw the project and we saw that there are not many men attending the training; project members should recruit more young men'. Elderly men were cooperative but could not use computers. In most cases people from marginalised communities prefer to live life traditionally in the way they have been used to. They do not accept change easily. In the perception of some community members, the introduction of technology has never seemed appropriate to the traditional way of life. However, those who sent their children to school believed it would be a good thing if the children could learn to use ICTs.[4]

Age

The use of social media by older people is currently booming, as this group has significantly increased its use of information and communication technologies in daily life, on both personal and professional levels.[5] In this respect, the advantages of using new technologies to develop social relationships, leisure and entertainment opportunities, and life-long learning habits and access services and care could be considered factors for successful autonomy and aging in the life of older people.[6]

"As the availability of electronic resources for older adults increases, the quality of the aging experience will be enhanced" and in order to achieve involvement and counteract resistance to using these technologies, we need to bridge the "digital gap" experienced by older users by providing interfaces and tools adapted to suit their physical and cognitive characteristics. Suitable training and support systems are required according to seniors' objectives, abilities, and experience, so as to reduce anxiety about using computers and to promote motivation, especially in the initial stages of learning. Although qualitative research indicates that for some older adults computer use does lead to self-perceived improvements in well-being, there is no research-based evidence to support the assertion that computer use alone has a more general (and measurable) affect on well-being among older adults.[7]

Age also proved to have an impact on the way individuals adopted ICTs the coastlands of Puducherry. All age groups showed there were people who became first adopters and also laggards. Elderly men and women accepted the project but could not really adapt to ICT. Young people were perceived as the ones who should learn to use ICTs, as they might be relevant to their lives. During meetings which were called to introduce the project formally, elderly people promised to support the project. For example, when extra equipment was needed, the community rallied around members, collected money and bought the equipment. Teachers and young people were asked to help to upload the products on the Internet for advertising and marketing.

4.2.2. Frequency distribution of You Tube users based on their Age

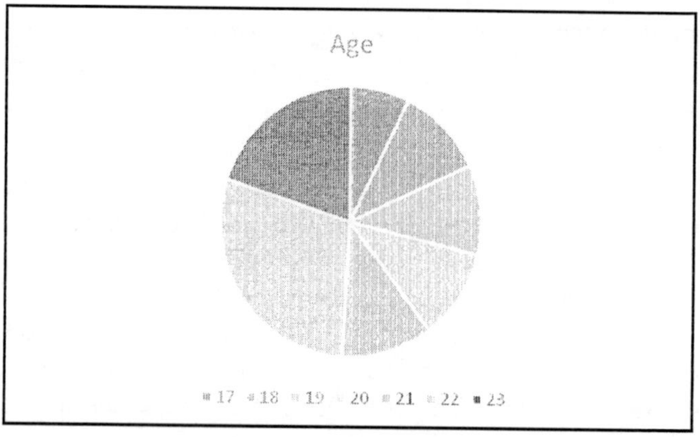

Pie chart 4.2.2: showing the percentage of various age group.

Age	*Frequency*	*Per cent*
17	18	7
18	27	11
19	27	11
20	27	11
21	28	11
22	73	29
23	50	20
Total	250	100

Age has been divided into 6 groups with equal scale. Age is one of the most important demographic characteristics as it directly links with the usage rate. The age group was set between 17 and 22. The grouping was set this way, as the people get more active and start using You Tube from 17 on a continuous basis. However, this would get reduced as they enter the work life.

As one can see from the table given above, 7% of users belong to the age group of 17, whereas the users between the age group of 18 - 21 show an equal proposition of 11%. Users belonging to age 22 showed 29% and the rest 20 % belongs to the age group of 23. Teenagers posted fewer pictures than adults since they are less exposed to the outer environment. And other researchers have already proved that more than 90% of the You Tube users aged below 35 (Pennsylvania State University, 2015).

Conclusion

Seventy percent of India's population lives in rural areas, with no access to modern Internet infrastructures. Rural politics is the area where social media networks have not reached to the required potential. But there still remains a lot of room for improvement for social networking services as with better technology, the connectivity of these places should improve and provide the economic opportunity to take benefits from the system.[8] As shown in this study, there are three factors that influence Internet infrastructure adoption in a marginalised community in India. The factors are education, age and gender. There are several indications that show that coastland community can fully adopt social media use. If the arts and craft women were able to adopt Information technology and develop their businesses, it would be a practical example for everyone in the community. People would see the benefits of Information technology and start developing interest in the project. Learners who would like to advance their education elsewhere would find they could also use computers to access information about different institutions. This suggests that learners in coastland community should participate in the computer training programme, so they can acquire the necessary skills. All community members need to take a more leading role in internet infrastructure use. Use of Information technology helps to create job opportunities in the villages. For this to happen, a range of training programmes should be introduced. All schools would need a permanent trainer and most teachers should include Information and Communication technology use in their curriculum. With improved computer skills, businesses would develop and young people would be able to find jobs in their communities rather than migrate to the cities in search of jobs.

References

Cullen, R., 2002, 'Addressing the Digital Divide', online information review http: / /informingscience.org/proceedings/inSITE2006/IISITJaco113.pdf#Search= %Cullen%20Rao%202003%22.

Dalvit, L; Alfonsi, R; Isabirye, N; Terzoli, A & Thinyane, M., 2006, A Case Study on the Teaching of Computer Training in a Rural Area in South Africa, Granada, Spain: Comparative Education Society of Europe.

Gelb, E., Wagner, P., Rosskopf, K., Parker, C., & Schiefer, G., 2004, 'ICT Adoption– A Summary of EFITA Questionnaire', Proceedings AFITA Conference, Bangkok, available online at: http://departments.agri.huji.ac.il/economics/gelb-gelbparker.pdf

Harris, R., 2001, 'Research Partnerships to Support Rural Communities in Malaysia with Information and Communication Technologies,' in J. Lazar (ed.) Managing IT/Community Partnerships in the 21st Century, United States of America: Idea Group Publishing,

Human Sciences Research Council, 2005, Emerging Voices: A Report on Education in South African Rural Communities, Cape Town: HSRC Press/Nelson Mandela Foundation.

LaRose, R. & Mettler, J., 1989, 'Who Uses Information Technologies in Rural America?' Journal of Communication, 39 (3).

McTaggart, R., 1989, '16 Tenets of Participatory Action Research', website accessed November 2006 at: http://www.caledonia.org.uk/par.htm.

Nedevschi, S, Sandhu, J, Pal, Fonseca, R, & Toyama, K., 2006, 'Bayesian Network: A Statistical Approach for Understanding ICT Adoption.' First International Conference on ICT and Development, University of California, Berkley. Oppenheim, A.N., 1992, Questionnaire Design and Attitude Measurement, New York: Pinter.

Osborn, D., 2005, 'Localising ICTs to African Languages and Arabic', available online at: http://www.idrc.ca/en/ev-87747-201-1-DO_TOPIC.html, date accessed: 20/08/06.

Palmer, R., Timmermans, H. & Fay, D., 2002, From Conflict to Negotiation: Nature based Development on South Africa's Wild Coast, Pretoria: Human Sciences Research Council; Grahamstown: Institute of Social & Economic Research, Rhodes University.

Patterson, S. & Kavanaugh, A., 1994, 'Rural users' Expectations of the Information Superhighway,' Media Information Australia, 74 (4), available online at: http://abs.sagepub.com/cgi/content/refs/45/3/496

Patton, M, Q., 1990, Qualitative Evaluations Research Methods, 2nd Edition, Newbury Park, California: SAGE, available online at: http://www.sas.upenn.edu/anthro/ICPIA/METHODS/Interviews.html Pierson, J., 2002, 'ICT Adoption and Use by Small Businesses', Chapter 5 of Final Report of the Capability Group, COST269 Group, available online at: http:// www.cost269.org.

Dickinson, A., Gregor, P., Computer use has no demonstrated impact on the well-being of older adults. International Journal of Human Computer Studies. 2006; 64(8):744–753. doi: 10.1016/j.ijhcs.2006.03.001. [CrossRef] [Google Scholar]

Rao, S.S., 2003, 'Information Systems in Indian Rural Communities', Journal of Computer Information Systems, available online at: http:informingscience.org/proceedings/inSITE2006/IISITJaco113.pdf#Search=%Cullen%20Rao%20 2003%22%20Rao%202003%22.

Rogers, E., 1995, Diffusion of Innovations, 4th Edition, New York: The Free Press, available online at: http://www.gdnet.org/middle.php?oid=884.

Sekaran, U., 1992, Research Methods for Business, a Skill Building Approach, 2nd Edition, New York: John Wiley and Sons Inc.

Shields, P. & Samarajiva, R., 1993, 'Competing Frameworks for Research on Information Communication Technologies and Society: Toward a Synthesis'. Communication Yearbook, 16, available online at: http://ci-journal.net/index.php/ciej/article/viewFile/201/160.

Songan, P., Alvin, Y., Gnaniah, J., Zen, H. & Hamid, K., 2005, 'Lessons Learnt from the Implementation Approaches of the E Bario and E-Bedian Projects', in S. Marshall, W. Taylor and X. Yu (eds.) Encyclopedia of Developing Regional Communities with Information and Communication Technology. London: Idea Group Reference, available online at: http://www.digitalopportunity.org/ article/view/127939/1/

Wimmer, R.D. & Dominick, J.R., 2003, Mass Media Research: An Introduction. 7th Edition. California: Thomson Wordsworth Publishing.

Balasubramania Raja G (2011), "Mass Media and Rural Development" , THAVAN IJRMS, Vol. 01, No. 01, October.

Notes

1. In 1962, Everett Rogers, a professor of rural sociology, published: *Diffusion of Innovations*. He categorically synthesized research from over 508 diffusion studies across the fields that initially influenced the theory. Using his synthesis of various social disciplines, Rogers produced a theory of the adoption of innovations among individuals and organisations. It is to be noted that his methodologies are closely followed in recent diffusion research, even as the field has expanded into, and been influenced by, other methodological disciplines such as social network analysis and communication.
2. Thandeka Priscilla Mapi, Lorenzo Dalvit and Alfredo Terzoli (2006) expressed these above concepts vividly in their , "Adoption of ICTs in a Marginalised Area of South Africa".

3. Newell, S. (2001). "Management Fads and Fashions". Organisation. 8 (1): 5–15. doi:10.1177/135050840181001. Taken from Wikipedia date: April 11, 2020.

4. The Common Sense data echoes the findings of a 2011 study from the Pew Research Center's Internet and American Life Project, in which researchers concluded that 67 percent of 12- to 13-year-old girls used a social networking site, and a third of them believed their peers were mostly unkind to each other online, while only 9 percent of the boys concurred. The divergence in the Pew data disappeared for older teenagers, 14 to 17, however. Roughly 20 percent of both boys and girls in that age range claimed that social networking sites were hostile environments. It's interesting how differently worded questions appear to produce different gender splits.

   See Google June 27, 2012. Study: Girls More Plugged in than Boys. By Ariel Doctoroff

5. Tatnall, A. ICT, education and older people in Australia: a socio-technical analysis. Education and Information Technologies. 2014;19(3):549–564. doi: 10.1007/s10639-013-9300-x. [CrossRef] [Google Scholar]

6. World Health Organisation. Connecting and caring: innovations for healthy ageing. Bulletin of the World Health Organisation. 2012;90(3):162–163. doi: 10.2471/blt.12.020312. [PMC free article] [PubMed] [CrossRef] [Google Scholar]

7. Dickinson, A & Gregor, P. 2006. 'Computer use has no demonstrated impact on the well-being of older adults', International Journal of Human-Computer Studies, Vol. 64, No. 8, pp. 744-753. https://doi.org/10.1016/j.ijhcs.2006.03.001.

8. Ekta Bansal, IMPACT OF SOCIAL MEDIA ON RURAL INDIA * ISSN 2319-345X www.ijmrbs.com Vol. 4, No. 3, July 2015 © 2015 IJMRBS.

26

Women Street Vendors in Shillong City – A Sociological Enquiry

— *Dr. Surojit Sen Gupta*

Introduction

Vending has been a profession since time immemorial with street vendors an integral part of urban history and culture. Vendors constitute a significant part of the informal sector and an integral part of urban economy. Street vending provides job opportunity and means of livelihood to the urban poor. It is stated that a very low skill and capital investment is required to enter this trade. In comparison to other trades it is easier to enter this trade for the poor as well as lower income groups living in the city for some time. With the increase of urban population one can see the growth of urban poor, which constitutes the largest section of consumers for these street vendors, has led to an increase in the number in any given city (Ray and Mishra, 2011).

Today vending is an important source of employment for a large number of urban poor in India. People engaged in vending tries to solve their problems through their own meager resources. It appears that irrespective of the location and type of vendors, they try to live their lives with dignity and self-respect through regular vending activities.

Street vendor is described to those who are incapable to getting regular jobs in the formal sector. Street vendors are also recognised as self-employed workers in the informal sectors. According to the National Policy of Urban Street Vendors (NPUSN) 2006, "a street vendor is broadly defined as a person who offers goods for sale to the public without having a permanent built up structure but with a temporary static structure or mobile stall (or head load). Street vendors may be stationary by occupying space on the pavements or other public/private areas, or may be mobile in the sense that they move from place to place carrying their wares on push carts or in cycles or baskets on their heads, or may sell their wares in moving trains, bus etc. In this policy document, the term urban vendor is inclusive of both traders and service providers, stationary as well as mobile vendors and incorporates all other local/ region specific terms used to describe them".

The National Classification of Occupation 1968 defines street vendors as hawker, peddler, street vendor, *pheriwala* sell articles of daily utility and general merchandise such as vegetables, sweets, clothes, utensils and toys, on footpaths or by going from door to door. Normally they purchases goods from wholesale market according to their needs and capital (money) available. They load them in basket or on pushcart, wheel barrow or tricycle and moves in selected areas to effect sales. Some of them may also display goods or articles of sale on footpath and effect sales.

McGee (1977) defines vendors from an economic, cultural and legal position. To him vendors in different countries have different characteristics. The different dimensions considered by McGee are the functional role the vendors play in the market distribution system, the scale of operation and the legal definitions prescribed in each city. He defines vendors as those people who offer goods or services for sale from public places, primarily streets and pavements. To Jumani (1991) lower income self-employed people includes the hawkers/street vendors which have been termed as vendors engaged in the trade of essential commodities.

A street vendor is broadly defined as a person who offers goods for sale to the public without having a permanent built-up structure from which to sell. Street vendors may be stationary in the sense that they occupy space on the pavements or other public/private spaces or they may be mobile in the sense they move from place to place by carrying their wares or push carts or in baskets on their heads (Bhowmik, 2005).

Various studies have already confirmed the fact that street vendors comprise one of the most marginalised sections of the urban poor. Notwithstanding the fact that they play a very dynamic role in the urban economy, providing necessary items, which are largely both durable and cost-effective, to average income-earning households at cheap and affordable rates (Saha, 2011).

Street vending is surviving and growing not merely because it is an important source of employment but also because of the services it provides to the urban population. For the urban poor street vendors provide goods including food at low prices. Thus, one section of the urban poor namely, street vendors subside the existence of the other sections of the urban poor by providing them cheap goods including food. Street vendors sell different kinds of goods which are manufactured in small scale or home-based industries. Apart from non-agricultural products, street vendors also sell agricultural products like vegetables and fruits.

The Government of India has used the term 'urban vendor' as inclusive of both traders and service providers stationary as well as mobile and incorporates all other local/region specific terms used to describe them such as footpath *dukandars*, side-walk traders and more.

Thus, street vending is one of the fundamental constituents of urban economics and also a distinctive part of large informal sectors in urban areas. Street vendor means a person engaged in vending of articles, goods, food items etc. of everyday use or offering services to the general public in a street lane, side-walk, footpath pavements, and public parks or any other public place or private areas or from temporary built-up structure.

Studies on Street Vendors – A Brief Review

Street vending is an attractive economic strategy and source of livelihood for the unskilled and illiterate new arrivals to the city (Tshuma and Jari, 2013). With increasing rural to urban migration and the contracting formal sector, street vending and other forms of informal employment become the most attractive means of survival for the urban poor (Chirisa and Muchini, 2011; Adhikari, 2012 and Njya, 2015). To Ray and Mishra (2011) vending has become an important source of employment for a large number of urban poor.

According to Mengistu and Jibat (2015) most street vendors engage in street vending activities to supplement their low income or to cushion their spouse's low salary. Ray and Mishra (2011) also argued that despite the low incomes generated from vending activities, the simple fact that vendors do not wait for handouts and / or employment opportunities from the government or engage in begging, stealing or extortion is a clear sign that street vending is a form of income distribution with great economic potential.

Sharit Bhowmik (1999) conducted a survey on seven cities in India namely, Mumbai, Ahmadabad, Kolkata, Imphal, Patna and Bhubaneshwar. The study found that except in Kolkata, all other municipalities have provisions for providing licences for street vending. Bhattacharya and De (1987) in a study of street vendors of Calcutta explained that street vendors are those people who do not have a permanent place of their own and who offer goods and services without having proper trade licence for sale from public spaces.

Harlan Dimas (2008) discussed the roots of street vending phenomenon and suggested several street vending management solutions from best practices followed around the world. The study revealed that street vendors were a big challenge for urban management. The city managers eliminated them as they defaced city sights. The study also suggested a change in the mindset of urban decision makers.

Street vendors often face harassment and arbitrary restrictions from civic authorities (Kumari, 2015). Street vendors work in hostile environments without basic infrastructure and services. Generally street vendors face four common challenges: economic pressure, socio-cultural challenges, adverse political conditions and operational challenges (Tambuman, 2009). To Mkhize (2013) street vendors are harassed and in some cases assaulted and their goods confiscated by urban authorities. This negative perception of street vendors has resulted in conflicts with urban authorities (Hasan, 2015), despite the street vendors role in the economy. Dube and Chirisa (2012) observed that street vendors continue to struggle at the margins of the economy.

Street vendors also provide low-cost basic goods and food items to other lower income groups within the cities. Evidence shows that the monthly incomes from street vending are very low compared to the national average of formally employed individuals (Roever, 2014). In a study of street vendors in Asian countries (Sharit Bhowmik, 2005) analyzed the magnitude of street vending in different countries. The assessment found that the number of street vendors in the countries was on an increase.

Nidan's (2010) study was based on 600 street vendors in 72 wards in Patna city. The study found that most of the respondents chose vending as a profession because there were no other job available, entry was easier and investment was also low. To Wongtada (2014) street vendors all over the world face a common set of challenges ranging from harassment from civic authorities, arbitrary relocations from vending sites to confiscation of their goods.

Chakraborty and Koley (2018) indicates the poor working conditions of the vendors in the daily market at Jamshedpur city in terms of working hours in a day in addition to unhealthy and unsafe conditions in the work place. The study also revealed that the vendors have low earnings which expose the vendors' standard of living life.

Women Street Vendors

Street vending is one of the few readily accessible avenues of employment open to women who need to earn a living. The low cost of entry into many types of hawking and vending as well as schedule flexibility is an attractive factor for some women. For some women, vending and hawking are the only occupations they know, while for others they are occupations of last resort. With limited literacy and mathematical skills, poor women have few alternatives. Street vending is an important domain of poor women's economic activity that requires endless juggling of family and work responsibilities.

Research also shows that through street vending, most women have taken the role of bringing food on the table (Amankwaa, 2015; Chingono, 2016 and Roever, 2016). Therefore, street vending does not only enable the formally 'marginalised' peddlers to meet their minimum daily food, but also teaches and inspires women in particular to value work (Mazhambe, 2017).

Methodology of the Study

The present paper is an attempt to study the women street vendors in the capital city of Shillong of Meghalaya State. In India, the growth of women street vendors has been significant. The number of women street vendors has increased significantly over the years. Due to awakening and desire for economic independence among women, a large number of urban poor women are appearing on the field of street vending. The women who have been in street vending underline the fact that street vending is a natural sources of employment without any expertise of knowledge related to informal sector in urban areas.

Keeping the above conditions in mind, an attempt has been made to study the women street vendors in the city of Shillong, with the following objectives:

1. To analyze the socio-economic background of the women street vendors.
2. To identify the reasons behind for choosing street vending by the women.
3. To examine the challenges being faced by the women street vendors.

The universe of the study is four markets located at the Municipal areas of Shillong city, i.e., Police Bazar, Bara Bazar, Laitumkhrah Bazar and Polo Bazar. The study is based on the empirical survey of the respondents in these market areas. The unit of observation is the women street vendors. Through the use of random sampling method 89 women street vendors were selected for the present study. A random sampling was drawn from the universe in such a way that every unit in the universe has equal probability.

Findings and Discussion

The several components which make up the personal background of the respondents in the present study comprise of age, marital status, type of family and economic standing on personal and family level. Thus, there is an attempt to focus on the background of the respondents through component associations.

We have classified our respondents according to age-group and assume that their views are bound to be influenced by their age. The respondents have been divided into four age-groups. Out of total 89 respondents, the majority of the respondents that is 33 fall in the age-group between 41-50 years which accounts for 37.07 percent. This was followed by 28 respondents that is 31.46 percent who fall in the age-group 31-40 years, and another 19 respondents, that is 21.34 percent reported their ages between 51 and above years. And only 10.11 percent that is 09 respondents fall in the age-group of 20-30 years. Regarding the sex composition of the respondents, all were females.

The marital status of the sample studied constituted that out of 89 respondents, majority of them were married which accounted for 57.30 percent. This was followed by 28.08 percent of the respondents who were unmarried. Respondents who have reported that they were separated accounted for 10.11 percent. And a very small segment of the respondents have reported that they were widowed which accounted for 4.49 percent.

Regarding the religious background of the respondents it was seen that majority of them were Christians which accounted for 74.15 percent of the sample. And the remaining 25.84 percent of the respondents were the followers of Hindu religion.

In this study of women street vendors we tried to uncover from our respondents, about their place of birth. In response to the information whether their place of birth was a rural or urban area, it was found that majority of them were born in urban areas that is 69.66 percent and the rest 30.33 percent of them were born in rural areas.

The ethnic background of the respondents reveals that majority of them that is, 66.29 percent are from Khasi community. This was followed by Nepalese which accounted for 20.22 percent of the respondents. A section of respondents that is 10.11 percent of them were Bengalies. And a small segment of respondents that is 3.37 percent were Garos.

Family is the bridge between an individual and the community. It acts as the communicator of social expectations and norms, mediator of individual and collective interests and regulator of persons in the context of group relations. Keeping this view, the respondents of the present study were asked to provide information about their types of family. And to this response it was found that, majority of the respondents belong to the nuclear family which accounted for 67.41 percent and 32.58 percent said that they come from joint family.

Regarding the respondents level of education, it was found that majority of them that is 35.95 percent of the respondents studied till standard V. This was followed by 25.84 percent of the respondents who have completed their studies till primary level. 16.85 percent of the respondents have revealed that their level of education is that they could not complete their matriculation examination. A section of respondents that is, 12.35 percent have reported that they were illiterate. And a small segment of 8.98 percent of the respondents has said that they have completed their matriculation examination.

About the family size of the respondents, it was found that 57.30 percent of respondent's family members range from 5-8 members. This was followed by 32.58 percent of the respondents who have reported that their family members range between 1-4 members. And only 10.11 percent of the respondents have claimed for 08 members and above in their family.

It was interesting to know from the respondents about the reason behind for choosing this particular work that is street vending. To this it was found that 58.42 percent of the respondents have said that it was economic compulsion. Income supplementation was another response which accounted for 29.21 percent of the respondents. This was followed by 12.35 percent of the respondents who have said for independent income as a reason for choosing this particular type of work in the informal sector.

Our interest was also to know from the respondents from whom they got the idea for choosing this particular street vending work. And in response it was found that 44.94 percent of the respondents have said that it was from their friends/known persons. Family members also gave the idea of street vending, which accounted for 32.58 percent of the respondents. This was followed by neighbours giving the idea of street vending which accounted for 15.73 percent. And a small segment of respondents that is 6.74 percent of them got the idea of street vending from TV/movie where they come across of street vendors.

Moving forward it was interesting to know from the respondents about their type of vending in the street that they have come up with. To this it was found that 52.80 percent of the respondents were selling tea and food staffs. This was followed by 21.34 percent of the respondents who were selling vegetables and fruits and another 12.35 percent of the respondents were into the selling of household items respectively. Respondents who have claimed that they are into the selling of garments accounted for 8.98 percent. And the remaining 4.49 percent of the respondents have reported that they are into the selling of different types of craft products.

Further an enquiry was made from the respondents that whether they have a permanent location in the street for their business. And in response it was found that 59.55 percent of the respondents have said yes, they have a somewhat permanent place in the street for vending purposes. And another 40.44 percent of the respondents have said no, they do not have any permanent place in the street for vending purpose.

Regarding the respondent's engagement in this particular work of street vending it was found that 38.20 percent of the respondents are into this work for the last 11-15 years. This was followed by 30.33 percent of the respondents who have reported their engagement into street vending for the last 6-10 years. Respondents whose engagement is less than five years accounted for 23.59 percent. And the remaining 7.86 percent of the respondents have claimed their engagement for this work is 16 years and above.

We were inquisitive to find out from the respondents that who have helped them to get the capital for starting this particular work. The response received on this query was that 41. 57 of the respondents have said that it was their family members who have helped them in this matter. This was followed by relatives and friends who accounted for 24.71 percent and 20.22 percent respectively. 11. 23 percent of the respondents have reported that it was the other local vendors that helped them to start this particular work. Wholesalers were the other source of fund for initiating street vending, as stated by a small segment of respondents that is 2.24 percent.

Our inclination was also to know from the respondents that whether they get support from their family members for pursuing this particular work. And in response it was found that 59.55 percent of the respondents have admitted that they get the full support, whereas 40.44 percent of the respondents have claimed that they do not get any such support from their family members while working as street vendors.

Next it was desirable to know from the respondents that whether they find any changes in their financial position after starting their business as street vendors. To this 78.65 percent of the respondents have stated in affirmative, yes, it is better. And 21.34 percent of the respondents have admitted saying no, that there is no such improvement in their financial position till date.

It was also interesting to know from the respondents that whether as a street vendors and running a business have increased their confidence level. The response was that 80.89 percent of the respondents have said yes, it has increased their confidence level. And only 19.10 percent of the respondents have said no, it has not increased their confidence level till present date.

We were also interested to know from the respondents that whether they face any competition in their profession of street vending. And in reply it was found that 70.78 percent of the respondents do face competition in this profession also. Whereas 29.21 percent of the respondents have admitted that they do not face any such competition in their work of street vending.

Our interest was also to know from the respondents who are into street vending about their social position in their respective family level. For this particular query it was found that 48.31 percent of the respondents have said that they made their family financially stable. This was followed by 31.46 percent of the respondents who have admitted that they were given the decision-making power in their family. And the remaining respondent that is 20.22 percent of them has claimed to have greater respect in family.

We have also enquired from the respondents that whether there is adequate demand for their products in their business of street vending. In response it was found that 82.02 percent of the respondents have said yes, they have a good demand for their product. And on the other hand only17.97 percent of the respondents have revealed that they do not have a good demand of their products.

To know about the access to work place amenities such as toilet, availability of water, storage and alike, an enquiry was made from the respondents. And in reply it was found that 69.66 percent of the respondents have said yes, they have these amenities to some extent in their work place. Whereas another section of respondents have said no, they do not have any such amenities in their work place.

Our next query was to know from the respondents that does government take any initiative to protect their rights and interests. And the response received was that 33.70 percent of the respondents have said yes, there is some initiatives from the government side and another 66.29 percent of the respondents have said no, there are no such initiatives from the government side.

Moving forward it was also interesting to know from the respondents that whether they were being harassed or abused by the concerned city authorities. For this query it was found that 29.21 percent of the respondents have said yes, at times they do face such things. But on the other hand 70.78 percent of the respondents have reported by saying no, that they do not face such things from the concern city authorities.

Next it was desirable to know from the respondents that whether they feel safe and secure while working late hours in the markets. The answer for this query was that 52.80 percent of the respondents have said yes, they feel safe and secure, whereas 47.19 percent of the respondents have admitted that they do not feel safe and secure while working late hours in the market as at times they do have to come across with some anti-social elements.

An enquiry was also made from the respondents to know whether they suffer from any occupation related health disorders. To this it was reported by 30.33 percent of the respondents who do suffer from such health issues. And 69.66 percent of the respondents have reported that they do not have any such health issues relating to their occupation.

Our interest was also to know from the respondents that whether did they created any assets after meeting all their essential need of life. The response to this was that 65.16 percent of the respondents have said yes, they have created some assets like (TV, Furniture, and Households Goods etc.). And another section of respondents that is, 34.83 percent have said no, they could not able to create any assets with their present occupation of street vending.

To know about the saving potential of the respondents it was found that 29.21 percent of the respondents try to manage some savings at home. Institutional savings like in the Banks and Post-Office accounted for 47.19 percent of the respondents. No savings at all by respondents accounted for 21.59 percent.

Our curiosity was also to know from the respondents about their relations with other co-vendors in their place of work. The various responses received for this query was that 42.69 percent of the respondents reported for having cordial relations as against 33.70 percent of the respondents who reported for maintaining peaceful relations. 15.73 percent of the respondents have also claimed for having good relations. And a segment of 7.86 percent of the respondents has reported for having conflicting relations with their other co-venders.

Enquiring further from the respondents whether they get any help from others in times of difficulties, it was found that 40.44 percent of the respondents have reported that they get the help occasionally in times of difficulties with their occupation of street vending. This was followed by getting help always accounted for 29.21 percent of the respondents. Getting help only at the time of emergency was claimed by another 20.22 percent of the respondents. And about 10.11 percent of the respondents informed that they do not get any help at all in times of difficulties.

It was also interesting to know from the respondents that with their occupation as street vendors whether their participation in social activity get hampered. The answer for this query was that 65.16 percent of the respondents have said no, it does not get hampered. Whereas on the other hand 34.83 percent of the respondents have admitted that yes, at times with their occupation as street vendors their social activity gets hampered.

We were also interested to know from the respondents that how do they spent their leisure time. To this 35.95 percent of the respondents spent their leisure time by watching television. This was followed by listening to music which accounted for 28.08 percent of the respondents. 25.84 percent of the respondents have claimed that they spent their leisure time by visiting their known people in the city. And the respondents who spent their leisure time by gossiping accounted for 10.11 percent.

We enquired from the respondents about their dual responsibilities that is, as a street vending work and household work, and whether they face any role conflict. To this it was found that 64.04 percent of the women street vendors did not experience any role conflict. And the remaining 35.95 percent of the respondents have admitted that they do experience role conflict in varying degrees with their occupation and household work.

Our interest was also to know from the respondents about the nature of problems they face in their occupation of street vending. The response received for this query was that 34.83 percent of the respondents have reported for lack of support from Municipality and Government. This was followed by the response unfavourable working conditions which accounted for 28.08 percent of the respondents. Another 21.34 percent of the respondents have admitted that the problem they face is due to the lack of space. And the remaining respondents that is 15.73 percent have claimed for lack of capital as a problem they face in their occupation.

It was also inquired from the respondents that what could be the related steps to improve the condition of women street vendors. And in response it was found that 43.82 percent of the respondents have admitted for government support. This was followed by forming associations which accounted for 34.83 percent of the respondents. And the other response was that 21.34 percent of the respondents seek help from the NGOs.

An enquiry was also made from the respondents with regard to their position as women street vendors in the society in terms of recognition, importance and their social status. The response received against this was that 92.13 percent of the respondents have stated that they did not receive any such recognition and importance as women street vendors in the society as yet. And only 7.86 percent of the respondents have admitted that at times they do get such recognition, importance and social status as women street vendors.

Conclusion

To conclude, in the present micro-level study we have examined the socio-economic profile and the social life of the women street vendors in the city of Shillong. It is revealed from the study that many poor women have undertaken street vending to generate a source of income for their family which provides them the scope to sustain their life through small earnings. Thus, the women street vendors have plunged into this field of occupation as a push factor which is reflected in their poor socio-economic condition for choosing this particular work in the informal sector. As street vending provides livelihood and source of income to many poor women in the city, therefore the concerned city authorities should come forward for their protection and to promote self-compliance amongst women street vendors. At the same time government policies should be framed for women street vendors by identifying the importance of women participation in street vending.

References

- Adhikari, D., 2012, Income Generation in Informal Sector: A Study of the Street Vendors of Kathmandu Metropolitan City, Economic Journal of Development Issues, Volume 13.
- Amankwaa, E. F.., 2015, Women and Men at the Traffic Lights: The (re) Configuration and (re) Gendering of Street Water Vending I Ghana, Geo Journal, 82 (2).
- Bhowmik, Sharit, 2005, "Street Vendors in Asia: A Review", Economic and Political Weekly: May 28 –June 4.
- Bhattacharya, K. P. and De, P., 1987, Problems of Hawkers in Metropolitan Cities: Case Study of Calcutta, Occasional Paper – No. 20, Habitat Centre, Centre for Human Settlement, Calcutta.
- Bhowmik, Sharit, 1999, "Hawkers in the Urban Informal Sector: A Study of Street Vendors in Six Cities", National Alliance of Street Vendors of India, http.nasvi.net
- Chakraborty, P. and Koley, S., 2018, "Socio-Economic View on Street Vendors: A Study of a Daily Market at Jamshedpur", Journal of Advanced Research in Humanities and Social Science, Vol. 5, Issue 1.
- Chirisa, I. and Muchini, 2011, Youth, Unemployment and Peri-Urbanity in Zimbabwe: A Snapshot of Lessons from Hatcliffe, International Journal of Politics and Good Governance, 2 (2).
- Chingono, M., 2016, Women, The Informal Economy and the State in Lesotho, World Journal of Social Science Research, 3 (4).
- Dimas, Harlon, 2008, "Street Vendors: Urban Problem and Economic Potential", Working Papers in Economics and Development Studies, Department of Economics, Padjadjaran University.
- Dube, D. and Chirisa, I., 2012, The Informal City: Assessing its Scope, Variants and Direction in Harare, Zimbabwe, Volume (1).
- Hasan, M. and Alam, J., 2015, Street Garments Vendors' Contribution to the Economyand Local Community: An Empirical Study to the Street Garments Vendors in Dhaka City, Bangladesh, International Journal of Management and Business Research, 5 (2).
- Jumain, 1999, "Legal Status of Hawkers in India", Ahmedabad.
- Kumari, P., 2015, Issues and Challenges for Street Vendors in Delhi, University of Delhi, New Delhi.
- Mengistu, T. and Jibat, N., 2015, Street Vending as the Safety-Net for the Disadvantaged People: The Case of Jimma Town, International Journal of Sociology and Anthropology, 7 (5).
- Mkhize, S., Dube, G.and Skinner, C., 2013, Street Vendors in Durban, South Africa, Informal Economy Monitoring Study.
- McGree, T. C. and Yeung, 1977, "Hawkers in South – East Asian Cities: Planning for the Bazaar Economy", Ottawa, IDRC.
- Mazhambe, A., 2017, "Assessment of the contribution of Street Vending to the Zimbabwe Economy: A Case of Street Vendors in Harare CBD", IOSR Journal of Business and Management, Volume 19, Issue 9, Ver. 1, September.

- Nidan, 2010, "Study on Street Vendors at Patna (Bihar)", Centre for Civil Society (CCS), Study Report on Street Vendor, New Delhi.
- Njaya, T., 2015, Strategies for Daily Survival: The Role of Social Capital among Street Vendors of Harare Metropolitan, IOSR Journal of Humanities and Social Science, 20 (70).
- National Policy on Urban Street Vendors, 2006, (NPUSV).
- Ray, C. N. and Mishra, A., 2011, Vendors and Informal Sector : A Case Study of Street Vendors of Surat City, Working Paper – 15, Centre for Urban Equity, CEPT University, Ahmedabad.
- Roever, S., 2016, Informal Trade Meets Informal Governance: Street Vendors and Legal Reform in India, South Africa and Peru, Cityscape, 18 (1).
- Saha, Debdulal, 2011, "Working Life of Street Vendors in Mumbai", The Indian Journal of Labour Economics, Vol. 54, No.2.
- Tshuma, M. C. and Jari, B., 2013, The Informal Sector as a Source of Household Income.
- Wongtada, N., 2014, Street Vending Phenomena: A Literature Review and Research Agenda, Thunderbird International Business Review, 56 (1).

27

Study on the Migration of Tribal People and its Influence on the Education of their Children with Reference to Komuteri Village Tribes of Jamunamakarathoor Block, Tamil Nadu

— *A. Vasantha Jayaseelan*

Overview of the study

The study on the migration of tribal people and its influence on the education of their children are structured to make the people aware about the importance of education of their wards. Jamunamarathoor is a village panchayat which is located in the Thiruvannamalai district. It covers a small portion of Javadhu hills. The local tribes of Javadhu hills are called as 'Malayalee' meaning natives of the hill, the sources of income are from agriculture and honey extraction.

The researcher has adopted descriptive design for the study since the research on tribes is already witnessed by many researchers.

The sampling technique used by the researcher to extract data from the respondents is probability sampling- simple random sampling for the study. The tool applied to collect the data from the respondents is interview schedule since most of the respondents feel difficult to understand the questions. The main findings indicate that more than half (58 percent) of the respondents are female and (42 percent) of the respondents are male and regarding interest towards education, it is found that less than half (40 percent) of the respondent's interest towards education is excellent whereas (30 percent) of the respondents show moderate interest towards education and the left (30 percent) of the respondent's interest are poor towards education.

It is found that half (50 percent) of the respondents feel that their children have irregular attendance whereas less than half (30 percent) of the respondents feel that school dropout is prevalent among the children and (20 percent) of the respondents say that their children are losing interest in education because of migration.

Therefore from the finding the researcher comes to a conclusion that the children of the respondents have interest towards education but the temporary relocation influence their children to distract into various other activities. The researcher believes that next generation will prove that there will not be much gap between common people and tribes in terms of health, wealth, education and socio economic status.

Introduction

Tribes are an organisation among families (including clans and lineages), which generates a social and ideological basis for solidarity that is in some way more limited than that of an "ethnic group" or of a "nation".

Komuteri is one such small tribal community in Jamunamarathoor block which is located in the Thiruvannamalai district. It covers a small portion of Javadhu hills. Since it is a tribal zone, outsiders are not allowed to hold properties and that keeps the village away from commercial purposes. The local tribes of Javadhu hills are called as 'Malayalee' meaning natives of the hill. The sources of income are from agriculture and honey extraction, the native honey has its own taste and colour. Millets are the native crops which are largely cultivated by the tribes and this is because of climatic conditions and lack of water saving system in the hills.

Around 80 thousand people live in Javadhu block and out of which 98 percent of them are tribes and other 2 percent belongs to dalits and vanniyars. The native place is famous for sandalwood, teakwood and rosewood etc. the hill is around 2315 feet higher from the sea level. Elephants, forest buffalows, monkeys, foxes and deers are the native fauna present in the hills. There are 11 panchayats and 229 hamlets within the radius of 150 square kilometers.

It clearly indicates that people are not constantly yearning from agriculture for their livelihood and that is the reason the tribes move from one place to another to fulfill their basic needs, but on the other side the relocation creates negative impact in their education. As we all know the importance of education and the positive impact it createswith the life of an individual, a good education will always makes an individual to build his/her personality in a positive approach which in turn make them socially and economically fulfilled.

Research Methodology

AIM

To study the migration of tribal people and its influence on the education of their children with reference to Jamunamarathoor tribes.

Objectives

- To know about the demographic details of the respondents
- To identify the reasons for lack of education among the children
- To know about the influence of relocation on their children.

Research Design

The researcher has adopted descriptive design for the study since the research on tribes is already witnessed by many researchers. Therefore the researcher has planned to describe the influences of migration of tribes towards their wards.

Sampling

The researcher has used probability sampling- simple random sampling for the study.

Universe: The total population of the village is 450.

Sample size: The researcher collected data from 50 respondents using simple random sampling.

Tool used: The researcher used interview schedule to collect the data, since most of the tribes feel difficult to understand the questions and its inner sense.

Statement of the Problem

Jamunamarathoor block has one of the richest natural resources which are well preserved and protected by the local tribes (Malayalees). But the sad thing is that they do not have proper channels to store water and this makes the farmers to voluntarily leave the place for six months to look after their livelihood. The tribes of Jamunamarathoor are usually migrating to the nearby states like Andhra Pradesh, Kerala and Karnataka for cutting trees, construction works and chamber works. As per the income it is significantly higher than what they earn in their own place but the education of their children is never considered by them during the migration.

Need and Importance of the Study

The social development and economic status of the people are directly proportionate to education, but it is observed that education is not properly met by them. The education among the tribes and their wards are less than 30 percent which is the indicator that they lack education. It is noticed that government and many private organisations had studied the status of the tribes as a whole, but the researcher felt that this study on the education will focus on one particular village which will provide a wide understanding on various influences that stop the children from getting educated. Therefore the study on the migration of tribes and its influence on their children's education will ensure significant data for future references.

Limitations

- This study is limited to Komuteri village of Jamunamarathoor block
- This study is limited to tribes and not with other communities
- This study is limited only to the parents and not with their children.

Review of Literature

The Government of Tamil Nadu, forest department, expresses, the need of the hour of the tribal community is to break the gap between the tribal community and non-tribal community in the aspects of economic, educational and social status. The study says that out of 36 tribal communities 6 are identified as primitive tribes and it is noted that 50% of the communities come under integrated tribal development area but still government could not achieve the desired rate of development. Tamil Nadu Forest Department is successfully running 20 Tribal schools in Jawadis, Jamanamarathoor and Pollachi and have been able to attract tribal children due to the facilities offered in the school. Primary education to tribals in Jawadis where started by the Forest Department as early as 1951 at Jamanamarathoor and extended to other villages. With all these significant attempts children from village are lacking interest towards education and moreover the dropout ratio is gradually increasing among them.

Dr. K. Krithiga, in her thesis indicated that education is crucial to development as it provide the individual with adequate skill for participating in various economic activities. Education enables human beings to understand the interrelationship among the tangible phenomena surrounding them and give skill to translate the knowledge into action. Her research pointed out that 60 % of children shows positive sign towards education whereas 40% of the population turns to be negative attitude towards education.

S. Ramesh, Developmental issues in Jawadhu hills

Smoking and drinking is very common among youth. Even kids at the age of six starts smoking and they start consuming alcohol at twelve or fifteen years. This is of very serious concern. There are many widows in the villages, which can be seen as a result of these habits. A study has to be undertaken to know the health and social issues caused by smoking, drinking and dietary habits in their villages.

G.Anbuselvi, P. John Leeson, in their case study shared the education of tribal children in India. It says that the teachers appointed in the tribal school are from non-tribal community and which creates big gap between the languages. This creates lack of interest in attending classes on regular basis.

Mahalakshmi, government school teacher from Jamunamarathoor, while addressing to a news channel, expressed her challenges and difficulties in educating the tribal community children. She says that when she was appointed to the school in tribal area her first day experience seems to be misery, the children were not properly dressed and the class has the strength of 35 students out of which only 7 students were present on that day. This created her to come with alternative methods to handle children like going to their home and creating friendly relationship with the students, making ways to provide financial support to the family so that the parents can peacefully send their children to school. Thus, her attempt created positive impact towards education.

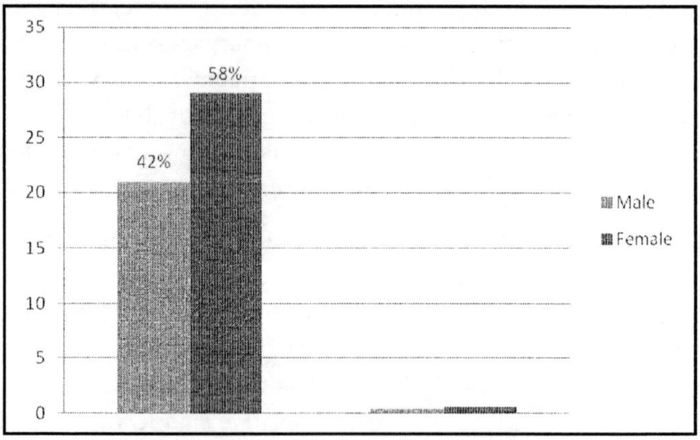

Figure 1: Gender of the Respondents.

Figure 1 represents the gender of the respondents. It is found that more than half (58 percent) of the respondents are female and (42 percent) of the respondents are male.

Table 1: Interest Towards Education of Tribal Children

Interest towards education of tribal children	*Respondents*	*Percentage*
Excellent	20	40%
Moderate	15	30%
Poor	15	30%
Total	50	100%

The Table 1 represents the interest of tribal children towards education. It is found that less than half (40 percent) of the respondent's interest towards education is excellent whereas (30 percent) of the respondents show moderate interest towards education and the left (30 percent) of the respondent's interest are poor towards education.

Table 2: Various Reasons for Children Dropout

Various reasons for children dropout	*Respondents*	*Percentage*
Financial crisis	18	36%
Child labour	8	16%
Migration	24	48%
Total	50	100%

Table 2 indicates the various reasons for children dropout. It is found that almost half (48 percent) of the respondents witness that children's dropout is because of migration and less than half (36 percent) of the respondents say that children's dropout is because of financial crisis and a meager (16 percent) of the respondents feel that dropout is because of child labour.

Figure 2: Gender Disparity in Education.

Figure 2 represents the gender disparity in education. It is found that more than half (56 percent) of the respondents believe that there is gender disparity in education whereas less than half (30 percent) of the respondents believe that there is no gender disparity in education and a meager (14 percent) of the respondents are not sure with both the cases.

Table 3: Reasons for Migration

Reasons for migration	***Respondents***	***Percentage***
Insufficient water for agriculture	36	72%
Income isinsufficient to run the family	10	20%
Forced migration	4	8%
Total	50	100%

Table 3 indicates the reasons for migration. It is found that a sizable majority (72 percent) of the respondents say that insufficient water for agriculture is the reason for relocation whereas (20 percent) of the respondents feel that income is insufficient to fulfill the basic needs and therefore they relocate. A meager (8 percent) of the respondents witness forced migration is the reason.

Figure 3: Influence of Migration in their Children Education.

Figure 2 represents the influence of migration in their children education. It is found that half (50 percent) of the respondents feel that their children have irregular attendance whereas less than half (30 percent) of the respondents feel that school dropout is prevalent among the children and (20 percent) of the respondents say that their children are losing interest in education because of migration.

Table 4: Other Influences of Migration

Other influences on migration	*Respondents*	*Percentage*
Child marriage	20	40%
Substance abuse	15	30%
Lack of family support	15	30%
Total	50	100%

Table 4 indicates the various other influences that arise because of migration. It is found that almost half (40 percent) of the respondents say that child marriage is found common among the tribes because of migration and less than half (30 percent) of the respondents say that substance abuse and lack of family support is found among the tribes because of migration.

Main Findings

- It is found that more than half (58 percent) of the respondents are female and (42 percent) of the respondents are male.
- It is found that less than half (40 percent) of the respondent's interest towards education is excellent whereas (30 percent) of the respondents show moderate interest towards education and the left (30 percent) of the respondent's interest are poor towards education.

- It is found that almost half (48 percent) of the respondents witness that children's dropout is because of migration and less than half (36 percent) of the respondents say that children's dropout is because of financial crisis and a meager (16 percent) of the respondents feel that dropout is because of child labour.
- It is found that more than half (56 percent) of the respondents believe that there is gender disparity in education whereas less than half (30 percent) of the respondents believe that there is no gender disparity in education and a meager (14 percent) of the respondents are not sure with both the cases.
- It is found that a sizable majority (72 percent) of the respondents say that insufficient water for agriculture is the reason for migration whereas (20 percent) of the respondents feel that income is insufficient to fulfill the basic needs and therefore they migrate. A meager (8 percent) of the respondents witness forced migration is the reason for migration.
- It is found that half (50 percent) of the respondents feel that their children have irregular attendance whereas less than half (30 percent) of the respondents feel that school dropout is prevalent among the children and (20 percent) of the respondents say that their children are losing interest in education because of migration.
- It is found that almost half (40 percent) of the respondents say that child marriage is found common among the tribes because of migration and less than half (30 percent) of the respondents say that substance abuse and lack of family support is found among the tribes because of migration.

Suggestions

- Jamunamarathoor is block is having few residential schools and very few non-governmental organisations run shelter homes, it is the duty of the parents to accommodate their wards to continue education.
- It is advised that parents should be given counselling on the importance of education and at least one should stay with their children for moral support.
- Government should increase the numbers of residential schools with better facilities.

- Teachers should given additional training to influence the students through activity based learning, skill lab sessions and practical exposure visits.

Conclusion

Tribal community acts as the hedges in protecting the natural resources; it is well observed that people are well attached with nature but when it comes to education their interest is not up to the mark. The tribes produce various reasons for lack of education among them but the main factor could be the migration of tribes on seasonal basis, which is witnessed in the study. As we all know education is the key to bring holistic development with the individuals, therefore with due social responsibility we should commit ourselves to create awareness with the community people, to increase the literary rate through skill development sessions and activity based learning. India is a secular country and we believe that everyone has equal rights towards law and let's not forget the tribal people who also the citizens of this country should enjoy all the rights like non-tribal people. The researcher believes that next generation will prove that there will not be much gap between common people and tribes in terms of health, wealth, education and socio-economic status.

References

https://www.forests.tn.gov.in/pages/view/Tribal_Development_on-going

http://shodh.inflibnet.ac.in:8080/jspui/bitstream/123456789/1049/1/synopsis.pdf

https://www.dhan.org/developmentmatters/2014/february/case4.php

https://www.researchgate.net/publication/313437127_Education_of_Tribal_Children_in_India_A_case_study

28

A Study on the Standard of Living of Resettled Bonded Labourers belonging to Irular Community at Palavakkam with Reference to Anna Nagar Hamlet, Chennai

—A. Mary Dayana

Introduction

In this jet-set age every country is competing to become scientifically advanced, economically superior and politically strong. India also has a dream to become superpower nation with its huge population, variety of culture, traditions, religions and many social issues. But the sad truth is still 21.9 percent of Indian does not have the basic living condition (Asian Development Bank). We have a number of legislation and policies to bridge this gap. It is going on as a never-ending process. During this development process, one of the majorly affected marginalised groups is tribal people. In ancient times tribal people were treated like any other community. But in later stage they were ill-treated. Their natural resources were looted in the name of development. Their traditional occupation is outdated and their livelihood is in great danger. They are forced to migrate leaving their ancestral land and occupation. Now-a-days many tribal people started contributing in almost all the fields. But still there are many tribals without proper identity and security. This study is focusing on the living condition of rescued and resettled bonded labourers working in brick chambers in Thiruvallur district, Tamil Nadu. These people are from a particular tribal community called 'Irular'.

About Irular

Tribal groups are homogeneous, culturally firm and they have their own lifestyle of live. According to 2011 Census, the population of Tamil Nadu is 72.1 million, in that 20.01 percent are Scheduled Tribal people. There 36 tribal groups in Tamil Nadu, among which six tribal communities are primitive tribal groups. Irulas are one among them. They are one of the second largest groups of tribes in Tamil Nadu. The word '*Irul*' means dark. They are called by this name because of their dark skin or because they perform their important rituals during night. The other opinion of the name is that 'Irular' means 'one who digs tubers'. Irular are good at honey harvest, preparation of ayurvedic medicines, cattle farming and agriculture.

Bonded Labourer

"Bonded labourer" means a labourer who incurs, or has, or is presumed to have, incurred, a bonded debt.

Bonded Labour System

The system of forced, or partly forced, labour under which a debtor enters, or has, or is presumed to have, entered, into an agreement with the creditor.

Standard of Living

A standard of living is the level of wealth, comfort, material goods, and necessities available to a certain socioeconomic class or a certain geographic area. The standard of living includes basic material factors such as income, gross domestic product (GDP), life expectancy, and economic opportunity. The standard of living is closely related to quality of life.

Research Methodology

AIM

To study the standard of living of resettled bonded labours of Irular community at Palavakkam with reference to Anna Nagar hamlet, Thiruvallur district. Tamil Nadu.

Objective

- To study the socio-demographic details of the community.
- To analyze the resources available in the resettlement area.
- To analyze the living condition of the respondents.

Research Design

The researcher has adopted descriptive design for the study. This helps to explore all the dimensions of the study topic.

Sampling

The researcher has used probability sampling- simple random sampling for the study.

Universe: The total population of the village is 250.

Sample size: The researcher collected data from 50 respondents using simple random sampling.

Tool used: Most of the respondent lack reading skill, so the researcher used interview schedule to collect the data.

Scope of the study

There is an unproportionate development happening worldwide in terms of globalisation and industrialisation. Marginalised people are the victims of this process. Especially tribal people have lost their land, indigenous culture and occupation. Due to their poor economic condition, they are forced to migrate and become bonded labours. There are many such bonded labourers in Thiruvallur district, Tamil Nadu. These people are employed in rice mills, brick chambers and other industries in the outskirts of Chennai. Nongovernmental organisations and the revenue department now and then make inspection and rescue those bonded labourers. Those rescued people are given rehabilitation. Anna Nagar hamlet in Thiruvallur district is one among those resettlement areas. This study explores the current living condition of the rescued bonded labourers in the Anna Nagar hamlet. This study will help to analyse the impact of rehabilitation and recommend the areas of improvement for future intervention.

Limitation

- This study is limited to Anna Nagar hamlet in Thiruvallur District.

Review of Literature

Standard of living in India is different from one state to another. There is a huge disparity. According to 61 round of **National Sample Survey (NSS)** there are 21.9% of the Indian population is living below poverty line. 55% of the population don't have toilet and 49% of the household have to travel minimum 30 minutes to get water. This disparity leads to human exploitation.

K. Gnanamoorthy, Research Scholar, Department of Economics, Presidency College, Chennai, in his study expresses that due to lack of rain and other factors people in rural area are facing economic crisis. And they started migrating for livelihood. Living on subsistence wages many are not able to afford even minimal fee for their children's education. Their traditional occupation also becomes outdated so they are forced to give up on it and choose some other means of living. Thus, they end up in low paid jobs. Due to their poverty they become prey to the money-minded owners. This is how they become bonded labours. In and around Thiruvallur district there are many rice mills and brick chambers has this bonded labour system. These labourers are brought from Odisha and other parts of Tamil Nadu. One such victim group is Irulas.

A report on **India together** states that on 2004 six hundred families were rescued from Thiruvallur district. They were given 2 cents of land in 'Natham porambokku' by the revenue department. 'Natham porambokku' is communal land that the government owns. Few families are also given help to construct houses under the Indira Awas Yojana. These people also try to get help from Tamil Nadu Adi Dravida and tribal welfare for the employment. One such resettlement hamlet is Anna Nagar, near Palavakkam village in Thiruvallur district.

Barathi Trust the Non-governmental organisation which works for bonded labourers in 5 districts. It has mentioned in the proposal that these hamlets lack basic living condition. These people are not aware about their basic right which make them to be left out from the main stream of society. They need schools and employability skills that will at least help them to protect themselves from further exploitations.

Table 1: Gender of the Respondents

Gender	*Respondents*	*Percentage*
Male	10	20%
Female	40	80%
Total	50	100%

The table shows that majority of the respondents are female and 20 percent of the respondents are male.

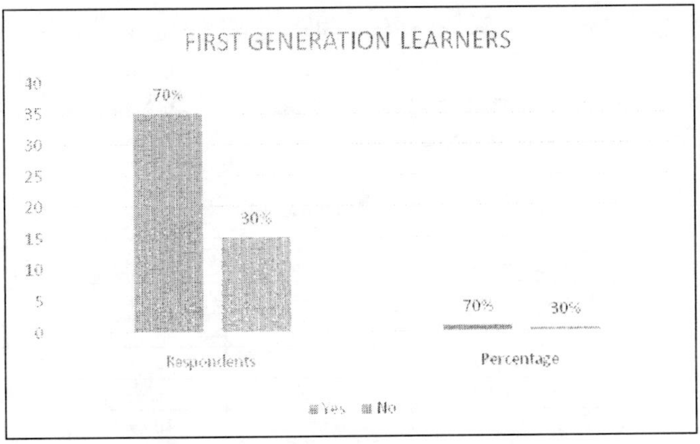

Figure 1: First Generation Learners.

Figure 1 two represents the first-generation learners. Majority of the respondents i.e. 70% of the respondents are first-generation learners and the other 30 percent of the respondents say that some from their family had access to education previously.

Table 2: Education Level of the Respondents

Education level	*Respondents*	*Percentage*
Primary	14	28%
High school	15	30%
Higher secondary	9	18%
No literacy	12	24%
Total	50	100%

The above table represents the educational level of the respondents. It is found that 28 % of the respondents had gone to the primary schooling. 30 percent of the respondents went up to high school and 18 % of the respondents studied till higher secondary school. 24 percent of the respondents are illiterate.

Table 3: Age of the Marriage

Age of the marriage	*Respondents*	*Percentage*
12-15	18	36%
16-20	24	48%
21-25	8	16%
Above 25	0	0
Total	50	100%

This table represents the respondents age of marriage. 48 percent of the respondents married between the age of 16-20. 36% percent of the respondents got married between the age of 12-15 and 16 % of the employees married between 21-25.

Table 4: Annual Income of the Family

Annual income	*Respondents*	*Percentage*
Less than 50000	43	86%
Less than 100000	6	12%
Less than 200000	1	2%
More than 200000	0	0%
Total	50	100%

The above table depicts the annual income of the respondents. 86 % of the respondents say that their annual income is less than 50000 rupees. 12 % of the respondents are earning 50000-1 lakh rupees per annum. Only 2 percent of the respondents are earning between 1 lakh to 2 lakh per annum. And no respondents earn more than two lakhs per annum.

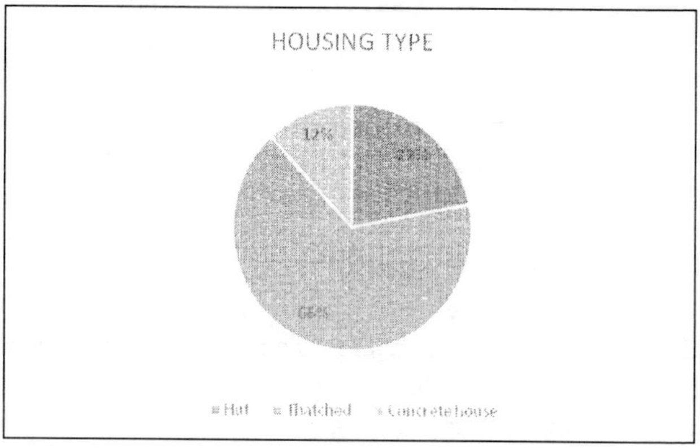

Figure 2: Housing Type of the Respondents.

The above figure shows the housing type of the respondents. 22 percent of the respondents live in hut type of houses. 66 % of the respondents are residing in thatched housing type and twelve percent of the respondents are living in concrete houses.

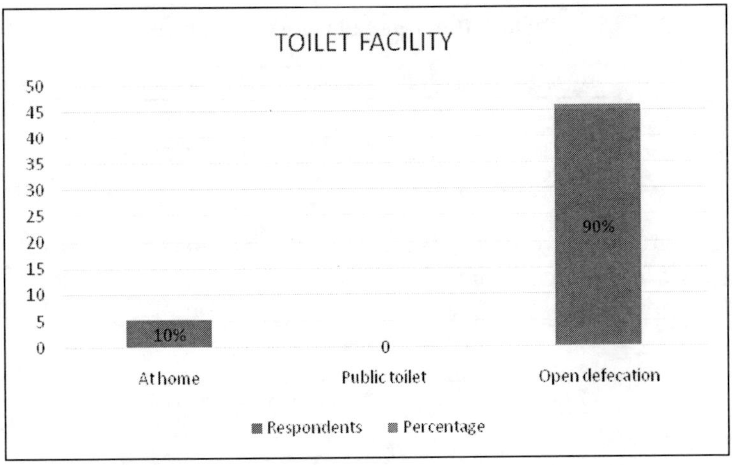

Figure 3: Toilet Facility.

The above figure shows that 90 percent of the respondent don't have toilets and the remaining 10 percent have it in their home.

Table 5: Mode of Transport of their Spouse

Mode of transport	*Respondents*	*Percentage*
Bi-cycle	10	20%
Scooter/bike	18	36%
Local transport	22	44%
Total	50	100%

Table 5 represents the mode of transportation of the respondents. Forty-four percent of the respondents use local transport and another 36% of the respondents use two wheelers. 10% percent of the respondents use bicycle for their transportation.

Table 6: Electricity Service

Electricity	*Respondents*	*Percentage*
Yes	50	100%
No	0	0
Total	50	100%

The above table shows that all the respondents houses have electricity connection.

Table 7: Drainage and Garbage Facilities

Drainage and garbage	*Respondents*	*Percentage*
Yes	0	0
No	50	100%
Total	50	100%

From the above table it is clear that there is no drainage or garbage disposal facility in the community.

Table 8: Gas Stove Facility

Gas stove	*Respondents*	*Percentage*
Yes	22	44%
No	28	56%
Total	50	100%

The above table shows that 44% percent of the respondents cook in the gas stove and 56% of the respondents use other means of cooking.

Main Findings

- Majority of the respondents i.e. 70% of the respondents are first-generation learners.
- 24 percent of the respondents are illiterate.
- 86 % of the respondents' annual income is less than 50000 rupees.
- 22 percent of the respondents live in hut type of houses. 66 % of the respondents are residing in thatched housing type.
- Forty four percent of the respondents use local transport.
- All the respondent's houses have electricity connection.
- There is no drainage or garbage disposal facility in the community.
- 56% of the respondents use fire wood and cow dung for cooking.
- 90 percent of the respondent don't have toilet and they go for open defecation.

Suggestions

- The government body should take necessary measures to construct the drainage system and remove the garbage periodically.
- Government and non-governmental agencies should do intervention to increase the literacy rate in the community.

- Encouraging the non-governmental organisations to take up as many as employability skill development programmes.

Conclusion

Indian economy growth is not even for different social groups and regions. Industrialisation, urbanisation and globalisation are aimed for development. But sadly, they concentrate only on the cities. That even more contributed to the disparity. Because 75% of the poor people are living in the rural area. Each and every individual in the rural area also should get access to healthcare, nutritious food, education, employment and welfare schemes of the government. There should be proper sanitation, clean drinking water and proper housing. Then the 'development of a nation' really has a meaning.

References

https://www.investopedia.com/terms/s/standard-of-living.asp

http://indiatogether.org/irulas-society

https://shodhganga.inflibnet.ac.in/bitstream/10603/815/14/14_chapter%207.pdf

Naganna, A. and Uma Mohan, C.H., Tribal development programmes and social transformation, Discovery Publishing House Pvt. Ltd., New Delhi.

29

Effect of Migration on Living Standards of Marginalised Communities of Murkula Basthi Hyderabad, Telangana

— Sr. Velangini Kumari, Dr. R. Komala

Introduction

This paper examined the effects of Migration on Living standards of rural to urban areas from neighbouring states of Telangana to Murukula Basthi near Nacharam, Hyderabad, Telangana. The study is taken up by the faculty and students of St. Pious X Degree and PG College for Women, Hyderabad. Data was obtained using mixed methods approach comprising questionnaire surveys and key informative interviews. This area is selected based on population size and location advantage of the institution. Seventy households were sampled for the study out of one hundred and sixty migrant families. The study focused on their livelihood, shelter, sanitary facilities, drinking water, electricity, healthcare and education.

Reasons for Migration

Rural-urban migration results from the search for perceived or real opportunities as a consequence of rural-urban inequality in wealth. The main reasons for migration are due to overwhelming concentration of wealth, assets, purchasing capacity, economic activities, and variety of services in the urban centres as well as the continued neglect and degradation of rural environments or areas. Most of the migrants of the slum area Murukula Basthi are from drought struck areas of Andhra Pradesh, Karnataka and Telangana. The only purpose of the migration was to get a livelihood around the year. These migrants own nothing in their native places. Most of them are labourers who worked for daily wages in their villages. Due to drought, they lost their livelihood and as there was no other alternative for the survival of their families migrated to **slums** of Hyderabad city in search of work.

Living Standards of Migrants at Murkula Basthi (Slum)

Slum is a place where migrants settle and are informal areas gradually improved, formalised and incorporated into the city itself, through extending land, services and citizenship to slum dwellers. The living standards of the slum dwellers are very poor. They are often overcrowded, with many people crammed into very small living spaces.

These migrants lack basic municipal services such as water, sanitation, waste collection, storm drainage, street lighting, paved sidewalks and roads for emergency access. They do not have easy access to schools, hospitals or public places for the community to gather. Many slums have been under-service and unrecognised for long periods, over 20 years in some areas.

Like all informal settlements, housing in slums is built on land that the occupant does not have a legal claim to and without any urban planning or adherence to zoning regulations. In addition, slums are often areas where many social indicators are on a downward slide; for example, crime and unemployment are on the rise.

All slums are not the same, and some provide better living conditions than others. Likewise, slum dwellers are not a homogeneous population, but a diverse group of people with different interests, means and backgrounds.

Following are the observations made after the survey on migrants of Murukula Basthi:

Identity Crisis: After migration they lose their native identity and try to establish themselves in urban areas. Their language, customs and traditions are affected due to migration.

Insecurity: Most of the migrants live in insecurity because of their non-inclusiveness in various activities of the society.

Education Background of Migrants: 50% of the rural migrants are illiterates and work as labour in nearby industries. Their children are first generation schooling kids.

Wages of the Migrants: The monthly income is ranging from Rs10,000 to Rs 15,000 per family. Most of the migrants are working as labour force for daily wages.

Basic Amenities: The Migrants have poor availability of basic needs. They don't get timely medical care. They don't have permanent houses. They don't have power and personal sanitation.

Socio Economic Standards: Due to illiteracy and lack of skills the socio-economic standards are very low.

Gender Inequality: Men and women are not paid equal wages for the same amount of work.

Education: Children from slum areas do not have proper facilities to get educated and most of them turn into child labour due to financial crisis.

Societal Status: The communities of Murukula Basthi are confined to the lower or peripheral edge of the society. They are denied from involvement in mainstream economic, political, cultural and social activities due to their living conditions and lifestyles.

References

Deepak, K. Mishra (Ed.): Internal Migration in Contemporary India, Sage Publications, New Delhi, 2016, 343 pp, 995 (Hardback: alk. paper), ISBN: 978-93-515-0857-1

https://en.wikipedia.org/wiki/Human_migration

https://en.wikipedia.org/wiki/Social_exclusion

30

The Plight of Women Domestic Workers in Urban India

— *Dr. Aarthi Deepak*

Introduction

Globalisation is a process of growing interdependence between people of all nations. It is an important term in 21st century. The term 'Globalisation' acquired a lot of considerable forces during the 1990s.

In India, globalisation is a process that encompasses the causes, courses, and consequences of transnational and transcultural integration of human. India currently accounts for 2.7% of world trade (as of 2015), up from 1.2% in 2006 according to the World Trade Organisation (WTO).

Migrants

The term migration means people moving from one place to another place in search of food, clothing and shelter, health and also for other specific purpose such as employment and education in their lives.

For a large country like India, the study of movement of population in different parts of the country helps in understanding the dynamics of the society better. At this point of time in the economic development in the country, especially when many states are undergoing faster economic transition, particularly in areas such as manufacturing, information technology or service sectors, data migration profile of population has become more important.

History of Globalisation of Migration in India

Migration has been a historical process shaping human history, economy and culture. Migration has globalised from a destination country perspective, but hardly from an origin country perspective, with migrants from an increasingly diverse countries concentrating in a shrinking pool of prime destination. The global migration map has thus become more skewed.

India has a long history of migration which has shaped its social history, culture and pattern of development. In pre-colonial times the reasons for the circulation of populations were mainly for religious and trade purposes. Migration on account of military movements also played an important role. People also travelled in search of pastures with their cattle. Nomadic migration even for short distances was an important feature outside the Gangetic valley. This practice is still found in some parts of Rajasthan and Madhya Pradesh located in central India and is one of the earliest forms of circulation in the history of human migration (Hutton, 1986: 61).

According to UNHCR (United Nations High Commission for Refugees it is estimated that 20 million of Hindus, Sikhs and Muslims were displaced during the partition of India in year 1947, the largest mass migration in human history. Apart from India the other largest documented voluntary migration in history was the Italian diaspora, which migrated from Italy between 1861 and 1970, with 13 million people leaving the country. Rural Urban Migration in India has re-emerged as a strong force shaping its cities and urbanisation since the time of industrial revolution in western countries. It had a greater impact in the Indian urbanisation since 19th century and is closely associated with urban transition influencing the demand and supply of labour, economic growth and human wellbeing.

Migrants enjoy certain unique socio-economic and cultural characteristics which differentiate the individual from the local people of the place of destination. Moreover, migrants occupies the position of marginal man by sharing the subsystems of both native village and present city respectively called as Donor sub-system and Recipient sub-system.

Migrating from one state to other state at the beginning these people have to face some obstacles to settle in that particular area as they are not the local people of that region. They have to grow to that culture, ethnic, traditions, linguistics and other habits to make their life better with patience and perseverance.

Thus, migrants by nature had to be adaptative to any vulnerable situations, and it is these unique qualities which make human beings to survive themselves. In addition to this they have to shoulder challenges that they may come across in their livelihood and need to bring out the best prospects in their life.

Objectives

(i) To explicate the main patterns and reasons behind Migrations from Rural to Urban areas.

(ii) To understand the Social Structure of Migrants.

(iii) To understand the Problems and Challenges.

(iv) To suggest policy measures for better living conditions.

Rural and Urban Migration in India

The Indian urban and rural life is viewed as the two faces of the same coin. They are mutually interdependent, and both have a great impact on globalisation.

Every minute, 25-30 people are migrating to Indian cities from rural areas in search of better livelihood and lifestyles. If the pace of migration from rural areas to urban centres continues Indian urban population is likely to reach 600 million by 2030.

Migrants' Social Structure

It is divided into three segments:

- Family and kinship,
- Marriage,
- Social Class.

Types of Migration

Basically there are two types of Migrants:

- **Internal migration.** This refers to a change of residence within national boundaries, such as between states, provinces, cities, or municipalities.
- **International migration.** This refers to change of residence over national boundaries.

Drivers of Migration

- Migrations due to Internal conflicts
- Human Security

- Income Inequalities
- Religious persecution
- Better prospects for future
- Education
- Aiming for better job opportunities
- Displaced population
- Natural calamities
- War

Characteristics of Migrants

Migration is also characterised by enormous economic and social diversity spanning socioeconomic variables such as caste, landholding size, age, sex, education, family size and composition, activity, consumption levels and more.

Socio-Cultural Impact of Migrants in Indian Society

- Indian society and culture has seen a drastic change in human behaviour.
- We are marching towards the changing pattern of living conditions which are easy to adapt.
- India has come long way in transformation of its culture from ancient to modern.
- There has been a lot of societal impact such as changing traditions and culture.
- The increasing migration coupled with financial independence has led to the breaking of joint families into nuclear ones.
- People in rural and urban area are also able to access education in any field of their choice.
- It has been estimated that by 2050 more than 50% of India's population will live in cities.

Migration and Urbanisation

Urbanisation has been a major driver of internal migration. Rates of urbanisation influence Rural- Urban wage differences. An increase in the demand for labour in urban areas can attract urban wages and increase migration.

The pull factors of better job facilities, good salary, and more income, medical and educational facilities are attracting the rural people to move to the cities.

The push factors of no job facilities, low salary, less income, drought, less medical and education facilities compel people towards cities.

Marriage: Marriage is a very important social factor of migration. Every girl has to migrate to her in-law's place of residence. Thus, the entire female population of India has to migrate over short or long distance. About 49% of people shifted their residence after marriage in 2011. Urban growth in towns and cities are expanding, covering a greater area of land. Urbanisation is an increasing proportion of people living in towns and Mega cities and those, over 10 million people are also enhancing.

Push-pull Factors

Expectation of Migrants

One-third of the total India's population are migrants. Half of this population has migrated from rural areas to cities in search of work. In addition to better prospects of life in general the following emerges as their expectations.

- Approach for better protection of rights of workers that defines the roles and responsibilities of the state, employers, workers/

trade unions/civil society organisations and emphasises the use of social dialogue and collective bargaining for promoting the rights of migrant workers.

- Ensuring access and portability of social security schemes, for example, access to public distribution network/ subsidised ration in destination areas.
- Providing identity documents to migrants, which enables them to open bank accounts and enrol for welfare schemes as they can avail the benefits for their better condition of living.
- Strengthening and setting up district facilitation centres, migrant information centres and gender resource centres.
- Strengthening the role of vigilance committees to guard against bonded labour and child labour.
- Educate migrants for their regional identities.
- Registering workers by organising enrolment camps.
- Promote education and provide health services.
- Providing skills training in particular for adolescents and young workers.
- Establishing a universal helpline for migrant workers and
- Special provision for women migrants.

Factors of Globalisation on Migrants

- Technology,
- LPG reforms,
- Faster transportation,
- Improved mobility of capital,
- Rise of multinational corporations,
- Operating in different geographies have led to diffusion of best practices.

By these factors it has helped the economic liberalisation and globalisation of the country and have facilitated India to become a benchmark in a **"Global Village".**

National Government Schemes

The Ministry of Rural Development are implementing several programmes as given below:

- Mahatma Gandhi National Rural Employment Guarantee Scheme (MGNREGS),

- National Rural Drinking Water Programme (NRDWP),
- National Rural Livelihood Mission (NRLM),
- Pradhan Mantri Awaas Yojana – Gramin (PMAY-G),
- Pradhan Mantri Gram Sadak Yojana (PMGSY),
- Shyama Prasad Mukherjee National RuRBAN,
- Integrated Watershed Management Programme (IWMP),
- Swachha Bharat Mission (SBM).

National Schemes for Women and Child Development

The Ministry of Women and Child Development is implementing various schemes/programmes for empowerment of women and development of children across the country.

- Beti Bachao Beti Padhao (BBBP),
- Pradhan Mantri Matru Vandana Yojana (PMMVY),
- Pradhan Mantri Mahila Shakti Kendra Scheme
- Rastriya Mahila Kosh (RMK),
- Integrated Child Development Services (ICDS),
- Integrated Child Protection Scheme (ICPS),
- National Nutrition Mission (NNM).

These programmes were necessary for the development of the rural and urban areas of the country, but all are not sufficient to stop rural-urban migration. The Provision of Urban Amenities in Rural Areas (PURA) is one of the five major components of late President Dr. A. P. J. Abdul Kalam's dream vision 2020 for a developed India.

The PURA refers from the conventional ideas of economic development of rural areas in different ways. It aims at a comprehensive development of rural areas to generate urban level income and not mere poverty mitigation to curtail rural urban migration.

Impact of FDI (Foreign Direct Investment)

The origin of FDI has its impact since the colonial era in 17th century. The invasion of East India Company in Indian subcontinent through the gate way of trade "Surat" Guajrat on August 24, 1608 AD for the purpose of trade and we have the subsequent history for which we had to pay for the foreign occupation through a long fight for Independence.

The British brought on the Industrial revolution to India which led to development of transportation (Railways and Roadways) and communication systems albeit for their benefits. The new innovations and inventions happening around the European countries got introduced to the Indian subcontinent too.

Later in 20th Century FDI was introduced in the year 1991 under Foreign Exchange Management Act (FEMA), by then finance minister Dr. Manmohan Singh. India is considered as second important destination for foreign investment. The major sectors that attracted FDI are services, telecommunication, construction activities and computer software and hardware.

FDI plays an important role in the economic development of a country. The capital inflow of foreign investors.

- Allows strengthening
- Infrastructure, Increasing productivity
- Creating Employment Opportunities in India
- It has promoted Trade Agreements
- Development of Human Capital Resources.

Rural-urban Migrant Hub

Ahmedabad, which is the seventh-largest metropolitan area in India with a population of over 6 million is an important economic and industrial hub. There are approximately 1.3 to 1.7 million migrants labour in the city. They come from all directions in north, west and eastern India. Over the years they have come to be identified with specific sectors:

- Tribal migrants from Madhya Pradesh and Rajasthan from the construction workforce.
- Seasonal migrants from Bihar are head-loaders and cart pushers.
- Migrants from Uttar Pradesh dominate as factory workers and drivers.
- Oriyas are mostly associated with plumbing work, and the diamond cutting industry is made up of people from Saurashtra.

A large majority of them hail from historically marginalised groups such as the Scheduled Case and Scheduled Tribes, which adds an additional layer of vulnerability to their urban experiences. These seasonal migrant workers have carved spaces for themselves in the most inhospitable places in Ahmedabad. The choices are varied: rented rooms, open spaces, slums, pavements, worksites, etc. While the rented rooms are severely congested, open spaces are insecure arrangements exposed to the public gaze and eviction drives by the Ahmedabad Municipal Corporation. The most vulnerable of these are the seasonal migrant workers who live on the worksites themselves – while it helps them save money, it also makes them available for work 24 hours a day.

A migration from different parts of the country to the city of Ahmedabad has formed numerous channels of exploitation. Recruited from villages through an elaborate network of contractors, migrant workers end up being a vulnerable workforce that can be subjugated and disciplined easily. The system has become so openly abusive and brutal that migrants find it easier to find work in other states rather than in their own. The contract labour system and a loose monitoring and regulating state apparatus has only helped strengthen these unfair models and practices in the migrant job market.

Case Studies of Migrants in Hyderabad

Below are the case studies which are taken from internet:

1. **Sultan Sahi:** Located near the Old City in Hyderabad, Sultan Sahi has a mix of migrants from all over India but mostly coming from the states of Uttar Pradesh, Bihar and West Bengal. The majority of the migrants in this location are engaged in traditional family occupations like footwear making, zardozi, embroidery, thread work, bangle making etc.
2. **Sayed Nagar:** Sayed Nagar, located near Banjara Hills, has a sizeable population of migrants mainly from Odisha, Uttar Pradesh, Bihar and Maharashtra. The migrants are engaged in various livelihoods in the informal sector as carpenters, plumbers, hotel boys, false ceiling workers, daily wage labourers, construction workers etc.
3. **Nallakunta:** Nallakunta is located near Vidyanagar in the eastern part of Hyderabad. The group of migrants in Nallakunta came from Lucknow and was engaged in zardozi work, for a limited duration every year. They would come to Hyderabad during the lean season in Lucknow when orders for chikan embroidery would thin out.
4. **Ferozeguda, Gandhinagar and Balanagar:** These areas are adjacent to each other and are situated in close proximity to the Cantonment area in Secunderabad. The migrant communities in

these areas mostly came from Odisha who are engaged in diverse occupations.

So the problems of the above migrants in Hyderabad are as follows:

- No fixed wages,
- No fixed working hours,
- No pay no work,
- Poor housing, sanitation, drinking water.

And their income is perhaps just adequate to their daily living which may not be beneficial to their health. They have to visit only government hospitals situated at different locations for which time and effort is needed. They may also face language difficulties as in Hyderabad Telugu is the main spoken language.

In spite of so many obstacles they look and hope for migrating in better cities.

Facts and Figures

- The Constitution of India (Article 19) gives the right to all citizens "to move freely throughout the territory of India and to reside and settle in any part of the territory of India.
- As per Census 2011, 45 million Indians moved outside their district of birth for economic opportunities (be it employment or business).
- In India, internal migration (fuelled by an increasing rate of urbanisation and rural-urban wage difference) is far greater than an external migration.
- India's urban population is expected to grow from 410 million in 2014 to 814 million by 2050. Instead of long-term migration, there is a huge flow of short-term migrants in the country.

Conclusion

Migration from rural to urban in intra state is been increasing slowly with industrialisation and modernisation in India. Rapid urbanisation is essential to sustain India's impressive 10-year growth trajectory and meet Prime Minister Narendra Modi's economic target of $5 trillion by 2025. The proposed network of small towns and industry clusters can become India's engine of growth and provide jobs at scale, thus improving overall economic prosperity. Sustainable urbanisation can be the force multiplier to mobilise India's potential.

References

https://www.drishtiias.com/to-the-points/paper1/human-migration-in-india

http://www.iesd.org.in/jesd/Journal%20pdf/2012-VIII-1%20Giribabu%20M..pdf

https://www.iom.int/sites/default/files/our_work/ICP/MPR/WMR-2015-Background-Paper-RBhagat.pdf

https://pib.gov.in/newsite/PrintRelease.aspx?relid=175325

https://rural.nic.in/press-release/status-rural-development-schemes-2

https://yourstory.com/2019/08/urban-development-india-growth-narendra-modi

http://censusindia.gov.in/Census_And_You/migrations.aspx

https://www.slideshare.net/geoslades/rural-to-urban-migration-in-india

https://is.mendelu.cz/eknihovna/opory/zobraz_cast.pl?cast=66570;fit_w=1

https://www.researchgate.net/publication/26498168_Globalisation_Migration_and_Development

https://shodhganga.inflibnet.ac.in/bitstream/10603/170915/1/thesis.pdf

Migration in India: Causes and consequences ISSN: 2455-6157; Impact Factor: RJIF 5. 12

http://www.shram.org/uploadFiles/20150417051128.pdf

https://shodhganga.inflibnet.ac.in/bitstream/10603/29746/7/07_chapter-i.pdf

https://www.civilsdaily.com/question/the-indian-urban-and-rural-life-is-viewed-as-the-two-faces-of-the-same-coin-they-are-mutually-interdependent-and-both-have-a-greater-impact-of-globalisation-in-the-light-of-the-giv/

31

Globalisation and Cultural Isolation

— ***Bushera Fatema***

Introduction

"For the first time in Human evolution, the individual life is long enough, and the cultural transformation swift enough, that the individual mind is now a consistent player in the global transformation of human culture" – by William Irwin Thompson.

The term globalisation based on culture view, is the process of transmission of ideas, meanings, values and cultures around the world in such a way as to extend and intensify social relations. Also, in general terms, globalisation can be defined as the spreading of political, economical and cultural phenomena across political and geographical boundaries. It involved the greater mobility of people and capital.

The Indian culture has absorbed and amalgamated many different customs and ideas throughout its long history which has led to a rich tradition and folk culture.

Social Customs & Protocol

Naming conventions

Meeting & Greeting

Communication style

Personal Space

Gift Giving

Visiting a home

Taboos, some basic etiquettes and moral values.

Overview

- Cultural identity is established on the core values shared on a living society. These values include language, dressing style, way of talking, habits and many others.
- **21st Century.** A century of globalisation where all the societies with different culture live together. Mostly, Western civilisation is sweeping away the traditions and culture of the society, affecting changes in the behaviour and thinking of people of different society. It is understood that a culture loss seems too apparent in some communities where the main culture is weak. Many think that if this trend keeps going on, the global diversity of culture identity will be lost forever. Societies think globalisation is a big threat as the young generation is sweeping away with different cultures mostly adapting the culture of western style, which unfortunately worry the societies as they think it will affect their culture and also won't take time is the disappearance of their cultures and values they follow.
- But, this can't be true all the time. There are some positive influence on people or society because of globalisation. Globalisation is also a way to learn and explore the culture difference and so much more. Globalisation gives us a chance to represent our culture in front of the whole world and give all different societies a chance to explore our culture. Nowadays different people from different society lives together in different culture society, so by seeing the surrounding culture shown by that society it gives a chance for the migrants to adapt and adjust with their culture and values as they can learn and explore that they are seeing in their surroundings.
- Cultures are the core values that cannot be disappeared just because of globalisation. Globalisation is system that helps us learn and explore different society culture by not forgetting our own culture because the mainstream of any culture of any society is not weak that it can be affected by any globalisation. But we can't say there is no effect on cultures but, they won't change the rituals and values of a culture of certain community or society.
- Educational institutes in Sharjah like Skyline University College, one of the accredited universities in UAE, has a multicultural environment that houses more than 70 nationalities. Despite the differences in language and culture, my university always come

up with initiatives that cater to all nationalities. It creates an atmosphere that accepts and respects different cultures. Skyline, being one of the best universities in UAE, prove that globalisation and culture differences are not a hindrance to creating a community where people from all corners of the world can co-exist harmoniously.

Effect of Globalisation on Language and Culture

- Language is intrinsic to the expression of culture. As a means of communicating values, beliefs and customs, it has an important social function and fosters feelings of group identity and solidarity. It is the means by which culture and its traditions and shared values may be conveyed and preserved.
- **Language:** One-way globalisation effects language is by spreading language globally, when one language is considered a dominant language, it tends to over shadow the native language. For example, English language came into culture and threaten to eliminate the native language of the indigenous people. Why it tends to happen that way is because, English language is used globally in doing businesses, media and internet. Its and international language and it has dominant factors.
- As the world becomes more connected, language diversity is plummeting at an unprecedented rate. 40% of the world's 7000 languages at risk of disappearing, according to estimates by the endangered languages project. That trend is linked to economic globalisation.
- People learn English language rapidly because in doing international businesses, English language is most highly preferred, so every culture try to learn English and put little effort in learning their local or native language. As the dominant language is being spread, also the dominant culture is spread too.
- The world languages are fast disappearing and the dominate ones are rampant across the globe. People want to speak English and other dominating languages in order to participate in the global activities.
- Globalisation has allowed languages and their cultures to spread and dominate rapidly on global scale, and it has led to extinction of other languages and culture putting them in endanger.

- Things have deteriorated considerably since Dr Johnson's time. Linguists estimate that by the end of the 21st century, over half of the world's languages will have been lost. Many of them will be dead without yielding the linguistic secrets they may hold.
- Linguists are understandably concerned that such a valuable part of human culture should disappear without a trace. Scholars have published an Atlas of the World's Languages in Danger of Disappearing.
- According to the 1961 census, India had 1,100 "living languages", but there has been a steady decline in their number since then. And in their study titled People's Linguistic Survey of India, the Bhasha Research and Publication Centre at Vadodara in Gujarat, India, revealed that the last 56 years have seen the death of 250 languages.
- More unnerving is that the study foresees the demise of another 400 languages in the next 50 years. For example, in spite of many people speaking Gondi – the language of the Gonds in Madhya Pradesh, Gujarat, Telangana, Maharashtra, Chhattisgarh and Andhra Pradesh – it is in the "vulnerable" category in UNESCO's Languages in Danger.
- The UNESCO list has also described Manipuri (Meitei), the Karbi language of Assam, and the Khasis in Meghalaya as endangered languages. And there are many other languages that are spoken by less than 10,000 people in Arunachal Pradesh.
- In the Andaman and Nicobar Islands, Onge is spoken by almost 100 people and Shompen by around 200. The risk of language extinction is high. Most of the tribal languages are in danger, while certain languages such as Pali and Ahom have already become extinct.
- The phenomenon is not uniquely Indian. Around the world, languages die at the rate of one every few weeks. The distressing feature is particularly evident in America and Australia, where hundreds of aboriginal languages are extinct. Many more are on the decline in Asia and Africa.
- In Europe, many languages are in danger, the main reason being the pressure from dominant languages – English, French, German, Russian, Spanish and mainstream Chinese.
- Researchers have mapped the hotspots from where languages are disappearing most rapidly – eastern Siberia, northern Australia,

central South America, south-west United States and the US-Pacific Northwest etc.

- Linguistic experts estimate that 96% of the world's languages are spoken by four percent of the world's population. At least 80% of the African languages have no orthographic. Bunuba, an Australian aboriginal language, has no more than 100 speakers left.
- Only after the study of several languages can it be concluded whether there are universal rules of grammar, which would indicate that it is under the control of genes rather than culture. It is generally agreed that more than half of the world's languages have no written form. With the death of the last speaker of many of these, these languages will be extinct.

Suggestions to Safeguard the Endangared Languages

- The 30th session of the general conference of UNESCO in 1999 decided that the organisation would launch and observe an International Mother Language Day on Feb 21 every year throughout the world. Such celebrations may play a significant role internationally.
- Its important for a culture to preserve their language despite the rapid growth of globalisation, there are ways to achieve it, such as language classes for young people and children's.
- Also, by promoting the native language in schools, homes etc by doing this there is chance of protecting our language from globalisation. Promoting is a strong national identity.
- It is important for the people to learn and respect their language, lest many of the languages and dialects should die their natural death. The crucial question is – how can their languages be preserved if young people are loath to speak them? – The Statesman (India)/Asia News Network.

Conclusions

In short globalisation has been helpful to intensify socio-economic and cultural relations of many nations. There are negative and positive effects of it in cultural diversity, but the benefits we get from it are useful in the development of our country.

32

Impact of Globalisation on Migrants: Plight of Libya

— K. Sai Jaahnavi

Introduction

Globalisation and Migration

Migration was not the recent trend, but it is an aspect of each of the livelihood for an individual by leaving many requirements of citizenship, knowing local language, education and many other where migration is from ages and habituated to many of us. Migration of people from one country to another country may severely affect the mob gaining country's economy but also social life and culture of natives of the host country, where this will be the impact of globalisation. The fact that what actually globalisation can be observed slightly that it is one of the cause for migration which effects the host country of migrants with lot of changes in its culture and traditional aspects of the natives as well the migrants too. But globalisation in other hand is helping migrants on the low rate by leaving a major contradicting aspect by leaving behind the rest. Due to the economic downfall and many aspects of migrants – children and young (or) equivalent the medium of language will be a problem to many of them. Countries like USA, Australia, Canada and many other European countries are vastly globalised because of high economy, social order, equality among every one, liberty and mainly equality education that they had from the country's growth. Also, imperialism and colonisation are the main factors for these countries to have a great economy and financial hold. Where these factors gave a great grip to be a globalised country than any other in maintaining world class ranking in maintain powerful army, high economic growth for better life standards.

Research Aim

To find how globalisation is impactful on lives of migrants & refugees.

Research Task

To define abstraction of globalisation impact on migrants, to observe migration process in Libya and problem faced by Libya migrants in process of migration to European countries.

The paper is divided into three parts. The first part is the abstraction of globalisation, the second part is about impact of globalisation on Libyan migrants to enter European boundaries by crossing Mediterranean Sea and lastly third part is on analysis of Libyan crises and difficulties that Libyan refugees face because of globalisation in developed countries.

The Abstraction of Globalisation

Globalisation has effected quite enormously from many years in terms of economic, social development and political affairs of many countries. Globalisation was so rapid that it almost turned aspects of economy crises, livelihood, social life and political affairs majorly. And their traditional change of trade, economy, social life had effected migrants as well, but the abundant growth of economy has not improved unemployment, unequal pay and many other in reality. Globalisation was demonstrated well in socio - economic provisions but not on migrations. The fact of what actually globalisation is not intersecting when it comes to migrants' division of labour, trade and economy across the world by creating a global wed is what actually globalisation meant for, further many companies are opting developing countries like African countries and South Asian countries for high job market, employability and mainly natural resources. But the anticipation of natives in countries like Africa are left behind for being uneducated to be employable in such companies. Globalisation has improved on communication between countries for trade and commerce. Everything has been digitalised from sending a fax to bank transactions. Well the margin of life parameters is not parallel here because of lack of economy and downfall of government and social order in countries like Syria, Libya and Iraq, many international migrations have happened while the half of the world is above modern age, but the rest is being back stabbed by old practices even after many good will organisations, human rights organisations and functioning around us. And as far globalisation was caused by changes in economy and social development, where mostly we can observe globalisation is above the middle station of life majorly than of lower station.

As the "inventions are mother of necessity", communication are highly developed, travelling become easier and technology is highly advanced that most of these simplifications are accessible to either higher or middle stations of life than the lower one. And another anticipation of globalisation is that global language is the medium for trade and commerce, employability for international migrants. Where the usage of English became more but it has made handy to make it easier by translating it into native languages from English to Spanish and many other, where the necessity of global language is not profound.

Impact of globalisation on Libyan migrants

The impact of globalisation in Libya in twenty-first century is because of Arab uprising in Libya which is later recalled that Tunisia blazed the tract of Arab spring. This Arab spring effected Libya and Tunisia on a parallel media before it got dissolved in other Arabian countries where it has to effect. This Arab spring is series of protests supporting democracy uprisings that award sensual largely populated Muslim countries including Egypt, Moscow, Libya, Bahama, Tunisia and Syria. These series of pro-democratic demonstrations were started in beginning of early spring of 2011. Which later named as the agitation, even after its being a decade of this Arab spring, being started it has never gone in office for a betterment of social order and lives of people. There was a greater impact of political and social order but these upsprings still remain common even today. Even after many years of globalisation every country is in the race of development and economic growth but some of the countries, like which are a part of this Arab spring are still fighting for uprising of democracy and freedom. After this great disturbance in social and political affairs this movement led to instability and oppression. The raise of Arab spring in December 2010, later lid to Jasmine revolution when Tunisian street vendor Mohammed Bouazizi set fire on himself to protect the arbitrary seizing of his vegetables cart by police of his failure to obtain a permit. Where Bouazizi sacrificed act is served as a catalyst for a new revolution called Jasmine Revolution in Tunisia. After street protects in Tunis, the capital of Tunisia, later eventually prompted authoritarian President Zine El Abidine Ben Ali to abdicate his place and flee to Saudi Arabia. This 20 years of dictatorship was like in iron fist. After the legion was inspired by the people and new regime came into existence in Tunisia. The country's first democratic parliamentary elections were held in October 2011 and later the same began to protest against authoritarian government in their own nations.

This later got spread many other places, this includes the Tahrir square uprisings in Cairo, Egypt and similar in Bahrain. Whereas in some countries like Libya and Syria, these protests morphed into full scale of civil war. As the series of protests became a chain which later morphed into a civil war in Libya. Where an authoritarian dictator Colonel Muammar Qaddafi was overthrown in October 2011, during upraise of violent civil war and he was killed with torture by opposition fighters. After the downfall of Qaddafi, Libya was still remained in civil war where the two opposition parties are ruling the country. Libyan civilians are suffered from many years with violence in the streets, no access to food, healthcare, where there are mere services even in emergency times. This later led to ongoing worldwide refugee crises, where thousands of Libyans are crossing the boundaries to enter Europe by crossing Mediterranean Sea in search of new hopes to restart a new life with good opportunities of survival. "And massive wave of migration is crashing through north Africa, but there is only one major gateway Europe – Libya". Qaddafi's ugliest rule trapped in European public. Fear of migrants that concerns, that their communities may affect lives of European people.

Analysis on Libyan crisis and Libyan migration

As after the overthrow of Qaddafi's dictatorship in 2011 in Libya, there was a serious disturbance among Libya in managing the political and social order all over the country. As the country has to enhance the globalisation in many ways which were protests for democracy and freedom even in this modern era of globalisation. But later after "ARAB SPRING", the power was taken over by the militants and after the assassination of prime minister Colonel Qaddafi which later resulted in serious economic and political downfall of Libyan economy. Even though after having many natural resources like crude oil and gas industries Libya has become "THE VICTIM OF GLOBALISATION" because of Arab expansion. Where it still shows that the strong countries in desert land are prioritising themselves by making market on Libyan crude oil in their country's name for expansion of trade and commerce. This can be seen in many parts of North Africa and middle East. The result of the globalisation in twenty-first century is expansion of severe crisis and international migrations to save lives where they are not regarded as people of any country with a birth tag. However, we can observe a membrane of colonisation and imperialism in twenty-first century which is an impacting factor of globalisation.As far as the analysis that I made by considering the reports, studies and many statistical evidences from many international organisations and United Nations organisation this is

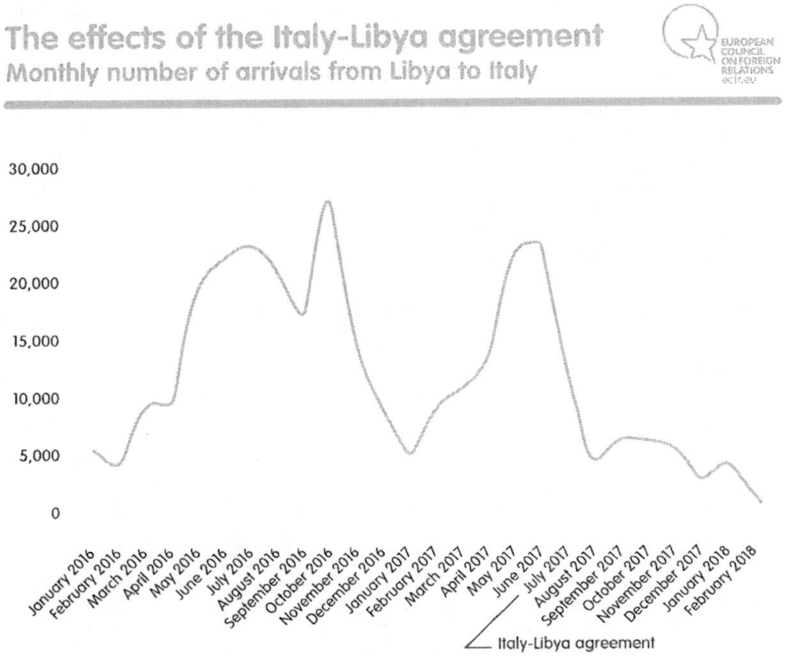

Source: UNHCR

the analysis of Libyans migrating Europe mostly ITALY across the Mediterranean Sea yearly and employment of this Libyans after migrating to the European countries.

Analysis

European countries particularly Italy, policy in Libya has made the migration difficult on entirely blocking the departure of migrations to Italy without any proper addressing evidences of migration. This led to internal security of the Italy to provide effective security in reducing the number of arrivals in Italy since 2017, which are not long term policies. Furthermore, the country's persistent inner conflicts are raging many activities in rise of militants. Also in the process of migration many Libyans are undergoing physical and psychological abuse, as well as extortion where profiteers of detention centre have simply replaced profiteers of human trafficking as well. Therefore, in Libya around 700,000 migrants, including almost 50,000 asylum seekers and 165,000 internally displaced persons. The UN High Commissioner for Refugees had begun to relocate asylum seekers from Libya to Niger and then to Europe, but the effort has stalled since last

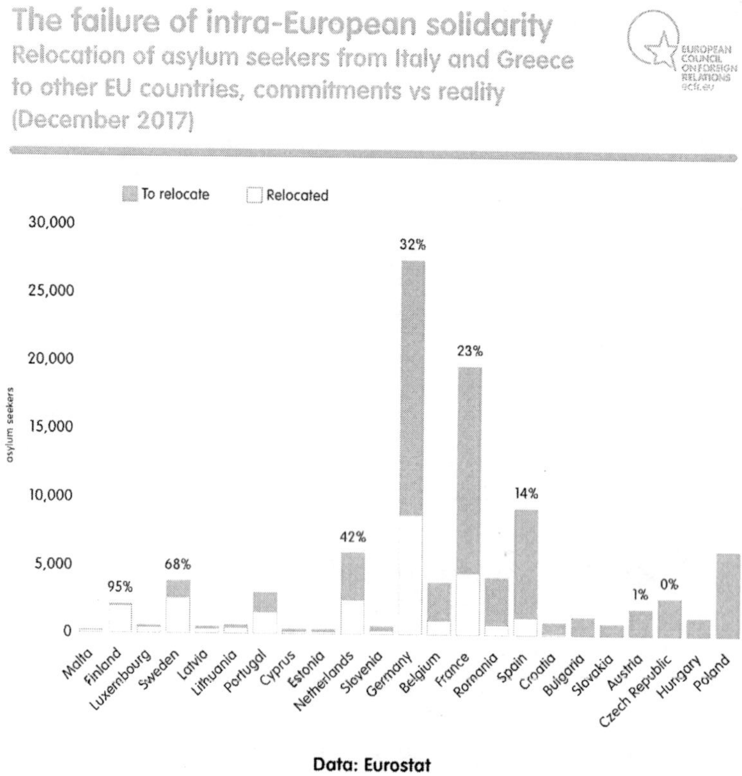

October: out of 1,300 people transferred to Niger, only 300 have been relocated to Europe, most of them to Italy.

The above graphical representations are about the African migrations who are called as asylum seekers and different countries allowing them from Italy and Greece where these all are from middle East and North Africa.

The majority of places from where most of the migrations occurring from militant acquired territories of Middle East and North Africa, which are highly impacted by factors of globalisation and ISIS.

As for the analysis of employability in European countries particularly for African migrants with raise in employment rates with low educated migrants appear more in Labour market than the natives. Where the level of employment is inversely proportional to high education levels.Indeed, the level of knowledge of the host country language has a meaningful impact on the employment rates of refugees. The highest jump in the employment

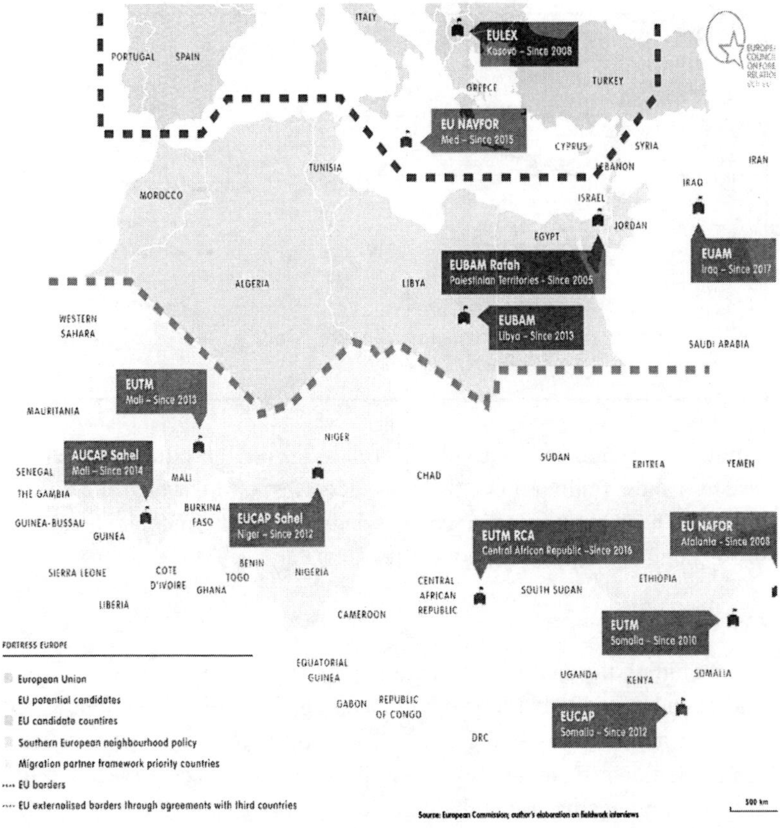

rate is found between those refugees who declare to have an intermediate level of host country knowledge and those with a beginner or lower level. Refugees with an intermediate level have an employment rate of 59%, more than twice that of those with a lower level (27%). The only exception to this relationship between language and employment is that refugees with an advanced level have a higher employment rate than those whose mother tongue is that of the host country (67% vs. 59%), an outcome which may be related to discrimination, cultural factors, legal obstacles to work and the ability of migrants to capitalise on their education and skills (European Commission, 2016a and 2016 forthcoming; see also Annex C). Overall, knowledge of the host-country language is such a key determinant of employment that refugees with an advanced level surpass the native-born in terms of employment rates (67% vs. 65% for the native-born). This also seems to hold across education levels. Even though knowledge of the host

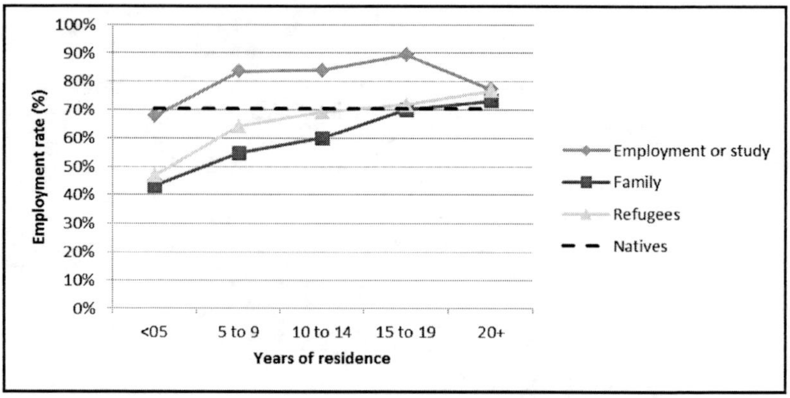

country language is positively correlated with the education level of refugees, these findings nevertheless suggest that efforts which aim bringing refugees' host country language knowledge to an intermediate level could bring along significant employment gains.

Conclusion

In concluding the analysis of Libyan crisis and migration process to enter European Union co-relating with impact of globalisation in various aspects of study and analysis that I made from migrations to Europe, cause of economic downfall and many other statistical evidences proves that lives of these migrants has severely affected because of globalisation.

References and sources

1. Through different modes of web-articles and websites.
   - https://ec.europa.eu/eurostat/statistics-explained/index.php/Migrant_integration_statistics_%E2%80%93_labour_market_indicators
   - https://www.ecfr.eu/specials/mapping_migration
   - http://www.msnbc.com/specials/migrant-crisis/libya
   - https://www.hrw.org/world-report/2019/country-chapters/european-union
2. Marquardt, M., Berger, N., O. (2003). The Future: Globalisation and New Roles for HRD. *Advances in Developing Human Resources*. Vol. 5, No. 3 August 2003 283-295 DOI:10.1177/1523422303254668.

33

Emerging Strategies to Ensure Health Equity of Marginalised Women Population

— *C. Vanisree, N. Swathisree,*
Syeda Meher Afreen

Introduction

Marginalisation is a process by which individuals or groups are kept or pushed at the margins of the society. At present, marginal groups include, women, children, SC, ST people with AIDS, mental illness or other health conditions, refugees; ethnic or religious groups homosexuals and the poor who are considered as the largest among the marginal groups in the world. This paper aims to highlight the discrimination and exploitation of these marginal groups especially in terms of women health.

India is still a patriarchal society where women is considered to be a weaker gender. Women have low status compared to men. Sexual and reproductive health is a key aspect of women's right to health. About 28% of girls in India get married below legal age, experience pregnancy and have serious repercussions on health including sexually transmitted diseases, aches, injuries, anaemia, nutritional problems and so on. About 21% of women have experienced domestic violence which leaves a major impact on both physical and mental health. As a result women can have fatal consequences like suicide, homicide and maternal mortality.

Collaboration through community health assessments and other strategic endeavours will play a foundation in identifying health priorities and providing efforts to address them. In addition hospitals and other community stakeholders will need to work together to identify barriers that could prevent populations from achieving good health. Unite around shared goals and work collaborating to implement changes that promote a healthier women community.

Women's health concern is influenced by biological, social and cultural factors. Indian women are generally vulnerable to poor nutrition, especially during pregnancy and lactation. Women in traditional set up are expected to eat only after rest of the family has eaten and the left over consumed one devoid of nutrient rich food.

Women's low socio-economic status, gender discrimination, and reproductive role not only expose them to various diseases but also their access to health services. Domestic violence, physical and sexual abuse affect their quality of life both physically and mentally. Gender biased discrimination is having age impact on women's health in India. According to joint study conducted researches at AIIMS from health records of patients who visited AIIMS, 37% of women got access to healthcare as compared to 67% of men.

Females between age groups of 31 & 44 and 45 & 59 years faced less degree of gender bias at 1.5 male patients per female patient respectively. Study also revealed the gender bias increased with different regions of state.

For example, States like Bihar, UP and NE states women patients reporting for treatment were comparatively less when compared to Delhi and Punjab.

Other reasons include irresponsible shortage of doctors and attitude of medical personal in rural areas. A large number of doctors unwilling to walk in remote areas had lead to healthcare facilities operated by private companies which are too expensive for marginalised women. National Health Profile report 2018 highlights low government spending on public health only around 1.3% of its Gross Domestic Product (GDP). National Health profile 2018 shows that 71.9% pregnant women in India do not have access to iron and folic acid tablets. Only 21.8% expectant mothers get full antenatal care. The practices of segregating menstruating women in areas like Nepal, Tamil Nadu is the main cause of anaemia and in turn leads to high infant of maternal mortality rates.

Maternal mortality is 57 fold higher in Indian woman than in other countries. Severe anaemia accounts to 20% of maternal deaths. Women are tend to visit hospitals more frequently than women to treat their ill-health more ever, Women are men prone to depression, anxiety and gender disadvantage and anguish related to domestic violence and finally suicidal deaths.

Methods to Improve

1. Assessing the disparities that affect access to healthcare (Eg: race, ethnicity, socio-economic status, age, sex, disabilities, gender identity and residential location).
2. By developing means to reach and use services such as transportation to services that may be located at a distance.
3. Determining changes in healthcare and developing in new models for delivering of primary care.
4. Promoting health literacy to understand their health and communicate with health instructors.
5. Expand training of maternal health provider in rural areas.
6. Incentive programmes should be initiated which provide scholarships, grants, student loan repayments other financial incentives to providers also commit to practising in undeserved areas.
7. Counselling by healthcare providers about malnutrition, pregnancy, menstrual health and other conditions to rural women.
8. Assess Network models to enhance access to rural communities.
9. Free medical camps and checkups.
10. Establish accountable care organisations to improve population health at lower costs.
11. Educating the young girls by organising maternal health programmes.
12. To keep a watch over mortality rates one can organise maternal mortality review committee.
13. Implementing programmes using phone applications. It has been said that when "I" is replaced with "WE" illness becomes wellness.

Common reasons of marginalisation

Various Marginalised Groups and their Problems

Most vulnerable marginalised groups in almost every society can be summarised as below:

1. Women

Under different economic conditions, and under the influence of specific historical, cultural, legal and religious factors, marginalisation is one of the manifestations of gender inequality. In other words, women may be excluded from certain jobs and occupations, incorporated into certain others, and marginalised in others. In general, they are always marginalised relative to men, in every country and culture. Women (or, men) don't present a homogeneous category where members have common interests, abilities, or practices. Women belonging to lower classes, lower castes, illiterate, and the poorest region have different levels of marginalisation than their better-off counterparts.

2. **People with disabilities**

People with disabilities have had to battle against centuries of biased assumptions, harmful stereotypes, and irrational fears. The stigmatisation of disability resulted in the social and economic marginalisation of generations with disabilities, and, like many other oppressed minorities, this has left people with disabilities in a severe state of impoverishment for centuries. The proportion of the disabled population in India is about 21.9 million.

The percentage of the disabled population to the total population is about 2.13 percent. There are interstate and interregional differences in the disabled population. The disabled face various types of barriers while seeking access to health and health services. Among those who are disabled women, children and age are more vulnerable and need attention.

3. **Scheduled Castes (Dalits)**

The caste system is a strictly hierarchical social system based on underlying notions of purity and pollution. Brahmins are on the top of the hierarchy and Shudras or Dalits constitute the bottom of the hierarchy. The marginalisation of Dalits influences all spheres of their life, violating basic human rights such as civil, political, social, economic and cultural rights.

A major proportion of the lower castes and Dalits are still dependent on others for their livelihood. Dalits do not refer to caste but suggest a group who are in a state of oppression, social disability and who are helpless and poor. Literacy rates among Dalits are very low. They have meagre purchasing power and have poor housing conditions as well as have low access to resources and entitlements.

Structural discrimination against these groups takes place in the form of physical, psychological, emotional and cultural abuse which receives legitimacy from the social structure and the social system. Physical segregation of their settlements is common in the villages forcing them to live in the most unhygienic and inhabitable conditions. All these factors affect their health status, access to healthcare and quality of life. There are high rates of malnutrition reported among the marginalised groups resulting in mortality, morbidity, and anaemia. Access to and utilisation of healthcare among the marginalised groups are influenced by their socio-economic status within society.

Caste-based marginalisation is one of the most serious human rights issues in the world today, adversely affecting more than 260 million people mostly reside in India. Caste-based discrimination entails social and economic exclusion, segregation in housing, denial, and restrictions of access to public and private services and employment, and enforcement of certain types of jobs on Dalits, resulting in a system of modern day slavery or bonded labour. However, in recent years due to affirmative action and legal protection, the intensity of caste-based marginalisation is reducing.

4. **Scheduled Tribes**

The Scheduled Tribes like the Scheduled Castes face structural discrimination within Indian society. Unlike the Scheduled Castes, the Scheduled Tribes are a product of marginalisation based on ethnicity. In India, the Scheduled Tribes population is around 84.3 million and is considered to be socially and economically disadvantaged. Their percentages in the population and numbers, however, vary from State to State. They are mainly landless with little control over resources such as land, forest, and water.

They constitute a large proportion of agricultural labourers, casual labourers, plantation labourers, industrial labourers etc. This has resulted in poverty among them, low levels of education, poor health and reduced access to healthcare services. They belong to the poorest strata of the society and have severe health problems.

5. **Elderly or Aged People**

Aging is an inevitable and inexorable process in life. In India, the population of the elderly is growing rapidly and is emerging as a serious area of concern for the government and the policy planners. According to data on the age of India's population, in Census 2001, there are a little over 76.6 million people above 60 years, constituting 7.2 percent of the population. The number of people over 60 years in 1991 was 6.8 percent of the country's population. The vulnerability among the elderly is not only due to an increased incidence of illness and disability but also due to their economic dependency upon their spouses, children, and other younger family members. According to the 2001 census, 33.1 percent of the elderly in India live without their spouses.

The widowers among older men form 14.9 percent as against 50.1 percent widows among elderly women. Among the elderly (80 years and above), 71.1 percent of women were widows while widowers formed only 28.9 percent of men. Lack of economic dependence has an impact on their access to food, clothing, and healthcare. Among the basic needs of the elderly, medicine features as the highest unmet need. Healthcare of the elderly is a major concern for society as aging is often accompanied by multiple illnesses and physical ailments.

6. Children

Children mortality and morbidity among children are caused and compounded by poverty, their sex and caste position in society.

All these have consequences on their nutrition intake, access to healthcare, environment, and education. Poverty has a direct impact on the mortality and morbidity among children. In India, a girl child faces discrimination and differential access to nutritious food and gender-based violence is evident from the falling sex ratio and the use of technologies to eliminate the girl child. The manifestations of these violations are various, ranging from child labour, child trafficking, to commercial sexual exploitation and many other forms of violence and abuse.

With an estimated 12.6 million children engaged in hazardous occupations (2001 Census), for instance, India has the largest number of child labourers under the age of 14 in the world. Among children, there are some groups like street children and children of sex workers who face additional forms of discrimination. A large number of children are reportedly trafficked to the neighbouring countries.

Trafficking of children also continues to be a serious problem in India. While systematic data and information on child protection issues are still not always available, evidence suggests that children in need of special protection belong to communities suffering disadvantage and social exclusion such as scheduled castes and tribes, and the poor (UNICEF, India).

7. Sexual Minorities

Another group that faces stigma and discrimination are sexual minorities. Those identified as gay, lesbian, transgender, bisexual, kothi and hijra; experience various forms of discrimination within the society and the health system. Due to the dominance of heteronomous sexual relations as the only form of normal acceptable relations within the society, individuals who are identified as having same-sex sexual preferences are ridiculed and ostracized by their own family and are left with very limited support structures and networks of community that provide the conditions of care and support. Their needs and concerns are excluded from various health policies and programmes.

Consequences of Marginalisation

Marginalisation is a group of systems or processes by which we will be able to make our life's hell with regular unhappiness. It's a ultimate short way to split up the country into different countries where permanent marginalisation will remain with fighting within different communities of same religion also with other religions.

Wrong implementation of diversity in social ground is "marginalisation" due to degradation in properties of human beings, particularly "leaders in power of parliament, leaders of different societies" along with general mass of all communities are more or less have been responsible for diversified in the name of marginalisation of societies in basis of caste, groups, social status, states and other different ways.

At present, Humans thoughts are concentrated within self-explanatory and self-interest. We totally lost the sense of responsibilities to others, fall down of morality, character, principle and human properties are the root causes of marginalisation. Till the leaders of societies, communities, political parties and members of parliament don't be united together with a sense of responsibilities to reform total humans irrespective of religions, caste and creed marginalisation will be in theory only as a subject to discuss among.

Marginalisation based on different castes is one of the most serious human rights issues in the world today, adversely affecting more than 260 million people mostly reside in India. The Scheduled Tribes population in India is around 84.3 million and is considered to be socially and economically disadvantaged.

But the so many castes in Hindu Dharma is not available and approved in any of the guideline spiritual books including Upanishads and Bhagavad Geetha and other spiritual texts.

There are certain laws which gives special right to women are:

Just and humane condition of work and maternity benefit (Art.42) Socio-economic legislations to provide protection to women.

1. Equal Remuneration Act 1976
2. The Workmen Compensation Act, 1923
3. Dowry Prohibition Act, 1961
4. Immortal Traffic Prevention Act, 1986
5. Commission of Sati (Prevention) Act 1987
6. Violence against Women: Law relating to Rape, Dowry, Domestic Violence.

Conclusion

Right to health is a basic human right unfortunately women in India do not access such basic right. Problem of health is deep rooted in the socio-cultural practices, socio-cultural norms which is responsible for gender inequality.

Thus, there is need to promote gender equity and positively erasing all the margins and boundaries for better health outcomes of women as well as economic development of Nation.

References

- Are marginalised women being left behind? A population-based study of institutional deliveries in Karnataka, India. *BMC Public Health* 12, 12-30.
- Primary healthcare services among a migrant indigenous population living in an eastern Indian city. *Journal of Immigrant and Minority Health* 12, 53-59.
- Migrant women's utilisation of prenatal care: a systematic review. *Maternal and Child Health Journal* 17, 816-836.
- *Applied Logistic Regression*, 2nd edn. John Wiley & Sons Inc, New York.

Index

A

G

H

I

J

K

L

M

N

O

P

Q

R

T

U

V

W

Z

Y

Z